THE
HORSE'S
HEALTH

FROM A to Z

THE
HORSE'S
HEALTH

FROM A to Z

AN EQUINE VETERINARY DICTIONARY

Peter D. Rossdale
& Susan M. Wreford

DAVID & CHARLES

A DAVID & CHARLES BOOK

First published in the UK in 1974
Second impression 1976
Third impression 1978
Fourth impression 1981
Fifth impression 1983
Sixth impression 1983
Seventh impression 1984
Eighth impression 1985
Ninth impression 1986
Tenth impression 1987
Eleventh impression 1988
Completely revised and updated edition 1989
Reprinted 1990
Reprinted 1993
Paperback edition 1993
Revised and updated paperback edition 1998

A catalogue record for this book is available from the British Library.

ISBN 0 7153 0714 2

Typeset by ABM Typographics Ltd, Hull
and printed in the UK by Redwood Books, Trowbridge
for David & Charles
Brunel House   Newton Abbot   Devon

CONTENTS

ACKNOWLEDGEMENTS

1st Edition

We would like to acknowledge many friends and colleagues who have helped with this book, in particular: Michael D.N. Hunt, MA, VetMB, MRCVS and Derek Thurlbourn for drawing the diagrams; Jenny Crossman and Elizabeth Wilson for preparing the manuscript; and Sidney W. Ricketts, BSc, BVSc, MRCVS for reading it in its final form.

We have also received much helpful advice from Raymond Hopes, BVMS, MRCVS, Colin K. Peace, MA, VetMB, MRCVS and Jack C. Sewell, BVSc, MRCVS (QDAH).

Figures 34 and 35 have been produced from *Lameness in Horses* by O.R. Adams, with the permission of the publishers Lea & Febiger, Philadelphia. Figures 5, 6, 7, 8, 13, 18, 19, 20, 29, 32, 36, 37 and 43 have been reproduced from Sisson & Grossman's *Anatomy of Domestic Animals* (W.B. Saunders & Co. Ltd. Philadelphia) with the permission of Mrs L.C. Grossman.

2nd Edition

We would like to acknowledge the help of Rachel Haldane, Kathy Holtan and Jan Wade in the preparation of this edition.

We would also like to thank Tim Greet, BVMS, MVM, CertEO, FRCVS, Rob Pilsworth MA, VetMB, MSc, CertVR, MRCVS and Terry Bushe for their advice and assistance.

3rd Edition

In the 23 years since this dictionary was first published some words have gone out of fashion, others have come into general use. New technologies and fresh discoveries have brought their own jargon. We have attempted to reflect these changes by omission or inclusion. In the process of this revision we have been ably assisted by Deidre Carson, MRCVS, Kate Robb and Brigitte Heard.

INTRODUCTION AND ETYMOLOGY

Veterinary language, especially that relating to the horse, is becoming increasingly difficult to understand. This is why we feel there is a need for an equine veterinary dictionary. We have tried to keep the book as simple as possible by defining diseases under their common names with the medical terminology included for reference. In this way we hope to improve communications between horsemen and veterinarians.

Horsemen, for example, talk about big or filled legs, veterinarians refer to oedema or lymphangitis. To some it is Monday morning leg.

Jargon in all walks of life creates barriers in communication. Professionals cannot converse freely with those who do not know the specialised terms they use. Even within a profession, groups of specialists can become isolated from each other. In compiling this book we aim to help reverse this trend as far as it relates to horses. Readers from countries which have generally dropped diphthongs will find anemia, cecum, diarrhea, edema, esophagus, estrus, fetus, hemorrhage and words from similar roots defined under traditional spellings, eg anaemia, caecum, diarrhoea, oedema, oesophagus, oestrus, foetus and haemorrhage.

Although the book is intended primarily as a dictionary, we have not resisted the temptation to expand on some entries. To make space for this extra information we have omitted many pronouns and are prepared for the style to be criticised as staccato. The following syllables should help the reader to understand medical words:

negative or away from, as in abnormal	a-/ab- or an-
hear, as in acoustics	acou-
near, as in adrenal (near kidney)	ad-
fat, as in adipose tissue	adip-
pain, as in analgesic (pain relieving) drug	-alg-
against, as in anti-inflammatory	anti-
joint, as in arthritis (joint inflammation)	arthr-
joint, as in articulation	articul-
ear, as in auricle (flap of ear)	aur-
go, walk, as in abasia (faulty walking)	ba-
small staff, rod as in description of bacteria	bacter-
two, as in bisexual	bi-
life, as in biochemistry	bi-/bio-
early stages of something growing, as in blastula	blast-
short, as in brachydonty (having short teeth)	brachy-

cardi-	heart, as in cardiologist (one who studies heart)
cav-	hollow, as in cavity
cephal-	head, as in encephalitis (inflamed brain or head)
cervic-	neck, as in cervical bones (vertebrae)
chondr-	cartilage, as in chondritis (inflamed cartilage)
-cid/e	kill, cut, as in bactericidal drug
contra-	against, as in contra-indicated drugs
crani-	skull, as in cranium
de-	away/lack of, as in dehydration
dent-	tooth, as in dentistry
derm-	skin, as in dermatitis (inflamed skin)
di-	two, as in diploid (having paired chromosomes)
dors-	back, as in dorsal vertebrae (bones of the back)
dys-	bad, as in dysfunction
ect-	outside, as in ectoderm (outer skin)
end-	inside, as in endometrium (uterus lining)
enter-	intestine, as in enteritis (inflamed intestine)
erythr-	red, as in erythrocyte (red blood cell)
extra-	outside, in addition to, as in extra-articular (outside a joint)
-facient	cause, as in abortifacient (agent causing abortion)
febr-	fever, as in febrile (characterised by fever)
gastr-	stomach, as in gastric juices
gloss/o	tongue, as in glossophanyngeal (of tongue and pharynx)
haem-/haemato-	blood, as in haemorrhage
helc-	ulcer, sore, as in helcoma (corneal ulcer)
hepat-	liver, as in hepatitis (inflammation of the liver)

impulse, as in hormone	**horm-**
inflammation, as in carpitis (inflammation of the knee)	**-itis**
milk, as in lactating mare	**lact-**
flank, as in laparotomy (surgery into flank)	**lapar-**
white, as in leucocyte (white blood cell)	**leuc-**
abnormal, as in malfunction	**mal-**
membrane, as in meningitis (inflamed membrane)	**mening-**
form, shape, as in amorphous (without shape, eg powdered drug)	**morph-**
new, as in neonate (foal)	**neo-**
kidney, as in nephritis (inflammation of the kidneys)	**neph-**
nerve, as in neuron (nerve cell)	**neur-**
nourish, as in nutrition	**nutri-**
eye, as in periodic ophthalmia (moon blindness)	**ophthalm-**
mouth, as in oral dose	**or-**
testicle, as in cryptorchid (rig)	**-orchi-**
bone, as in osteitis (inflamed bone)	**oste/o-**
near, beside, abnormal, as in paracentesis, qv	**para-**
drug, as in pharmacology (science of drugs)	**pharmac-**
throat, as in pharyngoscope (instrument to examine throat)	**pharyngo-**
vein, as in phlebitis (inflammation of vein)	**phleb-**
lung, as in pulmonitis (inflammation of lungs)	**pulmo-**
kidneys, as in adrenal glands (glands near the kidneys)	**ren-**
flesh, as in sarcoid (a growth of skin)	**sarc-**
clot, lump, as in thrombus (blood clot in heart or blood vessel)	**thromb-**
windpipe, as in tracheotomy (surgery through neck on windpipe)	**trach-**
bladder or sac, as in vesicle (small blister on skin)	**vesic-**

ABBREVIATIONS

Abbreviations most commonly used in the dictionary:

abbr	abbreviation	**LH**	luteinising hormone
approx	approximately	**lit.**	literally
Assn	Association	**μ**	micron (measure of size)
Ave	Avenue	(pronounced mew)	
b.i.d.	twice daily	**mg**	milligram (1,000th of a gram) measure of weight
C	Centigrade		
Ca	calcium	**ml**	millilitre (1,000th of a litre) measure of volume
cf	compare		
cm	centimetre (100th of a metre) measure of distance	**mm**	millimetre
		mmol	millimoles per litre
colloq	colloquial/ly	**mμ**	millimicron or micro μ (1,000th of a μ) measure of size
cu mm	cubic millimetre		
dim	diminutive	**N**	North/ern
dl	decilitre	**neg**	negative
E	East/ern	**opp**	opposite
eg	for example	**oz**	ounce
EU	European Union	**P**	phosphorus
F	Fahrenheit	**pl**	plural
Fr	French	**pos**	positive
FSH	follicle stimulating hormone	**q.i.d.**	four times daily
g	gram/s	**qv**	which see
g/kg wt	grams per kilo bodyweight	**RBC**	red blood cell
Gr	Greek	**Rd**	Road
h	hands	**S**	South/ern
Hz	cycles per second	**Soc**	Society
Hb	haemoglobin	**Sp**	Spanish
Hg	Mercury	**spp**	species
ie	that is	**St**	Street
IM	intramuscular/ly (by injection into the muscle)	**sub cut**	subcutaneous/ly (by injection into skin)
Ital	Italian	**syn/s**	synonyms
IU	international units	**t.i.d.**	three times daily
IV	intravenously (by injection into vein)	**viz**	namely
		W	West/ern
L	Latin	**wt**	weight
l	litre		

THE DICTIONARY

A

AAEP	Abbr American Association of Equine Practitioners, qv.
a-/an-	Prefix meaning negative (an is used before a vowel, eg in anorexia, qv).
ab	Prefix meaning away from, eg abduct, qv.
abdomen	(belly, possibly from L abdere, to hide) Body between chest and pelvis.
abdominal	Of abdomen. **a. cavity** The area bounded by diaphragm in front, **a.** muscles below and at sides, spine and lumbar muscles above, pelvic outlet behind. Contains stomach and intestines (see alimentary canal), liver, kidneys, urinary bladder and sex organs. Enlarged in some colics, ascites, pregnancy. **a. sounds** See borborygmus.
abdominocentesis	(abdomino + Gr kentesis, puncture) Withdrawal of fluid through needle inserted into abdominal cavity. Used in diagnosis of colic or similar cases. Colloq tap.
abduct	(ab- + L ducere, to draw) Draw one part of body away from the midline, eg to **a.** a limb is to move it out of line as in some lamenesses. Opp adduct, qv.
abberant	(L aberrans; ab, from + errare, to wander) Deviating from usual course, eg botfly larva's **a.** migration to equine brain.
ablate	(L ablatus, removed) Cut away or remove.
abort	(L aboriri, to miscarry) To expel foetus before it is viable. See abortion.
abortifacient	(L abortio + facere, to make) substance which causes abortion, ie makes uterus contract, eg oxytocin.
abortion	(L abortio) Expulsion of foetus too undeveloped to survive outside uterus; arbitrarily put at 300 days' pregnancy (after this usually termed premature birth). Signs of **a.** may be any or all of those at normal birth, although mammary development may be absent. **A.** usually follows death of foetus but sometimes foetus may breathe after delivery. **bacterial a.** Due to several types of bacteria, eg streptococcus (most common in first 150 days), *Escherichia coli* (common at 150–300 days), *Klebsiella*, *Salmonella abortus equi*, staphylococcus, pseudomonas,

Actinobacillus equuli and, occasionally, *Brucella abortus.* | *abortion*
fungal a. Due to fungus, eg *Aspergillus* spp, entering uterus through vagina when mare is in oestrus or after foaling. Fungus grows on placenta interfering with nourishment of foetus, causing **a.** usually at 200–300 days. Fungus may also enter foetal bloodstream and cause lesions in liver and lungs. Diagnosis: on thickened placenta covered by brown exudate, white spots in lung and fungus in placenta. **physiological a.** That due to unknown cause, eg hormone deficiency in mare or foetus, chromosome abnormality resulting in faulty development, mare's poor diet, illness or excitement. **twin a.** That due to one twin dying and causing **a.** of the other. (Mare cannot easily carry twins to full term because uterus is not large enough for two placentae of normal size.) Mammary development with wax on teats and running of milk may start days or weeks before **a.**, probably on death of first twin. **viral a.** That due to virus, most commonly equine herpesvirus I (syn rhinopneumonitis). Virus easily spread by infected mare aborting and all horses in contact are susceptible. Usually causes snotty nose in young horses but can cause **a.** in pregnant mares without preliminary signs, singly or in epidemic form, from 6 months to full term. Diagnosis: on laboratory evidence of inclusion bodies in nuclei of epithelial cells of liver and lungs. Virus can sometimes be grown in tissue culture.

(L abrasio) Break in continuity of body surface such as skin or mucous membrane. Usually caused by mechanical process, eg ill-fitting tack. | **abrasion**

(L abscessus from ab-, away + cedere, to go) Cavity containing dead cells, bacteria and exudate (collectively called pus). May be acute, forming and bursting rapidly, or chronic, ie developing slowly and not bursting unless near body surface. Found in all tissues and organs. Causes: presence of foreign bodies, infection with bacteria or fungus, migrating parasitic larvae. See summer pneumonia, *Corynebacterium*, inflammation, sleepy foal disease, staphylococcus, strangles, tuberculosis. | **abscess**

(L ab, from + scindere, to cut) Horizontal line which, with ordinate (vertical line) is used as reference for recording data, as on a graph. | **abscissa**

(Gr akakia) Gummy exudate from stems and branches of *Acacia senegal* tree. Used as suspending agent or emollient in medicines, ointments. | **acacia**

(Gr akantha, spiny + eidos, form) Abnormally shaped red blood cell. | **acanthocyte**

acariasis   (Gr akari, mite + iasis, a state of) Infestation with mites such as those causing mange, qv.

accessory carpal bone   One of 8 small bones of carpus (knee joint), placed behind and to outside of the other 7. In prominent position behind joint and may fracture, especially when jumping, causing lameness and pain. Diagnosis: on X-ray examination. Some cases suitable for surgery but most heal with fibrous union if rested 3–6 months.

acclimatise   To become used to new climate or management eg when horses travel from one country to another.

acellular   Not made up of cells (horn, hair, said to be **a.** but strictly they are cellular).

acepromazine maleate   (trade name: Acetylpromazine, ACP) One of phenothiazine group of drugs. Used as tranquillisers before handling or anaesthesia.

acetabulum   (in ancient Rome, cup to hold vinegar) Cup-shaped part of pelvis formed by ilium and ischium; receives head of femur to make hip joint. See hip.

acetylcholine   Substance associated with transmitting nerve impulses; used to cause parasympathomimetic (qv) actions, eg to stimulate alimentary canal in colic. See autonomic nervous system; carbachol.

acetylpromazine   (ACP) Tranquilliser, qv.

acetylsalicylic acid   (syn aspirin) Colourless crystals or white granules. Odourless with slightly acid taste. Used to treat muscular pain, arthritis and reduce temperature, eg in setfast. May cause indigestion and haemorrhage if given repeatedly.

aciclovir   (trade name Zovirax) Substance which inhibits DNA of viruses and is used therefore as an antiviral agent against herpes infection.

acid   (L acidus from acere, to be sour) Sour, with properties the opposite of alkali. Compound that dissociates in aqueous solution to form hydrogen ions, turns litmus red and unites with bases to form salts. **a. base balance** Used in connection with buffering system of blood. Responsible for maintaining pH (qv) at about 7.40 units. **a. fast** Used in the laboratory to denote that stained bacteria are colour-fast in acid. **a. poisoning** See poisons.

(acid + Gr haima, blood + -ia) Lowering of blood pH to below normal level of about 7.40 units. **acidaemia**

Disturbance of acid base balance. **respiratory a.** Due to accumulation of carbon dioxide. **metabolic a.** Due to any acid other than carbon dioxide. See neonatal maladjustment syndrome. **acidosis**

(syns contagious acne, Canadian pox, contagious pustular dermatitis, staphylococcal dermatitis) Skin condition caused by infection with *Corynebacterium pseudotuberculosis* (Canadian pox) or *Staphylococcus aureus*. Small lump develops in skin and forms pimple, the top of which breaks, exuding pus. This mats with hairs and comes away as a scab, leaving moist, red area with small hole in centre. Staphylococcal infection tends to spread from central pustule and cause large raw areas. Often seen in yearlings when first saddled. Condition may be mistaken for ringworm, warble fly maggot or mud fever. See separate headings. Diagnosis: on finding organism in laboratory examination of pus and scabs. Treatment: apply antibiotic to sores and, in severe cases, also inject. Tack and grooming kit should be disinfected, especially girths and rubbers, horse should be isolated and not ridden. **acne**

(L aconitum, Gr akoniton) Drug from dried root of *Aconitum napellus* (monkshood, wolfsbane, blue rocket). All parts of plant are poisonous and contain alkaloid aconitine. Previously used in liniments and for laminitis. **a. poisoning** Symptoms include colic, slowing of heart, muscular weakness, paralysis, dilated pupils, often resulting in death from asphyxia. No specific treatment. **aconite**

Fruit of oak tree. Can poison. See New Forest pony, oak. **acorn**

Combining form meaning hear or of hearing. **acou-**

Of/relating to **a.** acid or its derivatives. **a. acid** is used to form **a. resin**, a quick-drying, synthetic, glassy thermoplastic used to repair hoof cracks. Fibreglass and other synthetic materials also used. **acrylic**

See adrenocorticotrophic hormone. **ACTH**

(Gr aktis, aktinos, a ray) Prefix meaning relation to a ray. **actino-**

Genus of microorganisms of family Brucellaceae. Most common in horse is **A. equuli**, causal agent of sleepy foal disease. **Actinobacillus**

The substance responsible for effect of compound, eg morphine is **a.p.** of opium. **active principle**

acute	(L acutus, sharp) Sharp. In disease: having short, relatively severe course.
ad-	(L ad, to) Prefix meaning to or towards, between, in addition to or near.
additive	Something added, usually to diet, eg vitamin or mineral.
adduct	(L adducere, to draw towards) To draw towards midline of a body or structure. Opp abduct, qv.
aden-/adeno-	Combining form meaning gland.
adenitis	Inflammation of a gland. See strangles, lymphangitis.
adenoma	A benign glandular tumour. See growth.
adenocarcinoma	A malignant glandular tumour. See growth.
adenosarcoma	A sarcoma (qv) with glandular elements. See growth.
adenovirus	Virus causing upper respiratory tract disease. See virus.
adhesion	(L adhaesio from adhaerere, to stick to) Fibrous band or structure abnormally joining two parts, eg between two loops of bowel following peritonitis (see colic); between tendon and tendon sheath; between iris and lens. See eye, diseases of; moon blindness.
adipo-	(L adeps, fat) Combining form: relationship to fat.
adipose	(L adipatus, fatty) Of fatty nature; fat.
adjustment	Process of adapting to altered circumstances, especially used in connection with newborn foals and the change from intra to extra uterine environment. See neonatal maladjustment syndrome.
adjuvant	(L adjuvans, aiding) Substance or drug which aids another. **Freund a.** (after Hungarian bacteriologist) Mixture of mineral oil, water and emulsifying agent used as vehicle for antigens of vaccine to increase immunising stimulus.
ad lib	(L ad libitum, at pleasure) Used in connection with feeding unlimited quantities.
adrenal	(L ad, near + ren, kidney) In region of kidney. **a. glands** Two red-brown flattened organs about 10cm long and 4cm wide lying close to kidneys. They consist of capsule enclosing outer

cortical layer and inner medulla. Glands are ductless and secrete hormones: outer layer, cortisol; inner layer, epinephrine (adrenaline).

adrenal

Hormone secreted by medulla of adrenal gland. White or creamy-white crystalline odourless powder with slightly bitter taste. When injected causes rise in blood pressure (due to ability to constrict blood vessels and increase heart rate), dilation of pupils, inhibited movement of alimentary tract, formation of glucose from liver glycogen, sweating and fast breathing. Used locally to reduce bleeding by constricting blood vessel, combined with local anaesthetics to prevent rapid absorption from site of injection. Has no general action when given by mouth, so administered IV, 2–4ml of 0.1 per cent solution. See autonomic nervous system.

adrenaline

Term denoting relationship to that part of sympathetic nervous system in which nerve fibres produce the adrenaline-like substances, epinephrine (qv) and norepinephrine. Adrenergic drugs are classified according to whether they affect alpha or beta receptors within the sympathetic nervous system.

adrenergic

(ACTH) Corticotropin hormone secreted by anterior lobe of pituitary gland. It causes adrenal glands to produce corticosteroids. Synthetic ACTH injected to increase cortisone output for counteracting stress, shock, allergy, lymphangitis and oedema. Used in foals in preference to cortisone which, if given repeatedly, may cause adrenal gland to reduce output. Used as a short-acting test in foals to measure response of white blood cells (neutrophil:lymphocyte ratio) as indicator of maturity at birth. Narrow ratio failing to respond to ACTH indicates an immature adrenal cortex.

adrenocorticotrophic hormone

See corticotrophin, adrenocorticotrophic hormone.

adrenocorticotrophin

(L ad, to or near sorbere, to suck) Substance on which other substances accumulate eg intestinal adsorbents such as kaolin (qv).

adsorbent

Mature or fully-grown horse, ie one over 4 years. See maturity, immaturity.

adult

(Gr aer, air + Gr bios, life) Microorganism which grows and survives in oxygen.

aerobe

Within air. **a. bacteria** Those which thrive only in oxygen. Cf anaerobic.

aerobic

aerophagia | (Gr aero, air + Gr phagein, to eat) Excessive swallowing of air. See wind-sucking.

aetiology | (Gr aiatia, cause + logy, study of) Study of factors causing disease and their method of introduction to the host. Cf epidemiology.

afebrile | Without elevated temperature.

afferent | (L ad, to + ferre, to carry) Conveying towards a centre, eg **a.** nerves convey impulses from periphery to central nervous system, ie brain and spinal cord. Cf efferent.

African horse sickness | Acute or sub-acute virus infection endemic in Africa and present in Middle East and Asia since about 1960. It is spread by mosquitoes, not by direct contact. Horse family naturally affected (in horses mortality may reach 90 per cent, donkeys are more resistant) but dogs, goats and other animals can be experimentally infected. There are 9 known strains of virus, which is present in blood tissues and internal organs; immunity against one strain will not necessarily protect against others. Strains can cause one of 4 types: horse sickness fever, pulmonary, cardiac and mixed. Each begins with fever reaching maybe 41°C (105.8°F). Horse sickness fever is mild, causing conjunctivitis, increased pulse rate and deep breathing, incubation 5–30 days. Pulmonary form characterised by acute oedema of lungs, fits of coughing and yellow discharge from nostrils. Breathing is difficult and head and neck are distended. Finally animal chokes and appears to drown in its own secretions. Cardiac form incubates up to 3 weeks, fever develops slowly and persists longer than in pulmonary form. Swellings occur in head, neck and chest and small blood spots appear under tongue. There may be partial collapse, abdominal pain and restlessness. Recovery is more common than in pulmonary form. Mixed form common but often diagnosed only at post-mortem when heart and lung damage discovered. Often the result of double infection. Diagnosis: on symptoms and laboratory examination of blood. Immunity is produced by infection or vaccination, although vaccine must include all strains of virus to be effective. Control: vaccinate annually, kill mosquitoes, protect horses from being bitten. **A.h.s. vaccine, living** Mixture of several strains of virus weakened (attenuated) by repeated injection into mice. Used to protect against **A.h.s.** Injected in spring, 2–3 months before disease expected. Mares in advanced pregnancy should not be vaccinated and horses receiving first dose should be rested at least 3 weeks.

afterbirth | Foetal membranes consisting of placenta, amnion and cord (combined weight averages 7kg (15lb)). Normally expelled

from uterus 10–140 minutes after foal has been delivered. *afterbirth*
Unlike cows, mares rarely eat **a. a., retention of** Foetal membranes retained longer than 10 hours after birth. May be serious (cause of infection). Treatment: palpation, prostaglandin, qv, oxytocin, qv, intrauterine infusion of sterile fluids. **a. pains** Pain felt by mare following birth. Caused by contraction of uterus and expulsion of **a.** or uterine haemorrhage, qv. Mare may roll violently and sweat.

(a, neg + Gr gala, milk + ia) Failure of mammary glands to **agalactia**
secrete milk. May affect mares who give birth to premature or stillborn foals. Cause unknown but probably related to hormonal disturbances. See mammary gland.

Absence of immunoglobulins in blood. Result of failure of passive transfer in foals and seen in congenital anomaly in Arabian foals. **agammaglobulinaemia**

Time lived. Measure of life dating from birth; best assessed by **age**
development and wear of teeth, qv. Some breeds take their official age from arbitrarily chosen registration date, eg Thoroughbred: 1 January (N hemisphere), 1 August (S hemisphere). In first year horse is called foal or weanling, second year a yearling, after seventh year it is termed aged. Life averages 20 years although 50 years has been recorded.

Reaction between antigen and antibody causing clumping of **agglutination**
cells, bacteria or particles bearing antigen. Used in laboratory as test to identify bacteria or viruses. Also clumping together of any other cells, eg blood cells in the cross-matching of incompatible blood.

Drug which acts at receptor site normally stimulated by natural **agonist**
substance and which mimics its effects.

Colourless odourless gas of approx 1 part oxygen, 4 parts nitro- **air**
gen. Also contains ammonia, argon, carbon dioxide and organic matter. **alveolar a.** That contained in air sacs of lungs. **a. passages** Tubes of head (nasal passages), larynx (voice box), trachea (windpipe), bronchi and small tubes of lung ending at air sacs (alveolae). **a. sac** See alveolus. **a. way** Respiratory tract.

See artificial insemination. **AI**

(pl alae) One of cartilagenous plates which supports entrance **ala**
to nostrils. Consists of a broad lamina (qv) above and a narrow cornu (qv) below.

Curling up – off ground – of foundered horse's toe. Seen when **aladdin's slipper effect**

aladdin's slipper effect | feet left untrimmed for excessively long periods.

alanine aminotransferase | (ALT) Formerly GPT. A liver and kidney enzyme. Normal levels less than 25IU/l but not particularly useful to measure in the horse. Has been superseded by gamma glutamyltransferase.

albinism | (L albus, white + -ism) Congenital absence of pigment in skin, hair and eyes. Complete **a.** rare in horses, usually confined to loss of pigment of iris so that dark area of pupil is surrounded by ring of white (wall-eyed). (See Albino.) Mating of albinos results in albino offspring but **a.** in only one parent produces coloured foal which, when inter-bred, has one-in-four chance of albino offspring. See Albino, coat colouring.

Albino | Originally a colour, now developed to mean also a breed. True **A.** has pink iris to eye and entirely pink skin covered with white hair. Can be developed in almost any breed. Foundation sire of **A.** breed said to have been Old King, foaled in 1906 and believed to have been Arab-Morgan. Albinism may be aesthetically pleasing but must be suspect. Lack of pigment predisposes weakness, eg pink or blue eyes may have inferior vision. Pink skin, like white heels of coloured horses, tends to have low resistance to infection and is sunlightsensitive. Popular as ceremonial and circus horse. **International American A. Assn Inc,** Rt 1 Box 20, Naper, NE 68755. (402 832–5560).

albumen | See albumin.

albumin | (L albus, white) Protein found in animal and vegetable tissues; characterised by solubility in water and coagulation when heated; contains carbon, hydrogen, nitrogen, oxygen and sulphur. **serum a.** That in blood. See blood tests.

albuminuria | (albumin + Gr ouron, urine) Albumin in urine. Sign of inflamed kidneys or damaged urinary tract, ie bladder, ureter, urethra. Affected horses usually lose condition. See cystitis, kidney disease.

alcohol | (Arabic al-koh'l, something subtle) Colourless transparent volatile liquid used in laboratory (methyl **a.** or methanol) as antiseptic or astringent, or by mouth (ethyl **a.** or ethanol) as tonic, eg in beer.

aldosterone | Hormone produced by adrenal glands important for electrolyte and water balance in the body.

alg- | Combining form meaning pain.

(L alimentum) Food or nutritive material.

Colloq guts, intestines or bowel. Tube extending length of body from lips to anus, in which digestion occurs. Various parts developed according to function and named in order – mouth, pharynx, gullet (oesophagus), stomach, small intestine, caecum, large colon, small colon, rectum. Last four parts referred to as large intestines. Canal has three layers: an inner lining or mucous membrane containing digestive glands, middle muscular layer and outer peritoneal (qv) layer, except part from mouth to stomach and last part of rectum. Canal also receives products from salivary glands, liver, pancreas. It is suspended in abdomen by folds of peritoneum known as mesenteries, in which blood vessels pass to and from tube. Size and capacity of parts: oesophagus – 1–2 metres; stomach – relatively small, 8–15 litres; small intestine – 22 metres, 40–50 litres; caecum – 1.25 metres, 25–30 litres; large colon – 3–3.7 metres, 5,000 litres; small colon – 3.5 metres; rectum – 0.31 metres. See separate headings, colic. Cf gallbladder. **alimentary canal/tract**

(Arabic al-qaliy, potash) Compound such as soda, potash, ammonia, which neutralises strong acids. Sodium bicarbonate used to treat bites, acid poisoning, diarrhoea and to counteract acidity of blood. **acid/a.** Measurement is written pH. See neonatal maladjustment syndrome. **a. disease** See selenium poisoning. **alkali**

Enzyme mainly in liver, bone and intestine. Normal level varies with age: 3-year-old 375 (271–451 range) IU/l serum, increased in bones of young horses and in liver and intestinal pathology. **alkaline phosphatase (AP)**

(alkali + Gr eidos, form) Nitrogenous substance found in plants. Usually has bitter taste and strong physiological action. Term also used for synthetic substances, eg procaine, pethidine, which have actions similar to plant **a.**s. **A.**s common in equine practice include atropine, caffeine, cocaine, codeine, digitalis, digitoxin, ephedrine, ergometrine, hyoscine, hyoscyamine, morphine, physostigmine, pilocarpine, quinine, strychnine. **alkaloid**

Disturbance of acid base balance resulting in excess base or a deficit of acid or carbon dioxide. **metabolic a. / respiratory a.** Cf acidosis. **alkalosis**

Brown or yellowish-brown waste fluid, formed partly by placenta and partly by foetal urine secreted by kidneys and passing through bladder and urachus; surrounds foetus but is separated from contact by amnion. Quantity at 45th day of pregnancy is 100ml; at 100th day, 2,000ml; at 300th day, **allantoic fluid**

allantoic fluid	8,500ml. Contains flat rubber-like pad (hippomane, qv). Helps to protect foetus and lubricate birth canal at delivery. Escapes at beginning of 2nd stage labour when placenta ruptures. See birth: 2nd stage.
allantois	(allanto, sausage + Gr eidos, form) Outgrowth of hind gut of embryo which forms bladder, carries blood vessels in umbilical cord and later combines with chorion to form placenta. During development of foal, urine passes from foetal kidneys into bladder and then through urachus into sac formed by placenta. See allantoic fluid.
allele	(Gr allelon, of one another) One of two or more different genes which can occupy same locus (site on chromosome).
allergen	(allergy + Gr gennan, to produce) Substance which causes allergy; may be protein or nonprotein. See antigen.
allergic	Of allergy. **a. dermatitis** Syns sweet itch, Queensland itch, qv.
allergy	Body's reaction to contact with, inhalation or ingestion of, antigen qv. Form of sensitivity characterised by local reaction, eg rash or weals on skin. Horse injected with penicillin may suffer allergic reaction in form of filled legs and general malaise. Broken wind (qv) is allergic response to fungal spores or pollen which causes spasm of smooth muscle of small air passages (similar to asthma). Diseases caused by **a.** include haemolytic jaundice of newborn, purpura haemorrhagica, laminitis, nettle rash, photosensitisation.
allyltrembolone	See altrenogest.
aloes	Yellowish or reddish-brown powder with bitter taste, from various species of aloe. Used as purgative, now generally replaced by modern preparations such as danthron, qv.
alopecia	Loss of hair. See bald.
alpha	First letter of Gr alphabet, written α. See globulin, prostaglandin, radiation.
ALT	Abbr alanine aminotransferase, qv. Formerly termed GPT, qv.
altrenogest	(trade name Regumate) Synthetic progestagen, qv, composed of the substance allyltrembolone. Given by mouth to suppress oestrous and encourage development of ovarian activity.
alum	(L alumen) Colourless crystalline mass or white powder with sweetish taste. Used for astringent action in proprietary

medicines for diarrhoea, in lotions with zinc sulphate to counter proud flesh, and in toxoid preparations, eg tetanus toxoid. See lockjaw.

alum

(L dim of alveus, hollow) Small sac-like cavity. **dental a.** Socket of tooth. **pulmonary a.** Minute air sac, many together forming the interface between air and blood in lungs.

alveolus

(L ambire, to surround) That which prevails. **a. temperature** That surrounding patient. See temperature, neonatal maladjustment syndrome.

ambient

Of the Americas. **A. Assn of Equine Practitioners** (AAEP) 4075 Iron Works Pike, Lexington, KY 40511. Tel (606) 233–0147. Equivalent of British Equine Veterinary Assn, qv. **A. Farriers's Assn** Organised in 1971 to provide certification of farriers on two levels: farrier and journeyman farrier. Assn publishes *Farrier's Journal*. See blacksmith. **A. Horse Protection Society** See horse. **A. Quarterhorse** Fast, strong breed with especially muscled-up hindquarters. Named **A. Qh** because first races in USA were over a quarter-mile. Descended mainly from English Thoroughbred stallion Janus, whose stock, mostly from Spanish mares, flourished in North Carolina and Virginia in the 1700s. See hyperkalaemic periodic paralysis, wobbler syndrome. **Qh Registry** Box 500, Akron, CO 80720 (970 345 6800). **British Qh Assn,** 2 Tile Farm Rd, Orpington, Kent BR6 9RZ (01689 855021). **A. Saddlebred** Graceful breed, best examples being in USA. Now used primarily in show ring to display either 3 or 5 gaits, qv. Base of tail is vertical giving hair a fountain effect. This is achieved by nicking dock muscles and setting with a crupper (strap looped around base of tail and secured to saddle or roller). Breed influenced by English Thoroughbred, Morgan, Standardbred and, immediate forerunner, Kentucky Saddle horse. **A. S. Assn,** 4093 Ironworks Pike, Lexington, KY 40511 (606) 259–2742. **A. S. Assn of GB,** Uplands, Alfriston, E Sussex, BN26 5XE (01323 870295).

American

(trade name Amikin) Antibiotic (aminoglycoside, qv) particularly effective against pseudomonas, qv, infection of the mare's uterus and clitoris, and gram-negative infections of foals, instead of gentamicin (qv).

amikacin sulfate

An organic compound containing nitrogen, eg norepinephrine (noradrenaline, qv), dopamine, qv.

amine

(**a. a.**) Unit from which proteins are made. Essential **a.a.s** must be provided by diet. Non-essential ones can be derived from digestion of other substances in diet.

amino acid

aminoglycosides	Group of antibiotics that kill bacteria by interfering with the protein metabolism, eg streptomycin (qv), amikacin (qv) and gentamicin (qv). Kill gram-negative bacteria such as *Escherichia coli* and gram-positive bacteria such as staphylococcus. May be combined with penicillin.
aminophylline	White or yellowish powder which acts to dilate airways and stimulate heart.
ammonia	(after Ammon, near whose temple in Libya it has been found) Pungent, water-soluble gas, NH_3. **a. solution** Clear colourless liquid with characteristic odour. Used to blister legs or, diluted, to relieve irritation from insect bites.
amniocentesis	Withdrawal of fluid through needle inserted into the amnion. Not practised routinely in horses because amnion is surrounded by the allantois, qv.
amnion	Shiny transparent membrane surrounding foetus and containing amniotic fluid, qv.
amnionitis	Inflammation of amnion, producing thickened membrane due to fungal or bacterial infection; may be associated with brown staining due to premature passing of meconium, qv.
amniotic fluid	Clear colourless fluid surrounding foetus and containing acids, salts, cells and mucus; formed by foetal urine and secretion of amnion, volume increases from 120ml to 3,600ml during last 8 months of pregnancy.
amoeboid action	Moving or eating like an amoeba, ie absorbing food by surrounding it, eg white blood cell.
amorphous	(a, neg + Gr morphe, form) Having no definite form or shape; in pharmacy: not crystallised.
amoxicillin	(trade name: Clamoxyl) Antibiotic active against many gram-positive bacteria, eg streptococci and some gram-negative bacteria, eg salmonella. Occasionally used to treat foals with diarrhoea or septicaemia.
amphetamine	(trade name: Benzedrine) Synthetic powder which stimulates nervous system. Occasionally used to increase respiration during anaesthesia. Can be used dishonestly as stimulant drug.
amphi-	(Gr amphi, on both sides) Prefix meaning on both sides; also double.
amphiarthrosis	(amphi- + Gr arthrosis, joint) Form of articulation allowing

little movement, the surfaces being connected by fibrocartilage, eg vertebrae united by intervertebral fibrocartilages (discs). See vertebra. *amphiarthrosis*

(trade names: Amfipen, Duphacillin) White microcrystalline odourless powder with bitter taste. Synthetic penicillin particularly active against gram-positive and gram-negative bacteria. Given by mouth or injection. Not commonly used in horses. **ampicillin**

(Fr ampoule) Small glass container, usually used to store fluid drugs and sealed to preserve contents in sterile condition. **ampule**

(L a jug, pl. ampullae) Flask-like enlargement. **a. ductus deferentis** Enlargement in vas deferens. There is no increase in lumen of tube but a thickening of wall due to numerous tubular glands. **a. of semicircular canals.** Enlargement at one end of the three semicircular canals in inner ear. **a. recti** Terminal part of rectum which is not surrounded by peritoneum. **ampulla**

Surgical removal of limb or appendage. **amputation**

(amylo-, starch + Gr eidos, form) Abnormal material of complex nature, probably a glycoprotein, qv. May accumulate in abnormal quantities in various organs of body – particularly liver – causing amyloidosis disease. Can be a complication of wasting diseases such as glanders, strangles, tuberculosis. **amyloid**

(Gr) Prefix meaning upward, backward or repetition. (Second a is dropped before words beginning with vowel.) **ana-**

Hormone that causes anabolism (qv), eg testosterone, progesterone occurring naturally. Synthetic preparations now illegal for use in UK because of EU regulations. **anabolic steroid**

(Gr anabole, a throwing up) The cells' conversion of simple substances into complex ones, eg food into protoplasm; building of muscle and generally putting on condition. Can be increased by injecting drugs. **anabolism**

(Gr an, negative + haima, blood) Deficiency of red blood cells (erythrocytes) and haemoglobin per unit of blood. Normal RBC count is $7–12 \times 10^{12}$/litre and Hb 12–17/dl. Figures indicating **a.** would be $< 5 \times 10^{12}$/litre. Signs might be pale mucous membranes and increased rate and force of heartbeat. **a.** is due to: (1) loss of blood as a result of rupture of a vessel, external or internal bleeding (see haemorrhage); (2) increased destruction of RBCs (haemolytic **a.**) due to infection with bacteria, virus (see swamp fever), protozoa (see biliary fever), poisoning, **anaemia**

anaemia immunological reaction (see haemolytic jaundice); (3) nutritional deficiency – bone marrow may cut output of RBCs and/or Hb due to deficiency of iron, copper, cobalt or folic acid, or as a result of a generalised infection with toxin-producing bacteria such as streptococci, *E. coli*. **a.** classed as normocytic, microcytic or macrocytic according to size of red cells; or normo-, hypo- or hyperchromic according to concentration of haemoglobin in each cell (see swamp fever).

anerobe (an, neg + Gr aer, air + bios, life) Organism which lives only in absence of oxygen. **facultative a.** One able to live under anaerobic or aerobic conditions. **obligate a.** One living in complete absence of oxygen, eg *Clostridium tetani*. See lockjaw.

anaerobic Growing only without oxygen.

anaesthesia Loss of sensation especially pain. **epidural a.** Injection of 5–15ml of procaine or other local anaesthetic into epidural space, usually between 1st and 2nd tail (coccygeal) vertebrae. This blocks spinal nerves as they emerge from cord. Used for surgery of tail, vulva, anus, vagina, rectum, perineum, to repair rectovaginal fistula and in difficult birth to eliminate excessive straining. **general a.** Consciousness is lost. Used in major operations. A quick-acting anaesthetic is given intravenously to induce recumbency. Endotracheal tube (see volatile **a.** below) may be inserted into windpipe and **a.** can be maintained for several hours, depending on time needed by surgeon. **local a.** Where effect is confined to a small area. Includes procaine injection into skin causing loss of sensation in that area. Used for stitching wounds, removing growths and simple operations, eg castration, Caslick (see separate headings). Can also be injected over nerve. See nerve block. **volatile a.** Gases such as chloroform, halothane, ether. Administered through mask or through closed or open circuit apparatus of tube in windpipe (endotracheal tube). A cuff around tube is inflated, sealing windpipe so that gas can be introduced into horse's air supply.

anaesthetic Agent which produces anaesthesia, qv.

anal (L analis) Of the anus.

analeptic (Gr analepsis, a repairing) Drug which stimulates central nervous system, eg caffeine.

analgesic (an, neg + Gr algesis, pain) Drug which relieves pain without causing unconsciousness. Pain in skin, muscles, bones, joints, responds to aspirin, phenylbutazone, flunixin meglumine etc; pain in abdomen and alimentary tract to pethidine, Buscopan and morphine derivatives.

(ana- + Gr lysis, dissolution) Determination of exact composition of substance or material. **qualitative a.** Nature of constituents. **quantitative a.** Proportion of constituent. See dope test, laboratory.　**analysis**

(Gr anamnesis, a recalling) Collected medical history, ie previous abnormality or disease, date of appearance, duration.　**anamnesis**

(ana-, up again or backward + Gr phylaxis, protection) State of shock produced experimentally or unintentionally. Often result of hypersensitivity (allergy) to drug.　**anaphylaxis**

Accumulation of fluid in tissues below skin, particularly on wall of abdomen and chest. Caused by heart failure, allergy, malnutrition and septicaemia.　**anasarca**

To communicate, as in arrangement of arteries and veins which allows blood to flow past an obstruction, eg if one artery supplying foot is severed, other arteries **a.** so that bloodflow to area is not restricted; in surgery, portion of intestine can be removed (eg to correct a twist) and ends of gut anastomosed so that continuity is restored. See twist.　**anastomose**

(ana- + Gr temnein, to cut) Science of body structure and relationship of its parts. Knowledge of **a.** is based on dissection of body. **comparative a.** Comparison of different species. **morbid a.** That of diseased organs and tissues. **veterinary a.** That of domestic animals. See conformation, various breeds.　**anatomy**

Breed named after district of Spain. Influenced many breeds, including Criollo, Frederiksborg, Lipizzaner, Neapolitan and Friesian. Generally noble-looking with thick mane, although in Portugal a slighter type is used in bullring to jump away from the bull. **A. Carthusian** Descended from those **A.** horses bred by monks in Carthusian monasteries in Jerez and Seville. **A. Thoroughbred** Fine-looking riding horse, usually grey. **A. Zapatero** Descended from **A.** bred by Zapata family, now bred privately and at military stud in Cordova. Usually grey.　**Andalusian**

(Gr aner or andros, man) Combining form meaning relationship to male.　**andr-/andro-**

(andro + Gr gennan, to produce) Any male hormone. Substance which induces masculine characteristics, eg testosterone. Cf antiandrogen. See sex hormones, male.　**androgen**

An androgen in urine of both sexes which carries male characteristics. Can be injected to help improve libido of stallion.　**androsterone**

anemia	See anaemia.
anesthesia	See anaesthesia.
aneurine/ a. hydrochloride	(syns thiamine hydrochloride, vitamin B_1) White crystalline powder with meat-like odour and bitter taste. Made synthetically, from rice polishings or yeast. Forms part of enzyme system essential for metabolism of carbohydrate. Deficiency causes acids to accumulate in tissues and a reduced absorption of glucose from gut. (Deficiency is rare as **a.h.** widely distributed in foodstuffs.) Used to treat bracken poisoning and said to have quietening effect in high doses.
aneurysm	Sac-like dilatation of artery wall due to weakness caused by disease. **parasitic or verminous a.** That caused by migrating redworm larvae. Occurs in artery supplying intestines (anterior mesenteric). It may set up inflammation of artery (arteritis), causing blood to clot and stick to lining of vessel (thrombus), resulting in death; or blood clot may break into small parts which get carried in bloodstream (see embolus) until they lodge in a vessel, blocking blood supply to part of gut. Peritonitis and colic (verminous colic) follow. Treatment: scientists are trying to (1) perfect drug that will disperse blood clots (aspirin used for anti-clotting action), (2) find way of pinpointing clots, so that they can be surgically removed. Prevention lies in controlling the parasite. See redworm. Cf ulcerative enteritis.
angiography	Mapping of blood vessels by x-ray after injection of contrast medium.
angioma	(Gr angeion, vessel + -oma) Tumour formed of blood vessels. See growth.
angleberry	Wart-like growth on skin. See growth.
Anglo-Arab	Recognised cross of Thoroughbred/Arab. Popular as hack and hunter and to cross with pony breeds. To qualify for **A.A.** Stud Book, horse must be (1) produce of horse in Arab Stud Book or General Stud Book (Arabian section) and horse in GSB (not Arabian section); (2) direct descendant of horses eligible as in (1); (3) bred abroad, entered in the country's stud book and accepted by Arab Horse Society, body controlling breed in England. Breed flourishes in France through Arab and Thoroughbred stallions of National Stud (Le Haras du Pin, Orne). **A.A. Owners' Assn**, Gosford Farm, Ottery St Mary, EX11 1LX (01404 814998).

Three main types: draught, cavalry, trotter. Hybrid of latter two now being developed especially around Caen, Orne, for show-jumping. Originally developed in Normandy, France as powerful war horse. William the Conqueror said to have imported many into England. Breed deteriorated when haphazardly crossed with Mecklenburg and Danish carthorses. Later Arab, Thoroughbred and Norfolk trotter blood introduced, resulting in **A.N.** trotter, hardy type which tended to pull loads at the trot. Draught type, usually grey, developed with Percheron and Boulonnais strains and formerly used to pull mail carts. Cavalry type used by army and for sport. | **Anglo-Norman**

(an, neg + Gr hidros, sweat + -osis) Absence of or abnormal reduction in sweating. See drycoat. | **anhidrosis**

Enzyme concerned in removing water from a compound. **carbonic a.** This helps decompose carbonic acid into carbon dioxide and water, aiding transfer of carbon dioxide from tissues to blood and alveolar air. | **anhydrase**

(L anima, breath) Being with life, feeling and voluntary motion. **a.** kingdom contains about 24 large groups (number varies with classification), one of which (chordates) contains mammals (see Equidae). **a. health technician** Lay assistant to veterinarian in USA. **a. nursing auxiliary** See **Royal A. Welfare Foundation** Part of British Veterinary Assn. See Veterinary Record. | **animal**

(L animates, to give life to) Enhanced gait of show horses achieved by combination of shoeing, training and breeding. Characterised by high head, neck and tail carriage and accentuated elevation of limbs (especially forelimbs). | **animation**

(Gr anisos, unequal, uneven) Combining form meaning unequal or dissimilar. | **aniso-**

(aniso- + Gr kore, pupil + ia) Having pupils of unequal size. | **anisocoria**

(aniso- + Gr kytos, hollow vessel + -osis) Having red blood cells (erythrocytes) of unequal size. | **anisocytosis**

Preferred term for fetlock in N. America. | **ankle**

Abnormal fusion of joint surfaces by disease, injury or surgery. See arthritis. | **ankylosis**

(L anus, ring) Ring-like. **a. ligament** Band of ligamentous tissue forming part of tunnel through which flexor tendons run behind fetlock. Carpal **a.** ligament forms part of carpal tunnel. | **annular**

anoestrus	Absence of oestrus (literally no oestrus). Term used to describe period of sexual inactivity usually present in mares during winter. See also oestrous cycle.
anophthalmia	(an neg + Gr ophthalmos, eye) Absence of both eyes at birth. Rare cogenital fault requiring destruction on humane grounds. In some cases minute vestiges of eyeball are present (microphthalmia).
anoplocephala	See tapeworm.
anorchid	(an, neg + Gr orchis, testis) Male without either testis in scrotum. See rig, cryptorchid.
anorexia	Complete absence of appetite. See appetite, lack of.
anorgasmy	(an, neg + orgasm) State of failure to ejaculate. See behaviour, male sexual.
anovular	Not accompanied by discharge of an ovum. See oestrous cycle.
anoxaemia	(an, neg + oxygen + Gr haima, blood) No oxygen in blood.
anoxia	Absence of oxygen (also hypoxia - low oxygen).
antacid	Drug which corrects excessive acidity of gut, eg bicarbonate.
antagonism	(Gr antagonisms, struggle) Opposing, as between muscles, medicines, eg groups of muscles such as flexors and extensors of limb said to be antagonistic to one another; one type of antibiotic may be antagonistic to another, each reducing the other's capacity to kill bacteria, eg penicillin and Chloromycetin.
ante-	(L before) Prefix meaning before (time or place).
antenatal	Before birth.
anterior	A position which is forward, in front of or towards the head end of body, eg shin is anterior aspect of cannon bone. Descriptions of markings use **a.**, eg bay with white off-pastern extending to **a.** aspect of fetlock. Cf posterior. **a. presentation** Foetus head first during birth.
anterolateral	In front and to one side.
anteroposterior	(syn AP) Front to back, eg X-ray beam said to be **a.** when machine is in front of, and photographic plate behind, leg.

(ant- + Gr helmins, worms) (Syns worm powders, vermicide, vermifuge) Drug or substance which kills intestinal parasites (worms). Usually given in feed or by stomach tube. Acts only on those parasites in alimentary canal, not on larval forms which migrate through organs and blood vessels. In common use in horses: piperazine salts (seatworm and whiteworm), levamisole hydrochloride (lungworm), dichlorvos, phenothiazine, pyrantel tartrate, thiabendazole (redworm), oxyfenbendazole. Some are larvacidal eg ivermectin. **anthelmintic**

(Gr anthrax, coal, carbuncle) Infectious disease. Rare in horse and man, caused by anthrax bacillus. More common in cattle and sheep. See bacterial diseases. **anthrax**

Group of drugs used commercially as dyes which have a purgative action when given orally, eg danthron. **anthrocene dyes**

(Gr anthropos, man) Combining form meaning relationship to humans. **anthropo-**

Disease transmitted between man and animal; in the horse: glanders, encephalomyelitis. **anthropozoonosis**

Combining form meaning against, eg in antidote. **anti-**

Drug given to prevent abortion, eg progesterone, luteinising hormone. **antiabortifacient**

Any hormone which reduces effect of an androgen, ie decreases masculinity. **antiandrogen**

(syn bactericidal) capable of killing bacteria; drug or substance which does so, eg antibiotic, sulphonamide. **antibacterial**

(anti- + Gr bios, life) Substance or drug which kills or inhibits multiplication of bacteria. **bactericidal** or **bacteriocidal a.** One which kills bacteria, eg neomycin, penicillin. **bacteriostatic a.** One which reduces growth and reproduction of bacteria, eg chloramphenicol (Chloromycetin), chlorotetracycline hydrochloride (Aureomycin). **A.** may have both -cidal and -static powers, eg streptomycin. **broad spectrum a.** Effective against wide range of bacteria, eg neomycin, Chloromycetin. **fungicidal a.** Effective against fungal organisms, such as those causing ringworm and uterine infections, eg nystatin. Any **a.** may cause side-effects such as allergy, filling of legs, loss of appetite, diarrhoea. **antibiotic**

Substance produced by body as a result of an antigen, and which reacts specifically with that antigen. **A.** is classed **antibody**

antibody	according to its action, ie anti-enzyme, antitoxin, bacteriolysin, haemolysin, agglutinin, blood group **a.** Cf monoclonal **a.**
anticoagulant	Substance which prevents clotting of blood, eg sodium acid citrate or heparin. 120ml of solution containing 2 per cent sodium acid citrate and 2.5 per cent dextrose prevents clotting of 400ml of blood (eg when collected for transfusion). Heparin was used systematically to treat navicular disease.
anticonvulsant	Substance or drug which stops or relieves convulsions. Used to treat newborn foals.
antidiarrhoeal	Drug or substance that combats diarrhoea.
antidote	(L antidotum, from Gr anti, against + didonai, to give) Substance used to combat effect of poison. See poisons.
antifungal	Capable of killing/suppressing fungus. See antibiotic, ringworm, fungus.
antigen	Substance, usually a protein, which stimulates body's production of antibodies (immune bodies). Can be bacteria, virus, blood corpuscles, serum or toxin. **a./antibody reaction** Result when antigenic material contacts antibody in tissues or in laboratory experiment. Includes agglutination, precipitation, haemagglutination, complement fixation, neutralisation.
antigenicity	Property of being able to produce immune response.
antihaemorrhagic	Stopping haemorrhage; drug that prevents or stops it. See coagulation.
antihistamine	Drug that counteracts action of histamine, eg promethazine hydrochloride, corticosteroids.
anti-inflammatory	Reducing inflammation (qv); drug, substance or process which reduces or suppresses it. Those in common use in equine practice: phenylbutazone, oxyphenbutazone, corticosteroids, cold water, ice packs.
antipruritic	Drug, substance or measure which serves to allay itching and local irritation.
antipyretic	Temperature-reducing drug, eg pethidine hydrochloride, salicylate (aspirin), quinine (rarely used in horses). Acts by reducing production of heat or increasing its loss.
antiseptic	(anti- + Gr sepsis, putrefaction) Preventing decay; a drug or substance which acts by controlling, not necessarily killing,

organism. Cf disinfectant. (See benzalkonium chloride solution.) **a. poisoning** Result of contaminated water or accidental administration. Symptoms include convulsions, coma, shock. Treatment: give soothing substances (demulcents), saline (intravenously) and corticosteroids.

antiseptic

Serum that contains antibodies. Prepared by injecting horse or other animal with specific antigen so that large quantities of antibodies circulate in blood. This is then purified in laboratory to concentrate the antibody required. See tetanus toxoid, antigen, antibody.

antiserum

Preventing spasms, eg of painful, overactive gut; drug that does so.

antispasmodic

(anti- + Gr toxicon, poison) Counteracting the action of toxin; substance (antibody) that does so.

antitoxin

Fighting virus/es; drug or substance which destroys or suppresses their growth. See interferon. Cf vaccine.

antiviral

(an, neg + Gr ouron, urine) Little or no excretion of urine. Caused by lack of kidney secretion due to low fluid intake, excess sweating, obstructed urinary passage (see stone) or ruptured bladder. See bladder, rupture of.

anuria

Terminal part of alimentary tract. Sphincter muscle which keeps faeces in rectum. Is normally tense, but may become relaxed in diarrhoea. Is sometimes torn by forelegs of foal (see rectovaginal fistula). Should be noted for signs of parasite infestation (see seatworm).

anus

Trunk of main artery beginning at base of left ventricle. It passes upwards and forwards, then curves sharply backwards to reach spine at 8th or 9th thoracic vertebra; passes backwards underneath spine, lying first between the lungs then passing through diaphragm to enter abdomen, where it divides, under the 5th or 6th lumbar vertebra, into two common iliac arteries. May rupture causing fatal haemorrhage if its walls are weakened by redworm larvae or long-standing nutritional disturbance.

aorta

Of the aorta. **a. arch** See arteries, table of. **a. semilunar valve** One of three semilunar cusps, each with a nodule on the free edge. Valve opens during contractions of heart, allowing blood to pass from left ventricle into aorta. It closes as heart relaxes, preventing blood from returning. Closure of valve forms part of 2nd heart sound. May be infected by bacteria or redworm larvae (see endocarditis). Inefficiency of action is termed

aortic

aortic	incompetence, and hardening of cusps (with consequent narrowing of the opening), stenosis.
AP	Abbr (1) alkaline phosphatese, SAP qv. (2) anteroposterior, from anterior (front) to posterior (back) used, eg to describe x-ray view of leg. (3) anterior pituitary (see pituitary). (4) *Anoplocephala perfoliata*. See tapeworm.
apathy	Loss of interest in surroundings. Symptom of many illnesses especially those involving fever and pain.
apex	Pointed extremity or top of an organ or part, eg **a.** of heart.
aphonia	(a, neg + Gr phone, voice) Loss of voice, as caused by Hobday (qv) or similar operation. Rarely congenital.
apices	(L) Pl of apex.
apnoea	(a, neg + Gr pnoia, breath) Cessation of breathing, eg in asphyxiated newborn, during anaesthesia or in disease, when it may follow periods of rapid breathing. **terminal a.** State where heart beats but breathing stops. Horse will die in minutes without emergency measures. See neonatal maladjustment syndrome.
apo-/ap-	(Gr apo, from) Prefix meaning separation or derivation.
apocrine	(Gr apokrinesthai, to be secreted) Glandular secretion which is concentrated at one end of secreting cell then thrown off, eg milk from mammary gland. Cf holocrine and merocrine.
aponeurosis	Broad ribbon-like tendinous band of muscle attachment.
apoplexy	(Gr apoplexia) Condition associated with acute vascular lesions of brain, ie haemorrhage, thrombosis or embolism; marked by coma and paralysis. Rare in horses although similar signs found in newborn foals or adults with head injuries. See cerebellar degeneration.
Appaloosa	(spotted horse) Probably exported from Near East or Spain to Mexico about 1600 and named from breed developed by Indians of Palouse area of Washington State, N America. Now found in most parts of world and is popular as circus, drum and saddle horse. Body pink-skinned with predominantly white hair, spotted black or brown, the pattern often strikingly regular over quarters. Whatever the coat's appearance, **A.** strain easy to identify by feeling raised skin patches and noting patterned hoofs, possibly with vertical stripes. Some Arab blood present. **A. Horse Club**, PO Box 8403, Moscow, ID 83843 (208 882 5578); **British A. Soc**, 36 Clusterbolts, Stapleford, Hertford,

SG14 3ND (01992 558657); **British Spotted Pony Soc**, 7 Sand
Farm Lane, Weston Super Mare BF22 9UF.

Appaloosa

(L appetere, to desire) Conditioned reflex depending on past
associations (hunger describes sensation from stomach movements caused by lack of food). **a.** decreases in dehydration,
fluid imbalance, overwork, nervous tension, fever. Can be
increased by drugs such as anabolic steroids and possibly ton-
ics, most of which contain vitamins A, B_1 and B_{12} and minerals including iron, copper, cobalt, manganese and strychnine.
depraved a. (pica) Desire for substance not classed as food, eg
tree bark, soil, dung, afterbirth. May be result of mineral or
other deficiency, of boredom or of physiological upset, eg if
horse is given antibiotic it may nibble faeces to replace intestine's natural flora. (Fresh dung can be mixed with water and
given by stomach tube.) **lack of a.** (anorexia) Occurs in colic
and severe illness and is usually a sign of ill-health.

appetite

Breed thought to be the oldest (it was bred in Asia, more than
5,000 years ago). Later developed as it is today by jealously
guarded breeding in Arabian desert, where there were 5 strains
of Asil or pure-bred **A.**, most widespread being Kuhaylan.
(Word comes from kuhl, a paint women used around their
eyes, the connection being that **A.** has dark, kuhl-coloured
skin though the coat may be almost any colour.) **A.** has great
beauty, high spirits, proud carriage, long mane and tail, 19 (as
opposed to 18) pairs of ribs, wide deep-angled jaw and dished
profile with large, low-set eyes. Darley **A.** (imported 1704 and
bred by Anazeh tribe on fringe of Syrian desert) is ancestor of
majority of Thoroughbreds. Breed seems to be only one which
suffers cerebellar degeneration. Outperforms other breeds in
long-distance events such as endurance races and ride-and-tie.
See agammaglobulinaemia. **A. Horse Soc** Windsor House,
Ramsbury, Wilts SN8 2PE (01672 520782). **A. Horse Registry
of America**, 12000 Zuni St, Westminster, CO 80234 (303 450
4748).

Arab/Arabian

Class of Arthropoda which includes marine kingcrabs, spiders,
scorpions, parasitic ticks, mites and all their relatives. Those
important in equine veterinary medicine: sub-class Euarachnida,
order Acarina, sub-order Ixodides, family Ixodidae (see ticks), sub-
order Trombidiformes, genus Demodex (see mange) and genus
Trombicula (see harvest mite), sub-order Sarcoptiformes, family Oribatidae (see oribatid mite and tapeworm), family
Sarcoptidae, genus Sarcoptes (see mange), family Psoroptidae,
genus Psoroptes (see mange) and genus Chorioptes (see
mange).

Arachnida

(L arcus, bow) Part of circumference of a circle. **reflex a.** Term

arc

35

arc	describing route of nervous impulse reflex, eg from skin to central nervous system and returning to muscle, as in reaction to pin-prick.

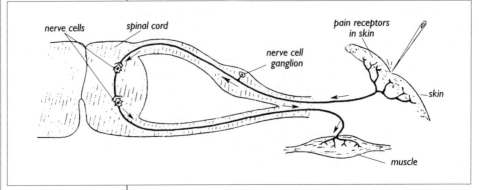

I Reflex arc (or nervous pathway); impulse is transmitted from skin to spinal cord and back to muscle, causing it to contract

arch	(L arcus, bow) Anatomical term, eg aortic **a.**, part of aorta from heart to beneath spine.
ARCS	Abbr Associate of the Royal College of Science.
Ardennes	Breed originally from **A.** mountains and area spanning French/Belgian border. Old-established, hardy type used by Napoleon's cavalry and in World War I. Crossing with Brabançon breed has produced some draught families, while other strains are 14–15 hands. Especially popular in Sweden, where they make up more than half the horse population. **A. Horse Soc of GB**, Weather Hill, Brancepeth, Crook, Durham, DL15 9AS. (01358 780159).
arecoline hydrobromide	White crystalline odourless powder with bitter taste. Alkaloid obtained from seeds of *Areca catechu*. Contracts involuntary muscle, eg in alimentary tract, uterus and air passages; contracts pupils, slows heart rate and stimulates salivary glands. Action reversed by atropine. See colic.
areola	(L dim. of area, space) Minute space in tissue. **a. tissue** Special cells which fill spaces between muscles or under skin.
areflexia	Absence of reflexes.
arrhythmia	(a, neg + Gr rhythmos, rhythm) Irregular heartbeat or rhythm, eg dropped beat. Diagnosed by electrocardiogram but can be heard with a stethoscope. **sinus a.** Disturbed SA (sino-atrial) node. See electrocardiogram; heart.

Medicinal forms include Fowler's and Donovan's solutions, now rarely used. **A.** tends to accumulate in liver and is slowly released to other tissues. Toxicity varies with solubility but in massive doses it causes rapid death. Symptoms include abdominal pain, staggering, collapse and paralysis; in less acute cases: salivation, thirst, diarrhoea (sometimes blood-stained), exhaustion, loss of appetite, trembling and subnormal temperature. At postmortem: acutely inflamed alimentary tract; swollen mucous membranes which come away when rubbed. Diagnosis: symptoms confirmed by urine analysis; at postmortem liver is most useful material for chemical analysis. Treatment: saline purgative followed by kaolin, sodium thiosulphate 10g in 100ml water IV and 30g in about 300ml of water by mouth. | **arsenic**

See equine viral arteritis. | **arteritis**

Of an artery. | **arterial**

(L arteriole) Minute artery which leads from a larger artery to a capillary, qv. | **arteriole**

Hardening of artery walls. | **arteriosclerosis**

(L and Gr arteria, from aer, air + terein, to keep, because **a.**s once thought to hold air) Tube, part of system which conveys blood around body. It has thick walls of elastic tissue and muscle formed of outer coat (adventitia), middle coat (media) and inner coat (intima). Carries bright red blood (due to high oxygen content) except pulmonary **a.**s, at high pressure, in contrast to vein or capillary. Most **a.**s divide and branch until they end in arterioles. For main ones see table. | **artery**
(Table of Major Arteries, see p38)

(Gr arthron, joint + -itis) Joint inflammation caused by trauma, infection or stress. Any joint affected but most common are knee (carpus), fetlock and intervertebral joints. **infective a.** See joint-ill. **osteo-a.** Ulceration of joint surface and rarification of bone below with growth of new bone (oesteophyte). See joint mice. **rheumatoid a.** Chronic disease not known in horses. **synovial a.** Inflammation of joint membrane producing increased joint oil (synovia) and swelling. See windgall, bog spavin. **ankylosing a.** Destruction of joint surface following infection or injury. Results in fusion of underlying bones, eliminating movement. | **arthritis**

Combining form meaning relationship to a joint. | **arthr-/arthro-**

(arthro- + Gr kele, tumour). Swollen joint. See windgall, joint. | **arthrocele**

TABLE OF MAJOR ARTERIES

Part	Artery	Origin	Area of supply or continuing artery
chest	coronary (right & left)	aorta	heart muscle
chest	pulmonary	right ventricle	lungs
chest/abdomen	aorta	left ventricle	all parts of body other than lungs
chest	common brachiocephalic	branch of aorta	forelegs, head and neck
chest	brachiocephalic	brachiocephalic trunk	head, neck and right foreleg
head & neck	occipital	common carotid	brain and spinal cord
head & neck	internal carotid	common carotid	brain
head & neck	external carotid	common carotid	upper jaw, pharynx, tongue, lips, face, eyes and ears
head & neck	internal maxillary	external carotid	lower jaw, meninges, eyelids, nasal passages and palate
right foreleg	brachial–right	brachiocephalic	right foreleg
left foreleg	brachial–left	common brachiocephalic trunk	left foreleg
forelegs	brachial	brachiocephalic and common brachiocephalic	shoulders and forelegs
forelegs	median	brachial	forelegs below elbow
forelegs	common digital	median	medial and lateral digital
forelegs	medial and lateral	common digital	forelegs below fetlock
hindlegs	femoral	external iliac	popliteal a., belly muscle, udder, penis, stifle region, muscles of hindquarters
hindlegs	popliteal	femoral	stifle joint, muscles at bases of 2nd thigh, hock, cannon bone and lower part of leg
hindlegs	common plantar	popliteal	medial & lateral plantar a.
hindlegs	medial and lateral plantar	common plantar	hindlegs below fetlock
chest	thoracic aorta	ascending aorta	oesophagus, intercostal muscles, substance of lungs
abdomen	abdominal aorta	thoracic aorta	contents of abdominal cavity
abdomen	anterior mesenteric	abdominal aorta	small intestine, caecum, part of large colon
abdomen	renal (left & right)	abdominal aorta	kidneys
abdomen	posterior mesenteric	abdominal aorta	colon and rectum
genital organs	internal spermatic (male) (left & right)	abdominal aorta	spermatic cord and testes
genital organs	utero-ovarian (left & right)	abdominal aorta	ovaries and uterus
back	lumbar	abdominal aorta	skin and muscles of back
hindquarters	internal iliac	abdominal aorta	contents of pelvic cavity, perineum, penis, clitoris, tail, muscles of hindquarters
abdomen	umbilical	internal	placenta in foetal life, round ligament of bladder (adult)
abdomen	external iliac	abdominal aorta	femoral a., uterus, muscles of back (psoas)

Puncture of a joint to draw off fluid. See synovial fluid. **arthrocentesis**

Inflamed joint cartilage. See joint. **arthrochondritis**

(G arthron, joint + G desis, a binding together) Surgical fusion of a joint. **a.** of two or more vertebrae occasionally used to treat wobbler syndrome, qv. **arthrodesis**

(Arthropoda) (Gr arthro-, joint + pous, foot) Phylum of animal kingdom of which Arachnida (qv) and Insecta are main classes. Members have hard exoskeleton and paired, jointed legs. Some are important in human and veterinary medicine because they suck blood and act as vectors. See insect, tick. **Arthropod parasites**

(arthro, joint + scope) Instrument for viewing interior of joint through tube containing lights and mirrors. Used also for removing chips of bone or cartilage, ie arthroscopic surgery. See endoscope. **arthroscope**

Junction between two or more bones. See joint. **articulation**

(L articularis) Of a joint eg **a.** cartilage (qv). **articular**

Unnatural; by mechanical process. **a. insemination (AI)** Putting stallion semen into mare's uterus. Fresh or frozen semen can fertilise egg after **AI**. (Freezing is more difficult than when using cattle semen.) **a. respiration** Breathing with help of, eg oxygen mask or ventilator (may be necessary in treating shock, respiratory stress). **a. vagina (AV)** Apparatus used to collect semen for laboratory examination. Usually rubber sheath surrounded by warm water inside flask-like cylinder. When stallion has mounted mare, penis is directed into **a.v.** See also condom. **artificial**

(Gr arytaina, ladle + eidos, form) Jug-shaped. **a. cartilage** See wind. **arytenoid**

(pl ascarides) Genus of nematode parasite. See whiteworm. **Ascaris**

(after German gynaecologists, Selmar **A.** and Bernhardt **Z.**) Pregnancy test in humans; female's urine is injected into mouse. Similar test adopted in horses, using blood instead of urine. See pregnancy tests. **Aschheim-Zondek test**

Collection of fluid in abdomen. Caused by toxins in blood (septicaemia) or obstructed blood flow to liver. May be accompanied by oedema in other parts of body. Fluid consists of blood plasma or exudate. (Urine may collect in abdomen in cases of ruptured bladder.) **ascites**

ascitic	Of, or characterised by, ascites.
ascorbic acid	(syn vitamin C) Odourless, colourless crystals or white crystalline powder with acid taste. Essential to all animals, but horses unlikely to suffer deficiency. Given to treat anaemia or chronic haemorrhage. See bleeder.
asepsis	(a, neg + Gr sepesthai, to decay) Absence of septic matter or freedom from organisms. See antiseptic, disinfectant.
ASIF	(syn AC/ASIF) Association for the Study of Internal Fixation. Applies biological and metallurgical research techniques to improve internal fixation (qv) in orthopaedic surgery. Encourages exchange of practical and scientific experiences in fractures, osteotomies, non-unions and reconstructive procedures. Developed manual of internal fixation techniques and also standardised surgical instruments. Secretariat: Clavadelerstrasse, CH-7270 Davos-Platz, Switzerland.
aspartate aminotransferase	(AST) Formerly known as GOT. Enzyme found in liver and muscle. Normal level less than 400 IU/l serum, increased in soft tissue/liver/muscle damage. Setfast levels may exceed 10,000 IU/l. Levels peak after 24–48 hours, returning to normal after 10–20 days. See creatine kinase (CK).
Aspergillus	Genus of fungus.
asphyxia	(a, neg + Gr sphyxis, pulse) Suffocation; condition of decreased oxygen and increased carbon dioxide in blood and tissues. **a. neonatorum** Faulty breathing in foal. Birth subjects foal to degree of **a.** from which it rapidly recovers, in normal situations, as breathing starts. See breath.
aspirator	Apparatus for sucking fluids and matter from a cavity; used in surgery.
aspirin	See acetylsalicylic acid.
ass	Member of Equidae similar to donkey and probably its ancestor. Two sub-species, Onager (the wild **a.** of Bible) and Kiang. Types include **Nubian wild a.** (*Equus asinus africanus*); **Somali wild a.** (*Equus asinus somalicus*); **Indian wild a.** (*Equus hemionus khur*). Usually about 12 hands; grey or dun with pale belly; dark dorsal stripe between short, dark mane and dark, tufted tail; long ears and boxy hoofs. Makes braying noise instead of whinny (see equine sounds). Has 62 chromosomes, qv. Cf mule.

Abbr aspartate aminotransferase, qv. Formerly termed SGOT (serum glutamic oxaloacetic transaminase). — **AST**

(Gr panting) Disease characterised by difficult breathing (dyspnoea) and accompanied by wheezing due to spasmodic contraction of bronchi, qv. Usually caused by allergy and complicated by bronchitis. See broken wind. — **asthma**

Drug or chemical which causes contraction of blood vessels and stops discharge. **a. lotion** Often mixture of copper and sulphate and used to check growth of proud flesh. — **astringent**

(Gr astron, star) Combining form meaning relationship to a star, eg star-shaped. — **astro-**

(astro- + Gr kytos, hollow vessel) Star-shaped cell; as found in nervous tissue, eg brain. — **astrocyte**

(a, neg + Gr symmetria, symmetry) Inequality in size, shape of parts of body on opposite sides. — **asymmetry**

Not showing or causing symptoms or signs. — **asymptomatic**

(L atavus, grandfather) Remote inheritance rather than from immediate ancestors, due to chance combining of genes. — **atavism**

(Gr ataxia, lack of order) Failure in muscle coordination. See wobbler syndrome, cerebellar degeneration. — **ataxia**

(Gr ateles, imperfect + ektasis, expansion) Incomplete expansion at birth, or subsequent collapse, of air sacs in lungs. See broken wind, neonatal maladjustment syndrome. Adjective: atelectatic. — **atelectasis**

(Gr athere, gruel + -oma) 1) Lesion of arteries characterised by degenerative changes. 2) Sebaceous (qv) cyst. — **atheroma**

Lesion of arteries in which deposits occur in inner lining resulting in yellowish plaques containing cholesterol and other fatty material. May occur in aorta of horses and cause heart murmurs or rupture of artery. — **atherosclerosis**

First cervical vertebra articulating with skull. — **atlas**

(a, neg + Gr tresia, a hole + -ia) Absence or closure of normal body opening. May be congenital as in absence of part of rectum and small colon. See meconium retention. — **atresia**

Condition in which heart beats irregularly (arrhythmia) due to — **atrial fibrillation**

atrial fibrillation	rapid and ineffectual contractions (flutter) of first chambers. Causes reduced performance and, months or years later, enlarged heart and death. Diagnosis: on ECG recordings. Treatment: digitalis and quinidine sulphate can sometimes revert heartbeat to normal rhythm.
atrioventricular valves	Those guarding opening between first and second chamber (atrium and ventricle) on left and right sides of heart. See mitral and tricuspid valves.
atrium	(L, Gr atrion, hall) A chamber; anatomical term, eg either of first chambers of heart, qv.
atrophy	(L and Gr atrophia) Wasting or diminution in size of cell, tissue, organ or part. **muscle a.** Wasting of muscle due to lack of use, in lameness or paralysis.
atropine	Alkaloid contained in plants of the family Solanaceae (deadly nightshade), dwale (blanewort), henbane and thornapple. **a. poisoning** Symptoms: dry mouth, increased pulse and respiratory rate, extreme dilation of pupils, blindness, restlessness, muscular trembling followed by fall in temperature, convulsions, paralysis and death. Diagnosis: place a drop of horse's urine into eye of a healthy animal, eg cat, and observe the dilation of pupil in bright light half an hour later. Treatment is largely ineffectual. **a. sulphate** (trade name Atrocare) Colourless odourless alkaloid crystals, synthetic or extracted from *Hyoscyamus muticus*. Antagonises effects of arecoline and diminishes secretions from salivary, bronchial and alimentary glands. Causes increased heart rate, dilated pupils. Used before operations or with purgative to reduce pain caused by excessive stimulation of alimentary tract. Given by injection, by mouth or in eye drops, ointments. See purgatives; eye, diseases of.
attapulgite	(trade name Forgastrin) Substance given in combination with charcoal to combat diarrhoea.
attenuation	(L attenuation from, add to + tenuis, thin) Altered virulence of a microorganism by passage through host species or by repeated growth on laboratory media; process used to prepare vaccine, qv.
atypical	(a, neg + Gr typos, type or model) Not conforming to typical pattern; of unusual type, eg signs of disease may be **a.** of a particular syndrome. **a. behaviour** See vices.
Aujeszky's disease	(after Aladar A., Hungarian physician) See rabies.

Combining form meaning ear.

aur-

Of ear or hearing.

aural

See chlortetracycline hydrochloride.

aureomycin hydrochloride

(L auricula, a little ear) The external ear, ie pinna or flap of ear. Also atrium or first chamber of heart. See ear, heart.

auricle

(L auscultere, to listen to) To examine by listening with or without stethoscope. See stethoscope, heart sounds, murmur, borborygmus.

auscultate

Act of listening for sounds within the body, eg of chest, heart, abdomen. Usually performed with a stethoscope.

auscultation

Breed developed in New South Wales. No other type recognised as national breed, but draught horses (developed from Shire, Suffolk Punch and Clydesdale), ponies (from Timor stock), polo ponies and Thoroughbreds bred in most states. See Brumby.

Australian Waler

(Gr autos, self) Prefix meaning relationship to self.

aut-/auto-

(auto- + L clavis, key) Apparatus used for sterilising instruments, swabs etc. Relies on heat produced by steam under pressure.

autoclave

Immune response to component of own body eg **a**. haemolytic anaemia in foals.

autoimmune

Effect of toxin generated by microorganisms normally present in body, eg those in gut can, in certain conditions, produce a harmful toxin causing diarrhoea or colic.

autointoxication

(auto-, self + Gr lysis, dissolution) Disintegration of cells and tissues by their own enzymes; process of dissolution after death.

autolysis

Arrangement of nerves regulating actions not under conscious (voluntary) control ie heart, smooth muscle and glands. Composed of sympathetic (or accelerator) and parasympathetic systems and characterised by a junction (synapse) between spinal cord and nerve-ending in organ or tissue. (Place of junction known as a ganglion.) Action of the 2 systems is usually antagonistic, eg pupil of eye dilated by sympathetic, constricted by parasympathetic; heart rate increased by sympathetic, slowed by parasympathetic; gut movement decreased by

autonomic nervous system

autonomic nervous system	sympathetic, increased by parasympathetic; secretion of glands in lungs and alimentary canal decreased by sympathetic, increased by parasympathetic; blood pressure increased by sympathetic, lowered by parasympathetic. Drug which mimics action of sympathetic nerves (energy) is adrenaline. Drug which mimics action of parasympathetic nerves (rest) is acetylcholine. Cf nervous system.
autopsy	(auto- + Gr opsis, view) See postmortem.
AV	Abbr artificial vagina, qv.
avitaminosis	Deficiency of vitamins in diet. See appetite.
avulsion	(L from a, away + vellere, to pull) The pulling away of a part eg in a fracture.
axilla	Area between shoulder and chest through which vital nerves and arteries travel.
axis	(L, Gr axon, axle) (1) Imaginary line dividing body or part of it symmetrically. (2) Second cervical vertebra. Also a main line of direction, motion, growth, or extension. **pastern a.** Imaginary line passing through centre of pastern when viewed from side. **foot a.** Imaginary line parallel to hoof wall at toe and, ideally, in a continuous line with pastern axis when viewed from side. When viewed from front, an imaginary line passing through centre of toe of hoof. Conformation in which pastern and foot axes are not continuous lines (viewed from front and side) predisposes limb to certain pathological changes. See conformation.
azotaemia	(azote + Gr haima, blood + -ia) Excess urea (qv) in blood.
azoturia	See setfast.

(after Victor Babès, Roumanian bacteriologist) Protozoan (qv) parasitic in red blood cells of man and animals. See piroplasmosis (babesiosis). **Babesia**

(pl bacilli) Rod-shaped bacterium eg *E. coli* – found in faeces, *Klebsiella pneumoniae* – cause of venereal infection, *Clostridium tetani* – cause of tetanus. Specifically, member of genus Bacillus. **bacillus**

Substance produced by gram-positive organism *Bacillus subtilis*. Used as antibiotic against gram-positive bacteria. **bacitracin**

Part of horse's body from withers to tail. **broken b.** Fracture of one or more vertebrae, may result in severed or pinched spinal cord causing paralysed hindlegs. **dipped or hollow b.** Depressed vertebral column behind withers giving sunken look. See muscles, vertebra. **back**

Vertebral column or spine. Series of bones (vertebrae) which form column extending length of body; acts as support for legs and ribs and forms bony canal for main nerve trunk (spinal cord, qv). **backbone**

Flow of fluid in an abnormal direction, eg **b.** of blood from second to first chamber of heart, due to faulty valve action. See heart. **backflow**

Removal of faeces from rectum, eg before rectal examination of colic case. **back-raking**

Bacteria in blood. **bacteraemia**

(pl of bacterium) Extremely small chlorophyll-free unicellular organisms which multiply by simple division. (Also called germs, microbes, microorganisms. Cf fungi, which are multicellular with sexual reproduction, and viruses, minute part icles invisible with standard microscope, which reproduce only in living cells.) **b.** classified by (1) reaction to stains (dye): eg gram-negative, gram-positive, acid-fast; (2) shape: eg coccus – round; bacillus – cylindrical rods; vibrio – comma shaped; actinomyces – with branching filaments; spirochaete – long and flexible, twisted around long axis; (3) size: eg average diameter of a coccus is about 1/25,000th an inch; (4) arrangement: eg strings – streptococci (distinguishable from staphylococci which have grape arrangement); capsules – around some **b.** and can be demonstrated by staining, eg klebsiella; (5) spore formation: oval **bacteria**

bacteria | or round bodies in framework and in cell membrane of **b.** eg *Clostridium tetani*; (6) flagella: long, delicate threads on motile **b.** eg *Escherichia coli*. **b., cultivation of** In laboratory **b.** should be grown on/in special substances known as media, eg fluid media containing meat extract, broth or peptone; solid media made of gelatine (albumin from tendons and cartilage) or agar (dried sea-weed); selective media, those favouring growth of certain **b.**, eg which are coloured by dye. Material containing the **b.** is placed on/in sterile media and incubated overnight at 38°C. Colonies grow on solid media and a sediment of **b.** accumulates in liquid media. Sediment or colony can then be examined under micro-scope and tested further. **b., identification of** Classification is by how **b.** grow in fluid and solid media, their biochemical activity, eg side reactions during growth as in klebsiella, which split urea, streptococci which ferment carbohydrate.

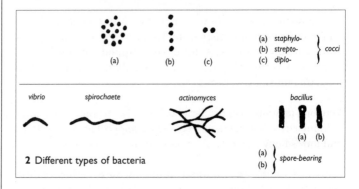

2 Different types of bacteria

bacterial | Of bacteria **b. abortion** See abortion. **b. diseases**

Specific disease	Causal organism
acne	*Staphylococcus aureus*
	Corynebacterium pyogenes
anthrax	*Bacillus anthracis*
botulism	*Clostridium botulinum*
brucellosis	*Brucella abortus*
glanders	*Loefflerella mallei* (syns *Pfeifferella mallei, Malleomyces mallei*)
leptospirosis	*Leptospira pomona*
lockjaw	*Clostridium tetani*
malignant oedema	*Clostridium septicum*
salmonellosis	*Salmonella typhimurium*
	Salmonella abortus equi
	Salmonella enteritidis
sleepy foal disease	*Actinobacillus equuli*
strangles	*Streptococcus equi*
summer pneumonia	*Rhodococcus equi*
tuberculosis	*Mycobacterium tuberculosis*
ulcerative lymphangitis	*Corynebacterium pseudotuberculosis*

Non-specific disease	Bacteria	*bacterial*
abscess (1,2)	1 *Staphylococcus aureus*	*Figures in brackets indicate*
diarrhoea (3)	2 *Streptococcus pyogenes var equi*	*most common causal bacteria*
	(*S. zooepidemicus*)	
joint-ill (1,2,3,4)	3 *Escherichia coli*	
lymphangitis (1,2)	4 *Klebsiella pneumoniae*	
meningitis (1,2,3)	5 *Pseudomonas aeruginosa*	
uterine infection	6 *Hemophilus influenzae*	
(metritis) (1,2,3,4,5)		
pneumonia (1,2,3)	7 *Bordetella species*	
snotty nose (1,2,6,7)		

(bacterium + L caedere, to kill) Able to destroy bacteria. **bactericidal**
Antibiotics are classified as **b.** or bacteriostatic. See antibiotic.

(bacteria + Gr phagein, to eat) Virus which kills bacteria. **bacteriophage**

Able to inhibit the growth/multiplication of bacteria, eg **bacteriostatic**
sulphonamide. See antibiotic.

Colloq for mammary glands, qv. **bag**

Of glans penis or glans clitoridis. **balanic**

Inflamed glans penis. **balanitis**

(balano + Gr posthe, prepuce) Inflamed glans penis and also **balanoposthitis**
prepuce.

Loss of hair over a part of the body due to eczema, dermatitis **bald**
(inflammation of skin), trauma eg rubbing harness, hormonal
disturbance.

(Fr a tossing about) See pregnancy tests. **ballottement**

(1) Part of upper gum between front teeth (incisors) and either **bar**
tusks (absent in mare) or premolars. Area bears no teeth and
takes bit of bridle. (2) Continuation of wall of foot; turns inward
at heel to run parallel with frog. See foot.

Native breed of Morocco, Algeria and W Africa around Lake **Barb**
Tchad. Delicate-looking, with particularly low-set tail. Can
thrive on poor food, like Arab, but is less spirited than its more
popular neighbour. Virtually extinct outside natural home due to
extensive crossing, particularly with Arab. **B.** and Arab are
ancestors of English Thoroughbred. **Spanish B.** Developed in
Spain from **B.** and bred in USA for endurance and hardiness.
S.B. Breeders' Assn,12284 Springridge Rd, Terry, MS 39170
(601 372 8801).

barbiturate	Class of drug used as sedative and anaesthetic (or, dishonestly, as stopper dope). Symptoms of **b.** poisoning: shallow breathing, lethargy, coma, absence of normal reflexes, dilated pupils. Can cause death from respiratory failure (due to depression of nerve centres). Treatment: give stimulant drugs. See dope test.
barium	A pale yellowish, metallic element belonging to the alkaline earths, whose acid-soluble salts are poisonous; its atomic number is 56; atomic weight 137.34. **b. swallow** Test where **b.** is inserted into mouth and its progress on swallowing monitored by series of radiographs. Used in diagnosis of grass sickness (qv) and other conditions causing dysphagia (qv).
barker	See neonatal maladjustment syndrome.
barley	Cereal grain often fed to horses. **b. straw** Used for bedding but considered inferior to wheat straw because horses tend to eat it. See food.
baroreceptor	Sensory nerve-ending stimulated by changes in pressure especially in blood vessels. See nerve-ending.
barren	Sterile; infertile. **b. mare** One that is not pregnant; also barreller. See infertility.
barrier	Obstruction. **blood-brain b.** Division between blood and central nervous system. Term means substances and drugs in blood cannot necessarily pass into nervous system. **placental b.** Placental membrane between maternal and foetal blood. It is selective, allowing only certain substances to pass to foetus.
base	(L, Gr basis) Foundation or lowest part; a substance which takes up hydrogen ions and thereby makes a solution more alkaline. **b. deficit** Lack of base (alkaline salts) in blood, resulting in acidity. Present in diarrhoea, convulsions. See blood tests, biochemical (7). **b. narrow/b. wide** Terms of conformation, qv.
basilar	(L basilaris from basis, base) related to lower part eg **b.** fracture of sesamoid bone.
basophil	(Gr basis, base + philein, to love) Histological term denoting structure or cell easily stained with basic dyes especially type of white blood cell. See blood tests (5).
bastard strangles	See strangles.
Basuto/Basuto pony	One of most sure-footed breeds. Developed in S Africa from Cape horse, Arab, Barb and, later, English Thoroughbred. Used

for polo and general riding in S Africa, where it is still crossed with Arab.

Basuto/Basuto pony

(or Deli) Pony of hills of Sumatra. Takes name either from island's **B.** inhabitants or port of Deli. Usually brown or skewbald with crested neck and delicate head due to Arab influence.

Batak

See coat colouring.

bay

(trade name BCG) Abbr bacillus Calmette-Guérin. Preparation of live bacteria used (1) to protect against tuberculosis, (2) to treat sarcoid (qv) growths.

BCG

See club foot.

bearfoot

A pulsation of heart or artery. See pulse. **dropped b.** An irregular **b. ectopic b.** Heartbeat originating at some point other than sino-atrial node. See electrocardiogram.

beat

Breed now dying out which resembled heavy Thoroughbred, usually over 16 h and chestnut or bay. Developed in **B.** region of E Germany from local mares, Arab and Thoroughbred stallions. Rule of **B.** breeding was that Thoroughbred-sired fillies were covered by only **B.** stallions. **B.** stud sold to Polish government after World War I.

Beberbeck

Alcoholic drink from barley and hops. Given as conditioner, especially to hunters and older Thoroughbreds racing in Britain and Ireland.

beer

Draught breed developed from mares around **B.** river, Veronej province, Russia, and Dutch stallions, with progeny being bred to Orlov trotters, qv.

Beetewk

Demeanour. Most horses' natural **b.** is inhibited by domestication but patterns do exist. Those described are typical of a normal, healthy horse – deviation may indicate ill-health. **atypical b.** See vices. **eating b.** The horse is now a continuous feeder, a grazer (see evolution) and seldom takes more than a mouthful or two before moving a step. When stabled it should be fed little and often, because its stomach is small for its size (see food). It sometimes nibbles tree bark or dung (see appetite, depraved) but does not usually graze where it defecates. Foal nibbles solid food at about 8 days old. **foal b.** Foal is born with head unsteady, eyes open, ears back and tail tucked down. It quickly rights itself onto brisket and paws with forelegs, moving away from mare, causing umbilical cord to break (see birth). Mare nuzzles and licks foal and when, a quarter of an

behaviour

behaviour | hour after birth, it tries to stand, she nickers (see equine sounds). After repeated efforts it finally stands, maybe three-quarters of an hour after birth. At about an hour old, foal's lips make sucking movements as it searches for mare's udder. It sniffs and licks any object and eventually finds way along mare's flank to stifle, which it may suck vigorously before finding teats. After about 2 hours it walks easily, gets up and down, nurses and, if humans approach, seeks mare's side. If mare appears in pain (qv), foal shows distress by whinnying and circling round her. Sleep and awareness of danger steadily increase, though foals carefully handled in first few hours show less fear and are more tractable later. (**abnormal foal b.** See neonatal maladjustment syndrome.) **general b.** (temperament) Probably inherited (see gene) and affected by training. Some claim sire is more likely than dam to pass on temperament and that energetic **b.** is more easily transmitted than passive **b.** White, palomino and grey horses are thought more tractable and tend to be cautious (because they are conspicuous to enemies) while chestnuts are less tractable. Few judges now claim aggressive nature for certain points of conformation, eg small ears, small eyes. Fighting, by kicking and biting, is usually between a stallion and any other entire male or gelding who tries to oust him as herd leader. **herd b.** In the wild, a herd roams little at night. As most foals are born during darkness, herd is unlikely to move before new foals can travel. Herd leader is usually a stallion who, especially during spring and summer, stays near whichever mare is in season. Herd leader (can also be old or large horse) can be identified by watching feeding order. Grey horses often act as look-outs (see **general b.**). **male sexual b.** Colt may show erection and mounting at 6–8 months, but is unlikely to mate before 10–12 months. Penis is comparable to human penis (vasculomuscular type) therefore entry into mare (intromission) depends on full erection. Stallion shows three phases: (1) courtship, (2) erection and mounting, (3) intromission and ejaculation. In courtship stallion neighs on seeing receptive mare, arches back and curls upper lip (flehmen posture), nudges mare, smells vulva and bites skin of her rump. Erection is gradual until, when complete, penis is 30–50cm (12–20in) long. (In captivity, experienced stallion may achieve erection when taken to covering yard, before seeing mare.) Immature stallion may try to mount mare sideways and might mount 1–4 times before intromission. Ejaculation, on average, is 13 seconds later and recognised by flagging of tail. Some stud grooms, to be certain it has occurred, hold base of stallion's penis to feel flow of semen. Sexual drive (libido) is keenest in spring, which coincides with mare's natural breeding season. **abnormal male b.** includes sometimes savaging mare instead of ejaculating, and masturbation (qv). **mare b.** Mare's bond with foal develops as she licks and sniffs it soon after birth. When she stands, maybe 30 minutes later, she will shelter it from intruders. Attachment increases until she weans foal, about 10 months later (in wild state), by being uncooperative when it wants to suck (see weaning). Occasionally mare lets another foal suck, but usually accepts only her own (see foster). (**abnormal mare b.** Some mares are hostile towards foal and may savage it. Occasionally mares show lesbian **b.** by mounting one another.) **b. during pain** See birth, colic, setfast. **resting b.** Horse sleeps intermittently for about 7 hours of the 24, mostly in hottest part of day, though habits vary according to breed. Most horses sleep standing up and rest by lying down to expose body to sun. Horse may paw ground before lying down, lowering first shoulders, then quarters. It rests on one side, with legs outstretched, or on side of chest with a forelimb and a hind limb flexed under body. (It cannot rest, dog-like, on sternum, as bone forms a sharp ridge.) On rising, forelegs stretch ahead and chest rises as hocks take weight. **social b.** When horses first meet they show 4 stages of acceptance: (1) they circle, watching one another; (2) touch nostrils; (3) investigate the other's body and tail with tip of muzzle; (4) if mutual tolerance is agreed, nibble one another's necks. Horses prefer particular herd-mates, usually of the same social rank (see also equine sounds). **voiding b.** Adult defecates 5–12 times a day and urinates 7–11 times, though figures depend on breed, climate, diet and amount of work. Horse does not defecate where it grazes, but will walk to a particular area. Entire horse tends to back into area, but mare faces patch, so that field of mares soon becomes horse-sick. A gelded animal may change habit from that of stallion to that of mare. Entire horse (but not mare) smells ground before and after defecating. He also sniffs ground after urinating. The sexes adopt similar stance to urinate – hind legs pushed back and apart. The stallion walks away, lashing tail and flexing penile muscles. Mare may wink vulva, as if in season. (If she has foal at foot she will defecate and urinate more carefully to avoid contaminating udder.) See ethology; equine sounds.

behaviour

(syn. deadly nightshade) (1) Plant poisonous to horses. See nightshade poisoning. (2) Fine green powder with slight odour and bitter taste. Prepared from leaves of *Atropa belladonna*. Similar action to atropine sulphate, qv.

belladonna

Fine white odourless powder. Stimulates central nervous system and used to lighten barbiturate anaesthesia after operations.

bemegride sodium

Non-malignant, eg growth which does not recur when removed. See metastasis, growth.

benign

benzalkonium chloride solution	Clear colourless liquid with aromatic odour and bitter taste. Used 1 part to 50 parts water or 1 in 500 with alcohol for pre-operative sterilisation of hands and arms. Instruments, but not rubber, may be stored in 1 in 2,000 dilution.
benzamine penicillin	White odourless tasteless powder. Antibacterial action which, when given by IM injection, is released slowly over several days.
benzene hexachloride	See gamma.
benzimidazole	Group of substances that kill internal parasites of gastrointestinal and respiratory tracts of horse such as strongyles (see redworm), ascarids (see whiteworms), oxyuris and dictyocaulus (see lungworm). Includes oxyphenbendazole, mebendazole, fenbendazole, thiabendazole and oxybendazole.
benzyl benzoate	(trade name Killitch) Colourless crystalline or oily liquid with faint aroma and sharp burning taste. Used to treat sarcoptic mange. See mange.
benzylpenicillin	(syn penicillin, penicillin G; trade names: Crystapen, Solupen) Fine white crystalline powder obtained by growing *Penicillium notatum* in suitable culture medium. Bacteriostatic drug and, in high dosage, bactericidal against gram-positive bacteria, eg clostridium, corynebacterium, leptospira, streptococci. Relatively inactive against gram-negative bacteria. See infection, strangles, joint-ill, pneumonia, uterus (infection of).
beta	Second letter of Gr alphabet. Designates certain cells. See insulin, globulin, radiation. **b. hemolysis** Clear zone round growth of streptococci on blood agar due to breakdown of blood (haemolysis) by toxins produced by the bacteria. See *Streptococcus pyogenes*.
betamethasone sodium phosphate	(trade names: Betnesol, Betsolan, Duphacort) Absorbent crystalline powder with slight odour. Potent anti-inflammatory steroid. For uses and side-effects see cortisone acetate.
BEVA	See British Equine Veterinary Association.
Bhutia	Native pony of India, sure-footed and hardy. Usually grey and about 13h (larger than other native of India, the Spiti).
bi-	(L bi, two) Combining form meaning two or twice.
bicarbonate	Salt with two equivalents of carbonic acid to one base, eg **sodium b.**, counteracts acidity in stomach and blood, makes urine more alkaline and is used to treat excess staling. See milkshake.

(bi- + L caput, head) Muscle having two heads. See muscles. | **biceps**

Relating to biceps muscle, eg **b.** groove on front of humerus bone. **b. bursitis** Inflamed bursa between biceps brachii muscle and **b.** groove. Symptoms are those of shoulder lameness, including shortened stride and stumbling. Diagnosis: on signs, swelling at point of shoulder, pain when joint is manipulated. Treatment: inject bursa with corticosteroids. | **bicipital**

(bi- + L cornutus, horned) Having two horns, eg uterus. | **bicornuate**

(bi- + L cuspis, point) Having two cusps, eg molar teeth or **b.** valve of heart. | **bicuspid**

Abbr for L bis in die, twice a day, eg in drug frequency. | **b.i.d.**

(syns osteodystrophia fibrosa, miller's disease) Disease of horses on unbalanced diets, high in phosphorus (P) and low in calcium (Ca) such as cereal, hays and bran. Usually affects horses 2–7 years old. Can be produced by diets with a ratio of Ca to P of 1:3 or greater, irrespective of total Ca intake. Low Ca intake (2–3g per day) and Ca/P ratio of 1:13 causes symptoms within 5 months. A Ca intake of 26g per day and a Ca/P ratio of 1:5 produces signs in a year. Normal ratio in a diet should be 1.3:1.0. Soft fibrous tissue forms in bones and first symptoms are lameness, arching of back and creaking joints. Erosions of joint cartilage develop and, in advanced cases, bones may break and tendons become sprained. If not treated, condition results in swollen lower jaw and enlarged face. Treatment: give diet with Ca/P ratio of 2:1. Cereal, hay should be supplemented with alfalfa, or clover and limestone (20–40g daily). See calcium. | **big head**

(syn capped knee, popped knee) See hygroma. | **big knee**

See lymphangitis. | **big leg**

(bi- + L latus, side) Having or affecting two sides. | **bilateral**

Brown or greenish-yellow fluid secreted by liver and carried in **b.** duct to intestines. It aids emulsification and absorption of fats and contains acids, pigments, carbonate, cholesterol and mucin. Constantly secreted by the horse which, unlike other species, does not have gallbladder in which to store it. See bilirubin, biliverdin. | **bile**

(L bilis, bile) Combining form meaning relationship to bile. | **bili-**

A serious condition caused by *Babesia caballi* and *B. equi* | **biliary fever** *biliary fever* (parasites which live in red blood cells and are transferred from host to host by ticks and possibly other blood-sucking insects). After a bite, parasite incubates 5–30 days. Symptoms: depression, thirst, watery eyes with swollen lids, intense jaundice (turning all tissues deep yellow) and minute haemorrhages on mucosal surfaces. These signs are followed by constipation or diarrhoea and in some cases oedema of limbs, head and abdomen. The urine is red due to presence of haemoglobin and there is severe anaemia. Can be fatal. Recovery takes weeks or months. Diagnosis: by examination of blood smears for presence of parasites. These begin to disappear from circulation soon after day of bite so smears should be made early. Carrier state exists and may occur in foals. Treatment: diminazene aceturate qv; phenamidine isethionate, qv; quinuronium sulphate.

3 Various stages of Babesia reproduction in red blood cells; the organism causes biliary fever

bilirubin (L bill + L ruber, red) Bile pigment formed from haemoglobin when red blood cells are destroyed by special cells. Liver normally changes **b.** into biliverdin (qv) but it may be found in urine and tissues in cases of jaundice. See blood (biochemical tests: 4), haemoglobin, red blood cells, jaundice.

bilirubinemia (bilirubin + Gr haima, blood) Abnormal amount of bilirubin in bloodstream.

bilirubinuria Abnormal amount of bilirubin in urine.

biliverdin (bili- + L viridis, green) Green pigment which liver forms from bilirubin, before it passes to intestines.

bimastic Having 2 mammary glands, eg mare.

biniodide An iodide with 2 atoms of iodine in each molecule, eg **b.** of mercury, used as blister, qv. See red mercuric oxide.

bio- (Gr bios, life) Combining form meaning relationship to life.

biologicals Medicines prepared from living organisms, eg serums, vaccines, antigens, antitoxins.

biomechanics Application of laws of mechanics to movement and action of living things.

(bio- + Gr metron, measure) Science of statistics applied to biological facts; mathematical expression of biological data. **biometry**

(bio + Gr opsis, vision) Removal of a minute portion of tissue to study in laboratory, eg portion of tumour, uterus, bone or liver. A **b.** punch or needle is used, depending on site and tissue involved, eg liver **b.** is performed through flank, uterine **b.** through vagina. **biopsy**

(trade names: Biometh-Z, Biotrition, Kerra Care) Member of B vitamin group necessary for healthy growth of hair and hooves. Used as dietary supplement. **biotin**

Condition found in Australia if horses graze *Indigofera dominii* plant. Symptoms: wandering in circles, pushing head against objects. Certain types of protein, eg peanut meal, gelatin, may help to counteract toxicity. **birdsville disease**

(syns labour, parturition, confinement, foaling) Act of expelling foal and its membranes from uterus, through **b.** canal. Occurs between 7pm and 7am in 90 per cent of mares. Relatively fast and completed in 3 stages. **birth**
1st stage b. (hotting up) Surface veins stand out and mare may run milk. Uterus contracts causing signs of pain/unease – pawing ground, looking round at flanks, flehmen posture, lifting hind leg, raising tail, hindquarter cringing. Signs appear in increasingly intense phases, between which mare may rest or eat. Muscles in uterus wall bear down on contents in waves passing towards cervix, which dilates. Foetal head and limbs are propelled into **b.** canal. This stage may last minutes to several hours. May occur hours, days or weeks before foaling and be repeated several times. Mare said to hot up and cool off. Finally, placenta ruptures.
2nd stage b. Starts when mare 'breaks water' (placenta ruptures, allowing escape of yellowish (allantoic) fluid). Mare shows most of signs of 1st stage plus straining. Many mares get up and down several times but 95 per cent complete delivery when down. Mare may half roll, apparently to alter foal's position for easier delivery, or lie with back against wall. Abdominal muscles contract to supplement action of uterus by reducing size of abdomen. Foal is forced along **b.** canal until only hind legs are left in vagina. 2nd stage lasts 5–60 minutes and averages 20 minutes.
3rd stage b. Foal paws with forefeet, dragging hind feet clear of vagina. Mare usually stays down for up to 40 minutes. She normally delivers foetal membranes (afterbirth) about an hour after foal, but it may be from 5 minutes to 10 hours. Mare may roll and show other signs of pain as uterus returns to non-pregnant size (involution) and placenta separates from uterine

birth | wall. **b. canal** Foetus's route from uterus to outside: cervix, vagina and vulva, encased in pelvis. **b., hazards of** Include trauma and **b.** haemorrhage. See dystocia; rectovaginal fistula; uterus, prolapse of; vaginal bruising; afterbirth, retention of. **b. haemorrhage** (syn parturient haemorrhage) Bleeding during or immediately after delivery of foal. Two types: internal and external. Internal is result of ruptured artery in membrane (broad ligament) supporting uterus. At birth this is enlarged to accommodate extra bloodflow necessary for pregnant uterus. Rupture allows blood to escape but it may be contained by peritoneum. If blood escapes into abdominal cavity, mare bleeds to death. External bleeding is from lining of uterus after separation of afterbirth. Some blood may be from placenta. Condition is not usually fatal but causes pain and can lead to uterine infection. Symptoms: pain, sweating, rolling, curling upper lip, pawing ground, rapid breathing and pulse, pale mucous membranes which became chalk-white in fatal cases. Swelling may appear to one side of vulva. Initially mare may be reluctant to proceed with 2nd stage labour, may roll during delivery and if she survives, may be jaundiced (best seen on sclera of eyes and lining of gums) after 24 or 48 hours. Treatment: quiet handling, rest, pain-relieving drugs, tranquillisers, blood-coagulating agents, transfusion of whole blood but this is ineffective unless plenty is available, ie over 17 pints. Prevention: no specific measures but copper deficiency may be associated with fatal haemorrhage. Avoid using twitch for at least 24 hours after foaling as its use may start haemorrhage. Cf vaginal bruising. **b. management** As far as possible mares should be allowed to foal without interference but should be watched for signs of abnormality. Many breeds foal outdoors but Thoroughbreds nearly always foal in a loose-box. This should be at least 3.65m x 3.65m (12ft x 12ft) with good ventilation and clean bedding, which should not be shaken as this can contaminate atmosphere with dust. Mare should be watched at a distance and breaking of water recognised. Within 5–10 minutes of this the shiny amniotic membrane should appear at vulval lips. After thoroughly washing hands, attendant should feel in vagina for foal's muzzle and forelegs and if mare's vulva has been stitched (Caslick operation) it should be cut with straight scissors. Further action unnecessary unless 2nd stage is delayed, ie straining does not occur or is not associated with a progressive appearance of foal. After complete delivery the umbilical cord should be left to rupture when mare gets to her feet or foal struggles. Mare should not be disturbed or made to get up prematurely. During final stages of delivery amnion can be removed from foal's head. This is unnecessary for normal healthy foal but may prevent an unhealthy one suffocating. Amnion can be tied to cord after it has ruptured, to provide a weight which helps delivery

of afterbirth. **pre-b. position** For about 4 months before **b.** foe- | *birth*
tus lies on back with head and limbs flexed. In 1st and early
2nd stage labour, body rotates and forelegs extend. Foal passes
into **b.** canal with forelegs stretched out, one slightly ahead of
the other. See dystocia; presentation; position; posture.

(after a **Mr B.** who originated deceitful marking of teeth) To | **bishop**
make grooves in front teeth (incisors) so animal appears
younger than it is.

(L, twice a day) See b.i.d. | **bis in die**

(trade names: BCK, Forgastrin, Pepto Bismol) Tasteless, odour- | **bismuth**
less creamy-white powder. Given internally to soothe stomach
and intestine, or applied externally as protective ointment,
lotion or powder.

(syn farrier) A smith, or maker, who forges iron. Frequently | **blacksmith**
used to denote farrier (horseshoer) because of close association
of the two trades in the past. See shoe, shoeing. **Worshipful
Company of Farriers,** 37 The Uplands, Loughton, Essex, IG10
1NQ (0181 508 6242). **American Farriers' Association,** 4059
Iron Works Pike, Lexington, KY 40511 (606 233 7411).

(L cystis) Any membranous sac, but usually means urinary **b.** | **bladder**
Hollow muscular organ roughly pear-shaped and capable of
holding up to a gallon of urine. **b., rupture of** (syn patent **b.**)
Colloq for condition of newborn foal in which hole or tear in
b. wall causes continual escape of urine into abdomen. May be
result of faulty development or injury during birth. Signs
appear 2–4 days after birth and include failure to pass normal
stream of urine, crouching and straining (must be distinguished from more common condition of meconium retention,
qv). Abdomen becomes distended with fluid which can be
drawn off. See paracentesis. Treated by operation under general anaesthesia to close tear. Most cases survive if diagnosed
early, otherwise foal dies from pressure of diaphragm on lungs,
causing suffocation.

Cell mass (blastoderm) and fluid-filled cavity (blastocoele) | **blastula**
formed from division of fertilised ovum. See embryology.

White marking (qv) over forehead and bridge of nose. | **blaze**

Fluid sac or vesicle beneath skin, eg **b.** of local anaesthetic. | **bleb**

Horse which suffers from nosebleeds (epistaxis). Several dis- | **bleeder**
tinct types of condition, the most common one occurring after
exercise and termed exercise-induced pulmonary haemorrhage

bleeder	(EIPH), qv. Other haemorrhages may occur spontaneously from the nasal passages or guttural pouch (qv). The latter results from ulcer forming in top of pouch often associated with fungal infection. Ulcer may penetrate branch of carotid artery which is immediately above pouch. Fatal haemorrhage may result. Treatment is to tie off branch of carotid in surgery under general anaesthesia.
blemish	Defect, pathological or otherwise, in tissue such as skin or bone, which does not interfere with horse's action; may diminish value but not function. Examples: bone spavin, bog spavin, capped hock, capped knee (see hygroma), crooked tail, firing marks, saddle sores, scars, splints (if not lame), shoe boil (capped elbow), thoroughpin, windpuff (windgall).
blepharitis	Inflammation of eyelids. Caused by injury, flies, infection with bacteria.
blepharo-	(Gr blepharon, eyelid) Combining form meaning relationship to eyelid or eyelash.
blepharospasm	(blepharo- + Gr spasmos, spasm) Spasm of eyelid muscles, occurs in painful conditions of eyeball, especially when subjected to light.
blister	(L vesicula) (1) Collection of fluid that causes horny upper layer of skin to rise, separating it from parts below. May be filled with blood. See blood **b.** (2) Colloq for fluids and ointments that cause counter-irritation and are used to treat tendon injuries or inflamed joints. **B.** may be cantharides (Spanish fly), red mercuric iodide or ammonia compound (which all cause small **b.**s) or mustard or turpentine, which make skin peel. Treatment dying out on humane grounds in favour of rest and/or physiotherapy.
bloat	See colic.
block	Obstruction or stoppage. Used in connection with impulse through heart muscle, local anaesthesia (nerve **b.**) or colloq for stoppage in alimentary tract. See colic, heart, nerve **b.**
blood	Red fluid circulating in arteries, capillaries and veins and driven by pumping action of heart. Consists of about 40 per cent cells and 60 per cent fluid (plasma). Cells are mainly red (erythrocytes) – 8,000,000 per cu mm; rest are white (leucocytes) 7 to 8,000 per cu mm (8×10^9/l) or platelets – 200,000 per cu mm (7-8 x 10^9/l). Plasma contains water, proteins, salt, sugars, enzymes, vitamins and minerals. **B.** takes nourishment and oxygen to body cells, carries waste material and gas (carbon

blood

dioxide) to organs of excretion, ie lungs, gut, kidneys, and transports hormones. It is one of 3 vehicles for body water, the others being intracellular and interstitial fluids (see fluid balance). **b. blister** (syn haematoma) Collection of **b.**-stained fluid in muscle. It lifts skin, area often becoming gradually larger until it needs lancing and washing out with antibiotics. Common sites: brisket and hindquarters, resulting from kick or other injury. **clotted b.** See coagulation. **cord b.** That in umbilical arteries and veins. **b. disease** Changes in composition of **b.** may be due to: (1) Condition in part of body, eg diarrhoea which causes loss of body fluid (see dehydration) and therefore **b.** becomes more concentrated (haemoconcentration). Liver disease may alter protein and enzyme levels (see liver disease). (2) Infection with parasites (see biliary fever), bacteria or virus (see swamp fever). (3) Haemolytic diseases (see haemolytic jaundice). (4) Primary conditions (see anaemia, leukaemia). **b. in faeces** Sign of enteritis due to bacterial/parasitic infection. **B.** is dark if bleeding is some distance from rectum and bright if it is close to anus. **b. groups/types** Various inherited systems are present in red **b.** cells (erythrocytes). Red cell systems are designated A, C, D, K, P, Q, U and further divided into factors. Serum polymorphism systems : albumin (Al), transferrin (Tf), esterase (Es), protease inhibitor (Pi), A1B, Gc, haemoglobin (Hb), 6PGD, PGM and PGI. These systems are divided into factors. Systems and factors can help establish parentage of a foal and widespread DNA testing is expected soon. A record of **b.** is necessary to qualify for General Stud Book (Thoroughbreds). **occult b.** That present in such small quantities that it can be detected only by laboratory tests. **peripheral b.** That circulating in, or close to, skin. **placental b.** That in placenta. **b. plasma** That part of whole blood in which red and white cells are suspended. If anticoagulated **b.** is allowed to stand, plasma is seen as clear fluid above sediment of cells; contains water, proteins and salts. **b. pressure** Pressure in arteries (high) and in capillaries and veins (low). During contraction (systole) of heart, pressure is about 120mm of mercury (Hg) in arteries, but during relaxation (diastole) it falls to about 80mm Hg. In veins pressure may be as low as 5mm Hg, and close to heart there may be small negative pressure when **b.** is sucked into chambers. Estimating arterial pressure impracticable in standing horse; has been tried using cuff around tail or limbs. Pressure can be gauged by inserting catheter into artery and connecting it to measuring apparatus, usually only during anaesthesia. **b. serum** Clear fluid which separates when **b.** clots. Similar to plasma but does not contain fibrinogen. **b. tests** Examination of **b.** samples in laboratory to aid diagnosis of disease. Haematology is examination of cellular content; biochemical tests determine levels of minerals, salts, enzymes, proteins; serological tests show **b.** groups and the presence of *blood* | antibodies. Haematology: (1) Red **b.** cell count – the number of red cells (erythrocytes) per litre. Normal range 7–12 x 10^{12}/litre depending on age and state of fitness. (2) Haemoglobin content – measured in g per dl, normal 12–17. (3) Packed cell volume (haematocrit or PCV) – proportion of cells to plasma expressed as litres/litre. Normal range, depending on age and fitness, 0.33–0.49 litres of cells/litre of plasma. (4) White **b.** cell count – number of white cells per cu mm of **b.** Normal range 5–10,000 (5–10 x 10^9/l). (5) Differential white **b.** cell count – polymorphs 50 per cent, lymphocytes 45 per cent, monocytes 2 per cent, eosinophils 1 per cent, basophils 2 per cent of total white cell count. (6) Platelet count, normal 150–300 x 10^9/litre. (7) Erythrocyte sedimentation rate (ESR) – rate at which red **b.** cells (erythrocytes) separate from plasma if sample of **b.** is left to stand. Samples usually left at room temperature and measured in mm per hour. Normal range 10–50mm per hour. Not usually significant in horses. For these tests **b.** is collected into bottles containing an anticoagulant to prevent clotting. Red cell count, haemoglobin and packed cell volume can show anaemia, qv. White cell count can indicate infection; see infection, diagnosis of. Platelets help clotting. Biochemical tests: (1) Total serum protein (TSP) – grams of protein per litre of serum. Normal 50–70g/l. (2) Albumin and globulin – albumin/globulin ratio of TSP. Normal ratio about 1:0.7 (that is 30–40g/l albumin and about 17–30g/l globulin). TSP increases in disturbed fluid balance and decreases in chronic conditions. Albumin/globulin ratio is reversed (eg 0.5:1.0) in infectious disease and albumin levels may fall below 20g/l in liver disease. (3) Serum enzymes – aspartate aminotransferase (AST), creatine kinase (CK) and serum alkaline phosphatase (SAP). Levels are measures of liver and muscle activity. They rise in disease of tissues (see setfast; heart, diseases of; liver, diseases of; bone, diseases of). Normal levels: AST – less than 400IU/l; SAP – less than 400IU/l depending on age, higher in young animals; CK – less than 200IU/l. (4) Bilirubin – bile pigment. Normal: total bilirubin less than 40μ/l; direct bilirubin less than 15μ/l. Tests can distinguish between bilirubin (bile pigment) which has entered **b.** before passing through liver from that which entered afterwards (see jaundice). (5) Calcium and phosphorus levels – normal range: calcium 2.5 – mmol/l. Calcium/phosphorus ratio in young animals is normally about 4:2.5 and in 3-year-olds and over, 3:1. Changes occur in bone disease, rickets and dietary deficiency, or excess of either mineral (see calcium/phosphorus ratio). Most biochemical tests are performed on serum. **B.** is collected into clean bottle and left at room temperature, so that it clots, leaving serum separate. (6) Plasma is used to measure hormone levels – progesterone, oestrogen, cortisol. **B.** is collected into an anticoagulant (eg heparin) and centrifuged to separate cells from plasma. (7) **b.**

gases (oxygen and carbon dioxide) and acidity (pH) can be *blood* measured in **b.** collected from a vein but arterial samples are necessary to study lung function. These tests are not routine but help diagnose acid states of **b.** (as a result of metabolic or respiratory dysfunction), foal conditions, diarrhoea, broken wind and other diseases of lungs and liver. **B.** can form basis of function tests, eg using dye, such as bromosulphalein (qv), to measure its rate of disappearance from **b.** (This shows liver function.) **B.** can also be examined for unnatural substances, such as dope (barbiturates, minerals, toxins, see dope test). Serological tests: levels of antibody can be measured in serum and expressed in titre, ie the lowest dilution of serum at which antigen/antibody reaction occurs in test tube, eg in brucellosis 1 in 10 titre is negative and 1 in 40 positive. These tests are used to diagnose virus infections. Initially (acute phase) the body has not reacted to infection and level of antibodies in **b.** has not been affected. A sample at this stage can be compared with one taken 2 or 3 weeks later (convalescent phase) when titre is higher. This is evidence of an infection of the antibody used in test, eg a horse with fever and cough is tested for levels of influenza virus antibodies in acute phase (result 1 in 100). In convalescent stage, serum level is 1 in 640 (definite evidence of infection with influenza). See also pregnancy tests, cross-matching. **b. transfusion** Giving **b.**, usually of one horse to another. The donor **b.** is collected into bottle containing anticoagulant and transfused with apparatus attached to a needle or catheter inserted into recipient's vein, usually the jugular. Before transfusion it is usual to cross-match to ensure compatibility. See cross-matching. **b. in urine** Sign of setfast, infection or stone in bladder or urethra. Stallion may bleed from the urethra after repeated attempts at service due to rupture of small vessel at distal end of penis. **b. vessels** Arteries, capillaries and veins. The system of tubes carrying **b.** from heart to body tissues and organs and returning it to heart to complete circulation. **whole b.** That which contains all its elements. See anaemia; plasma; red cells; white cells.

Colour of dye, eg methylene **b.** used as antiseptic and in labo-   **blue** ratory for staining. **b. roan** See coat colouring.

(L corpus, Gr soma) Whole of horse, or main part. **inclusion b.**   **body** Particle in cell infected with virus.

Swollen hock joint due to increased synovial fluid. Caused by   **bog spavin** faulty conformation, OCD injury, nutritional deficiency, anaemia, allergy or infection with bacteria or virus. Symptoms: fluctuant swelling over front inside of hock and two smaller swellings on outside of joint about hand's breadth below point of hock. Treatment: identify cause, treat accordingly and

bog spavin possibly inject corticosteroids into joint and apply deep heat. See spavin.

boil External abscess. Treatment: apply warm poultice until ripe; lance or allow to burst, use antibiotics. **blind b.** Abscess which does not form a core and may not burst. Affects saddle area in particular. Cf warble fly, acne.

bolus (L, Gr bolos, lump) (1) Mass of food before swallowing or in intestines. (2) Substance in which to hide pill, eg **b.** of honey. (3) Rapidly administered volume of drug.

bone Hard substance making up body's skeleton, on which soft tissues hang. Consists of 35 per cent living and 65 per cent non-living material. Half the weight of **b.** is non-living calcium phosphate which, with fluid of **b.**, is constantly changing; entire calcium content of skeleton is replaced about every 200 days. Covered by membrane (periosteum) and if, as in a long **b.**, it has a hollow (marrow) this is lined with membrane (endosteum). Consists mainly of a ground substance or matrix arranged around living cells in concentric rings. These rings form cylinders (lamellae) through which fine (Haversian) canals travel along axis of **b.** These canals contain small arteries and veins to supply **b.** cells. Cells immediately around Haversian canals are osteoblasts, which secrete matrix of **b. B.** varies according to place in skeleton and may be compact, spongy, or a mixture, eg hind cannon (metatarsal) has a compact shaft with a spongy inside which helps to give lightness and strength. Long **b.**s grow at either end from cartilage in which calcium is laid down, so changing calcium into **b.** Life of molecule of calcium can be examined by making it radioactive and following it with a geiger counter. Typically, a molecule of calcium might stay in **b.** for 10 days, then travel in bloodstream. Equine blood contains 4 parts calcium (12mg per 100ml) to 1 part phosphorus (4mg per 100ml). **b., diseases of** Can affect structure, outer lining (periosteum), growth rate (epiphysis) or cavity and marrow. Conditions are caries, rickets, osteoarthritis (see arthritis), epiphysitis, osteitis, periostitis, osteoarthropathy, exostosis, osteodystrophy, fracture. **b. flour/b. meal** Source of calcium and phosphorus; included in some compound feeds. See calcium/phosphorus ratio. **b.s of foreleg** Shoulder blade (scapula), arm (humerus), forearm (radius and ulna), knee (carpus, containing 8 small **b.**s), cannon **b.** (metacarpus, equivalent of **b.**s between human wrist and knuckles), digits, (1st, 2nd and 3rd phalanx **b.**s, equivalent to human finger). **b.s of hind leg** Hip (pelvic girdle or os coxae), which joins its fellow on opposite side at symphysis and articulates above with sacrum – hip is composed of ileum, ischium and pubis; thigh (femur) which articulates with pelvis at top end and with tibia and patella below; second thigh (tibia and fibula), hock (tarsus, containing 6 small **b.**s, equivalent to human ankle), cannon (metatarsal); digits similar to those of foreleg. See skeleton; cartilage.

bone

Colloq 2nd or subsequent dose of vaccine, qv.

booster

Leather and metal cover for part of limb, eg hock **b.**, ankle **b.**, foot **b.** Used to protect when travelling, racing etc or to hold dressing in place.

boot

Salt of boric acid, qv.

borate

(pl borborygmi) Sound from food, fluid and gas passing through intestines by movement of alimentary tract. Can be heard with naked ear or stethoscope. Loud in diarrhoea and spasmodic colic; decreased in cases of blocked alimentary tract. See colic, peristalsis, twist.

borborygmus

Genus of gram-negative aerobic bacteria which is implicated in some respiratory infections.

Bordetella

White shining scales, crystals or powder; odourless, nonirritant, with slightly bitter taste. Can be applied to wounds, ulcers, mucous membranes and as mouthwash or eye lotion.

boric acid

An infectious viral disease affecting brain. Causes fever, paralysis, muscular tremors and hypersensitivity with death 1–3 weeks later. Similar to encephalomyelitis, qv.

borna disease

Genus of spirochete. Tick-borne bacteria causing borreliosis. **B. burgdorferi**. Cause of Lyme disease (qv).

Borrelia

Botfly larva which lives in horse's stomach. Belongs to order Diptera, family Oestridae. Five species of genus *Gasterophilus*, 3 of which live in Britain – *G. intestinalis, G. nasalis* and *G. hemorrhoidalis*. (Others are *G. pecorum* and *G. inermis*.) Fly is about 13mm (¹/₂ in) long, resembles bee but cannot suck, bite or feed because its mouth parts are degenerate. Life cycle: adult fly is active in early summer and September, making humming sound as it flies. On warm days it hovers close to horse, with egg ready at rear (ovipositor) and lays up to 300 eggs an hour. Each hatches in 9–12 days but first larvae cannot develop until licked into a horse's mouth. The larvae of *G. inermis* and *G. hemorrhoidalis* can pierce cheek to enter mouth. In mouth, larva penetrates mucosa and burrows down wall of gullet. *G. intestinalis* wanders in tongue 20–30 days. The 2nd and 3rd larvae (**b.** maggots) live in stomach, although those of *G. inermis* and *G. pecorum* are also found in pharynx and gullet.

bot

4 Botfly (*Gasterophilus intestinalis*) – female

bot | Maggot is thought to live on host's food for about 10 months. It drops off stomach wall and either attaches to rectum or passes straight out. On the ground it wriggles to a crevice to pupate. The pupal stage lasts about 3 weeks, then adult fly emerges and cycle is complete. Adult flies can cause horses to panic and gallop into each other or into fences; maggots cause inflamed stomach or other parts of digestive tract and disrupt digestion. Treatment: haloxon.

botulism | Paralysis of muscles caused by action on their nerves by the toxin of *Clostridium botulinum*. Toxin prevents action of acetylcholine (qv) at junction of nerve with muscle. Horses very susceptible. Toxin eaten with forage causes forage poisoning, loss of tone of the tail and tongue, which hangs out of mouth. Swallowing difficulty results in saliva drooling from mouth and spilling of food/water, with food in nostrils. Affected horse 'plays' in feed and water buckets. Weak, shuffling gait develops and muscle tremors appear as the individual tires. Death occurs from paralysis of respiratory muscles. Antitoxin available and prognosis is favourable but if horse becomes cast or disease develops rapidly, mortality is high. Disease follows similar course in foals and term 'shaker' denotes characteristic muscle tremors and standing difficulty.

Boulonnais | Draught horse named after breeding area in Pas-de-Calais dept of France, around Boulogne. Two types: Abbeville, medium size and Dunkirk, larger and heavier. Improved by Arab and Barb stallions brought home by French crusaders. Generally strawberry or blue roan, dapple grey or black, resembling Percheron, qv.

bowed tendon | Colloq for inflamed deep and superficial flexor tendons and their sheaths (tendinitis) of forelimb. Shows as bulge in normally straight line (seen in profile) behind cannon bone. Treatment: (1) physiotherapy, hot and cold applications, ie poultice or deep heat by shortwave plus cold water from hose or iced bandages; (2) massage and supporting bandage; (3) surgery by stabbing, splitting, transplant; (4) blistering or firing, now dying out on humane grounds; (5) injections of glycosaminoglycans IM or into tendon; (6) superior check ligament division. Requires 3–24 months' rest depending on severity.

boxy | Colloq, club-footed. See club foot.

brace | Device that transmits, directs, resists, or supports weight or pressure. **shoe b.** Therapeutic shoe designed to support fetlock after severe tendon injury. **surgical leg b.** Similar to **shoe b.** to assist in supporting surgically or traumatically damaged sites while they heal; usually a portion is hinged or bolted on to allow access for treatment.

brace

Of the foreleg. **b. plexus** See nerves, table of.

brachial

Area from shoulder to elbow. Adj: brachial.

brachium

(Gr brachys, short) Combining form meaning short.

brachy-

Caused by eating young bracken; it contains an enzyme which inactivates thiamine, causing deficiency. Symptoms: incoordination, staggering and unnatural stance, eg feet well spread and back arched. Severe muscular tremors develop, death is preceded by chronic spasms and drawing back of head (opisthotonos). Treatment: 50–100ml thiamine sub cut.

bracken poisoning

(Gr bradys, slow) Combining form meaning slow.

brady-

(Gr bradys, slow + Gr kardia, heart) Slow heart rate.

bradycardia

(L encephalon, Gr enkephalos) Part of central nervous system occupying skull (cranium). Weighs about 650g (23oz) and forms about 0.7 per cent of bodyweight in medium-sized horse. It consists of 3 main segments: cerebrum (or cerebral hemispheres), cerebellum and medulla. These are divided into secondary segments and derivatives: medulla oblongata; pons cerebellum; anterior cerebella peduncles; anterior medullary velum; corpora quadrigemina; cerebral peduncles; optic thalami; hypothalamic tegmen; pineal body; pituitary body; optic nerves and retinae; cerebral hemispheres; olfactory tracts and bulb. All segments contain nerve cells (grey matter) and nerve fibres (white matter) and parts are specialised to control certain functions, eg cerebellum, movement; medulla oblongata, breathing. **B.** also contains cavities: 4th ventricle, cerebral aqueduct, back and front parts of 3rd ventricle, lateral ventricles and olfactory continuations. **b. cortex** External layer of any part of **b. b., diseases of** Include abscess and growth. Both are rare. Abscess causes drowsiness and incoordination (similar to encephalomyelitis, qv) and may be due to *Streptococcus equi* infection. Growth (syns neoplasm, tumour) is usually a slowly developing abscess which causes chronic changes in **b.** See also cerebellar degeneration. **b. haemorrhage** Bleeding into **b.** Result of kick, knock etc or, in foals, of difficult birth. See neonatal maladjustment syndrome. **b., injury of** Most common after collision or rearing. Symptoms, which vary with extent and site of injury, include semi- or complete unconsciousness, convulsions, incoordination, failure of eye pupils to contract in bright light, blindness, bleeding from nostrils and/or ears. Any of these may continue to some degree after initial recovery. **b. parasites** Botfly or redworm larvae occasionally wander to **b.**, damaging tissue.

brain
(see illus, page 66)

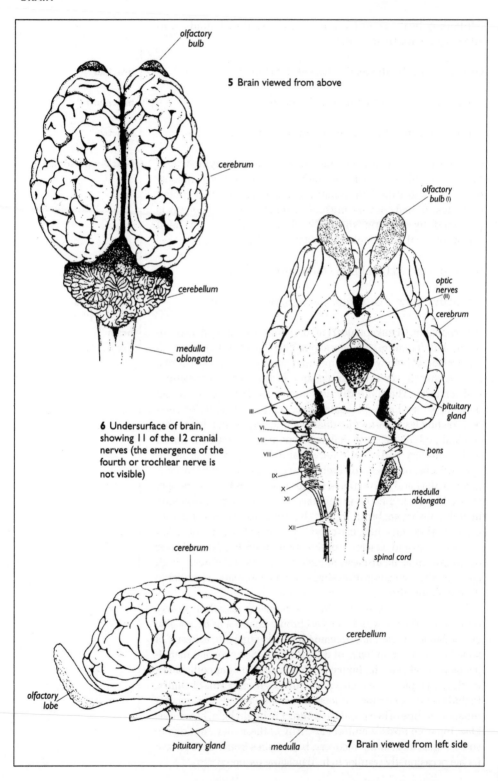

olfactory
bulb

5 Brain viewed from above

cerebrum

olfactory
bulb (I)

optic
nerves
(II)

cerebrum

cerebellum

medulla
oblongata

pituitary
gland

6 Undersurface of brain,
showing 11 of the 12 cranial
nerves (the emergence of the
fourth or trochlear nerve is
not visible)

III
V
VI
VII
VIII

IX

X
XI

XII

pons

medulla
oblongata

spinal cord

cerebrum

cerebellum

olfactory
lobe

pituitary gland

medulla

7 Brain viewed from left side

Food obtained from outer coat of cereal grain, usually wheat. See food.	**bran**
Colloq for escape of fluid from vagina at start of 2nd stage labour. See allantoic fluid, birth.	**breaking of water**
Front part of chest, usually pectoral region, ie in front of forelegs. Cf brisket. **b. bone** (syn sternum) Bone in centre of chest, keel-shaped in horse.	**breast**
(L spiritus, halitus) That air taken into lungs due to expansion of chest (inspiration) and expelled by contraction of chest (expiration). **bad b.** Sign of constipation, colic, decayed teeth, sinusitis, some forms of pneumonia. **first b.** That taken by foal when born as it struggles to break amnion; may be series of gasps followed by rhythm. Cf asphyxia neonatorum.	**breath**
Alternate inspiration and expiration of air. **b. rate** (respiration) Adult: 12–20 breaths per minute at rest. The younger the horse, faster the rate. Increased in exertion, fever, pneumonia, acidity of blood (acidaemia), anaemia. See broken wind; wind.	**breathing**
See dystocia.	**breech**
(1) To reproduce. See behaviour, oestrous cycle, embryology. (2) A division within species *Equus caballus*. See names of various breeds.	**breed**
Bred in Brittany, France. Three types: **B.** heavy draught, usually grey or bay with light 'feathers', about 16 h; **B.** mountain draught, up to 14/15 h; **B.** draught post, lighter type.	**Breton horse**
(L brevis, short) Combining form meaning short.	**brevi-**
Harness for horse's head, usually leather straps attached to metal piece (bit) in mouth. Used by veterinarians to control horse being examined when twitch (qv) would be unnecessarily severe or dangerous. See birth haemorrhage.	**bridle**
Area of body over sternum (breastbone). Horses said to lie on **b.** when head, neck and withers are off ground, forelegs flexed and one hindleg is beneath body. More common position of rest than lying flat on one side of body. See behaviour.	**brisket**
Of Gt Britain. **B. Equine Veterinary Assn** (BEVA) Hartham Park, Corsham, Wilts SN13 0QB (01249 715723). Founded in 1960 as a division of **B. Veterinary Assn. B. Field Sports Soc.** See hunter. **B. Horse Soc** (BHS) Body which oversees horse societies, sets show standards and examines riding instructors.	**British**

British | See horse. **B. Pharmacopoeia Veterinary** Booklet of use, action and dose of drugs and vaccines, distributed by Pharmaceutical Press, 1 Lambeth High St, London SE1 7JN (0171 735 9141). **B. Show Jumping Assn** A division of **B. Horse Society**. **B. Veterinary Assn** (BVA) See Veterinary Record. **B. Veterinary Journal** See Veterinary Journal.

broken wind | (syns heaves, atelectasis, chronic pulmonary emphysema) Now referred to as chronic obstructive pulmonary disease (COPD). Condition affecting 2-year-olds and older, becoming more common with age. A chronic respiratory condition due to pulmonary hypersensitivity to organic dust antigens, probably the most common cause of chronic coughing in horses. Most frequently occurs in stabled horses and is associated with dusty atmosphere and mould in hay and straw. *Micropolyspora faeni* (cause of farmer's lung in man and cattle) and *Aspergillus fumigatus* are predominant causes increasingly associated with pollen hypersensitivity, especially rape pollen. Antibody reaction induces spasm of muscles in wall of small air ducts and bronchioles so that air is trapped in air sacs (alveoli). These may eventually rupture so that two or more fuse (emphysema). Condition often accompanied by infected and inflamed air passages (bronchitis). The acute form occurs suddenly with difficult breathing (dyspnoea) and is similar to acute human asthma. Attack may coincide with change of environment, eg from field to stable. Attacks more common during hot, humid weather. Signs include heaving belly, flared nostrils, rhythmic movement of anus and surrounding area (perineum) coinciding with breathing, restlessness, profuse or patchy sweating and tendency to resent handling, deep, non-productive cough and loud wheezing. Attacks are not fatal but may last several minutes and occur daily if management is not altered. Case then progresses into chronic form. This may have history of mild respiratory fault. Horse may cough when walked from warm air into cold and breathing becomes faster, with double expiration. Bronchitis usually develops, with more coughing and slight nasal discharge. Condition may have functional or structural basis. In functional form, air sacs are enlarged and their walls undamaged, so horse may become normal. In structural form, air sacs have been damaged. This usually takes months or years to develop and is irreversible. Diagnosis: on symptoms, sounds from lungs and positive skin reaction to test doses of common moulds. Treatment: fresh, dust-free air is essential. Stabled horses should be placed on peat moss or paper bedding and fed good-quality hay. Sodium cromoglycate (qv), beta adrenergic (see adrenergic), and antihistamine drugs together with antibiotics may help, especially if bronchitis is present. Corticosteroids might be needed.

(trade name: Bisolvan) Drug used, often in conjunction with antibiotics or sulphonamides, to control respiratory disease. Acts to assist flow of mucus in airways. **bromhexine**

(trade name: Parlodel) Derivative of ergot and has dopamine activity. Used to treat Parkinson's disease in humans and to suppress lactation in mares. **bromocriptine**

See BSP. **bromsulphalein**

Pl of bronchus. **bronchi**

(L bronchialis) Of bronchi, bronchial, bronchioli, bronchiolus, bronchus. **bronchial**

Inflamed bronchioles when tubes may become full of exudate (cells and fluid). Associated with viral and bacterial infection, eg herpesvirus, streptococci, staphylococci or inhalation of irritant substance. See bronchitis; catarrh; cough; snotty nose. **bronchiolitis**

Inflammation of larger bronchial tubes of lungs due to infection or irritation by foreign material, eg dust. May accompany broken wind (emphysema) or follow infection with a virus, eg one belonging to herpes group. See bronchiolitis; broken wind; snotty nose; abortion, viral. **bronchitis**

Bacterial, viral or fungal infection of small air tubes and air sacs of lungs. **bronchopneumonia**

(pl bronchi) One of large air passages in lungs. Adjective: bronchial. **bronchus**

(after Sir David Bruce) Abortion caused by Brucella genus of bacteria. Rare in horses but possible if mares graze near infected cattle. See abortion. **Brucella abortus**

Infection by bacteria of family Brucellaceae, order Eubacteriales. Characterised by stiffness which is due to abscesses/infection in joints. Can be spread by drainage of fistulous withers. Diagnosis: on blood tests, qv. **brucellosis**

(syn stone bruise). See foot. **bruised sole**

Noise heard on auscultation, qv. See heart sounds. **bruit**

Feral horse of Victoria and New South Wales, Australia. Descended from Basuto (qv) imported from S Africa in 1800s and from many domesticated horses freed during the 1850s gold rush. Despite being hunted for years to preserve grazing **Brumby**

Brumby	for cattle and sheep, there are about 160,000 Brumbies today.
brushing	A mild form of interfering of one foot with opposite limb.
BSP	Abbr bromsulphalein, dye (used in liver tests) of sulfobro-mophthalein (chemical name: phenoltetrabromophthalein). Abnormally long BSP clearance indicates liver malfunction. A baseline serum sample is taken from jugular vein, BSP given IV and serum taken from opposite jugular at 2, 4, 8 and 16 minutes.
buccal	(L buccalis, from bucca, cheek) Of the cheek.
bucked knee	Carpal joint which is semi-permanently flexed. Usually seen in foals and improves by 6 months.
bucked shin	(syn sore shin, metacarpal periostitis) Periostitis of dorsal surface of metacarpal (or metatarsal). Seen most often bilaterally in forelimbs of young Thoroughbreds during first few weeks of training; sometimes in adult horses. May be associated with fissure fractures. Most likely aetiology is concussion. Signs include a warm, painful swelling on anterior surface of cannon bone. Cold packs may help in first 24 to 48 hours. Rest (minimum one month) essential in alleviating condition. Fissure fractures might be refractory to healing and require surgical drilling.
Buckskin	Dun-coloured horse developed in USA for ranch work. **International B. Horse Assn**, PO Box 268, Shelby, IN 46377 (219 552 1013). **American B. Registry**, PO Box 3850, Redding, CA 96049. (916 223 1420).
Budyonovsky	Russian breed popular for eventing and first in Britain found to harbour *Parafilaria multipapillosa*, qv.
buffer	Substance in fluid which lessens change in acidity or alkalinity when acids or alkalis are added.
bulbo-urethral	Of bulbs of urethra, qv. Two **b.-u.** glands – 4cm (1½ in) long and 2.5cm (1in) wide – open into urethra via 6–8 ducts and their secretion (seminal plasma) nourishes and transports spermatozoa.
bulbs of heel	Back part of foot, qv.
bulla	Large blister filled with serous fluid.
bull-nosed foot	See foot.

Anatomical term for collection of fibres eg nerves, muscle fibres. **b. branches**. See heart impulse.	**bundle**
(syn Shan) Strong but slow pony, bred by hill tribes of Shan state in central Burma. Similar to Mongolian and the faster Manipur.	**Burmese**
(Sp) General term used in western USA for donkey. See Mustang.	**burro**
(L, Gr a wine skin, pl bursae) Sac or cavity filled with fluid (synovial) at places where friction is likely, eg joints.	**bursa**
See stomach worm.	**bursatti**
Inflamed bursa caused by injury or infection, eg brucellosis. Common sites include bursa at point of elbow (syns shoe boil, capped elbow), at hock (syn capped hock), at hip (trochanteric **b.** syn whorlbone), on back – due to ill-fitting saddle. See whorlbone lameness, hygroma, bicipital **b**. Treatment: drain fluid with needle and inject corticosteroids.	**bursitis**
(trade name: Receptal) Drug equivalent to the natural hormone GnRH produced in hypothalamus of brain causing pituitary to release hormones LH and FSH. See luteinising hormone and follicle stimulating hormone.	**buserelin**
See phenylbutazone.	**bute**
(trade name: Torbugesic) Drug which acts on central nervous system producing analgesia and is therefore used to relieve moderate to severe pain including colic pain. Often given with detomidine (qv).	**butorphanol/ b. tartrate**
Anatomical term for knob-like structure, eg lower end of second and fourth metacarpal and metatarsal bones. See splint.	**button**
(syns pyramiditis, pyramidal disease) Swelling on front of coronary band/pedal bone, usually from injury, eg fracture, abscess. May lead to malformed hoof.	**buttress foot**
Abbrs Bachelor of Veterinary Medicine and Surgery.	**BVMS/BVM&S**
Abbr Bachelor of Veterinary Science.	**BVSc**
Divert flow, eg of ingesta through only part of normal route to avoid site of disease or obstruction.	**bypass**

C

Ca	Symbol for calcium.
cachexia	(cac- + Gr hexis, habit) Wasting and malnutrition. See metabolism, wasting.
cadaver	(L from cadere, to fall, perish; syn carcass) Corpse, dead body. See carcass, rigor mortis.
cadmium	Toxic metal. **c. poisoning** Rare condition of horses grazing near zinc smelters. Main symptom: acute diarrhoea.
caecum	(L, blind gut) Large comma-shaped sac between small intestine and colon; about 1.25m (4ft) long with capacity of about 25 litres (5¹/₂ gallons) in adult horse. Consists of base, body and apex and occupies central lower abdomen. See alimentary canal.
caesarean section	Surgical removal of foetus, performed under general anaesthesia. The flank or abdomen is opened (laparotomy), uterus exposed and foetus extracted. **c.s.** necessary if foetus cannot pass through birth canal because part or parts are lodged against mare's pelvis. (Attempts should first be made to correct malalignment by manipulation, see dystocia.) **c.s.** has replaced embryotomy (cutting foetus into pieces with a special instrument – embryotome – so it can be delivered through birth canal).
caffeine	White powder or silky glistening odourless particles with bitter taste. From dried leaves of *Camellia sinensis* (black tea). Stimulates central nervous system and helps muscle efficiency, increases breathing rate and acts as diuretic. Stimulant illegal in most sports.
calcaneus	(syn fibular tarsal bone) Bone which forms the point of the hock.
calcareous	(L calcarius) Of lime or calcium. **c. deposits** May form in ligaments after chronic inflammation.
calciferol	White or colourless crystalline powder, odourless and tasteless. Has action and uses of vitamin D. See concentrated vitamin D solution.
calcification	(calcium + L facere, to make) The depositing of calcium salts, eg **c.** of cartilage at growing ends of bones. See growth plate.

Hormone involved in calcium regulation.

calcitonin

(L calx, lime; abbr Ca) Yellow metal or basic element; atomic weight 40.08; present in body tissues and important in coagulation of blood. **c.** and phosphorus are main minerals in bone. **c. borogluconate** White odourless powder or transparent scales. Given as 10–40 per cent solution to treat poisoning by chloroform, carbon tetrachloride or lead; also in rare cases of mares showing signs like milk fever after foaling, ie unsteadiness, twitching of superficial muscles, lying down for long periods. **c. carbonate** See chalk. **C. Disodium Versenate** Trade name. See sodium calcium edetate. **c. hydrogen phosphate** White crystalline odourless slightly salty-tasting powder. Given as source of calcium and phosphorus. Dose 4–8g. See bone flour. **c. and phosphorus** (abbrs Ca, P) Minerals required for bone and teeth formation; they account for more than 70 per cent of mineral content of body. Too little of either limits usefulness of the other. Adequate quantities in a proportion of Ca to P of 1.3:1.0 and adequate vitamin D are essential for proper utilisation in body. Mature horse of 450kg (1,000lb) needs about 10g of Ca and 8g of P. **c./phosphorus ratio** Proportion of Ca to P in diet. See big head. **c. sulphate** See plaster of Paris.

calcium

See stone.

calculus

A formation of new bone in soft, fibrous tissues between and across ends of broken bone; may project from beneath skin as hard lump, as in fracture of splint bone. See splint.

callus

Unit of heat, 4.2 joules. **large c.** (written kilocalorie or C.) Heat required to raise temperature of 1kg of water 1°C Equivalent to 1,000 calories (**small c.**).

calorie

(L calor, heat + facere, to make) Heat-producing.

calorific

(L calor, heat + Gr metron, measure) Instrument that measures heat exchange.

calorimeter

Pony of marshy **C.** district of France, S of Arles. Usually grey or white (but not albino, qv). Some still roam and breed in feral (qv) herds of about 15 mares per stallion. Renowned for their looks – they have particularly long manes and tails – stamina and ability to sprint. Used to round up **C.** bulls. Many geldings and barren mares ridden by tourists in summer and turned loose with stallions, mares and foals to spend bitter winter on marshes. Country of origin doubtful, possibly N Africa, Tibet or China. Julius Caesar said to have created stud farms before **C.** pony reverted to its feral life. **British C. Horse Society,** Valley Farm Riding & Driving Centre, Wickham

Camargue

Camargue	Market, Woodbridge, Suffolk, IP13 0ND (01728 746916).
camped	Fault of conformation in which forelegs (**c.** in front) or hindlegs (**c.** behind) are extended too far from body.
campylobacter	Bacteria previously called vibrio. May be implicated in diarrhoea (qv) in foals and gastric/duodenal ulcers (qv).
Canadian pox	See acne.
canal	Narrow tube or channel in body, eg alimentary **c.**, qv, birth **c.**
cancellous	Spongy or lattice-like. Used in connection with bone tissue.
cancer	Malignant tumour. See growth.
Candida	(L candidus, glowing white) Genus of yeast-like fungus. **C. albicans** May infect uterus and genital tract or foal's tongue, causing greyish-white coating; infection may follow antibiotic treatment. Sometimes associated with seedy toe, qv.
canine	Dog-like. **c.** tooth – pointed tooth which erupts between incisor teeth and molars in males and some females.
canker	(syn hoof cancer) Chronic hypertrophy (vegetative growth) of the sensitive frog and occasionally the sole. Caused by persistent exposure to strong ammonium compounds, although spirochaete organisms have been isolated in this condition. Most commonly seen in draught horses and is characterised by a ragged, oily-appearing frog with a distinctive foul odour. Horse may be very tender in the bulb of the heel and affected area. Treatment: remove all diseased tissue and pack the hoof; add penicillin to hoof or give systemically. Bar shoe or metal plate over affected area helpful. Condition best prevented by regular stall and hoof cleaning.
cannon	Bone between knee or hock and fetlock. See metacarpal.
cannula	(L canna, reed) Tube for inserting into body to transfuse or collect fluid. **trocar and c.** Metal instrument for cannulating organ or part inflated with gas, pus or fluid. Cf catheter. See stiletto.
cantharadin	Glistening colourless crystals obtained from cantharides, qv. Irritates skin, causing redness, burning and blistering. See blister.
cantharides	Dried Spanish fly, cantharis (blister bug) or dried beetle.
canthus	Inner and outer angle of eye, qv.

(L capacitas from capere, to take) Expression of measurement. **capacity**
cranial c. Amount of space in skull. **vital c.** Amount of air that
can be forcefully expelled from lung after full inhalation.
C. measured metrically in cubic centimetres (cc); 1cc = 1ml
(millilitre).

Extinct ancestor of Basuto pony bred from first horses imported **Cape horse**
into S Africa (4 Arab/Barb types) in 1650s. Highly prized for
looks and stamina in Boer War but breed later deteriorated.
Used in 1820s in Basutoland by the invading Zulus, then
developed into today's Basuto.

(L capillaris, hair-like) Minute tube; smaller type of blood ves- **capillary**
sel connecting arteries with veins. Has extremely thin wall,
which allows exchange of gases, nutritive and waste materials
between blood and tissues through which it passes. Lymph
vessels also have **c.** system.

(syn shoe boil) Swollen point of elbow (over olecranon) due to **capped elbow**
inflamed bursa and/or bruising of skin and underlying tissues.
Often caused by hind foot when getting up. **c. hock** See hock.

(L capsule, a little box) Structure which encloses organ or part, **capsule**
eg fibrous **c.** surrounding kidney or ovary; **joint c.** Membrane
enclosing cavity of joint, qv.

Inflamed joint capsule. See arthritis. **capsulitis**

Small colourless crystals or white powder with faint fishy **carbachol**
odour. Stimulates movement of alimentary canal and bladder,
also smooth muscle of pregnant uterus. Antidote: atropine.
Mainly used in eyes to constrict pupil.

(syn sugar) Substance in vegetable and animal tissue, viz cel- **carbohydrate**
lulose, lactose, glucose and fructose. In plants starch and fructose are built up from carbon dioxide under influence of light;
in animals glucose is derived from breakdown of **c.** in food and
built up into glycogen (qv) and glucose. (Herbivores produce
no enzymes to process cellulose and rely on microorganisms.)
Lactose is produced in mammary glands from glucose and
secreted in milk.

(a tetrachlormethane) Clear colourless liquid with burning **carbon tetrachloride**
taste. Used as anthelmintic; largely replaced by piperazine
salts, qv. **c.t. poisoning** Death may occur 3–4 days after administration. Symptoms: spasm and coma. Antidote: calcium
borogluconate IV.

(L carbunculus, little coat) Type of abscess involving skin and **carbuncle**

carbuncle   subcutaneous tissue, usually has multiple drainage points and caused by staphylococcal germ. See abscess.

carcass   (Fr carcasse; syn cadaver) Dead body. Parts of equine **c.** can be utilised: hooves to make glue; flesh to feed carnivores. Meat has sweet taste and is eaten by humans in some countries, eg France and Belgium. See phenylbutazone.

carcinogen   Substance or virus which induces formation of tumour, eg wart. See growth.

carcinoma   (Gr karkinoma from karkinos, crab, cancer) Type of malignant growth composed of epithelial cells. See growth.

cardiac   (L cardicus from Gr kardiakos, heart) Of the heart. **c. output** Amount of blood pumped from heart during each beat (stroke volume), or amount pumped per unit time. Falls in heart disease such as atrial fibrillation. See heart rate.

cardiogram   (cardio- + Gr gamma, a writing) Tracing made by machine known as cardiograph, as in electrocardiogram, qv.

cardiograph   (cardio- + Gr graphein, to write) Instrument which records a cardiogram.

caries   (L rottenness) Decay or death of bone. See bone, diseases of; teeth.

carotid   (Gr karotis from karos, deep sleep) Main artery of neck. See arteries, table of. **c. body** Collection of special cells sensitive to alterations of oxygen and carbon dioxide concentrations in blood. Able to affect breathing by nervous reflex to help keep concentrations normal. **c. sinus** Part of **c.** artery sensitive to alterations in blood pressure.

carpal   (L carpalis) Of the carpus (knee). **c. bones, fracture of** Any of 8 may be broken, but third **c.** bone and accessory most likely. Small pieces of bone may chip off from **c.** bone. See joint mouse/mice. Trauma most common cause. Symptoms: similar to those of carpitis, ie heat, pain, swelling and lameness. Diagnosis: by careful X-ray examination from several different angles; number of bones involved may mask fracture in one. See slab fracture. **c. canal syndrome** (syn **c.** tunnel) Lameness resulting from inflammation and pressure on contents of **c.** canal. Frequently seen in jumping horses or following fracture of accessory **c.** bone. Symptoms: pain on extreme flexion of limb, absence of lesions in anterior **c.** bones and distension of sheaths of flexor carpi ulnaris and ulnaris lateralis muscles proximal to the annular ligament. Treatment: resection of an elliptical strip of the annular ligament on the medial side of the carpus. **c. hygroma** See hygroma. **c. joint** Formed by 8 bones in 2 rows: proximal and distal. Proximal: radial, intermediate, ulnar and accessory (pisiform). Distal: first, second, third and fourth **c.** bones. Radial is largest bone of proximal row and its front edge is usually where arthritis develops. **c. joints** The 3 small joints which make up knee joint: (1) between radius and proximal row of **c.** bones; (2) intercarpal joint, between the two rows of **c.** bones; (3) carpo-metacarpal joint, between distal row of **c.** bones and upper end of metacarpal (cannon and splint bones). Joint capsule is common to all 3 joints. Synovial membrane is arranged so that second 2 compartments communicate, but first is separate.

carpal

(syn popped knee) Inflammation of joint(s) of knee.

carpitis

(L, Gr karpos) Joint between forearm and cannon, commonly called knee; equivalent to human wrist.

carpus

Individual harbouring microorganisms capable of causing disease but without producing signs; a distributor of infection, eg individual carrying strangles germ in glands may cause outbreak of disease when in contact with susceptible horses. **c.**s help spread encephalomyelitis, swamp fever, etc.

carrier

(L cartilago; colloq gristle) Specialised connective tissue of cells. Provides embryo's skeleton, most of which gradually hardens into bone. **articular c.** Caps bones forming joint to provide surface for movement. **costal c.** That at ends of ribs where they join sternum. **cricoid c.** That forming a ring. **elastic c.** Pliable, occurs where muscles and membranes need support, eg voice box, windpipe and between nostrils (nasal septum). **fibro c.** Fibrous **c.** in, eg, skull. **growth (epiphyseal) c.** That at ends of long bones and which forms new bone. See growth plate.

cartilage

(L caseus, cheese) Main protein of milk.

casein

(after American veterinarian E.A. **C.**; syn stitching) Operation performed under local anaesthesia in which lips forming upper part of vulva are stitched together to prevent air entering vagina. Necessary in mares that have poor conformation (ie vulva sloping from normal vertical position). Mare that has had **C.** should be cut, with straight scissors, immediately before foaling and re-stitched afterwards. Cf Pouret.

Caslick

Rediscovered in 1965 around **C.** Sea. Some run wild, others are used as pack ponies. Usually 9–11 h. May be ancestor of Arab and direct descendant of horse which roamed Zagros

Caspian pony

Caspian pony	mountains on Iran/Iraq border in prehistoric times. **C. P. Soc**, 87 Hawkins St, Liverpool L6 6BY (01512 604398).
cast	(1) Rigid bandage or dressing applied to limb for support eg in fracture repair or serious wounds. Materials used include plaster of Paris (qv) or fibreglass. (2) To cause to lie down either using ropes or other apparatus. Largely replaced by use of anaesthetic drugs. (3) Become trapped or unable to stand eg due to position in stable or under fence.
castor oil	Colourless or pale yellow liquid from seeds of *Ricinus communis*. Has slight odour and nauseating taste. Sometimes used in foals up to 12 hours old to help passage of meconium (qv). Also used with zinc in soothing ointment for sores etc. **c.o. plant poisoning** Symptoms, several days after ingestion: incoordination, sweating, diarrhoea, muscle spasms and head tremor. May cause death. At postmortem gut lining is inflamed, lymph glands swollen, and gut, liver, kidney and possibly windpipe and lungs are fluid-filled. Treatment: specific antiserum, but this is unlikely to be available, so use anti-shock measures. See shock.
castrate	(syn alter, cut, emasculate, geld) To remove testes, rendering individual sterile.
castration	(L castratio) Surgical removal of testes; either under sedation and local anaesthesia with horse standing, or under general anaesthesia. (**C.** in Britain illegal without an anaesthetic.) Usually performed at 1 or 2 years; sometimes at 3 months. Castrated male (colloq gelding) does not develop stallion's physique, eg thick, slightly crested neck or, often excitable, temperament and rarely shows any sexual interest in females. Cf vasectomy.
catabolism	(Gr katabole, a throwing down) Breaking down of protein and loss of muscle. One of 2 types of metabolism (cf anabolism). Rate of **c.** (catabolic rate) usually increases with age.
cataplexy	Diminished responsiveness usually characterised by trance-like state, eg in foals.
cataract	See eye, diseases of.
catarrh	(L catarrhus from Gr katarrhein, to flow down) Purulent or semi-purulent discharge produced by an inflamed mucous membrane. May be in nose or in alimentary canal. See snotty nose; colic.
catecholamine	Compound having a sympathomimetic (qv) action. Aromatic

portion of compound is catechol. See dopamine; adrenaline; noradrenaline. — *catecholamine*

Pale-brown odourless powder with bitter taste. Powerful astringent, used to treat persistent diarrhoea. — **catechu**

Material prepared from sheep's intestine and used to stitch wounds. **chromic c.** That sterilised and impregnated with chromium trioxide. See suture. — **catgut**

See purgative. — **cathartic**

(Gr katheter; syn cannula) Surgical instrument, usually made of nylon or plastic, for drawing fluids from, or introducing them into, any cavity of body. **uterine c.** One used to infuse infected uterus with, eg antibiotic solution. **indwelling c.** One left in place for a long time, eg in vein or uterus. — **catheter**

Tail or tail-like appendage, eg **c.** epididymis, tail of epididymis, qv. — **cauda**

(1) Of or related to a cauda (tail-like structure, eg cauda epididymis). (2) Anatomical reference meaning towards tail, also caudad. Opp cephalad. — **caudal**

(L cauterium, Gr kauterion) Application of caustic (corrosive) substance, hot iron or electric current. See firing, diathermy. — **cautery**

(L cavitas) Space or potential space in body, eg abdominal **c.** — **cavity**

Pony of Red Indians of America. Descended from Mustang (qv) by careless cross-breeding. — **Cayuse**

(trade name Excenel) Bactericidal antibiotic belonging to the group cephalosporins. Used for treating respiratory and other infections. — **ceftiofur sodium**

(L cella, compartment) Minute unit of protoplasm, singular in such organisms as bacteria or certain protozoa, eg amoeba; or organised into complex systems forming tissues of body. Differs widely in size, structure and functions but usually consists of protoplasm divided into cytoplasm and nucleus, although nucleus absent in bacteria and red blood **c.s**. Main **c.** types: adipose (fat), blood, bone, cancerous (see growth), cartilage, connective tissue, egg (see gamete, ovum, embryology), endothelium, follicle, germ (see gamete), granulosa, hepatic (see liver), muscle, nerve, phagocytic (see phagocyte), sensory (see nerve), spermatozoon (see sperm). — **cell**

cellulitis — Inflammation, usually diffuse and oedematous associated with infection, especially in lower limbs. Requires antibiotic treatment. May progress to lymphangitis (qv).

CEM — Contagious equine metritis. See metritis.

centrifuge — (centre + L fugere, to flee) Machine which spins, exerting a centrifugal force; used in laboratory for separating, eg cells from plasma in blood (see haematocrit; blood tests), sediment from water in urine.

centrum — (L, Gr kentron) Anatomical term for a central structure, eg **c.** of vertebra.

cephalic — (L cephalieus, Gr kephalikos) Of head or head-end of body, eg **c.** vein. Same root used in cephalad, towards head. Opp caudad.

cephaloridine — Antibiotic with wide range of activity against gram-positive and gram-negative bacteria. Particularly useful in kidney, bladder and lung infections.

cerebellar — Of the cerebellum (part of brain, qv) **c. degeneration/hypoplasia** Rare disease of cerebellum which causes muscle incoordination (ataxia), head tremor and faulty blink response. Usually appears in first few months and worsens until foal dies or has to be destroyed. May be hereditary. Arab seems to be particularly affected, though similar disease reported in Gotland and Oldenburg breeds.

cerebellum — (from L cerebrum, brain) Part of brain controlling coordination. See brain.

cerebrospinal — Of the brain and spinal cord. **c. fluid** (CSF) Fluid which bathes spinal cord and brain stem; contains salts, minerals, sugar, small amounts of protein, a few cells. Can be withdrawn for laboratory examination by inserting needle into cisterna magna at base of skull (see occiput) or into space above spinal cord in back (lumbar puncture). Protein and cell content increase in inflammatory conditions.

cerebrum — Part of brain (qv).

cervical — (L cervicalis from cervix, neck) Of the neck (eg **c.** vertebra) or cervix (eg **c.** swab).

cervicitis — Inflamed cervix. May be due to infection or to injury (eg during foaling).

cervix — (pl cervices) Muscular neck of uterus, can be seen through speculum inserted into vagina; changes in tone, colour and moistness in various states of oestrous cycle and pregnancy. See oestrous cycle. | *cervix*

See caesarean section. | **cesarean**

See tapeworm. | **Cestoda**

(calcium carbonate) Fine white or off-white odourless tasteless powder. Absorbent and antacid, used in mixtures to treat diarrhoea. | **chalk**

To evoke an immune response by exposing to virus, bacteria or other antigen. | **challenge**

(L camera, Gr kamera) Enclosed space. **anterior c. of eye** Space between cornea and lens. **c.s of heart** Atrium (auricle) and ventricle, also known as first and second **c.s**. See eye, heart. | **chamber**

Nature of object or organism. **acquired c.** Modification as result of environment, such as some behaviour or stunted growth. **mendelian c.** Used in genetics (Mendel's law) for distinct characteristic dependent on inherited material (gene); may be recessive or dominant. **sex c.s**. Those of reproduction and differences between male and female. **sex-linked c.** One transmitted to only one sex, the genes for which are carried on sex chromosome. See Mendel's law; chromosome. | **character**

System of ligaments forming part of stay apparatus, qv. Foreleg: superior and inferior check ligaments, superficial and deep flexor tendons; hindleg: tarsal (inferior) check ligament and deep digital flexor tendon. Structures help support lower part of leg and prevent overextension. | **check apparatus**

Side of face. **C.s.** of some breeds, eg Arab, appear more bulbous than most. **c. teeth** Molars. See teeth. | **cheek**

Nerve cell (qv) sensitive to chemical substances, eg those of smell and taste; or to chemical changes in blood, eg reduced oxygen or increased carbon dioxide tension. | **chemoreceptor**

Treatment of disease by chemicals which affect causative germ but do not harm patient. See antibiotic. | **chemotherapy**

(syns thorax, thoracic cavity) Part of body bounded by ribcage and diaphragm. Contains heart, an important artery (aorta), a main vein (vena cava), lungs, gullet (oesophagus), thymus and lymph glands. | **chest**

chestnut	(1) Horny growth just above inside of each knee (carpal) joint and 7.5cm (3in) below inside of each hock. May be vestige of hoof of 2- or 3-toed horse (see evolution) and probably as individual as human fingerprint. Photographed to use in racehorses' identity papers in some states of America. Cf ergot. See donkey. (2) See coat colouring.
chewing	Contact of upper and lower teeth by which food is prepared for swallowing. **c. disease** Incessant abnormal **c.** after eating yellow star thistle, qv. **nervous c.** Symptom of brain damage. See neonatal maladjustment syndrome.
cheyne-stokes respiration	Gradual increase and decrease in depth of breathing. Occurs in heart failure, during excessively deep anaesthesia or after brain injury.
chigger	See flea.
chill	Attack of involuntary muscular contractions accompanied by sense of cold. Term used by horsemen for undiagnosed ailment if individual is off-colour. Has no scientific meaning. See shiverer.
chip	Small piece of bone fractured from joint surface. See osteophyte.
chiro-	(also cheiro-) Combining form meaning relationship to hand (from Gr cheir, hand).
chiropractic therapy	(chiro- + Gr prattein, to do) Treatment by manipulation. Based on theory that health and disease are related to function of nervous system.
chloral hydrate	Colourless crystals with pungent odour and bitter taste. Used as sedative or anaesthetic. Irritates locally so should not be injected sub. cut. Overdose can cause relaxation of voluntary muscles, staggering, dilation of pupils, subnormal temperature and death from respiratory failure. Infrequently used today.
chloramphenicol	(trade name: Chloromycetin) Fine white to greyish-white crystals with bitter taste. Obtained from *Streptomyces venezuelae* mould. Antibiotic effective against *E. coli*, Salmonella, Klebsiella. Used in gram-negative infections of alimentary tract and joints. **c. sodium succinate** Sodium salt of **c.** Antibiotic used in foals.
chlorhexidine gluconate/ c. hydrochloride	(trade names: Hibitane, Savlon) White crystalline odourless powder with bitter taste. Potent antiseptic, effective against wide range of gram-positive and gram-negative organisms.

Used for disinfecting wounds and burns (in 0.02–0.05% aqueous solution) and uterus in pessaries or solution. — *chlorhexidine gluconate/ c. hydrochloride*

Colourless heavy liquid with characteristic odour and sweet burning taste. Historically used as anaesthetic; may cause period of excitement. Little used now. — **chloroform**

White or cream-coloured powder with slight odour and bitter taste. Used to tranquillise excitable or aggressive animals for handling, minor surgery, induction of general anaesthesia (or dishonestly as stopper dope). Overdose causes paralysis of hindquarters, staggering, incoordination. Little used now. — **chlorpromazine/ c. hydrochloride**

(syn aureomycin hydrochloride, trade names: Achromycin, Aureomycin) Yellow odourless crystals with bitter taste; antibiotic produced from *Streptomyces aureofaciens*. Given by mouth, used in ointment or eye drops. — **chlortetracycline hydrochloride**

Completely or partially obstructed gullet (oesophagus), caused by hay, straw, dry grain, partially chewed wood. Symptoms: distress with repeated arching of neck, anxious facial expression, saliva mixed with food drooling from mouth and nostrils. Recovery may be spontaneous if horse is tranquillised. Severe or long-standing cases require passage of stomach tube to clear obstruction. Can cause inhalation pneumonia. See pneumonia. — **choke**

Combining form meaning relationship to bile. — **chol-**

(chol- + Gr agogos, leading) Drug or substance which stimulates flow of bile from liver. — **cholagogue**

(chole- + Gr stereos, solid) Fat-like substance in animal fats and oils, bile, blood, brain and milk. Deposited in arterial walls as atheroma. — **cholesterol**

One of B vitamins in animal and vegetable tissues. See acetylcholine. — **choline**

Of choline (acetylcholine). Also applied to nerve fibres which liberate acetylcholine at junction where nerve impulse passes. — **cholinergic**

Substance (an esterase) in body tissues which splits acetylcholine into choline and acetic acid. — **cholinesterase**

(Gr chondros, cartilage) Combining form meaning relationship to cartilage. — **chondo-/chondro-**

Inflamed cartilage. — **chondritis**

chondroblast	(chondro- + Gr blastos, germ) Cell which produces cartilage qv.
chondrocyte	(chondro- + Gr kytos, hollow vessel) Cartilage cell.
chorda	(L, Gr chorde, cord) Cord or sinew, eg **c. tendineae cordis** Tendinous cord connecting cusps of valves which guard entrance of ventricles of heart.
chorioallantois	Placenta.
chorion	Outermost membrane of embryo; nourishes and protects it and fuses with allantois to form placenta. See allantois, gonadotrophin, placenta. Adjective: chorionic.
chorionic	Produced by placenta, eg **c.** hormone such as **c. gonadotrophin** (trade names: Chorulon, LH 1500, Nymfalon) Sterile white water-soluble powder obtained from urine of pregnant humans. Stimulates gonads. Given to mares IV to induce ovulation and to stallions to stimulate secretion of testosterone. See oestrous cycle.
chromatin	(Gr chroma, colour) The portion of cell nucleus most easily stained. Carries DNA (qv) and proteins of chromosome, qv. **sex c.** Mass of **c.** at edge of nucleus. Present in normal females, but not normal males. See intersex.
chromatography	(chromato- + Gr graphein, to write) Chemical analysis in which different substances in solution produce bands of colour. Basis of method used for analysing saliva and urine samples in dope test, qv. See also electrophoresis.
chromic catgut	See catgut.
chromosome	(chromo- + Gr soma, body) Structure, in nucleus of cell, which carries hereditary material, ie genes; constant number in each species – domestic horse (*Equus caballus*) 64. Evolutionary trend may be loss of **c.**s (reference: Roger Short, Cambridge), as Przewalski (qv), probably most recent of domestic horse's antecedents, has 66. Short found the following **c.** figures: donkey (*Equus asinus*) 62; Nubian wild ass (*Equus asinus africanus*) and Somali wild ass (*Equus asinus somalicus*) 62; onager (*Equus hemionus onager*) 54; Grevy's zebra (*Equus grevyi*) 46. **c.**s usually paired and animal with odd number likely to be infertile, eg mule has 63 (mean average of its parents' **c.** numbers – male donkey: 62, female horse: 64). Laboratory examination of tests of such hybrids show odd **c.** unable to find a partner, plus paternal and maternal **c.**s which differ in size and shape. Fertile crosses such as Przewalski/horse inherit from each parent **c.**s so alike that they

can fuse and overcome the odd **c. sex c.** One concerned with determining sex and designated X (female) and Y (male). Normal male mammals have an XY pairing; normal females XX. Abnormal forms may have XXY, XYY (ie triploid numbers) or XX and XY cells, 2 sorts of cells in same individual (mosaicism). See gene. | *chromosome*

(COPD) See broken wind. | **chronic obstructive pulmonary disease**

(L chylus, juice) Lymph fluid which travels from intestine, in lymph ducts, to enter veins in chest. | **chyle**

See contra-indicated. | **CI**

See combined immunodeficiency disease. | **CID**

(pl cilia) Minute hair-like filament attached to free surface of a cell and which, with others, moves fluid and matter over area. See epithelium. Cf flagellum. | **cilium**

(trade names: Cimetidine, Tagamet) Drug which inhibits release of histamine and gastric acid secretions. Used to treat gastric/duodenal ulcer in foals. | **cimetidine**

(L circulatio) Movement of fluid through vessels in a regular course, eg blood and lymph. **collateral c.** Fluid which is diverted; eg if blood vessel is obstructed, blood will find **c.c.** as other vessels open up. See heart; arteries, table of; lymphatic system. | **circulation**

(Gr kirrhos, orange-yellow) Liver disease characterised by destruction of liver cells which are replaced by fibrous tissue. Liver becomes hard, enlarged and cuts like cardboard. See liver, ragwort poisoning. | **cirrhosis**

(L, pl cisternae) Space in which lymph or other body fluid accumulates, eg **c. magna** Space at base of skull. See occiput. | **cisterna**

Abbr creatine kinase, qv. | **CK**

Device to compress, eg prevent bleeding during operation, reduce hernia, qv. | **clamp**

Hydrated aluminium silicate. Used in drugs, ointments, poultices. **China c.** See kaolin. | **clay**

(syn fissure) Space or opening made by splitting. **hoof c.** Horizontal separation or hole in the hoof wall caused by | **cleft**

cleft	injuries to coronary band. **C.** usually descends as hoof grows but may interfere with nails of shoe. **c. palate** See palate.
clenbuterol hydrochloride	(trade name: Ventipulmin) A direct-acting sympathomimetic agent (mimics action of sympathetic nervous system). Used as a bronchodilator in horses suffering from chronic obstructive pulmonary disease (COPD), qv. Banned in some countries.
Cleveland Bay	Strong but light horse developed in Yorkshire. Only small white head-markings permissible on bay coat. Often crossed with Thoroughbred to produce hunter though pure-breds still popular; they provide some royal carriage horses, probably because breed has Yorkshire coach horse blood. Many exported, especially to USA. **C. B. Horse Soc**, York Livestock Centre, Murton, York YO1 3UF (01904 489731).
clinch	That part of a horseshoe nail that is seen on the outside hoof wall after having been driven through the hoof, shortened, tightened, flattened against the hoof wall (clinched), and rasped smooth by the farrier. The act of turning down a driven nail flat against the wall of a hoof.
clitorectomy	Surgical removal of clitoris and clitoral fossae. Used to treat and prevent venereal disease such as CEM.
clitoris	Female counterpart of penis, in floor of vagina just inside vulva. Made up of corpus, glans clitoridis and prepuce. About 4cm x 2cm ($1^1/_2$ x $^3/_4$ in), capable of becoming erect and exposed during eversion (winking) of vulva.
cloak fly	See tabanid fly.
cloprostenol	(trade name: Estrumate) Synthetic prostaglandin. See prostaglandin.
Clostridium	(Gr kloster, spindle, pl Clostridia) Genus of bacteria which are gram-positive, spore-bearing, rod-shaped and live only without oxygen. See bacteria. **C. tetani** See vaccine.
clot	Coagulated mass, eg blood **c.** See thrombosis, blood.
cloxacillin sodium	(trade names: Kloxerate eye ointment, Opticlox, Orbenin) White odourless crystals with bitter taste. Antibiotic particularly useful against penicillin-resistant staphylococci. Used to treat pneumonia, abscesses, eye infections.
club foot	Abnormal conformation of foot when angle of hoof wall from ground is greater than 60° and heel is high in relation to the toe. Foot may be knuckled over; affects one or both feet. May be

inherited, due to incorrect use of foot, secondary effect of contracted tendons, or due to nutritional deficiency or over-feeding (especially in combination with lack of exercise). May cause lameness and eventual separation of pedal bone from horn of hoof. Adjusting the feed and frequent corrective shoeing helps alleviate the condition. In some cases, when condition develops in foals the pedal bone becomes u-shaped and foot permanently clubbed. Surgical treatment involves cutting inferior check ligament, qv.

club foot

Scottish draught breed founded around River Clyde south of Glasgow; possibly descended from Scottish mares and a Belgian stallion imported about 1700. **C.** has more white than other 3 main draught breeds of Britain: Suffolk (which has none), Percheron and Shire. Breed popularised in USA by brewers of Budweiser beer who use **C.** teams for corporate promotion. **C. Horse Soc of GB** 3 Grosvenor Gdns, Edinburgh EH12 5JU (0131 337 5577). **C. Breeders of the US**, 17378 Kelley Road, Pecatonica, IL 61063. (815 247 8780).

Clydesdale

(L coagulatio) Forming of blood clot by process which occurs only if blood is in contact with roughened surface or damaged tissue. Blood contains about 12 factors which, under certain circumstances, react in 3 stages to produce clot (ie fibrin). (1) Damaged blood platelets and tissues release thromboplastin. (2) If thromboplastin and calcium are in contact with prothrombin (inactive thrombin) they form thrombin. (3) If thrombin is in contact with blood protein (fibrinogen) it forms fibrin. See blood.

coagulation

(L cotta, tunic) (1) Outer covering of organ. (2) Hair covering horse's skin. **c. colouring** Colour of horse's hair; determined by inheritance and sometimes age (grey horse can be born black and coat gradually turn grey, until in old age it is pure white). Some breed societies recognise only those horses of a particular colour, eg Suffolk Punch must be chestnut. Others, eg Albino, Appaloosa, Palomino, are more a colour than a breed. Colours include: Albino (qv); Appaloosa (usually white with black/brown spots and perhaps striped hooves), cf Knabstrup; bay (any shade of brown from dark mahogany to pale sandy but must have black mane and tail and often has black points (hocks, knees downwards) with white on face and around feet. Pony breeds sometimes have dark dorsal stripe. Can be picked to breed true, as in Cleveland Bay, though some produce chestnut or other colour); black (body no lighter than mane and tail but white markings allowed, usually breeds true, though 2 blacks can produce bay foal); blue roan (roaned black, ie black with sprinkling of white hairs); brown (almost black but lighter areas around eyes, muzzle and legs); chestnut (golden red or

coat

coat	reddish/brown – liver chestnut – without black points of bay, 2 chestnuts can produce only a chestnut foal. Cf Palomino); dappled grey (barely perceptible spots in lighter grey coat, may be equivalent of hammer spots in dark coat. Common in some breeds, eg Percheron); dun (sandy cream, ie dark palomino, but with dark mane and tail and often dorsal stripe. Dun to buckskin reflects sunlight so horse able to tolerate heat better than some colours. Common in native types, eg Highland, Iceland, Mustang); grey (seems particularly susceptible to melanotic growths (see growth) around anus and is especially suspicious (see behaviour). Those whose sire or dam were other than grey produce about 75 per cent grey foals when crossed with another grey); grey roan (grey with sprinkling of white hairs in darker coat, colouring similar to dappled grey, but more evenly distributed); Palomino (qv); piebald (black and white patches); pinto (qv); skewbald (patches of white and anything except black); sorrel (pale chestnut); spotted (see Appaloosa, Knabstrup); strawberry roan (roaned chestnut); striped (see zebra). Also see markings. **Coloured Horse and Pony Soc**, Fennemore Farm, Oakley, Bucks HP18 9PY (01844 237783).
cob	Type of horse rather than breed, though may be similar to Welsh cob (qv). Up to 15.2h, usually used as heavyweight hack. Shown with hogged mane and docked tail in the past, but docking now illegal. Sometimes driven, when action is higher than in ridden horse. **Welsh Pony and C. Soc** 6 Chalybeate Street, Aberystwyth SY23 1HS (01970 617501).
cobalamin	Cobalt complex of vitamin B_{12}.
cobalt chloride	Red slightly absorbent crystals contained in Vitamin B_{12}. Minute quantities are essential. Deficiency not known in horses, though **c.c.** included in most supplements and tonics. Also available as oxide or sulphate.
cocaine	Drug used as a local anaesthetic (or stimulant dope). Toxicity causes excitement, then depression, which ends in unconsciousness and death from respiratory paralysis. Treatment ineffectual, but oxygen and artificial respiration may help. See dope test.
coccus	(pl cocci; L, Gr kokkos, berry) Round bacterial cell. See bacteria.
coccygeal	Of area of coccyx ('tail bone') in man, especially used about **c.** vertebrae ie vertebrae of tail.
codeine phosphate	Colourless crystals or white odourless powder derived from morphine. Actions similar to morphine. Used to treat cough.

Joint between second and third phalanges and navicular bone. See navicular disease: foot.

coffin

(after Dr Leroy **C.** of Cornell University, USA) Laboratory test to diagnose swamp fever (equine infectious anaemia). Test takes 2–8 hours and is based on detecting antigen and antibody in infected horse's blood, by special technique (agar-gel-immunodiffusion).

Coggins test

(syns spots, pox) Infectious disease of mares and stallions caused by equine herpesvirus. Transmitted by coitus, insects, personnel handling mares and stallions and without obvious contact. Not thought to affect fertility. Causes small blisters (vesicles) on mare's vulva and stallion's penis. Blisters rupture, leaving ulcerated, inflamed areas which may be round or joined to form irregular patches. Scabs form on ulcers, which may persist up to 3 weeks. Individual may refuse food, suffer malaise and rise in temperature. Condition may leave areas without pigment. Treatment not essential. Ulcers heal spontaneously, but may be helped by ointment or lotion containing antibiotics or corticosteroids. Horse should be sexually rested.

coital exanthema

(colloq covering, mating, service) Sexual intercourse. See behaviour, fertility.

coitus

Low temperature. **c.-blooded** Colloq for horse tracing to prehistoric type of central Europe. Most heavy, slow horses are **c.b.** Cf hot-blooded. **c. fitting/shaping** Levelling hoof, shaping shoe, achieving correct fit without heating shoe. Ready-made/keg shoes used. Faster than hot shoeing but requires skilled farrier. **c. shoe** (syn ready-made shoe, keg shoe) Short-heeled, machine-made shoe fitted **c.** Many types, sizes, weights available. **c.** Also colloq for catarrhal disorder of upper respiratory tract. See snotty nose, temperature.

cold

Diseases caused by *Escherichia coli*. See septicaemia of the newborn; diarrhoea.

colibacillosis

Pain in tubes or ducts of abdomen. 3 main types: (1) **biliary c.** Disturbance in bile duct. Rare in horses; caused by growth or parasites blocking duct. (2) **renal c.** Disturbance in ureters (ducts carrying urine from kidneys to bladder). Rare in horses, may be due to kidney stones (calculi). See stone. (3) **alimentary c.** Disturbance in alimentary tract; only type common in horses. **impaction c.** Simple stoppage due to dry food material, usually in colon at pelvic or diaphragmatic flexure (bend) in caecum, or at point where small intestine enters caecum. **sand c.** Form of impaction **c.** due to accumulation of sand in caecum; occurs in horses grazing on sandy soil. **spasmodic c.**

colic

colic *(italic)* Excess activity of gut, causing spasm. May include diarrhoea. **twist c.** (volvulus) Acutely obstructed small intestine due to it becoming twisted or due to larger organs, such as caecum, rotating on suspending membrane. **tympanitic c.** Fermentation of food so that gas accumulates, usually in stomach, caecum or colon. **verminous c.** That due to blood clots in arteries supplying small or large intestines so that blood supply to part of gut is cut off. The clot (thrombus) occurs because blood vessel is damaged by migrating redworm larvae (see aneurysm). Pain in **c.** caused by (1) gut wall distended by gas or food, causing stretched peritoneum (membrane) in which there are many pain receptors; (2) inflamed peritoneum; (3) spasm of muscle in gut wall. Symptoms: refusal to eat, sweating, looking round at flanks, pawing ground, getting up and down, rolling, lying on back, anxious expression. In tympanitic **c.** horse may straddle its limbs or crouch. In impacted **c.** it may show signs of full bladder and straddle in urinating position. Pulse rate may increase and temperature rise, according to severity of pain. Diagnosis: on symptoms plus absent or increased gut sounds (borborygmi). Rectal examination is useful to determine type of **c.** Prognosis: poor if pain fails to respond to treatment, if pulse is fast and weakens, haematocrit rises (above 50 per cent) and mucous membranes of mouth and eye are red or purple. Treatment: (1) impacted **c.**, liquid paraffin and purgative drugs by stomach pump; (2) tympanitic **c.**, anti-spasmodic drugs by injection or by stomach tube; (3) twist, surgical operation essential. In all types, pain is relieved by injection of pethidine, anti-spasmodic and tranquillising drugs, analgesics such as equipalazone, flunixin meglumine, butorphanol.

colitis Inflamed colon. **c. X** Disease of unknown cause (possibly toxins from *E. coli* germ) characterised by acute pain, diarrhoea, shock and death in 1–2 days. At postmortem massive haemorrhage in wall of colon.

collagen (Gr kolla, glue + gennan, to produce) Main protein of skin, tendon, bone, cartilage and connective tissue.

collapse (L collapsus) Prostration and depression, usually applied to heart. **c. of lung** (atelectatic lung) Airless state of lung. See emphysema.

collateral (L con, together + latus, side) Secondary, not direct. See also circulation.

colostrum (colloq first milk) Thick milk secreted by mammary glands at birth, characterised by high protein content, especially globulin, which gives newborn foal its immunity. Close to birth drops of **c.** may exude from teats and form wax-like beads at end of teat, mare then said to be waxing up. See also tetanus toxoid, running of milk, haemolytic jaundice.

colostrum

(L color) See coat colouring.

colour

Male of Equus (qv) until he is: (1) castrated, (2) adult (usually considered 4/5 years old though growth not complete until 7), (3) used for breeding. Then termed respectively gelding, horse, stallion. Cf filly.

colt

(L columna) Grey matter of spinal cord. See cord.

column

(Gr koma) Unconsciousness from which it is difficult or impossible to arouse sufferer. See neonatal maladjustment syndrome.

coma

(CID) Condition resulting in lack of lymphocytes due to genetic defect in Arabian and part-Arabian horses. Once maternal antibody levels drop, foals lack functional immune system and succumb to variety of infections. Fatal.

combined immunodeficiency disease

(L com-, together + mensa, table) Organism living on or in another but not damaging host. Cf parasite.

commensal

Site of meeting of parts, eg **c.** (angle) of lips.

commissure

Complex substance in blood serum, probably formed by white blood cells. Necessary for antigen/antibody reaction and used in laboratory in **c.** fixation test for diagnosis of some bacterial and other diseases, eg brucellosis and haemolytic jaundice in newborn foal.

complement

Intensified. **c. vitamin A solution** Obtained from oils of fish liver and many vegetables, in most of which it exists as carotene. Vitamin necessary for healthy epithelial tissue, bone growth and formation of pigment in retina. Minimum daily requirement: 20IU per kg/bodywt. **c. vitamin D solution** Suitable fish-liver oil or blend of oils and calciferol. Vitamin necessary for absorbing calcium and phosphorus from gut. Deficiency may cause rickets. Min daily requirement: 10IU per kg/bodywt.

concentrated

(L concussio; syns jar, shock, trauma) Stress caused by knock. Word used of head injury where consciousness is impaired or lost; or of damaged skeleton, especially legs. More likely to affect forelegs (which bear 65 per cent of horse's weight) than hindlegs. See bucked shin, bowed tendon, foot.

concussion

(L condus, a receptacle, or possibly after Condon, the inventor) Sheath for penis applied to stallion before coitus to collect

condom

condom

semen for laboratory examination. Cf artificial vagina; semen.

condyle

(L condylus, Gr kondylos, knuckle) Rounded projection of bone, eg **c.** of humerus. Adjective: condylar.

conformation

Anatomical arrangement and proportion of parts of body. A major factor in soundness of legs. Poor **c.** may predispose to sprains of joints, ligaments, tendons, bone injuries and navicular disease. **c.** of body varies between breeds, eg Arab has short back compared with Thoroughbred; American Quarter-horse has heavy body compared with Thoroughbred. **faulty c.** Includes over at the knees/back at the knees (syn calf-kneed), base narrow/base wide (legs set on body too closely together/too far apart), toe narrow/toe wide (feet too close/too far apart), long/upright pastern affecting angle of hoof. See axis. **functional c.** The way horse uses its legs (in contrast to static **c.** of standing horse). They do not necessarily match. **c. of foot** Sole should be concave, bars well developed, frog large and in centre of sole. Front feet more rounded (less narrow) than hind. Angle formed by ground surface of hoof and front of wall should be 45–50° in front and 50–55° behind (see foot). **c. of vulva** Should be vertical line between anus and lower angle of vulva. Poor **c.** encourages infection. See Caslick, Pouret.

congenital

Present at birth, eg **c.** abnormality such as hare lip, cleft palate, contracted tendons.

congestion

(L from congeries, heap) Excessive accumulation of blood or other fluid in a part. **passive c.** That caused by obstructed blood flow. See inflammation, sprain.

conjunctiva

Membrane lining eyelids and covering exposed surface of eyeball.

conjunctivitis

Inflamed conjunctiva. May affect one or both eyes; characterised by red, perhaps swollen, eyelid, pus flecks and tears which run down face causing scalding and loss of hair. Spasm of eyelids and closure of eye is common. Cause: infection, foreign body, injury, allergy, irritation from flies. Treatment: antibiotic and hydrocortisone eye drops. See also eye.

connective tissue

One of 4 basic tissues in body (cf epithelial, muscular and nervous). So called because it holds tissues together and to the skeleton. Special property of **c.t.** cells is that they produce non-living substances to lie between cells. Some of these are hard, eg bone. **C.t.** is subdivided into (1) ordinary, including fat and soft tissue, binding skin to underlying muscles, bone etc; (2) special, including blood-forming cells and supporting structures composed of bone and cartilage.

Native breed of **C.** district in W Ireland. Hardy type, thrives on poor land. Now most often grey, must be 13–14 h to be eligible for stud book, though taller examples exist after introduction of Thoroughbred blood. Breed's origin obscure, could be Celtic type (like Norwegian, Highland etc) tracing to Mongolian; could have developed from oriental horses who swam ashore from wreck of Spanish Armada; or could trace to Irish Hobby (qv). Some **C.** ponies tend to amble (see gait). **C. P. Breeders' Soc**, 73 Dalysford Road, Salthill, Galway (01035391 22909). **English C. P. Soc**, Woodland St Mary Cottage, Lambourn, Berks RG16 7SL (01488 73313).

Connemara pony

(L constipatio, a crowding together) Infrequent defecation due to dry or hardened dung. See colic; meconium, retention of; obstipation.

constipation

(L contagiosus) Able to spread from one animal to another as in disease, eg influenza. See veterinary rules. **c. equine metritis** (CEM) Uterine infection of mares spread by stallions who carry the causal bacteria but do not exhibit symptoms. First identified in mid-1970s. Highly **c.** disease caused by gram-negative bacterium *Taylorella equigenitalis*, qv.

contagious

Combining form meaning against. **c.-indicated** (CI) Not advisable, usually used about drugs, eg phenylbutazone **c.i.** in heart, liver or kidney disease.

contra-

Reduced. **c. heels** Heels that are too narrow. They should be wide, compared with the toe. May be partially corrected by increasing pressure on frog. Can be done by using T or bar shoe and by increasing flexibility of hoof wall by grooving at quarters. See shoeing. **c. tendons** (syn hyperflexion of leg) Condition of newborn foals and yearlings. Flexor tendons and suspensory ligaments are too short and cause permanent flexion of fetlock and sometimes knee, in one or both forelegs; may affect hind legs. Animal knuckles over at fetlock and, in severe cases, may walk on front of joint. Congenital cases may result in dystocia due to inability of forelegs to straighten normally to pass through birth canal. Some foals born normal, then develop condition at any age up to 2 years. Mild cases are described as being straight and upright. Cause unknown, probably inherited or result of abnormal inherited material, ie chromosomes. Other possible causes: infection, malnutrition and dietary deficiency. Treatment: fit splints and special boots to counteract abnormality. Surgical treatment involves cutting superior check ligament. Severe cases might be helped by surgical cutting of flexor tendon and ligaments behind knee. Cf hypoflexion.

contracted

contraction | (L contractus, drawn together) A shortening as in ligaments, tendons of fore- or hindlegs of foal. Also muscle in sustained **c.** ie tetanic. See lockjaw.

convection | (L convectio from convehere, to convey) Route by which heat is lost through circulation of air or fluid. See temperature.

convulsant | Producing convulsions, eg drug. **anti-c.** Drug controlling convulsions, eg phenytoin.

convulsions | (L from convellere, to pull together) Violent involuntary muscle contractions. **clonic c.** Jerky movements due to alternate contracting and relaxing of muscles. **epileptic c.** Jerky movements accompanied by loss of consciousness, does not occur in horses. **general c.** Incoordinated movements, eg when foal lies on ground making galloping movements. **tetanic c.** Spasms, as in lockjaw. See neonatal maladjustment syndrome.

COPD | Chronic obstructive pulmonary disease. See broken wind.

copper sulphate | Blue odourless crystalline powder with astringent taste. Used in lotions to reduce proud flesh.

copro- | (Gr kopros, dung) Combining form meaning relationship to faeces.

coprophagia | Feeding on dung. See appetite, depraved; behaviour.

cord | (L chorda, Gr chorde) Long, rounded body or structure. **genital c.** Formed in embryo by union of mesonephric and mullerian ducts. **c., rupture of** Usually refers to umbilical **c.** which breaks naturally as foal struggles or mare stands. See birth. **spermatic c.** From abdomen, through inguinal ring to testis. Contains vas deferens, testicular artery, pampiniform plexus, nerves and muscle, enclosed by fine membrane. **spinal c.** Tissue made up of white matter (column) which extends from brain to level of third lumbar vertebra. Lodges in vertebral canal and gives off nerve branches to various parts of body. See nerve. **umbilical c.** Connects umbilicus (navel) of foal to placenta and contains two arteries, one vein and urinary duct (urachus).

cordectomy | Removal of vocal cord. Sometimes performed with Hobday operation.

corium | Modified vascular tissue inside horn of hoof. Divided into 5 parts all of which nourish horn (1) **perioplic c.** Narrow band above coronary border and merging with skin. (2) **coronary c.** Together with (1) forms coronary band. Responsible for growth, bleeds easily when damaged. Can be likened to bed of human nail. (3) **laminar c.** Membrane attached to surface of pedal bone, bears sensitive laminae. (4) **sole c.** Membrane lining ground surface of pedal bone. (5) **frog c.** Membrane nourishing frog.

corium

(L cornu, horn) (1) Bruise of sensitive and insensitive laminae of sole of foot. Most common at seat of **c.** in angle formed by wall and bar. Causes: poor shoeing, stones, improper trimming when heels are too low. Symptoms: lameness, evidence of pain on pressure, especially when turning. **dry c.** Due to haemorrhage on inner surface of horn, ie between the sensitive and insensitive laminae. **moist c.** Dark brown, moist area seen at seat of **c. suppurating c.** Due to infection of corn. Treatment: cut area of **c.** and dress with astringents, antibiotics and, if severe, bandage. Special shoes can be used. See shoeing. (2) Type of food, qv.

corn

(L corneus, horny) Transparent structure forming front part of eye and continuous with sclera. Adjective: corneal. See fig 12, eye.

cornea

(L horn; pl cornua) Anatomical term meaning horn-shaped. **uterine c.** One of horns of uterus.

cornu

(L, Gr korone; pl coronae, coronas) Anatomical term meaning crown-like or encircling. **dental c.** Part of tooth crowned with enamel.

corona

(L corona, Gr korone) (1) Of the heart, especially its vessels. See heart; arteries, table of. (2) Part of hoof farthest from basal surface at any given point and adjacent to hair of the foot. **c. band** (syn sensitive coronary band) The sensitive hoof structure around upper border of hoof under its junction with skin from which hoof wall is produced. It is the combined perioplic corium, coronary corium and coronary cushion and is the primary growth and nutritional source for the bulk of hoof wall and bars. Consists of a stratum germinativum (horn-producing layer of cells) which produces hoof wall (stratum medium) and horny laminae (stratum lamellatum). Injuries to this structure usually leave a permanent defect in the growth of the hoof wall. See hoof, corium, quittor. **c. cracks** See hoof cracks. **c. cushion** Elastic portion of **c.** corium which aids in reducing concussion. See hoof, corium.

coronary

A leg marking describing white above the hoof. Sometimes inaccurately used as a syn for coronary or coronary band.

coronet

(L body; pl corpora) Main part of a structure, organ or part.

corpus

corpus	**c. cavernosum penis** Vascular structure forming greater part of penis. **c. luteum** See yellow body.
corpuscle	Small mass or body, eg red or white blood **c.**
Corsican	Pony of Italian island of Corsica, similar to Sardinian, qv.
corrective trimming/ shoeing	Trimming and shoeing hoof so it is level, balanced and has normal hoof shape, foot-pastern axis, and foot flight pattern to provide a normal gait (qv). May be achieved by changing lateral balance, hoof angle, hoof length or hoof wall thickness. See shoeing.
cortex	(L, bark, rind, shell) External layer. **adrenal c.** Outer layer of adrenal gland which secretes corticosteroids. **renal c.** Consists of filtering units (glomeruli) and secretory ducts of kidney. Adjective: cortical. See adrenal glands, corticosteroids, kidney, urine.
corticosteroids	Hormones produced by adrenal cortex. (See adrenal gland.) Three classes: glucocorticoids (affect carbohydrate metabolism and have anti-inflammatory action); mineralocorticoids (affect mineral/salt balance); sex corticoids (affect male and female characteristics).
corticotrophic	Having specific effect on cortex of adrenal gland, eg hormone produced by pituitary gland. See adrenocorticotrophic hormone.
corticotrophin	Hormone (obtained from anterior lobe of pituitary gland) which stimulates adrenal cortex to secrete cortisol. Used as adjunct to cortisone therapy.
cortisol	Hormone produced by adrenal cortex. See hydrocortisone.
cortisone/c. acetate	Small white odourless crystals with bitter taste. Hormone affecting carbohydrate metabolism and with anti-inflammatory action, converted by body into hydrocortisone. Causes rise in glycogen in liver and sugar in blood. May affect water and mineral metabolism and modify growth of fibrous tissue; reduces resistance to infection and suppresses inflammation. Used with an antibiotic to treat arthritis, allergies and other inflammatory processes, such as in sprained tendons. See adrenal gland, corticosteroids, betamethasone sodium phosphate, dexamethasone.
Corynebacterium	(Gr koryne, club + bakterion, little rod) Genus of gram-positive bacteria of family Corynebacteriacae; straight or slightly curved rod and generally aerobic. **C. equi** Former name for causal

organism of pneumonia in foals (now *Rhodococcus equi*). See pneumonia.	*Corynebacterium*
(L costalis) Of a rib, eg **c.** cartilage.	**costal**
Subdivision of surface of placenta in which union between that organ and uterus is microscopic.	**cotyledon**
Reflex movement controlled by nervous pathways to and from brain. Analysed as: (1) closing of glottis (larynx entrance) by epiglottis; (2) deep inhalation when abdominal muscles push against diaphragm until air pressure in lungs is enough to expel mucus, dust, etc; (3) opening of larynx to allow sudden gush of air. **C.** caused by inhaling dust, pollen or other irritant, structural change in lung (eg emphysema) or viral infection especially with A/equi or herpesvirus. May be accompanied by rise in temperature except if caused by lungworm. Should never be treated lightly, especially in Thoroughbred. **Newmarket c.** Syn for influenza, qv.	**cough**
(L computare, to reckon) Numerical index of composition. **blood c.** Number of cells in measured volume of blood (red or white cells per cu mm, see blood tests). **egg/faecal/parasite c.** Numbers of strongyle (red) and ascaris (white) worm eggs per gm of faeces.	**count**
Drug or chemical causing increase in bloodflow to a part. See blister.	**counter-irritant**
Colloq to serve; have coitus/sexual intercourse.	**cover**
See dourine.	**covering disease**
(*Cicuta virosa*) Plant which, if eaten, causes nausea, dilated pupils, colic, convulsions and death from asphyxia. No obvious changes at postmortem. See poisons.	**cowbain**
Poor conformation, best seen from behind horse, in which hocks are too close together and feet splayed wide. Tends to produce bog spavin, qv.	**cow hocks**
Spiral arrangement in coat hairs. Cf whorl. See marking.	**cowlick**
(L hip) Hip or hip joint.	**coxa**
Abbr creatinine phosphokinase, now termed creatine kinase, qv.	**CPK**
Sores, fissures and eczematous lesions on heels. See mud fever, staphylococcus.	**cracked heels**

cranial	(L. cranium, head) Towards front of horse, related to head.
cranium	(Gr kranion, upper part of head) Bones of head except lower jaw; those surrounding brain. See skull.
creatinine clearance test	Method of determining ratios of creatinine, phosphate, calcium and electrolytes between urine and blood samples taken simultaneously. Indicates calcium and phosphate metabolism and electrolyte balance.
creatine kinase	(CK) Enzyme in skeletal muscle, heart muscle and brain tissue. Normal levels in serum less than 200IU/l, increased in muscle damage (heart and skeletal). In setfast, qv, level may reach 30,000IU/l, peaking at 6–12 hours, returning to normal in 3–4 days. See aspartate aminotransferase.
creosote	Strong-smelling liquid, colourless or pale yellow when neat. Distilled from wood tar. Acts as bactericide, parasiticide and deodorant. Should not be applied to skin as may be absorbed causing toxic symptoms. Active principle: phenol, qv.
crepitus/crepitation	(L crepitare, to crackle) Grating noise made by ends of fractured bone rubbing together. Likely to be serious if **c.** can be heard with naked ear.
critical care	See intensive.
cribbing/crib-biting	Vice in which animal grasps manger or other object with front teeth, arches neck and usually swallows air. Regarded as vice, qv. Diagnosed on sight and by noting worn front edge of teeth and marks on manger, box door. Cf wind-sucking.
cricoid	(Gr krikos, ring + eidos, form) Resembling a ring, eg **c.** cartilage.
Criollo	Argentinian pony noted for endurance. Usually dun or skewbald, about 14h. Developed from Andalusian horses imported into S America in 1530s, which escaped captivity and bred freely. Now under auspices of Argentine government which keeps stud book. Virtually same as Peruvian **C.** or Costeno.
Crioulo	Hardy Brazilian breed similar to Criollo and with many local names, eg Mangalarga, Campolino, Nordestino, Courraleiro.
crofton weed	(*Eupatorium* spp) If eaten causes Numinbah horse sickness of New South Wales. Symptoms: acute oedema of lungs, followed by haemorrhage.
cromolyn	(syns cromoglycic acid, sodium cromoglycate, qv). Antihistamine.

Condition in which inside of toe or wall of hind foot strikes inner quarter or undersurface of opposite forefoot. Cf forging.

cross-firing

(1) Used in embryology to describe exchange of genes between chromosomes, qv. See embryology. (2) Used to describe action of hindlegs, eg in brain disorders such as encephalomyelitis and spinal cord disorders, eg wobbler syndrome, segmental myelitis.

crossing-over

Process of testing blood from one individual against that of another; laboratory test: mix red blood cells from recipient with plasma from donor. Incompatibility is demonstrated by clumping together (agglutination) of red cells. Test used before blood transfusion. See blood tests, haemolytic jaundice.

cross-matching

Various species in USA, Australia and S Africa are poisonous if eaten, including **C.** *globifera* (wild lucern). Symptoms: difficult breathing, rapid and weak pulse, collapse and death. **C.** *retusa* causes dullness, wasting, irritability, yawning, muscular spasms and aimless galloping (Kimberley horse disease). No known cure.

crotalaria plants

(1) Part of hindquarters from highest point to top of tail; varies from virtually flat to generous slope. See Dutch Draught. (2) Acute obstruction of voice box.

croup

(L corona) Upper part of organ or structure, eg surface of tooth; colloq temporary premolars shed between $2^1/_2$ and $3^1/_2$ years (also known as caps). See teeth. **c. to rump** Measurement of foetus, qv.

crown

Shaped like a cross, eg **c. ligament** Two strong, round bands in stifle attached between femur and tibia in form of X.

cruciate

(Gr kryos, cold) Surgery using processes including freezing, eg of wart or sarcoid (qv), causing it to become insensitive.

cryosurgery

(L crypta from Gr kryptos, hidden) Blind-ended tubule or minute depression. eg **c.**s of Lieberkuhn glands in inner lining of small intestine.

crypt

(crypto-, combining form meaning hidden, + Gr orchis, testis) Male suffering from cryptorchidism, ie abnormality in which testes fail to descend into scrotum. See rig.

cryptorchid

Protozoa (one cell) organism which causes diarrhoea in calves and piglets. Not yet identified as being cause of diarrhoea (qv) in foals but may play a role.

cryptosporidia

See epithelium.

cuboidal epithelium

Culicoides — Genus of biting fly which can cause sweet itch. See Queensland itch.

culture — (L culture) Process of growing microorganisms in laboratory, on media or in tissue cells. **c. medium** Substance or preparation used to cultivate bacteria, virus or fungus. Virus is cultivated in tissue culture as it will not grow without living cells (**c.** media include egg embryo and kidney cells). Bacteria and fungus are cultivated on blood agar and other substances.

cunean tendon — Middle part of tendon of tibialis anterior muscle, hindleg. It forks from main tendon in middle of hock and travels to insert on second tarsal bone. Sometimes cut to relieve bone spavin.

cuneiform — (L cuneus, wedge + forma, form) Shaped like a wedge, eg **c.** cartilage, foot of voice box (larynx).

curare — Dried extract of various species of Strychnos. Highly toxic, used in general anaesthesia and to reduce spasm in lockjaw (tetanus). Overdose causes paralysis and death. Treatment: artificial respiration.

curb — Enlargement at seat of **c.** ie at back of upper end of cannon, about 15cm (6in) below point of hock. Causes include conformation (sickle hocks, curby hocks), putting strain on ligaments. May be result of trauma or sprain. Symptoms: soft, sometimes painful, swelling on upper end of cannon. Best seen standing at right angles to hock. Horse may be lame. Treatment: reduce acute inflammation, eg with cold water application, corticosteroids, irradiation.

curettage — (Fr) Removal of growth or other tissue from wall of cavity or skin surface using instrument known as curette. Used to treat barren mares (by scraping surface of uterus) so that new lining forms.

Cushing's disease — Condition caused by overgrowth of basophil cells of anterior lobe of pituitary gland. Most marked symptom: extreme overgrowth of coat which becomes shaggy, excessive thirst and urination and increased susceptibility to laminitis. Some drugs may reduce severity of signs.

cusp — (L cuspis, point) Triangular segment of cardiac valve. See heart valves.

cut — Colloq to castrate. See castration.

cutaneous papillomatosis — See milk warts.

Outer covering of body. See skin. **cutis**

White tasteless odourless powder. Used against lungworm, rendering parasites inert so they can be coughed up. **cyacetazide**

(including hydrocyanic acid, prussic acid) Occurs in contact with fertilisers or plants including family Sorghum, certain clovers and linseed meals. Acid is liberated when plant tissue is damaged or decayed. Symptoms: convulsions, paralysis, stupor and respiratory failure, followed by quick death. Diagnosis: on chemical analysis of stomach contents. Treatment: (where possible) solution of 3g sodium nitrate, 15g sodium thiosulphate in 20ml water, sub cut. **cyanide poisoning**

Vitamin B_{12} essential for red blood cell formation. **cyanocobalamin**

(Gr kyanos, blue) Bluish colour of mucous membranes due to blood's abnormally low oxygen content. Causes: heart failure, severe pneumonia. Sign of impending death, best seen in gums. **cyanosis**

General name for group of strongyles (parasitic worms) which includes genera Cyathostomum, Cylicocyclus, Cylicodontophorus. Normally less than 1.5cm in length. Larvae invade muscular lining of gut and develop there. When they emerge, inflammatory reaction can cause colic and enteritis. Ivermectin, pyrantel, benzimidazoles effective against adult stages. Ivermectin, or pyrantel on five consecutive days reported to have some effect on larvae. **cyathostomes**

(Gr kyklos, ciliary body + -itis) Inflamed ciliary body. See eye, diseases of; moon blindness. **cyclitis**

Abnormal sac lined with epithelial cells and coated with fibrous cells. Contains fluid or other matter; several varieties, eg **dermoid c.** qv. **ovarian c.** One in ovary. **stifle c.**, qv. **cyst**

Inflamed urinary bladder. Symptoms: repeated urination, possibly red-coloured urine. May accompany stones, qv. **cystitis**

(L cysto, bladder + scope) Instrument for viewing interior of bladder. See endoscope. **cystoscope**

(Gr kytos, hollow vessel + ology, study of) Study of structure and function of cells. Cf histology. **cytology**

(cyto- + Gr penis, poverty) Deficiency of cells in blood. **erythro-c.** Deficiency of erythrocytes in blood, as in anaemia. **leuco-c.** Fewer than normal white cells, as in viral infections. See anaemia; virus. **cytopenia**

cytoplasm	(cyto- + Gr plasma) Protoplasm of cell outside nucleus. See cell.
cytotoxic	(Gr kytos, hollow vessel + toxic, relating to, due to or with nature of, a poison) Capable of damaging cells.

D

Pony of N England, similar to Fell pony (qv) but with some cob and Clydesdale blood. Originally used to ferry weight in mines, now popular for pony trekking. Up to 14.2 h with fine mane, tail and feathers (long hairs on pastern). Often black, also bay or grey, but not chestnut or mixed colours. **D. Pony Soc**, Greystones, Glebe Ave, Gt Longstone, Derbys DE45 1TY (01629 640439).	**Dales**
Orange odourless tasteless powder. Purgative acting on involuntary muscle of large intestine, given in food or by stomach tube. Acts in 12–24 hours; more effective if mixed with water. May produce red-coloured urine.	**danthron**
(trade name Dantrium) Muscle relaxant used to treat setfast.	**dantrolene sodium**
See coat colouring.	**dappled grey**
Hardy pony, up to 12.2 h, of **D.** district of SW England. Long-lived, usually handled only at round-up and breeding times. All colours except piebald and skewbald. Domesticated **D.** is popular child's pony. **D. Pony Soc**, 57 Pykes Down, Ivybridge, Devon, PL21 0BY (01752 897053). **D. Pony Soc of America**, 292 Butler Rd SE, Milledgeville, GA 31061.	**Dartmoor**
(syn Eohippus) See evolution.	**dawn horse**
See nightshade poisoning.	**deadly nightshade**
Impaired or lost sense of hearing. See ear.	**deaf**
End of life shown by lack of heart beat and respiration. **foetal d.** Abortion. **early foetal d. D.** of foetus in early pregnancy, ie before 100 days. See postmortem; rigor mortis.	**death**
Remove contaminated and/or devitalised tissue from wound.	**debride**
(L from deciduus, falling off) Loss of tissue; usually applied to that from uterus, thrown off with placenta after birth in most mammals, but not in mares.	**decidua**
Drug or substance that reduces congestion or swelling especially of respiratory passages.	**decongestant**
(L, a lying down) Ulcers or sores formed by prolonged lying down. Common sites: point of hip, stifle region, elbow, hock. (colloq bedsore).	**decubitus**

deep heat Colloq for treating injury with heat. See physiotherapy.

defecation (L defaecare) Act of voiding rectum. See also behaviour; colic; diarrhoea.

defect Imperfection. **acquired d.** Result of accident or disease after birth, eg loss of eye. **congenital d.** Present at birth, may be inherited or due to faulty environment in uterus, eg parrot jaw, contracted tendons. **septal d.** Hole in heart wall between opposite chambers. See bladder, rupture of; contracted tendons; parrot jaw; unsoundness.

degeneration (L degeneratio) Pathological term meaning death or deterioration of cells. **hyaline d.** Tissue transformed into translucent material. See degenerative joint disease.

degenerative Adj of degeneration (qv). **d. joint disease** (syns DJD, osteoarthritis) Group of disorders characterised by progressive deterioration of cartilage cells lining joint surface resulting in damage to underlying bone, synovial membrane and ligaments, loss of mobility and pain. See osteophyte; osteochondritis dissecans (OCD).

deglutition (L deglutitio) Act of swallowing; may be strained in, eg grass sickness, some colics.

dehiscence Splitting or breaking down, eg wound **d.** breakdown of wound repair.

dehydration Condition in which more water is lost from body than is absorbed; this causes reduced circulating blood and relatively dry tissues. Caused by decreased water intake and/or excess fluid loss through sweating, diarrhoea, shock or urination. As water content of body decreases, fluid is drained from tissue spaces, cells and blood; haemoconcentration is recognised by increase in packed cell volume (haematocrit). Dry skin loses its pliability, so if pinched it stays raised instead of sliding back into place normally. Eyeball recedes into socket (especially noticeable in dehydrated foal); there is weight-loss, small dry faeces, decrease in urine; blood may become increasingly acid (acidosis); pulse becomes small, there is depression and, in extreme cases, coma. Treatment: give fluids IV or by mouth. See also blood, diarrhoea, fluid balance, temperature. Cf drycoat.

dembrexine hydrochloride (trade name: Sputolosin) Drug which is given to treat symptoms of respiratory disease. Acts by reducing viscosity of mucus in respiratory tract.

(Gr demos, fat + dex, worm) Genus of mite. See also mange, demodectic. — **Demodex**

Soothing, bland drug or substance. — **demulcent**

(Gr dendron, tree) Part of nerve cell, qv. — **dendrite**

To remove nerves to a part, eg horse's foot can be denerved by cutting volar nerves at level of fetlock. See neurectomy. Cf nerve block. — **denervate**

(L dens, tooth + gerere, to carry) Bearing teeth. **d. cyst** See also dermoid cyst. — **dentigerous**

(L dens, tooth) Chief substance surrounding tooth pulp and covered by enamel and cement. See teeth. — **dentin/dentine**

Diploma in Equine Orthopaedics, awarded by Royal College of Veterinary Surgeons, qv. — **DEO**

See DNA. — **deoxyribonucleic acid**

See appetite. — **depraved appetite**

Genus of tick, qv. — **Dermacentor**

(1) Concave area in organ or body, eg prophet's thumb mark (**d.** in muscle of neck). (2) Dull state of health, often present with fever, conditions of central nervous system, infections, liver disease. — **depression**

(Gr derma, skin + -itis, pl dermatitides; syn eczema) Inflamed skin caused by bacteria, fungus, virus, allergy or chemicals. Types include acne, nettle rash, Queensland itch, photosensitisation, ringworm, mud fever, dermoid cyst. See separate headings. — **dermatitis**

See mud fever. — **dermatophilosis**

Genus of microorganism with bacterial and fungal characteristics. **D. congolensis** Causal organism of mud fever, qv, and rain scald. — **Dermatophilus**

(pl dermatoses) Any skin disease. — **dermatosis**

See skin. — **dermis**

Egg-shaped growth with thick walls and cavity containing yellowish, greasy matter and, sometimes, a tooth (dentigerous — **dermoid cyst** *dermoid cyst* | cyst). Can occur anywhere on body, but usually on head, eg in nostril, eye, below ear. Often opens onto skin surface. Treat surgically.

derris | Dried resin and roots of *D. elliptica* and other plant species of Thailand and Malaysia. Active principle: rotenone. Widely used as dusting powder or wash to control parasites, especially warble fly, qv.

descent of testes | (testicles) In foetal life testes develop in upper part of abdomen, close to kidneys. Towards full term, each testis migrates down inguinal canal into scrotum. Testes have usually descended by birth but one or both may be retained in inguinal canal or abdomen. Migration is not clearly understood; the ligament known as gubernaculum testis, from tail of epididymis to inguinal ring, may exert traction. Retention of testis is cryptorchidism; absence of both testes: anorchidism or bilateral cryptorchidism. See rig.

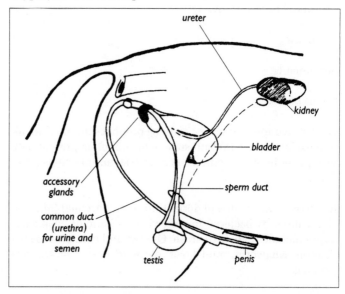

8 Male horse seen from off-side, showing route of descending testis

DESM | Diploma in Equine Stud Medicine, awarded by Royal College of Veterinary Surgeons, qv.

desmitis | Inflamed ligament. See sprain.

desoxycorticosterone acetate | (DOCA) Crystalline steroid, same as corticosteroid except hydroxyl group is replaced by hydrogen atom. Has marked effect on metabolism of water and electrolytes. See cortisone.

detomidine | (trade name: Domosedan) A premedication before anaesthesia with ketamine (qv), halothane (qv) etc. Also used as tranquilliser IV or IM.

detomidine

(trade names: Azium, Colvasone, Decadron, Dexadresson, Dexafort, Soludex) White crystalline odourless powder with slightly bitter taste. Actions and uses similar to cortisone, qv.

dexamethasone

(1) White odourless crystals or grains with sweet taste. Given in solution by mouth or IV to treat shock, blood loss, severe dehydration. (2) Product of digested carbohydrate in the alimentary tract.

dextrose

(Gr diabetes, a syphon) **d. insipidus** Increased production of urine (polyuria). It is of low specific gravity and free from protein and sugar. Associated with growths of pituitary gland but in horses may occur after eating mouldy hay or oats, in glanders or tuberculosis causing kidney damage. **d. mellitus** Condition in which sugar cannot be stored in body. Causes increase in blood sugar (hyperglycemia) and excessive discharge of sugar in urine (glycosuria). Rare in horses. Symptoms: thirst, abnormally high blood sugar concentration, weight-loss and coma.

diabetes

To identify disease or condition.

diagnose

(dia- + Gr gnosis, knowledge) Nature of disease deduced by observing, examining, special tests and laboratory measures. May or may not be specific, eg colic or certain type of colic, such as twist. **clinical d.** One based on signs. **differential d.** Distinction between diseases with similar symptoms, eg cough caused by influenza or broken wind. **laboratory d.** Based on lab tests, eg haemolytic jaundice of newborn foal. **D.** can be based on departure from normal, eg lameness, eating, movement, stance, defecation, urination. **D.** by physical examination includes palpation (feeling part) and percussion, qv.

diagnosis

Broad, domed, muscular partition between chest and abdomen. Chest side is covered by pleura, abdominal side by peritoneum. **D.** is attached to ribs, cartilage of sternum and lumbar vertebrae. It can change volume of chest to help breathing and can exert pressure on abdomen, eg during foaling (see birth). **D.** forms complete membrane except for 3 openings through which pass an artery (aorta), oesophagus and a vein (posterior vena cava).

diaphragm

Shaft of a long bone.

diaphysis

(syns scour, purge and, in foal, wet tail) Loose, very runny faeces. Symptom of increased water in faeces due to disturbed

diarrhoea

diarrhoea | fluid exchange between body tissues and gut contents. Often associated with increased gut movement (peristalsis) and inflamed intestinal mucous membrane (enteritis). Caused by (1) dietary factors such as composition and quantity of milk (foal **d.** more likely when dam in oestrus) or, in adult, excessive protein in fast-growing grass; poor-quality food; imbalanced diet; (2) bacteria (certain strains of *E. coli*, salmonella, campylobacter) fungus or virus (rotavirus); (3) protozoa (cryptosporidia); (4) antibiotics disturbing natural flora of bacteria in gut; (5) purgative drugs and poisons taken by mouth. Symptoms: dung of cow-like consistency or watery, sometimes blood-stained, odourless or strong unpleasant smell; relaxed anus, allowing air into rectum; dehydration, qv. Treatment: correct the diet, give antibiotics if cause is bacterial, or antifungal drugs if fungal, plus soothing drugs such as kaolin, chalk, sodium bicarbonate.

diastole | Period when heart fills with blood and muscle is relaxing, before contraction (systole). See heart.

diathermy | The use of electrical currents to heat tissues – in physiotherapy tissues are warmed. In surgery, tissues are destroyed. Used to control surgical haemorrhage.

diazepam | (trade name Valium) Tranquilliser with anticonvulsant, sedative and relaxant properties used in foals to combat convulsions. In older individuals used to control muscle spasms caused by tetanus.

dichlorvos | Drug used to treat most worms and botfly larvae. Should not be used in horse with broken wind, diarrhoea or constipation. Chickens etc should not be allowed to forage in dung of treated horse, as drug can kill birds. Antidote: atropine.

dicoumarol | Substance produced in fermentation of sweet clover. Interferes with prothrombin formation and prevents blood clotting. Antidote: vitamin K. See coagulation.

Dictyocaulus | Genus of lungworm, qv.

diethylcarbamazine-citrate | (DEC) White crystalline odourless powder with acid taste. Used to control lungworm, qv.

diethylstilboestrol/ diethyl stilboestrol | See stilboestrol.

digestion | (L from dis, apart + genere, to carry) Process of converting food into materials fit to be absorbed through lining of alimentary canal (qv) so that they enter bloodstream. From here they are transported to organs and tissues of body (eg hay is converted into the simpler carbohydrate, fat and protein). **D.** starts in mouth as food is mixed with saliva (which contains digestive enzyme) and continues in stomach (which contains enzyme pepsin) but main organs of **d.** in horse are caecum and large colon. See food.

digestion

Finger or toe. See evolution.

digit

Fibro-elastic fatty pad at back of foot, above frog and below second phalanx. Forms bulbs of heel and reduces concussion. See foot.

digital cushion

Green powder with slight odour and bitter taste, from leaf of *D. purpurea* (foxglove). Used in heart conditions. Prolongs time taken by nervous impulse to travel through heart muscle enabling force of contraction to be increased while rate is decreased. Dose: 1–4g. Effects are cumulative and may cause toxicity. See heart impulse; neonatal maladjustment syndrome.

digitalis

White crystalline odourless powder with bitter taste; prepared from digitalis and given by mouth or injection. See digitalis, alkaloid.

digitoxin

(trade name: Lanoxin) Colourless odourless crystals with bitter taste, obtained from leaves of *Digitalis lanata.* See digitalis.

digoxin

Being dilated or stretched beyond normal. **d. of cervix** Before birth or at mating. **d. of pupils** See eye. **d. of heart** Enlargement of chambers with thinning of walls and therefore weakened beat. **d. of stomach** See colic.

dilatation/dilation

(abbr DMSO) Drug used to treat muscular pain. Unusual in that it can penetrate skin and carry other drugs into underlying tissue. Used alone, it has anti-inflammatory and some antifungal and antibacterial action. Used to treat bucked shins, qv.

dimethyl sulphoxide

(diminazen) Yellow odourless powder effective against parasites *Trypanosoma* and *Babesia* spp also bacteria *Brucella* spp and streptococci.

diminazene aceturate

(di- + Gr morphe, form) Having two forms. **sexual d.** With characteristics of both sexes (hermaphrodite). See intersex.

dimorphism

Not in oestrus (heat). Time between two oestrous periods. See oestrous cycle.

dioestrus

(trade name Benylin) White odourless bitter-tasting powder. Used as antihistamine, qv, also applied externally in cream.

diphenhydramine hydrochloride

diplococcus	Spherical bacterium occurring in pairs; does not generally cause disease. See bacteria, streptococcus.
diploid	(Gr diplous, twofold) Having full set of paired chromosomes, ie 32 pairs for a horse. Opp haploid. See chromosome.
diprenorphine	(trade name Large Animal Revivon) Drug used to reverse effects of etorphine hydrochloride (qv). Injected IV.
Diptera	(Gr dipteros, two-winged) Order of insects including flies, gnats and mosquitoes. All can trouble horses and carry disease. See tabanid fly.
dirty	Colloq for mare discharging catarrhal fluid from vulva. See endometritis. **d. nose** See snotty nose.
disc	(L discus, Gr diskos) Flat, circular plate, eg **optic d.** See eye.
disease	(Fr dès, from + aise, ease) Any abnormal process associated with characteristic signs; may affect whole body or any part. Its cause, consequences and outlook may be known or unknown. See various organs; also bacteria; fungi; virus; newborn foal, **d.s of. Notifiable d.s** See veterinary rules.
dish	(1) Shallow vessel as in culture **d.** or Petri **d.** used in laboratory. (2) Faulty action when foreleg below carpus (knee) is thrown outwards (syn paddle). **d.-faced** Face with concave profile, as in typical Arab. See Arab. **d. foot** (syn flare foot) See foot.
disinfectant	Substance that reduces or destroys infective microorganisms, eg chlorinated lime, potassium permanganate, phenol, sodium hydroxide.
dislocation	(dis- + L locare, to place) Displacement of part, especially a joint.
dispensary	(L dispensarium from dispensare, to dispense) Place where medicines and remedies are dispensed. See also veterinary hospital.
distal	(L distans, distant) Anatomical reference meaning farther from given point. Opp proximal.
distress	(L distringere, to draw apart) Difficulty or suffering, as in distressed breathing.
distressed breathing	(syn dyspnoea) May be due to obstructed air passages, including nasal cavities, voice box, windpipe; diseased lung using extra effort to compensate; biochemical disturbance in blood, affecting breathing centres of brain. Occurs in growths in

nostrils, paralysed vocal cords, pneumonia, haemorrhage of brain, acute infection causing high fever, broken wind. Symptoms: anxious facial expression, dilated nostrils, laboured movements of chest and abdomen, stentorious or wheezing sound. — *distressed breathing*

(Gr diourein, to urinate) Process of passing urine. See diuretic. — **diuresis**

(Gr diouretikos, promoting urine) Substance which promotes excretion of body fluids by increasing urine flow. May help treat Monday morning leg, fever. Natural **d.**s. include potassium salts, alcohol, hay-tea, small amounts of caffeine, turpentine oil and oil of juniper. Digitalis and strychnine, which increase blood pressure, have **d.** side-effect. See hydrochlorothiazide; furosemide. — **diuretic**

(L dies, day) During day. Opp nocturnal. — **diurnal**

(L divertere, to turn aside) Anatomical term meaning pouch or sac. — **diverticulum**

Abbr deoxyribonucleic acid, present in all living cells. It is the genetic code in cell nucleus and, with proteins, makes up chromatin, qv. **DNA**, with RNA (qv) controls metabolism of cells. — **DNA**

(trade name Dobutrex) Synthetic drug which increases rate and strength of heart contractions. — **dobutamine**

Abbr desoxycorticosterone acetate, qv. — **DOCA**

Squatting on hindquarters with forelegs erect. Rare; symptom of bloat (see colic), nervous disease, eg encephalomyelitis. — **dog-sitting posture**

(*Mercurialis perennis*) Plant, common in woods, which can poison. It contains mercurialin which causes acute irritation of stomach, diarrhoea, blood-stained urine. Chronic cases develop anaemia, subcutaneous oedema and nettle rash. — **dog's mercury**

(*Equus asinus*/domesticated ass) Member of horse family which varies in different parts of the world; 4 heights often used to classify: miniature (under 9h), small standard (9–10.1h), large standard (10.2–12h), Spanish (above 12h). Colours from black through all shades of brown, grey and dun to white (**D.** Breed Soc recognises 20 colours). Probably introduced to Britain by Celtic traders in Roman times; differs from most Equidae as it has large head, ears and eyes; short neck; small, boxy hooves; especially thick coat, often with dorsal stripe and stripe across shoulders. (Stripes are rare in white **d.**s and will not be visible in black ones, but these animals may — **donkey**

donkey   have bands of particularly coarse hair.) Tail is usually short-haired with tufted end; ergots and chestnuts are absent (site of chestnut is a hairless patch); male has vestigial teats on sheath. **D.** has 62 chromosomes (qv) and is aged from 1 Jan of year born. It may be willing pack animal or live up to reputation for stubbornness; seems particularly susceptible to glanders, strangles, influenza and lungworm, so should not graze with horses unless checked. Only minimum dose of tranquillisers should be given, as **d.** likely to suffer incoordination. See Zeedonk. **D. Breed Soc**, The Hermitage, Pootings, Kent TN8 6SD (01732 864414).

dopamine   A substance (amine, qv) in body as an intermediary in synthesis of norepinephrine (noradrenaline). Has action in transmitting nervous impulses through central nervous system.

dope test   Colloq for laboratory analysis of fluid collected from horse to discover presence of drug (dope). Official Jockey Club **d.t.** performed on saliva and/or urine (see urine sample, veterinary rules). Blood or, less commonly, faeces can be used. Methods include radio-immunoassay (RIA) qv, electrophoresis and thin-layer chromatography (TLC), in which substances in fluid are split by special process which causes each to travel at differing speeds on paper. Presence and quantity of non-normal nutrient can be determined because separation of particular substance is specific and typical of that substance. A more conclusive test, gas chromatography and mass spectrometry (GCMS), can then be used. Difficulties are: (1) body metabolises drugs, so they may be excreted in another form, eg phenylbutazone (bute) as oxyphenbutazone; (2) horse may excrete drug faster or slower than average; (3) large numbers of drugs available and **d.t.** limited to those suspected; (4) doping drug might be masked by legal drug, eg furosemide, allowed by some racing authorities.

dorsal   (L dorsalis from dorsum, back) Of the back, eg **d. position** Normal position during birth, ie foal's back uppermost. **d. stripe** Band of colour, darker than majority of body, along line of backbone from poll to tail. Often seen in donkeys, mountain and moorland breeds.

dose   (Gr dosis, a giving) Quantity of medicine given at one time. **lethal d.** Sufficient to kill. **toxic d.** Amount causing toxic signs. **sensitising d.** First **d.** of protein or antigen, second of which will cause allergic reaction. **skin d.** Amount of radiation at surface of skin, eg where radiation therapy is applied to deeper structures, as in treating carpitis. See allergy, anaphylaxis, poisoning, radiation, toxicity.

(syns equine syphilis, covering disease, genital glanders, mal **dourine**
de coit) Contagious disease which is caused by *Trypanosoma
equiperdum* parasite; transmitted by coitus and characterised
by inflamed genital organs, skin lesions and paralysis. Occurs
in Africa, Asia, SE Europe, S America; kills 50–70 per cent of
infected animals. Treatment: see quinapyramine salts,
homidium bromide.

(trade name: Dopram V) Drug used as respiratory stimulant, **doxapram**
eg to initiate respiration in foal often following difficult birth **hydrochloride**
or caesarean.

Dose of liquid medicine. **Dutch D.** qv. **d. horse** Originally one **draught**
used to pull vehicle (colloq cart horse), now also any heavy,
Shire type, usually cold-blooded. Does not thrive in hot cli-
mates; is particularly susceptible to flies, ticks, etc. **Irish D.
Horse Soc**, 4th St, National Agricultural Centre, Stoneleigh,
Warwicks CV8 2LG (01203 696549).

Colloq to unsheath penis. See behaviour, masturbation. **draw**

Abbr Doctor of Veterinary Medicine; followed by (Bern) or **Dr Med Vet**
(Zurich) depending on which university awarded degree. See
veterinary surgeon.

Fallen. **d. elbow** (syn radial paralysis) Condition when horse **dropped**
cannot take weight on affected foreleg due to paralysed triceps
muscle supporting elbow joint. Causes: injured radial nerve,
fracture of humerus or olecranon (point of elbow) or possibly
of 1st rib. Elbow drops, fetlock joint is flexed and horse cannot advance leg. Partial recovery possible, but chronic cases are
incurable. **d. sole** (syn pumiced foot) Sole protruding below
hoof wall, associated with seedy toe, rotation of coffin bone,
laminitis.

(L hydrops from Gr hydor, water) Abnormal accumulation of **dropsy**
fluid in tissues or body cavity. See oedema.

(syns anhidrosis, non-sweating syndrome, puff disease) Failure **drycoat**
to sweat. Occurs in hot, humid climates such as India,
Malaysia, Australia. May be due to repeated sweating, causing
insensitivity of sweat glands. Results in reduced heat loss and
rise in temperature, especially on exercise; difficult breathing
and death from heart failure if exercise is not restricted. Horses
usually recover capacity to sweat when returned to cool
climate. Cf ichthyosis; sweat.

Channel. **d. arteriosus** Blood vessel connecting pulmonary **ductus**
artery to aorta; open in foetus, closes during first 4 days of life

ductus	when murmur can be heard on left side of chest, over position of line from shoulder joint to intersection with edge of triceps muscle. See muscles. **d. deferens** See vas deferens. **d. venosus** Foetal vein in liver; connects umbilical vein to posterior vena cava, allowing bypass of liver. Closes in equine foetus at about 4th month so that all blood returning from placenta has to find its way through liver.
dull	(1) Not resonant on percussion, qv. (2) Lacking brightness, spirit. Dullness is symptom of most diseases, especially those connected with fever.
dummy/d. syndrome	See neonatal maladjustment syndrome.
dun	Coat colouring (qv). **D. Horse and Pony Soc**, 14 Queens St, Chipperfield, Herts WD4 9BT (01895 825949).
dung	Colloq faeces, qv.
duodenal ulcer	See gastric ulcer.
duodenum	First part of the small intestine, not usually differentiated from this part of alimentary canal (qv) in the adult horse. Adjective: duodenal.
dupp	Syllable representing second heart sound, which is short and high-pitched. Caused by closure of pulmonary and aortic valves. Complete beat termed lubb-dupp. See heart.
dura mater	(L hard mother) Outermost and toughest of 3 membranes covering brain and spinal cord. Cf pia mater. See brain.
Dutch	Of Holland/The Netherlands. **D. Draught** Possibly heaviest breed in Europe. Carefully controlled by Royal Netherlands Draught Horse Soc. Distinguished from other breeds by particularly sloping croup and low-set tail. Colours: bay, grey, chestnut, occasionally black. **D. Warmblood** See Warmblood.
Duvaxyn EHV 1,4	Equine herpesvirus vaccine (inactivated). **D. IE Plus** Equine influenza vaccine (inactivated). **D. IE T Plus** Combined equine influenza vaccine (inactivated) and concentrated tetanus toxoid. **D. T** Tetanus vaccine, inactivated. Manufacturer: Fort Dodge Animal Health.
D. Vet. Med.	Abbr Doctor Veterinary Medicine (London)
DVH	Abbr Doctor of/Diploma in Veterinary Hygiene.
DVM	Abbr Doctor, Veterinary Medicine.

Abbrs Doctor of Veterinary Medicine and Surgery. **DVMS/DVM&S**

Abbr Doctor of/Diploma in Veterinary Science/Surgery. **DVS**

Abbr Diploma in Veterinary State Medicine (RCVS). Same **DVSM**
initials followed by (Edin) or (Vict) indicate diplomas
from Edinburgh or Victoria University, Manchester. See also
veterinary surgeon.

(L dysenteria from Gr dys- + enteron, intestine) Acute **dysentery**
diarrhoea, qv.

Term used to describe full-term foals that show symptoms of **dysmaturity**
prematurity. Probably results from interference with normal
transfer of nutrients to foetus related to placental dysfunction.
Cf prematurity.

(dys- bad, difficult + Gr phagein, to eat) Difficulty in swallow- **dysphagia**
ing. Causes include fracture of the hyoid (qv); guttural pouch
mycosis (qv); excessive traction on the tongue; abscesses of the
lymph nodes of the head; chronic lead poisoning; botulism
(qv); grass sickness (qv) and painful conditions and/or irregu-
larities (such as hooks) of molar teeth. Common complication
is pneumonia caused by aspiration of food into windpipe. See
barium.

(dys- + Gr plassein, to form) Abnormal development, eg epi- **dysplasia**
physeal **d.**, faulty growth of epiphysis (growth plate, qv).

Distressed breathing, qv. Cf apnoea. **dyspnoea**

See arrhythmia. **dysrhythmia**

(Gr tokos, birth) Impeded birth. **foetal d.** That caused by abnor- **dystocia/dystokia**
mal size, position, presentation or posture of foetus so that it
lodges against mare's pelvis at entrance to birth canal. Common
d. includes flexed legs, head turned backward, foal presented
backward or in upside-down position. May be result of defor-
mity, eg contracted tendons (preventing forelegs extending in
normal manner) or foetal illness, so that muscular tone is lost.
maternal d. Caused by subnormal strength of uterine contractions (uterine inertia) or lack of voluntary straining. Treatment:
realign foetus by manipulation (usually with mare standing,
with help of muscle relaxants injected intravenously, intramuscularly or with spinal anaesthesia to abolish straining). If
possible, foetus is aligned to lie in normal manner for delivery
(see birth); if not, caesarean section (or possibly embryotomy)
is performed. **D.** occurs in about 2 per cent of severe abnormalities and 3 per cent of minor ones.

dystrophy   (L dystophia from dys- + Gr trephein, to nourish) Wasting of organs or tissues. **muscular d.** Wasting of muscles; can be caused by lack of vitamin E or lack of selenium.

dysuria   Difficulty in passing urine. Usually associated with bladder stones and inflamed bladder (cystitis). Symptoms: repeated attempts to stale, with grunting, swishing of tail, kicking at belly. See stone.

E

ear (L auris, Gr ous) Organ of hearing; consists of external, middle and internal **e**. **external e.** Funnel-like movable organ which collects sound waves and conveys them to **e**. drum. Formed of skin and cartilage, controlled by muscles. **middle e.** Comprises **e**. drum, an air cavity containing 3 small bones (auditory ossicles), the malleus, incus and stapes, plus eustachian tube including the guttural pouch. Bones form a chain along which sound vibrates from **e**. drum to internal **e**. **internal e.** Membraneous sac (containing fluid and supporting sensitive cells which convey nervous messages to brain in auditory nerve) and series of cavities in skull containing semicircular canals and other structures concerned with balance. **E**.s vary greatly between breeds of equidae (compare donkey's long large **e**.s with Arabian's small pointed **e**.s). **E**.s can move independently in relaxed horse; alert animal usually points both **e**.s towards source of sound. **E**.s laid flat denote anger/aggression. A hood which muffles sounds may prevent highly-strung horse being distracted or startled when racing or being transported. See equine sounds.

earwax (syn cerumen) Waxy secretion in ear canal.

ecchymosis (Gr ekchymosis; pl ecchymoses) Small, abnormal splash of blood under mucous membrane or skin, eg inside nostrils in allergy or infection. Cf petechia.

ECG Abbr (1) electrocardiogram, qv, (also written EKG). (2) equine chorionic gonadotrophin (also written eCG).

echocardiogram Record produced by echocardiography (qv).

echocardiography The use of ultrasound (qv) to study action of heart muscle and valves. See echography.

echography Use of ultrasound (qv) as a diagnostic aid. Ultrasound waves (qv) are directed at the organ or tissues; waves are reflected as they pass through changes in structure (eg at skin, outer surface of heart, inner surface of heart). The energy of reflected waves is then received by the instrument (scanner) and changed by electronic means into a picture. Picture is interpreted according to form produced by changes in density within the tissues through which ultrasound waves pass. Used for early pregnancy diagnosis, twelve to twenty days, also to assist elimination of one member of twins by squeezing uterus on rectal palpation. Also used in examinations of heart (echocardiography), kidney, liver and other organs. Particularly

echography	useful for imaging soft tissue structures of lower limbs e.g. tendons, ligaments etc. Arrangement of crystals in transducer and frequency of waves they produce give rise to descriptions such as linear (straight), sector (wedge-shaped), real time (continuous movement), mode (fixed beam and moving image). Length of waves produced by crystals is measured in megahertz (MHz): 3, 5 and 7 are those in use. Shorter waves (7 MHz) achieve less penetration but produce higher-quality image.
E. coli	Abbr *Escherichia coli*, qv.
ecraseur	(Fr crusher) Surgical instrument used instead of knife (causes less bleeding), eg in removing ovary.
ectoderm	(Gr ektos, outside + derma, skin) Outermost of 3 main (germinal) layers of embryo; it develops horn (of hooves) hair, skin, nervous system, external sensory organs (ear, eye) and mucous membranes of mouth and anus. Cf endoderm, mesoderm. Adjective: ectodermal.
ectoparasite	Parasite which lives on outside of body, eg tick, mite, louse.
ectopia	(Gr ektopos, displaced) Displacement, especially of part when congenital.
ectopic	Of ectopia; not in usual position. **e. beat** See heart impulse.
ectropion	(Gr 'an everted eyelid') Turning outward of eyelid margin.
eczema	(Gr ekzein, to boil out) Nonspecific inflammatory skin disease normally pruritic (itchy). See dermatitis, Queensland itch.
edathamil calcium disodium	See sodium calcium edetate.
edema	See oedema.
EDTA (ethylene-diaminetetraacetic acid)	Anticoagulant used for blood samples and also to treat lead poisoning.
EEE	Eastern equine encephalomyelitis. See encephalomyelitis.
efferent	Conveying away from a centre, eg **e.** nerves pass messages from central nervous system. Cf afferent.
effusion	(L effusio, a pouring out) Escape of fluid into cavity, part or tissue, eg blood blister. **pleural e.** Presence of fluid around lungs. Likely in septicaemia, pneumonia, abortion caused by equine herpesvirus 1.

Voiding of faeces. Cf excretion.	**egestion**
(L ovum) (1) Female sex cell containing hereditary material in haploid (qv) form. See embryo transfer, ovum. (2) **e.** of parasite. See redworm; stomach worm; whiteworm.	**egg**
Microbe (rickettsia-type) which causes Potomac horse fever, qv.	**Ehrlichia risticii**
See equine herpesvirus.	**EHV**
Equine infectious anaemia. See swamp fever.	**EIA**
(Exercise-induced pulmonary haemorrhage) See bleeder. Modern theory for cause is that exceptionally high pressure in capillaries of the lungs causes rupture and escape of blood into lungs. Treatment: furosemide.	**EIPH**
(L ejaculatio) To expel semen. See behaviour, male sexual; semen. Noun: ejaculum (colloq **e.**)	**ejaculate**
(colloq ejaculate) The fluid (semen) expelled at ejaculation.	**ejaculum**
(L elasticus) The protein in connective tissue giving elastic properties.	**elastin**
(L cubitus) Hinge joint between humerus and radius. See capped **e.**, dropped **e.**	**elbow**
(ECG, electro- + Gr kardia, heart + gramma, mark) Graphic tracing of electric impulse passing through heart during each beat. Wave form of **e.** represents change of electric potential in heart muscle as it contracts and relaxes. The waves are designated P,Q,R,S and T. Record is formed by attaching electrodes of apparatus (electrocardiograph) to skin, usually on legs and chest. **E.** leads labelled I, II, III, aVL, aVF. (Chest leads usually designated VI–4, CR.LA, CL.LA, CF.LA.) Deviations from normal pattern indicate damaged heart muscle. **E.** particularly helpful in diagnosing general irregular heartbeat (arrythmia), fast, irregular movements of first chambers (atrial fibrillation) and beat originating outside usual starting point (ectopic beat). See heart impulse.	**electrocardiogram**
Instrument for recording electrocardiogram.	**electrocardiograph**
Tape recording of heart sounds (so they can be studied later or translated into visual record, ie graph).	**electrocardio-phonogram**
Instrument for recording electrocardiophonogram.	**electrocardiophonograph**

electroencephalogram	Graphic record of electrical impulse passing through brain.
electroencephalograph	Instrument for making electroencephalogram.
electrolyte	(electro-, relationship to electricity + Gr lytos, soluble) Any substance which conducts electricity by its ions. In horses, usually a salt of body, eg sodium.
electrophoresis	Technique in which molecules can be separated and identified by their rate of movement in electric field.
ELISA	(enzyme-linked immunosorbent assay) Non-isotopic immunoassay as opposed to isotopic assay ie, radioimmunoassay (RIA). **ELISA** also called EIA (enzyme immunoassay). Cf radioimmunoassay. Mainly used for steroids and thyroid function assays.
emasculate	(L emasculare, to castrate) See castrate.
embolism	(L embolismus from Gr en, in + ballein, to throw) Sudden blocking of artery or vein by clot carried in blood stream. Common site of **e.** is branch of anterior mesenteric artery, ie that supplying small intestines; often result of redworm damage to blood vessel at junction with aorta. See aneurysm, redworm, thrombus, colic.
embolus	(Gr embolos, plug; pl emboli) Blood clot carried in bloodstream from large vessel to smaller one, which it obstructs.
embryo	(Gr embryon) Conceptus until approx 40 days, after which it is termed foetus. **e. transfer** Technique of collecting **e.** from fallopian tube (by flushing tube or surgery) or from uterus via vagina, then transferring it to another female. Recipient must have recently formed yellow body (qv) in ovary when **e.** is placed (during surgery) in horn of uterus. **E.t.** has been achieved from mare into mare and jenny; donkey into mare and mule; zebra into mare and donkey and also into a temporary host such as rabbit so that **e.** can be transported and/or stored until recipient mare is ready.
embryology	Science of development of fertilised egg to fully formed foetus (developing foal). Individual begins as a single cell (zygote or fertilised egg) formed by fusion of spermatozoon and egg (2 gametes, one from each parent). This cell contains all inherited material (chromosomes and genes) which gives foal its individuality. Zygote divides repeatedly until it is a ball of cells (blastula). A cavity (blastocoele) develops inside. A process (gastrulation) follows, in which primitive gut cavity and 3 germ layers are formed, ie ectoderm, mesoderm and

endoderm from which skin, organs and lining of internal passages (nose, alimentary tract) develop. Then, brain, body cavity, organs of sense, alimentary canal, kidneys, gonads, arteries and veins and soft (cartilaginous) skeleton are formed. Amnion and placenta grow from embryo to surround it and placenta becomes attached to wall of uterus, so that it can exchange nourishment for waste material. **E.** is not limited to precise period (see embryo). Most organs are formed by about 30th day of pregnancy, although development of bone from cartilage occurs much later and hair forms only in last 8 weeks. Congenital abnormalities, eg cleft palate, probably occur in first 30 days. — *embryology*

(embryo- + Gr tome, a cutting) Dismemberment of foetus to allow delivery. Generally replaced by caesarean section, qv. See dystocia. — **embryotomy**

Drug which softens and allays irritation. — **emollient**

(Gr inflation) Swelling due to air; applied to abnormal distension of air sacs (alveoli) of lung, also to skin lifted by air entering through wound. See broken wind. — **emphysema**

(Gr) Accumulation of pus in body cavity, especially chest; may occur in foals due to bacteria. See newborn foal, diseases of; guttural pouch. — **empyema**

(L emulsio, emulsum) One liquid distributed in small globules throughout a second liquid, eg paraffin emulsified in water, used as laxative in foals. See meconium retention. — **emulsion**

White, compact, very hard substance that covers and protects crown of tooth. See teeth. — **enamel**

Inflamed brain. — **encephalitis**

(Gr. enkephalos, brain) Combining form meaning relationship to brain. — **encephalo-**

Inflammation involving brain and spinal cord; may be caused by virus ie equine viral **e.** Three strains important because they can affect man, viz, Western (WEE), Eastern (EEE) and Venezuelan (VEE). Disease is spread by blood-sucking insects, contaminated instruments, direct contact and infected bedding. Occurs June–November and usually dies out when frost kills mosquitoes. Horses of all ages are susceptible, though older ones may develop resistance. Symptoms: fever, depression, restlessness, excitement, walking in circles, wandering into obstacles, refusing food and water, sleepiness, adopting — **encephalomyelitis**

encephalomyelitis	strange postures, eg sitting on quarters (dog-sitting posture), possibly with forelegs crossed, pressing head against wall, paralysis, collapse. Death occurs in 2–4 days. Diagnosis: on symptoms and lab innoculation of guinea pigs with blood from suspected cases. Treatment: hyperimmune serum may help, also supportive measures, eg feeding by stomach tube. Control: vaccines. TC83 (containing live virus grown in foetal guinea pig cells) was used for first time in 1971 outbreak in N America. Insects should be controlled and horses stabled at night. Pathology: damaged nerve cells of brain, but no inclusion bodies, which helps distinguish **e.** from borna disease and rabies. Notifiable disease in many countries. See veterinary rules.
encephalopathy	Degenerative disease of brain.
endarteritis	(from Gr arteria, artery + -itis) Inflamed inner lining of an artery caused by migrating redworm larvae. See redworm, thrombus.
endemic	(Gr endemos, dwelling in a place) Disease or condition usually present in area but affecting only a small number of animals at one time. Cf epidemic.
endocarditis	Inflamed lining (endocardium) of heart chambers and/or valves (valvular **e.**) Caused by bacteria, usually streptococci, or migrating larvae of *Strongylus vulgaris* (redworm). Nodules and cauliflower-like growths cause leaking valves, heart murmurs. Associated with intermittent fever, loss of body condition and lack of stamina.
endocardium	(endo- + Gr kardio, heart) Membrane lining heart chambers and their valves. Formed of endothelium, qv.
endocrine	(Gr endon, within + krinein, to separate) Any gland (qv) which secretes hormones into blood or lymph stream, eg pituitary. (Hormone then carried to organ or part to exert influence.) Cf exocrine.
endocrinology	Study of endocrine glands and their hormones.
endoderm	(endo- within + Gr derma, skin) Epithelium (qv) of throat, respiratory and digestive tracts, bladder and urethra. Cf ectoderm, mesoderm. See embryology.
endogenous	(endo- + Gr gennan, to produce) Developing or originating inside organism. Cf exogenous.
endometrial	Of endometrium (qv). **e. cups** Develop about 35th day of pregnancy. See equine chorionic gonadotrophin.

Inflamed lining of uterus. Caused by irritation eg chemical or by infection with bacteria, fungus and possibly virus. Predisposing causes: hormonal influences, poor conformation of vulva, pregnancy, birth, coitus, constantly dilated cervix (rare). Phagocytes and other cells collect close to surface and mix with secretions of glands to produce catarrhal fluid that drains to outside through cervix and vagina (colloq dirty mare). Treatment: antibiotics injected and infused into uterus. — **endometritis**

(endo- + Gr metre, uterus) Mucous lining of uterus. — **endometrium**

Pain-relieving substances produced mainly by central nervous system, particularly brain stem. See twitch. — **endorphins**

(Gr endon, within + skopein, to examine) Instrument through which to examine interior of body. Early instruments straight and rigid. Modern instruments – based on fibreoptics – are flexible. Contains mirrored light system enabling viewer to see interior of bladder (with cystoscope), joint (arthroscope), larynx (laryngoscope), also lungs, windpipe, stomach, duodenum, rectum, uterus, etc. — **endoscope**

Visual inspection of any body cavity by means of an endoscope, qv. — **endoscopy**

(endo- + Gr thele, nipple; pl endothelia) Layer of epithelial cells lining cavities of heart, blood and lymph vessels. — **endothelium**

Toxin in bacterium, particularly a gram-negative one, and usually in cell wall. When freed and absorbed by horse **e.** raises temperature, increases permeability of blood vessels and results in malaise, diarrhoea and pain, often with fatal results. See colitis X. — **endotoxin**

See tube. — **endotracheal tube**

Liquid put into rectum with syringe or gravitated from container; rarely used on adult horses (see temperature, raised) but frequently on newborn foals to help passage of meconium, qv. May be paraffin and water or soap and water at blood temperature; quantity about 600ml (1 pint). Blunt, soft rubber tube should be used to avoid damaging anus and rectum. — **enema**

(Gr energeia) Power source. **nutritional e.** That from food, qv. — **energy**

(trade name: Imaverol) Synthetic antifungal drug used in treatment of ringworm. — **enilconazole**

(Gr enteron, intestine) Combining form meaning relationship to intestines. — **enter-/entero-**

enteric	Of intestines.
enteritis	Inflamed intestine (strictly, small intestine) Used nonspecifically in cases of diarrhoea or inflamed alimentary tract. Caused by agent which disturbs natural flora in intestine, eg fungus, excess protein, antibiotics, bacteria. Can be fatal, especially in foals. See also newborn foal, diseases of; and dehydration. Cf ulcerative **e**.
Enterobacteriaceae	(enteric bacteria) Rod-shaped, gram-negative organisms. E. family contains Escherichia, Aerobacter, Klebsiella, Proteus, Shigella.
enterotomy	Surgical incision into the intestines.
enterotoxaemia	Infection of alimentary tract by bacteria of toxin-producing groups which poison blood. Causes severe enteritis and diarrhoea. Not common in horses but well recognised in lambs, calves; may account for sudden death in horses and foals fed too rich diet, eg pelleted rations containing corn.
enterovirus	Group of viruses infecting alimentary tract and discharged in dung. Includes Poliovirus, Coxsackie. Horses not known to be affected by **e**. but infection probably occurs.
entropion	(Gr en, in + tropein, to turn) Inversion of an edge, eg eyelid. Result of dehydration (qv) when eyeballs sink into sockets, or of rubbing head on straw. Common in foals. Treatment (essential to prevent serious damage to eye): stitch lid parallel to its edge. Cf ectropion.
enuresis	(Gr enourein, to void urine) Urinary incontinence; more common in old mares (with weak sphincter muscle at bladder exit) than in geldings. Hindquarters may be lightly scalded by continual dribble of urine.
enzootic	(Gr en, in + zoon, animal) Old English for endemic (qv) within animal population.
enzyme	Organic compound, usually a protein, acting as catalyst and producing a specific change. Cf hormone, pheromone.
Eohippus	(syns dawn horse, Hyracotherium) Fox-sized animal of Eocene period about 55 million years ago. Ancestor of today's horse. See evolution.
eosin	(Gr eos, dawn) Rose-coloured stain or dye used in laboratory for histological sections.

(Gr eos, dawn + philain, to love) Special blood cell belonging to white cell type but containing granules which stain red with eosin (rose-coloured dye) in lab. work. See white blood cell. Eosinophilia denotes abnormally large number of **e.**s in blood or tissues.	**eosinophil**
Abnormally large number of eosinophils in blood or accumulating in tissues.	**eosinophilia**
Colourless odourless crystals with bitter taste and action similar to adrenaline, qv.	**ephedrine**
(Gr epi, on) Prefix meaning on.	**epi-**
(epi- + Gr kardia, heart) Layer of the pericardium (qv) on outer surface of heart.	**epicardium**
Rounded projection of bone, above condyle, which does not articulate with another bone, eg medial **e.** of femur (thigh bone).	**epicondyle**
(Gr epidemios, prevalent) Any disease outbreak affecting many animals in a region at same time. **e. cerebrospinal nematodiasis** See filaria.	**epidemic**
The study of epidemics.	**epidemiology**
(epi- on + Gr derma, skin) Outermost, non-vascular part of skin, qv. Adjective: epidermal.	**epidermis**
(from Gr didymos, testis; pl epididymides) Tube attached to testis. Has head (consists of 12 or more small coiled tubes), body (single tube) and tail (where tube joins vas deferens, qv). **E.** stores spermatozoa prior to ejaculation.	**epididymis**
On or outside dura mater, qv. See anaesthesia.	**epidural**
(epi- on + Gr glottis, vocal apparatus of larynx) Small flap of cartilage covering entrance to voice box. See wind.	**epiglottis**
(See adrenaline) Hormone secreted by middle (medulla) of adrenal gland. Synthetic **e.** given to increase blood pressure and heart rate.	**epinephrine**
(Gr sudden burst) Overflow of tears. Often due to blocked nasolacrymal duct.	**epiphora**
(Gr an outgrowth; pl epiphyses) Expanded end of long bone. Term often used for growth plate (qv).	**epiphysis**

epiphysitis | Inflammation of long bone growth plate, caused by infection, trauma or dietary imbalance (eg excess protein, incorrect calcium/phosphorus ratio). Most common during periods of rapid growth in lower end of radius at 12–24 months and in lower end of cannon at 6-8 months. Also occurs at lower end of tibia at 12–24 months. Symptoms: swelling, pain on palpation, lameness. Treatment: reduce exercise, correct diet, reduce food intake if horse growing rapidly.

epistaxis | (Gr) Nosebleed. See bleeder.

epithelium | (epi + Gr thele, nipple) Layer of cells covering internal and external surfaces of body, including lining of vessels and small cavities. Classified by shape and structure. **ciliated e.** Bearing cilia on free surface; lines air passages. **columnar e.** Tall, narrow cells; lines digestive tract. **cuboidal e.** Square cells; covers ovaries. **germinal e.** Lines ducts of gonads and produces germ cells, ie ova or spermatozoa. **glandular e.** Cells of glands or secreting cells. **scaly e.** Forms horn of hoof. **squamous e.** That of skin. **transitional e.** That of bladder.

episiotomy | (Gr epision, pubic region + tome, cutting) Cutting vulva, especially if previously stitched (see Caslick) to avoid tearing during mating and foaling.

epizootic lymphangitis | (syns pseudoglanders, mycotic lymphangitis, equine blastomycosis) Chronic contagious disease causing inflamed lymphatic vessels and glands, skin ulcers and pneumonia. Occurs in Asia, Africa and Mediterranean countries as epidemics with death rate of about 15 per cent. Important because it is similar to glanders and because it incapacitates victim for up to a year. Cause: fungus Histoplasma. Horses under 6 are most susceptible and fungal spores enter through small wounds and are carried by bedding, grooming tools, harness etc. Symptoms after 6–8 weeks' incubation: ulcer at site of entry, lymph vessels nearby thicken and develop nodules. These rupture, discharging thick, creamy pus; abscesses form in lymph nodes (especially around hocks, back, sides, neck, vulva/scrotum). Horse may also suffer inflamed eyes and nostrils and pneumonia. Recovery may be spontaneous after 3–12 months. Diagnosis: on laboratory examination of pus containing fungus cells. Must be distinguished from glanders, strangles, and corynebacterial infection. Control: observe strict quarantine, destroy or disinfect bedding, saddlery, etc.

EPM | EPM Equine protozoal myeloencephalitis, qv.

epsom salts | See magnesium sulphate.

Adjective from Equidae, qv. Generally replaced by equine.

equid

(L equus, horse). Includes horses, asses, zebras and onagers within order Perissodactyla (qv).

Equidae

An oestrogen hormone. See sex.

equilenin

Oestrogen hormone produced by foetus and passed in mare's urine from about 120 days' pregnancy to full term. Used in human medicine as hormone treatment and additive for cosmetics.

equilin

(L equinus, relating to horses) Of horse family Equidae. **e. behaviour** See behaviour. **e. blastomycosis** See epizootic lymphangitis. **e. chorionic gonadotrophin** (eCG) Hormone produced between day 38 and about day 120 of pregnancy from structures known as endometrial cups at junction of uterine horn and body. The hormone is produced by cells which transfer from developing foetal membranes into mare's uterus. Cells have limited lifespan so hormone, which is produced in large quantities, is present in mare's bloodstream only for a defined period (about 40–120 days pregnancy). Forms basis of MIP test, qv. **e. cutaneous papillomatosis** See milk warts. **e. encephalomyelitis** See encephalomyelitis. **e. flu** See influenza. **e. herpesvirus** (EHV) now classified as four strains: Type I (rhinopneumonitis) causes virus abortion and paralysis. Can also cause respiratory infection. Type II believed to be non-pathogenic. Type III causes coital exanthema (qv) in mares and stallions. Type IV causes respiratory disease and occasional abortion. **e. infectious anaemia** see swamp fever **e. influenza**: See influenza. **e. metritis** See contagious equine metritis (CEM). **e. protozoal myeloencephalitis** Infection of central nervous tissue by *Sarcocystis neurona*. Disease first reported in 1970s and predominantly where opossum roam as they excrete organism in faeces. Horses most frequently affected are young adults. Symptoms may be droopy eyelids or uncoordinated hindlegs. Treatment: trimethoprim and pyrimethamine. **e. sounds** Divided into vocal and internal. George Waring (S Illinois University) named categories: squeal, nicker, whinny, groan (all vocal) and blow, snort and snore (non-vocal). Squeal: high-pitched, typically used as threat, noted during aggression; sexual rejection; when mare running milk is touched near flank or mammary gland. Nicker: low-pitched and pulsating, used before being fed; by stallion investigating mare; by mare concerned for foal. Whinny: one of the loudest sounds, begins as squeal and ends as nicker; used for calling, especially between mare and foal at weaning. (Some members of Equidae, eg donkey, bray instead of whinny. Bray is harsh, rasping sound, almost a bark.) Groan:

equine

equine used during pain, especially when horse is lying on side. Blow: expulsion of air through nostrils (horse cannot breath through mouth), used before being fed, when suspicious. Snort: strong, pulsating blow, used to clear nasal irritation; after cough (in which case cough thought less serious); during colic; occasionally if in conflict situation. (Some consider snort sign of contentment.) Snore: rasping sound when inhaling, sometimes used before blow; sound of alarm; during colic. Other sounds include cough, chew, flatus, hoof beats and movements in male sheath. Internal sounds, sometimes audible with naked ear, include borborygmi and heart sounds. See separate headings. **e. syphilis** See dourine. **E. Veterinary Journal** and **Veterinary Education** Published bimonthly by EVJ Ltd, Graseby House, Exning Road, Newmarket, Suffolk CB8 0AU (01638) 666160. **e. viral arteritis** (EVA) Acute virus disease of respiratory tract. Symptoms: fever, nasal discharge, inflamed mucous membranes of eyes, respiratory and alimentary tracts, oedema of eyelids and legs, reduced circulating white cells (leucopenia), abortion. Was once confused with influenza, qv. Virus causes degeneration of middle layer (media) of small arteries (arterioles) and is present in nasal secretions, saliva, blood, faeces, urine and occasionally semen. Diagnosis: not always possible due to number of forms, but signs described appear in an outbreak. Incubation: 2–10 days; virus can be recovered from nasal swabs during fever, blood serum can be tested in acute and convalescent phases. Abortion occurs simultaneously with symptoms, which distinguishes it from abortion due to herpesvirus. Treatment: vaccinate (Artervac). Antibiotics can suppress secondary infection. Horse should be rested and isolated 4–6 weeks. Stallions may become permanent carriers of virus in their semen.

Equip F Trade name of flu vaccine with ISCOMS, qv. **E. FT** Flu and tetanus vaccine with ISCOMS.

equisetum See horsetails.

Equus (L horse) Genus of horse family (Equidae) which includes all living members of family and their immediate ancestors and close relatives during Ice Age. Genus is followed by species name, eg **E. asinus** (donkey). **E. caballus** Species which includes all breeds of domesticated horse and those feral or wild relatives so closely related that they can, or could, interbreed and produce fertile offspring. See chromosome, wild.

ergometrine maleate White crystalline odourless powder. Alkaloid drug which promotes contraction of uterus. Given, by mouth or injection, after birth to help restore uterus to non-pregnant size.

(Fr, L ergota) (1) Small, horny area in tuft of hair behind fetlock joint. May be vestige of another hoof (see evolution). Cf chestnut. (2) Fungus (Claviceps purpurea) of plants, particularly rye, poisonous if ingested.	**ergot**
Scottish pony, often grey, flourishing in/around Perthshire. **E. Pony Breed Soc**, Houston Mill, East Linton, East Lothian, EH40 3DG (01620 860307).	**Eriskay**
(Gr erythros, red + kytos, hollow vessel) Red blood cell, qv. **e. sedimentation rate** (ESR) See blood tests, haematology (7).	**erythrocyte**
Increase in number of red blood cells, qv.	**erythrocytosis**
(trade names: Erythrocin, Erythroped) White crystalline odourless powder with bitter taste. Produced from *Streptomyces erythraeus*. Antibiotic with bacteriostatic and bactericidal activity against gram-positive and some gram-negative bacteria. Given to foals with conditions caused by bacteria, eg joint-ill.	**erythromycin**
Genus of gram-negative microorganisms of tribe Escherichieae, family Enterobacteriaceae, order Eubacteriales. Have motile or non-motile short rods. **E. coli** Intestinal flora (mainly in caecum, large and small colon, rectum) connected with digestion. Strains can cause diarrhoea, septicaemia. See newborn foal, diseases of.	**Escherichia**
Tribe of family Enterobacteriaceae, order Eubacteriales; non-motile or motile rods that ferment glucose and lactose, producing acid. Comprises coliform bacteria including 5 genera: aerobacter, alginobacter, escherichia, klebsiella and paracolobactrum.	**Escherichieae**
(after German surgeon Johann von E.) Rubber bandage used to reduce blood flow to an area before surgery.	**Esmarch bandage**
See oesophagus.	**esophagus**
Abbr erythrocyte (red cell) sedimentation rate. See blood tests, haematology (7).	**ESR**
Body substance which breaks link between 'biological compounds such as esters and fatty acids, eg choline **e.** of blood, which destroys acetylcholine, qv.	**esterase**
See words beginning oestro-.	**estro-**
Clear colourless volatile liquid with characteristic odour and sweet, burning taste. Used as anaesthetic; less effective than chloroform.	**ether**

ethmoid (Gr ethmos, sieve) Sieve-like, eg **e.** turbinate bones of the nasal passages.

ethological Of ethology. **E. Society**, c/o Liverpool University Veterinary Field Station, Leahurst, Neston, South Wirral L64 7TE (0151 794 6071).

ethology Study of animal behaviour. **equine e.** The study of horses' behaviour. In USA, Colorado State University has extensive equine breeding behaviour programme. See behaviour, equine sounds. **Int. Society for Applied E.**, North Wyke, Okehampton, Devon, EX20 2SB.

etiology Science of causes of disease. See aetiology.

etorphine hydrochloride (trade name: Large Animal Immobilon) Drug producing narcosis and analgesia used for restraint and minor surgery. Reversible effects: diprenorphine (qv). Used in association with tranquilliser acepromazine.

eugenics (eu- + Gr gennan, to produce) Study of ways of improving hereditary characters in a breed.

euthanasia (Gr eu, well + thanatos, death) Mercy killing or humane destruction. May be necessary in cases of fractured leg, pelvis, vertebrae or painful conditions with no apparent chance of recovery. Carried out by IV injection of drug or humane killer consisting of bolt placed against forehead (at intersection of lines drawn from base of ear to opposite eye), then hammered home. Gun and bullet require great care because of danger of accident/ricochet.

EVA See equine viral arteritis.

evisceration (L evisceratio from e, out + viscus, the inside of the body) Disembowelment; rare congenital fault in which floor of abdomen is not formed.

evolution (L evolutio, from volvere, to roll) A rolling out, continual change and development; generally of a species over a long period. That of horse family (Equidae) can be traced from Eocene (Gr dawn, new) period, which began 55 million years ago. The animal living then, Eohippus (scientific name Hyracotherium), was considered forerunner of today's horse. It was fox-like with arched back; 4 horn-covered toes (padded underneath) on each forefoot and 3 on each hind foot. Small, primitive brain, 44 teeth and browsed on shrubs. (Usual number of teeth now: 40 in male, 36 in female. See teeth.) Eohippus (syn dawn horse) developed (via Orohippus and Epihippus)

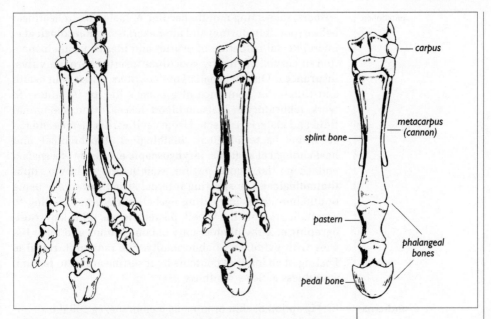

carpus

metacarpus
(cannon)

splint bone

pastern

phalangeal
bones

pedal bone

(left) **9** Eohippus (the dawn horse): skeleton of lower part of foreleg shows
the first horse-like animal had 4 toes on each forefoot;
(centre) **10** Merychippus; *(right)* **11** Equus, the present-day horse

into Mesohippus, pad-footed animal with 3 toes on each foot.
It lived in Oligocene period (which began 35 million years
ago) and its brain was much larger than that of Eohippus.
Mesohippus gradually evolved (via Miohippus and
Parahippus) from pad-footed animal into spring-footed one
(Merychippus) better adapted for running fast to escape ene-
mies. It had 3 toes but outer 2 (dew hooves) had shortened,
leaving middle one to take most weight. Ulna and radius bones
of leg had fused and lengthened and Merychippus looked
much like today's pony – perhaps striped or patchy for camouflage. Merychippus was a grazer, so its teeth were longer
(hypsodonty); it had grown (probably to 10h) and its eyes were
farther back in skull (so that it could see horizon when grazing). After Merychippus came Pliohippus (of Pliocene period
which began 10 million years ago). This had lost dew hooves
(see chestnut, splint, ergot) and it evolved into today's *Equus*
by continual streamlining. Today's domestic horse belongs to
kingdom Animalia, phylum Chordata, class Mammalia, order
Perissodactyla, family Equidae, genus Equus, species Equus
caballus, qv. See also chromosome, Przewalski.

(L examinare) Investigation or inspection. **clinical e.** Looking
for abnormality; listening to chest and abdomen; recording of
heart, pulse and breathing rates and rectal temperature;
watching behaviour; palpation (feeling) of legs, poll, back,

examination

examination withers; inspecting mouth. **cardiac e.** Listening to heartbeat before (possibly during) and after exercise. **gynaecological e.** (mare) Rectal palpation of ovaries and uterus; visual inspection of cervix, vagina by speculum inserted through vulva. **insurance e.** One on behalf of underwriters to ascertain health and fitness for insurance of a horse's life, or its fitness to work. **laboratory e.** Tests on blood, faeces, urine, abdominal fluid and material collected from cavities, discharges and tissues, for bacteriological, histological, biochemical and haematological analysis. **laryngoscopic e.** Passing of a special endoscope (laryngoscope) for examination of larynx. **ophthalmological e.** Inspecting internal structures of eye using ophthalmoscope, inspecting eyeball surface and feeling to ascertain pressure in eyeball. **postmortem e.** (PME), qv. **radiographic e.** X-ray photography of bones, joints and other tissues with evidence of abnormality. See radiation. **rectal e.** Feeling of abdominal contents by inserting arm into rectum. **soundness e.** See soundness.

exanthema (Gr) Eruption of skin or mucous membrane, eg coital **e.**

excipient (L excipiens, from ex, out + capere, to take) Inert substance acting as vehicle for drugs, eg in pessary or pill.

excretion (L excretio) Colloq voiding of waste material, especially faeces, urine. Strictly speaking, **e.** refers to carbon dioxide and urine. Cf egestion. See behaviour.

exercise-induced pulmonary haemorrhage (EIPH) Term given to nosebleeds occurring immediately after exercise, often first apparent when horse lowers its head. Not all individuals exhibit blood at nostrils and visual inspection of the windpipe through an endoscope (qv) reveals that most racehorses have some evidence of blood following exercise, from microscopic traces to substantial quantities which may collect at lower end of windpipe at its junction with lungs. Recent work suggests bleeding occurs from upper hind part of lungs (dorsal diaphragmatic lobe). Authorities divided whether cause is tearing of air sacs and blood vessels or bleeding from bronchial blood vessels, ie those supplying small air tubes (bronchi). Most authorities agree infection with virus/bacteria, causing bronchiolitis and obstruction to airways, may play a role in development of condition. No reliable cure found although furosemide (qv), coagulant drugs, vitamin C, antibiotics, and homoeopathic remedies have been claimed to help. Rest seems essential to allow lesions to heal. Some racing authorities in USA allow bleeders to race on furosemide, while bleeders are banned from racing in many countries of the southern hemisphere.

Term given to the study of body functions on which performance depends.

exercise physiology

Possibly oldest-established of England's mountain and moorland types; roams **E.** district of SW England. Extremely hardy and strong. Will carry full-grown man hunting or make good child's pony. Has prominent 'toad' eyes and mealy (ie light-coloured) muzzle, eyelids, insides of ears and belly. Colours: bay, brown or dun, without markings except those mentioned. Mares up to 12.2 h, stallions up to 12.3. Cf Dartmoor. **E. Pony Soc**, Glenfern, Waddicombe, Somerset TA22 9RY (01398 341490).

Exmoor

(Gr exe, outside + krinein, to separate) Any gland which secretes outwardly or externally, ie its products act locally, eg salivary gland. Cf endocrine. See gland.

exocrine

(from Gr gennan, to produce) Developing outside organism.

exogenous

See hyperthyroidism.

exophthalmic goitre

(ex- + Gr oesteon, bone) Bony growth on the surface of bone; usually follows inflammation. See also osselet, ringbone, splint.

exostosis

Toxin formed by bacteria and having its effect at a distance.

exotoxin

(ex- + L pectus, breast) Drug or substance which promotes coughing up of mucus from lungs and air passages.

expectorant

(ex + L spinare, to breathe) Act of breathing out. See breathing, wind.

expiration

(L exploratorius) Investigation to make diagnosis eg **e.** laparotomy (operation to open abdomen in case of colic).

exploratory

(L expressio) Facial appearance. **anxious e.** Seen in painful conditions, eg colic. **mask e.** Seen in lockjaw, qv.

expression

Any muscle or tendon which extends joint. Opp flexor. See contracted tendons.

extensor

(L extirpate, to root out) Removal of a part.

extirpation

(L outside) Prefix meaning beyond, outside, eg **e.** capsular, outside capsule.

extra

See heart impulse.

extrasystole/ extrastolic beat

extravasation   (extra- + vas, vessel) Escape of blood or fluid, from a vessel into tissues. Types include haemorrhage, oedema, petechia, ecchymosis.

extremity   Any part far from body centre, eg ear, hoof.

exudate   (L exsudare, to sweat out) Mixture of fluid, cells and cellular debris which has escaped from blood vessel into tissues or onto surface of mucous membrane; result of inflammation. Adjective: exudative.

eye   (L oculus, Gr ophthalmos) Organ of sight, one either side of face in **e.** socket (orbit) in skull. Provides mainly monocular vision (not binocular vision as in human eye) except when looking at close objects. Consists of ball, flattened on front surface with tough, fibrous coat (sclera) modified in front to form cornea. Middle vascular coat is uvea. Ball is bordered by angle (canthus) at either side of **e.** lid. Inside, lens divides ball into front (anterior) and back (posterior) chambers. Pupil is formed by iris, which dilates to admit more light and constricts to cut out light. Light falls on retina, a sensitive nervous membrane lining inside of **e.** and conveying messages to brain. Optic disc is pale area in retina where optic nerve and blood vessels leave and enter **e. E., diseases of: amaurosis** Blindness resulting from fault in nervous mechanism of brain; unrelated to abnormality in **e.** Occurs suddenly, usually after shock. Signs include rapid ear movement, reluctance to move from dark into light, or to pass through gate or doorway. **cataract** Opacity of lens or its capsule, caused by trauma or occasionally inherited or congenital; varies in size from pinpoint to complete coverage of lens, so interference with sight varies. **conjunctivitis** qv. **corneal perforation** Penetration of cornea by foreign body (eg straw), trauma (eg kick) or ulcer, allowing escape of aqueous humour (fluid in front chamber) and collapse of eyeball due to lowering of internal pressure. **dermoid cyst** (qv) Wart-like growth on cornea, contains hairs up to 2.5cm (1in) long. Surgical removal necessary. **glaucoma** Abnormally increased pressure in eyeball causing changes in retina and blindness. Common only in injury. **hypopyon** Pus in front chamber of **e.** Result of inflamed cornea (keratitis), ulcer on cornea or complication after infectious disease, eg strangles. **keratitis** Inflamed cornea; result of trauma, foreign body, turning in of lids (entropion), viral or bacterial infection. Symptoms: white spot on surface of cornea, blood vessels growing towards area. Ulcer may develop and, in severe cases, penetrate front chamber, resulting in prolapse of fine membrane lining inside of **e.** As healing takes place, blood vessels disappear, white scar (opacity) remains and eventually disappears. Treatment: antibiotic drops or ointment, weak astringent, eg silver argentum, corticosteroid (use sparingly because it may cause ulcer to penetrate deeper). If horse dislikes drops, place ointment on upper lid near lashes. Ointment will melt and seep into **e. luxation of lens** Displacement of lens, usually as result of blow. **moon blindness** (syn periodic ophthalmia) Inflamed ciliary body and iris (iridocyclitis). Affected horses suffer recurring attacks, each of which is increasingly severe until eventually internal structures of **e.** are irreversibly damaged, **e.** loses tension and collapses. Signs: spasm of lids when exposed to light (photophobia), inflamed surface of **e.** (scleritis) and membranes. Lids may swell, tears run down face and pupils constrict. Cause unknown, but infections with leptospira bacteria, virus and parasites have been blamed. Treatment: keep horse stabled in dark during attack, drop corticosteroids and atropine into **e.** to dilate pupil. Condition unlikely to improve. **retinitis** Inflamed retina; often occurs after moon blindness or infections such as arteritis and purpura haemorrhagica, qv.

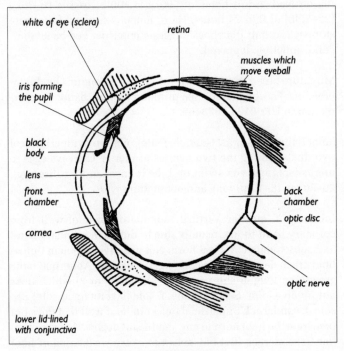

white of eye (sclera)

retina

muscles which move eyeball

iris forming the pupil

black body

lens

front chamber

back chamber

optic disc

cornea

optic nerve

lower lid-lined with conjunctiva

12 Section through eye

eyelid (syn palpebra) One of 3 membranes: 2 main (upper and lower) and third lid (syn nictitating membrane) which sweeps across eye from inner to outer angle.

F

facelessness (aprosopia) Rare congential fault in which eyes, nostrils and mouth have not formed. Foal usually dies immediately after birth.

F. (1) Abbr fahrenheit. See temperature, weights and measures. (2) Abbr Fellow (of Royal College of Veterinary Surgeons, qv). F_2 alpha. See prostaglandin.

facultative Ability to adjust, as in **f. anaerobe**, an organism which can live without air. See anaerobe.

faeces (L, pl of faex, refuse; syns dung, droppings) Excreta passed from intestines through anus; may be formed or soft, depending on feed. Adult horse of 500kg (1,100lb) passes 10–25kg (22–55lb) of **f.** in 24 hours. Hard, mucous-covered **f.** indicate stoppage in gut; diarrhoea suggests enteritis. See behaviour; colic; appetite, depraved.

Falabella/Fallabella Miniature breed, about 7 h, developed in S America by down-breeding Thoroughbred. See miniature horse, hand. **F.** information in UK: 01243 573469.

fallopian tube (after Italian anatomist Gabriele Falloppio; syn oviduct) One of two ducts joining the two ovaries to uterus. Conveys eggs to uterus (spermatozoa swim up tube to meet and fertilise egg). 20–30 cm (8–12in) long and about 3mm wide.

false Incorrect. **f. quarter** Vertical indentation of hoof wall from coronary band to toe, usually due to defect in coronary band and subsequent abnormal horn. Not usually a problem unless hoof crack develops. **f. rig** See rig. **f. ringbone** Abnormal bone growth on long or short pastern (phalanx 1 or 2) which does not involve joint. See ringbone. **f. sole** (syn retained sole) See sole. **f. sandcrack** Superficial defect in hoof wall that does not penetrate the hoof horn to any significant degree. Appears similar to sandcrack (qv) but does not cause weakening of hoof wall or lameness.

faradism (after English physicist Michael Faraday) Treatment using electricity to produce a rhythm of contractions in muscle. See physiotherapy.

farcy See glanders.

farrier More specific term for horseshoer than blacksmith, qv.

(L band) White fibrous sheets beneath skin or between muscles.	**fascia**
(syn adipose tissue) White or yellowish material laid down around, or in, various organs and muscles of body.	**fat/f. tissue**
Chemical symbol for iron (stored in body as ferritin).	**Fe**
See ferrous.	**Fe^{++}**
See ferric.	**Fe^{+++}**
Colloq for long hair of lower legs. Generally heavier horses and pony breeds have more feathering. F.s can be trimmed, (taking care to avoid chestnut, qv, ergot, qv, and skin) if they attract fly eggs, parasite larvae or caked mud.	**feather**
(L febrilis) Characterised by fever.	**febrile**
See faeces.	**feces**
(L fecunditas) Ability to produce offspring. See fertility.	**fecundity**
To eat or give food. Colloq ration provided, typically grass, hay, oats. See also behaviour, eating; food. **artificial f.** See food by stomach tube, parenteral nutrition qv.	**feed/ing**
Native pony of Pennine hills in N England. Made to carry great weights in past, now popular for pony trekking. Originally similar to Dales pony, but few inches smaller and unchanged by influence of other breeds. Most commonly black without any markings, also bay, and less commonly grey or dun. See pit pony. **F. Pony Soc**, Keeper's Cottage, Guyzance, Northumberland NE65 9AA (01670 761117).	**Fell**
Consist of 2 ovaries which produce eggs (ova) and secrete hormones, oestrogen and progesterone; 2 fallopian tubes (oviducts) in which egg is fertilised; uterus in which foal develops; cervix (neck of uterus) which guards contents of uterus and separates it from vagina; vulva, which acts as a valve preventing air entering genital tract; mammary glands (udder). See under separate headings. Diseases and conditions: see birth, hazards of; virus; bacteria; Caslick operation; cervicitis; endometritis; haemorrhage; mastitis; metritis.	**female genital organs**
(syn thigh bone, pl femora) Large bone between hip joint above and stifle joint below. Adjective: femoral.	**femur**
(trade name: Panacur) A benzimidazole (qv). Anthelmintic to	**fenbendazole**

fenbendazole	treat intestinal parasites. Effective against large and small strongyles, roundworm, pinworm, lungworm.
feral	Free-roaming; animal whose ancestors have escaped from captivity. **f.** breeds include Camargue, Sable Island. Cf wild.
fermentation	(L fermentatio) Decomposition of carbohydrate by enzyme action. See colic.
ferric	(L ferrum) Iron in trivalent form, Fe^{+++}.
ferrin	Iron-containing substance found in bile pigment.
ferritin	Form in which iron is stored in body.
ferrous	Iron in divalent form, Fe^{++}.
fertile	(L fertilis) Capable of causing pregnancy or becoming pregnant. Male usually **f.** at $2^1/_2$ years, female at 2 years, although colts and fillies under $1^1/_2$ years have been known to be **f.**
fertilisation	Process when spermatozoon fuses with ovum (egg); results in restoration of diploid number of chromosomes and establishes inherited characters of new individual. Occurs in upper part of fallopian tube. See embryology.
fertility	Ability to conceive or fertilise. **f. rate** (1) Percentage of mares particular stallion gets in foal. In captivity usually 60–80 per cent, claimed (unsubstantiated) to be higher in the wild. (2) Percentage of mares producing foals in any given season. Cf infertility.
fetal/fetus/foetal	See foetus.
fetlock	Foreleg or hind leg joint formed by cannon (metacarpal or metatarsal), pastern (first phalanx) and sesamoid bones. Joint capsule surrounds bones, and bursa is between capsule and extensor tendons on front of joint. Behind, a thin-walled pouch extends between cannon bone and suspensory ligament (see windgall). Joint often develops arthritis, with distension of joint capsule due to excess joint oil (synovia), pain on flexion and lameness. May become dislocated or affected by fracture of pastern bone if break extends to joint surface. See osselet; joint mouse/mice.
fever	(L febris) Abnormally high temperature, ie above 39°C (102°F.) Accompanied by fast pulse and breathing, rise in skin temperature and, possibly, patchy sweating. Symptom of infection by bacteria or virus, eg strangles, influenza, septicaemia. See temperature. **f. rings** See hoof rings.

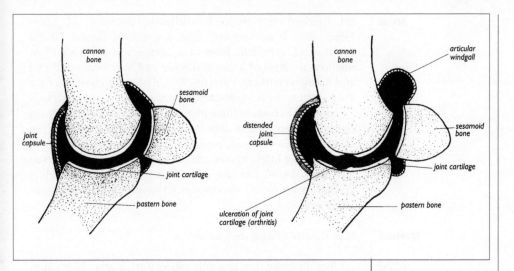

(left) 13 Fetlock joint, from left – normal;
(right) 14 Fetlock showing arthritis and articular windgall

Elongated structure, usually refers to nerve cells. See nerve. In diet, refers to undigested material.	**fibre**
Rapid contraction as in atrial **f.**, qv. Early degenerative change in arthritis.	**fibrillation**
Whitish protein formed from thrombin. See coagulation.	**fibrin**
(fibrin + Gr gennan, to produce) Plasma protein converted to fibrin by action of thrombin; also called coagulation factor 1. See coagulation.	**fibrinogen**
Type of cartilage, qv.	**fibrocartilage**
Benign tumour of fibrous tissue. See growth.	**fibroma**
Laying down of fibrous tissue in organs where not normally present, eg cardiac **f.** follows inflamed heart muscle infected with virus or affected by bacterial or other toxins.	**fibrosis**
(syn gristle) Densely or loosely arranged elongated cells (fibroblasts). They produce inert substance collagen, which forms basis of tendons, joint capsules, ligaments and scars.	**fibrous tissue**
Small slender bone attached at upper and lower ends to tibia.	**fibula**
(L filamentum) Delicate fibre or thread, eg nerve fibre. Some cells, eg spermatozoa, have **f.**	**filament**

filaria	(pl filariae) Nematode (roundworm parasite) of order Filarioidea. It is long and thin, resembling thread. Genus *Onchocerca cervicalis* lives in a ligament of the neck (ligamentum nuchae) of horse and mule and may cause poll evil and fistulous withers. Parasites live in blood from which they are sucked up by midges. Genus *Onchocerca reticulata* similar – and some experts believe identical – to *O. cervicalis*. Genus *Setaria equina* lives in abdomen, scrotum or lungs and is not known to cause disease. *Setaria digitata* is natural parasite of cattle but can infect horses and, in Japan, the migrating larvae have been found to cause disease of central nervous system known as epidemic cerebrospinal nematodiasis. Can also affect eye.
filariasis	Infection by filariae. See filaria.
filling	(1) Blood's entry into heart chambers during relaxation (diastole). (2) Colloq oedema of limbs or soft swellings on body. See oedema; joints.
filly	Female of Equus (qv) until she is termed mare, usually aged 4/5, earlier if used for breeding. Cf colt.
filter	(L filtrum) (1) Device for straining liquid. (2) In radiation, **f.** permits passage of some wavelengths but absorbs others. (3) Used to separate virus from bacteria (which are larger). **Wood's f.** Glass containing nickel oxide which allows only ultraviolet waves to pass and which causes hairs infected with some types of ringworm to fluoresce.
firing	Traditional treatment, usually for leg injuries, now dying out in face of evidence that it is cruel. Skin over flexor tendon, splints, fetlock and knee joints, ringbone or curbs is burned with red-hot iron. Penetration varies from superficial to underlying tissues and causes scar tissue to form, hardening the area; carried out under general or local anaesthesia. **line f.** Lines or bars burned into skin surrounding flexor tendons and continuing at intervals for length of cannon bone. **pin/point f.** Individual puncture marks made around joints or over tendons (most common **f.** now in use). All cases need rest after treatment, up to a year or more depending on severity of injury and whether horse is required to do fast work.
first	Initial/earliest. **f. aid** The help any attendant should be able to give to injured horse. **f.a. kit** Bandages (cotton and elastic), cotton wool, gauze, poultices, disinfectant, detergent, petroleum jelly, liquid paraffin, gentian violet, fly repellent, wound powder/ointment. See wound. **f. breath** See breath. **f. dung** See meconium. **f. milk** See colostrum; running of milk.

(L pipe) Abnormal passage connecting internal structures or between these and body surface. See rectovaginal **f.**, pervious urachus. **fistula**

Abscess in region of withers, usually result of wound infected with *Brucella* spp or other bacteria. See filaria. Cf poll evil. **fistulous withers**

(L fixatio) Act of holding or fastening, eg internal **f.** of fractured bone. **complement f. test** See complement. **internal f.** Method of repairing fractures by surgical intervention. Usually involves screws and plates to immobilise fracture ends. Most commonly used technique is ASIF (AO) and involves compression of bone ends by these implants. **fixation**

Substance used to preserve sample, eg skin or organ, to study later in laboratory, eg 10% formalin in saline solution. **fixative**

(syns Westland, Vestland) Stocky, good-tempered Norwegian pony of Celtic or Baltic type. Often dun with black dorsal stripe; widely used for farm work. **F. Horse Soc of GB**, Cilyblaidd Manor, Pencarreg, Carmarthenshire SA40 9QL (01570 480090). **Fjord/ing**

(L whip, pl flagella) Whip-like thread on some rod-shaped bacteria which moves the bacterium. Cf cilium. **flagellum**

See foot. **flat foot**

(L, a blowing) Gas in alimentary tract expelled through anus. See colic. **flatus**

Internal parasite belonging to phylum Platyhelminthes including classes Trematoda (fluke, qv) and Cestoidea (tapeworm, qv). **flatworm**

Parasite insect belonging to order Siphonaptera. Does not normally live on horses although two genera may attack those in tropical regions, viz., stick-tight **f.** of poultry; chigger (or jigger) in S America, Africa and West Indies. **flea**

(after German, Flehmen) Extended neck and curled upper lip. Seen in sexually aroused male, during colic and in mare in 1st stage labour. See behaviour, male sexual; birth. **Flehmen posture**

Muscle or tendon that flexes joint. Opp extensor. See muscle. **flexor**

(syns filing, rasping) Removing sharp edges on molar teeth with a rasp. See teeth. **floating**

See influenza. **flu**

fluid (L fluidus) Liquid or gas; elements or particles which change position without separating, eg allantoic **f.** (see allantois). **f. balance** Proportion of water in the 2 major compartments of body, ie in bloodstream (intravascular) and in tissues (extravascular); extravascular fluid is further divided into that outside/inside cells (interstitial and intracellular). The water in compartments relates to salts of the body and is therefore a measure of salt concentration, eg shortage of water (dehydration) may reduce cellular, intercellular or intravascular water (see haemoconcentration). Bodywt is normally 70 per cent water (intracellular 50 per cent bodywt, intercellular 15 per cent bodywt and blood 5 per cent bodywt).

fluke (*Fasciola hepatica*) Parasite of liver belonging to class Trematoda. (The **f.** of sheep and cattle can live in other animals, including horses.) It is leaf-shaped with conical projection at front, measures up to 26mm (about 1in) by 13mm (¹/₂in), is hermaphrodite (having male and female tissue) and is without alimentary canal – its simple excretory system consists of small canals. Life cycle: adult lives in bile ducts of liver where it lays eggs that pass, with the bile, into the small intestine. Eggs are then passed out in faeces. The larva (miracidium) develops in warm, moist conditions then hatches and swims in water until it penetrates an intermediate host. In Britain this is mud snail (*Lymnaea truncatula*). A second larva (sporocyst) then develops. Each sporocyst produces 5 to 8 radiae and finally a cercaria, a young fluke that can infect main host. The cercariae develop in snail, then form a cyst and are swallowed by the main host. They penetrate intestinal wall and travel to liver, causing chronic disease with anaemia, unthriftiness and diarrhoea. **F.**s of family Schistosomatidae live in tropical areas. They are elongated, worm-like and live in blood vessels. *S. japonicum* lives in veins of liver and abdomen causing schistosomiasis. Worms can penetrate skin, causing dermatitis, and will inflame intestines or other organs. *S. indicum* affects horses and camels in India. *S. nasalis* affects horses in India and America (especially Louisiana) causing inflamed nostrils. Control: remove intermediate host, the snail. Treat with carbon tetrachloride, qv.

flunixin meglumine **flunixin meglumine** (trade names: Binixin, Finadyne) Potent, nonsteroidal anti-inflammatory drug with analgesic and antipyretic properties (see pyrexia). Used in colic and soft tissue swellings, IV or IM.

fluorescein Orange-red odourless tasteless powder. **f. sodium** Used as solution for detecting ulcers on cornea. If drops of 10% solution are put into eye, ulcer will look green if studied in sunlight 5–10 minutes later. See eye.

May follow misuse of sodium flouride as anthelmintic against roundworms. Symptoms: gastroenteritis, abdominal pain, diarrhoea, muscular weakness and, in severe cases, collapse and death. Horses are relatively resistant. Can also occur near industries, eg aluminium, glass, enamel, stone, steel and metal works and potteries. Plants collect **f.** dust on leaves which horses then eat. **F.** is deposited in bones and teeth and, in high concentration, causes bony outgrowths in skeleton. Symptom: lameness, which may shift from one leg to another, spontaneous fractures which take 2 or 3 months to heal. Diagnosis: best on bones from dead animals. Over 5,000 p.p.m. (parts per million) of **f.** confirms poisoning. In life, urine values of 15 p.p.m. and above indicate poisoning. | **flourine poisoning**

Synthetic prostaglandin. See prostaglandin. | **fluprostenol**

Two-winged insect belonging to order Diptera. See bot, tabanid **f.**, warble **f.** | **fly**

Young horse from birth (newborn **f.**) to weaning time (weanling) or 1 year old (yearling). **f., diseases of** See newborn. **f. heat** Colloq name given to first oestrus after foaling. Occurs usually between days 5 and 17. First ovulation after foaling: 9–11 days. See oestrus. | **foal**

(L fireplace; pl foci) Chief centre of disease, eg foci of infection in strangles are the lymph nodes. See strangles. | **focus**

Of foetus. **f. membrane** See afterbirth. | **foetal**

(L) Unborn foal. Measured by weight and length (crown to rump, ie just in front of poll to top of tail). See embryology; gestation; growth. | **foetus** *(illus p144)*

Age in days	Weight	Length
60	10 – 20g	4 – 7.5cm
120	700 – 1,000g	15 – 20cm
180	3 – 5kg	35 – 60cm
240	12 – 18kg	60 – 80cm
300	25 – 40kg	70 – 130cm
340 (full term)	30 – 50kg	100 – 150cm

Small fluid-filled sac or gland. **hair f.** Sac at root of hair. **graafian f. of ovary**. This develops round egg during oestrus. Eventually ruptures when 2.5–6cm (ovulation) to allow escape of egg; lined by cells which secrete fluid and help to form yellow body, qv. **f. stimulating hormone** (FSH) Hormone produced by part (anterior lobe) of pituitary gland of both | **follicle**

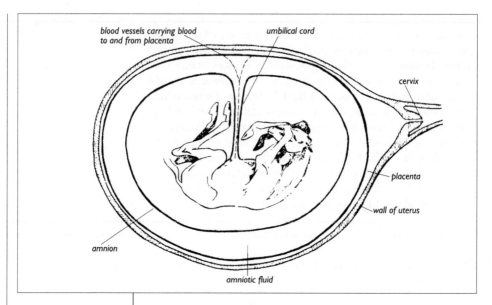

15 Position of foetus before it revolves ready for birth

follicle | sexes. In mare it acts on ovaries, causing increase in size of **f.** and production of hormone oestrogen. As level of oestrogen in blood rises, pituitary stops producing FSH and liberates luteinising hormone (LH) which causes ovulation. FSH in male stimulates production and growth of spermatozoa in testes.

follicular | (L follicularis) Of a follicle.

folliculitis | Inflammation of hair follicles, causing pustules, often due to *Staphylococcus aureus*.

food | Amount and type varies with age and status, ie barren or pregnant mare, horse in training or resting, stallion, horse during long sea voyage, illness or convalescence. General considerations: (1) Digestion. Poor-quality **f.** less digestible than good quality. (2) Fibre. Plant material of carbohydrate nature gives necessary bulk; heavy work demands some concentrates but horse's digestive system cannot deal with these alone and requires some coarse fodder such as hay. Daily minimum: about 320g per 45kg (0.7lb per 100lb) bodywt though double this is usually fed. Colorado State University workers recommend 900g per 45kg (2lb per 100lb) live weight per day (the average horse: 450kg (1,000lb) should get 9kg (20lb) hay per day). (3) Protein. Essential for building muscle. Mature horse needs about 250g (9oz) of digestible protein per day; about 8 per cent of diet. Pregnant mare needs 14 per cent during the last third of pregnancy and in the first three months of lactation.

Weaned foal or yearling needs 15–20 per cent protein; 2-year-olds, 12–15 per cent. (4) Energy. Supplied by cereal grains such as oats; usually fed rolled, flaked or cracked. (5) Minerals. Typical ration of grass, hay and grain is usually deficient in calcium, adequate in phosphorus and deficient in salt and iodine. On average, horse eats about 85g (3oz) of salt daily, according to work and temperature. Calcium/phosphorus should be given in a ratio of 1.5:1.0–1.2: 1.0 (see calcium and phosphorus). (6) Vitamins. Necessary for growth, health and reproduction. Rarely deficient in grazing horses but stabled ones may suffer vitamin A, D and E deficiency. Lack of vitamin E (alpha tocopherol succinate) may contribute to infertility. Recommended amount: 600–1,000 IU daily. (7) Water. Essential; average adult horse consumes 22–45 litres (5–10 gal) daily depending on amount of work and weather conditions. Horses should always have free access to water. (8) Specific requirements: brood mare – when barren should not be allowed to get fat, when pregnant must have adequate protein, minerals, vitamins in last third of pregnancy and during lactation; stallion – balanced ration that discourages obesity; foal and yearling – adequate protein. Foal with access to spring grass may get too much protein. Avoid overweight. If possible use scientifically formulated ration to ensure proper balance. Adult's **f.** should include carrots and bran mashes. Adult in light work: 225g (½lb) grain, 675g (1½lb) hay per 45kg (100lb) bodywt; in medium work: 340g (¾lb) grain, 570g (1¼lb) hay per 45kg (100lb) bodywt; in hard work: 900g (2lb) grain, 225g (½lb) hay per 45kg (100lb) bodywt. **F.** should be given in 3 or 4 equal feeds. (Horses are continuous feeders, unlike say, dogs, whose digestion is tuned to occasional large meals.) Dung is a guide to feeding; small hard faeces indicate too little water. Can be counteracted by mashes and more salt, causing horse to drink more. Pellet (cube) **f.** is cleaner, needs less storage space and labour and is a balanced diet. (Faeces of pellet-fed horses are softer than those on traditional feeds.) Horses at pasture show preference for the following grasses and herbs: crested dogstail, perennial ryegrasses, sceempter, melle, petra, midas S.23 and S.321, Timothy S.48 and S.50, dandelion, chicory, yarrow, ribgrass, burnet, sainfoin and, particularly, wild white clover (but not red clover). Grasses which should not be sown for horses: perennial ryegrass S.24, creeping red fescue, brown top, meadow foxtail, red clover. **f. by stomach tube** (qv). Should be given if foal has lost suck reflex. Pass tube, lubricated with water or liquid paraffin, when foal is standing or lying. Push end gently into one nostril, but not past entrance to thorax. After feeding, flush tube with saline so that milk is not left in nostrils. (Foal can be fed by bottle if suck reflex present but ability to suck from mare is absent.) **F.** can be colostrum, mare's milk, skimmed cow's milk or dried milk. Feed mare's or

food   skimmed cow's milk at 80–100ml/kg bodywt per day, divided into a minimum of 10 equal feeds. Foal of 50kg (110lb) would then be fed 4–5 litres (9–11 pints) per day. Ensure cleanliness and give milk at 38°C (100.4°F) or below – never above.

foot   (L pes; syn hoof) Horny box surrounding third phalanx (pedal or coffin bone), navicular bone, ligaments, tendon (insertion of the deep flexor), digital cushion, sensitive laminae, coronopedal (coffin) joint, blood vessels and nerves. Hoof consists of wall divided into toe and quarters, with sole, bars and frog underneath. Hoof wall is about 25 per cent water and is modified skin or nail. Outer layer (periople) helps protect wall from evaporation; middle layer forms dense portion of wall and contains pigment; inner layer or laminar layer forms insensitive membranes (laminae) which bind hoof to pedal bone. (Hundreds of thin primary laminae, each of which bears a hundred or so secondary laminae, interlock with sensitive laminae lining pedal bone.) Hoof wall grows approx 6mm (¹/₄ in) per month, taking 9 months to grow from coronary band to toe. See also bars, frog, white line, corium, contracted heels, evolution. **f., abscess of** May be caused by embedded stone, etc. See abscess. **f., anticoncussion mechanism** Frog represents most elastic structure of **f.** When this strikes ground, heel expands and forces of concussion are distributed. Digital cushion expands outward putting pressure on cartilages of pedal bone. The blood in veins and vascular bed of **f.** adds to the efficient cushioning. **f. blood supply** Comes from the medial and lateral digital arteries, which arise from common digital artery at lower end of cannon bone. See arteries, table of; corium. **bull-nosed f.** (syn dubbed **f.**, dumped **f.**) Condition in which toe

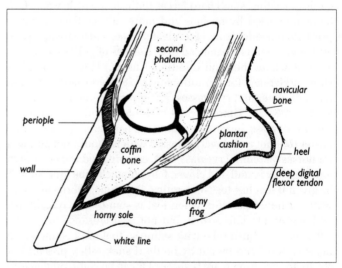

16 Section through foot

ends in abrupt angle. May be due to heredity, excessive wear at toe from poor conformation or lameness, or from excessive rasping of toe during improper trimming or shoeing. **brittle f.** (syn shelly **f.**) One that splits or crumbles easily. Most common in dry weather. See seedy toe. **f., diseases of** See dropped sole; contracted heels; club foot, laminitis; pedal osteitis; abscess; corn; bruised sole; sandcrack; navicular disease; quittor; sidebones; seedy toe. **dished/flare f.** (syn wry **f.**) Walls are distorted outwards (dished) due to imbalance/uneven weight distribution. **flat f.** One in which sole lacks normal concavity. Often seen in draught breeds. May be congenital, due to laminitis or poor environment, eg damp stabling. **f., nerve supply** Comes from medial and lateral volar nerves (see nerve block). **f., weight-bearing structures** Walls, bars and frog contact the ground. The sole does not bear weight, except for a strip about 6mm (¹/₄in) wide inside the white line. Bottom of wall should be level with frog to distribute weight evenly. | *foot*

(L, pl foramina) Anatomical term for natural opening, especially into or through bone. | **foramen**

Instrument with two blades and handles used in surgery to grasp or compress tissue. **artery f.** Used to clamp artery to reduce bleeding during surgery. **dental f.** Used to extract teeth. | **forceps**

Action when toe of a hind foot strikes bottom of front foot of the same side as it leaves ground. Cf brushing, cross-firing, overreaching, interfering. | **forging**

Colourless liquid with characteristic pungent, irritating odour and burning taste. Powerful antiseptic, reacts with proteins. Used to treat proud flesh, to fumigate after infectious disease and in laboratory to preserve specimens. | **formaldehyde solution**

(L arch, pl fornices) Anatomical vault formed by arch-like structures, eg **f.** of pharynx. | **fornix**

To raise young other than natural offspring. Foal can be reared on a **f.**-mother if dam had died, has insufficient milk or is hostile. Foal can be transferred to **f.**-mother at any age but it is increasingly difficult after one month. Some mares accept orphan foal better than others. Methods include (1) confusing **f.** mare by rubbing strong-smelling ointment onto nostrils before introducing orphan foal; (2) clothing orphan in amnion or skin of **f.**-mother's foal. Restraint of mare, injection of tranquillisers, and careful, patient handling of foal to avoid injury can usually make fostering successful. See National Foaling Bank. | **foster**

See laminitis. **f. ring** See hoof rings. | **founder**

foxglove	See digitalis.
fox-trot	See gait.
fracture	(L from frangere, to break) Break in bone: hairline (minute), greenstick (bending of young bone), spiral (corkscrew-like), comminuted (many pieces), impacted (one end driven into other), compound (bone exposed by skin wound). See lameness, sclerosing agent.
FRCVS	Abbr Fellow of the Royal College of Veterinary Surgeons. See veterinary.
Frederiksborg	Denmark's best-known breed developed by King Frederick II, in 1570s from Andalusian and Neapolitan horses. Related to Lipizzaner, usually chestnut and about 15.3 h.
frenulum	(L dim of frenum; pl frenula) Small fold of mucous membrane that curbs movement of an organ or part. **f. linguae** Fold of membrane beneath tongue (qv) attaching it to floor of mouth.
fremitus	Thrill or vibration which can be felt, eg in extremely loud heart murmur, by placing fingers on chest. See heart murmur.
Friesian	(syn Harddraver) One of Europe's oldest breeds, descended from horses which survived Ice Age. Reared in **F.** district of Holland and breed society given royal title by Queen Juliana. **F.** popular for willingness, especially in harness. Usually about 15 h, often with jet-black coat and exceptionally long mane. **F. Horse Assn,** Wingfield Castle, Diss, Norfolk IP21 5RB (01379 388088). See Morgan.
frog	Wedge-shaped mass in central back part of undersurface of hoof, ie bounded by bars and sole. Contains about 50% water; shaped as narrow triangle with point (apex) and base. Part of weight-bearing structure of foot (qv), particularly suited to absorb concussion.
frontal	Of forehead. **f. sinus** Cavity in skull from line in front of eye sockets (orbits) to back of skull, in front of cranium. See sinus.
fructose	(L fructus, fruit) Carbohydrate or sugar in foetus and newborn foal, which disappears from bloodstream after two days.
frusemide	See furosemide.
FSH	See follicle stimulating hormone.
fuller's earth	An impure aluminium silicate used in dressings.

Bottom or base of organ, eg **f.** of bladder, **f.** of eye.   **fundus**

See abortion.   **fungal abortion**

(L, singular fungus) Organisms belonging to vegetable kingdom but different from plants in that they do not contain chlorophyll. Composed of mycelium and a reproductive portion of spores. 4 main classes: (1) phycomycetes, (2) ascomycetes (containing the yeasts), (3) basidiomycetes (including mushrooms, toadstools), (4) hyphomycetes (containing pathogenic fungi). The following (see separate headings) are caused by yeast and fungi: **fungi**

Conditiom	Causal organism
epizootic lymphangitis	*Histoplasma farciminosus* (formerly *Cryptococcus farciminosus*) yeast family
ringworm	*Microsporum* spp; *Trichophyton* spp
fungal abortion (see abortion)	*Aspergillus* spp
broken wind	*Aspergillus* spp *Alternaria* spp *Hormodendrum* spp
mud fever	*Dermatophilus* spp
guttural pouch mycosis	*Aspergillus* spp

Drug or substance that destroys fungi. Can cause poisoning if treated food is given to horses. Symptoms: skin irritation, inflamed windpipe and urinary tract. May also affect central nervous system, causing incoordination.   **fungicide**

(trade name: Neftin) Yellow odourless powder. Antibiotic effective against many types of bacteria, especially Salmonella; is poorly absorbed from gut, and is sometimes used to treat diarrhoea in foals.   **furazolidone**

(frusemide) (trade name: Lasix) White odourless tasteless powder; increases flow of urine (diuretic drug) and excretion of sodium potassium and chloride from kidney; used to treat filled joints and other types of oedema. See EIPH.   **furosemide**

(trade names: Fucidin, Fucithalmic Vet) Steroid antibiotic used against staphylococci, especially skin infections.   **fusidic acid**

G

g Abbr gram/s, also written G and gm.

gad fly Colloq warble fly, qv.

gag Device for holding mouth open. Useful in dentistry, anaesthesia etc. Popular type: Haussman (colloq American). Half-moon pieces fit on to front teeth of upper and lower jaws and join crossbars on either side. Crossbars, held in place by strap over horse's poll, have ratchet (with quick release) to hold mouth open.

gait Sequence of leg movements, usually forward. First effectively recorded in 1870s by British photographer E. J. Muybridge. (Before this horses were thought to gallop as depicted in old paintings, ie with forelegs outstretched together and hind legs back together, which does not occur.) Horses move similarly to other 4-legged animals (quadrupeds) and are 3-gaited (walk, trot, canter) or 5-gaited (walk, trot, canter plus rack and a slow **g.**). About 6 support sequences are identifiable as **g.**s viz, walk, trot, canter, gallop, (natural **g.**s); amble, similar to rack and running walk, and pace (natural or false **g.**s). **amble** 4-beat, walking speed **g.** Legs move in lateral pairs, ie near-fore and near-hind virtually together. No period of suspension (when all 4 feet off ground); classed as slow **g.** See Connemara; Spanish Jennet. **asymmetrical g.** One in which either pair of feet, fore/hind, moves in uneven time, eg gallop. **canter** 3-beat **g.** (may be 4-beat in some horses); puts greatest wear on leading foreleg and opposite hind leg. Horse usually leads with same foreleg but may change legs negotiating a bend (if left-hand bend it should lead with near-fore; if right hand, with off-fore). **flat-foot walk** Similar to walk, but looser. Natural to Tennessee Walking horse, qv. **fox-trot** Classed as slow **g.** A slow, broken trot, usually with nodding of head. **gallop** Fastest **g.** virtually an uncollected canter so may be 3- or 4-beat. Fastest breed (Thoroughbred) can gallop at more than 65kph (40mph) over short distances. **pace** Fast, 2-beat lateral **g.** seen mainly in Standardbreds that race in harness (as it is unnatural to most horses, pacers usually race in hobbles). Pace slightly faster than trot (trotters also race in harness). Devotees of Peruvian Paso (qv) say this horse can pace, (camel is a natural pacer). **paso g.** (normal and marching) That of laterally gaited Peruvian Paso. Similar to pace. **rack** (syns singlefoot, broken amble) Exaggerated, regular 4-beat walk. Comfortable for rider but tiring on horse. See also American Saddle Horse. **running walk** 4-beat **g.** between walk and rack. Hind foot oversteps print left by forefoot in smooth, gliding motion. Accompanied by bobbing of head; easy on horse and rider. A **g.** of Standardbred (as well as pace). See also American Saddle horse. **symmetrical g.** One in which fore or hind legs are evenly timed, eg walk, trot (syns jog, parade **g.**, stepping pace, pacing walk, but meanings vary enormously). **trot** 2-beat **g.** in which opposite fore and hind feet meet ground virtually together. Can be slow or extended (when forging is common in some horses). Cf pace. Hackney (qv) renowned for particularly high-stepping trot. **walk** 4-beat **g.** slower than flat-foot walk and running walk. See lameness. Cf cross-firing, brushing, forging, over-reaching, interfering. | *gait*

(Gr gala, galaktos, milk) Combining form: of milk. | **galacta-/galacto-**

Mexican pony with characteristic running walk. Probably descended from Minho ponies imported from Portugal. | **Galiceno**

Reservoir, in species other than horse, for storing bile, qv. | **gallbladder**

See gait. | **gallop**

Extinct strain of Highland pony which influenced Lundy. | **Galloway**

(after Luigi Galvani) Uninterrupted current of electricity. Cf faradism. See physiotherapy. | **galvanism**

Third letter of Greek alphabet. See globulin, radiation. **g. benzene hexachloride** White crystalline powder with slight odour. Effective against fleas (rare in horses), ticks, mites, lice. **g. glutamyltransferase** (Gamma GT or GGT) Enzyme in liver, kidney tubules and pancreas. Levels increase in toxic liver damage, pancreatitis and selenium deficiency. Normal less than 40 IU/l. **g. camera** Detects gamma rays in investigation of soft tissue or bone damage after injection of radioactive dye. See nuclear scintigraphy. | **gamma**

(Gr gamete, wife; gametes, husband) Male (spermatozoon) and female (ovum) sex cells which unite to form new individual (zygote). See embryology. | **gamete**

Pl of ganglion. | **ganglia**

(Gr knot, pl ganglia) Any group of nerve cell bodies found outside spinal cord (central nervous system). See nerve cell. | **ganglion**

(L gangraena, Gr gangraina) Death of tissue because it is separated from blood supply. Rare in horses, but may occur in severely damaged foot, artery blocked by clot, strangulated | **gangrene**

gangrene	blood supply (possibly if wound is bandaged too tightly). Part becomes cold, decayed and foul-smelling. Treatment: cut away dead tissue. Amputation or destruction may be necessary in severe cases.
Garrano	See Minho.
Garron	See Highland pony.
gas	Colloq for flatus. See flatus, colic.
gaskin	(syn second thigh) That part of hindleg between stifle and hock.
gasterophilus	See bot.
gastric	(L gastricus, Gr gaster, stomach) Of the stomach. **g. dilatation** Distension associated with colic or grass sickness, qv. Symptoms: depression, excessive sweating, tendency to crouch in dog-sitting position or extend front and hind legs, vomiting (rare in horse and usually sign of impending death or rupture of stomach). Condition often eased by passing stomach tube. See colic. **g. ulcer** Ulcer (qv) in stomach especially of foal. Symptoms: grinding teeth, drooling saliva and evidence of pain especially after eating. **g.u.** may occur separately or with duodenal ulcer. See also campylobacter.
gastritis	Inflamed stomach.
gastro-	(Gr gaster, stomach) Combining form meaning relationship to stomach.
gastrocnemius	(gastro- + Gr kneme, leg) Muscle acting on hock. See muscles, table of.
gastroenteritis	Inflamed stomach and intestines. See colic, diarrhoea.
gastroscopy	Visualising lining of stomach by endoscope, qv.
gastrula	Early stage of embryo after blastula. See embryology.
gastrulation	Process by which blastula acquires three tissue types (germ layers). See embryology.
gauze	Open-mesh muslin or similar material. Can be impregnated with antiseptic and used for dressing, qv.
GCMS	Abbr gas chromatography and mass spectrometry. See dope test.

Abbr glutamate dehydrogenase, qv. — **GDH**

(L gelatina from gelare, to congeal) Produce of bones and other tissues, used as food and to make capsules in which drugs can be given by mouth. — **gelatin**

Developed in **G.** province of Holland last century by crossing native mares with many types of imported stallion. Equally good for riding, driving or light agricultural work. Often bright chestnut marked with white and usually about 15 h. — **Gelderland**

Gelded (castrated) male. See castration. Cf colt, stallion. — **gelding**

(after Jean Baptiste **G.**, French neurologist) See narcolepsy. — **Gelineau's syndrome**

(Gr gennan, to produce) Hereditary unit in definite position on chromosome. **allelic g.**s At corresponding places on pair of chromosomes. **dominant g.** One which produces effect regardless of state of corresponding allele, ie if one parent possesses **d.g.** that characteristic will appear in progeny (cf recessive **g.**). **lethal g.** One that kills individual. **recessive g.** One effective only when transmitted by both parents. **sex-linked g.** One carried on X or Y chromosome. See chromosome; embryology. — **gene**

Of inheritance. — **genetic**

(L genitalia, belonging to birth) Of reproduction or reproductive organs. — **genital**

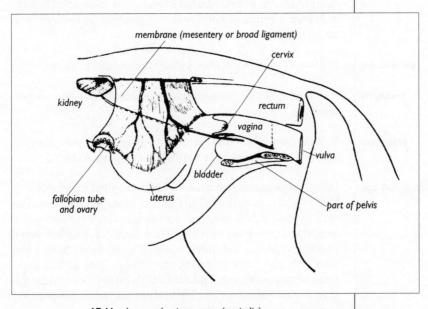

17 Mare's reproductive organs (genitalia)

genitalia	Reproductive organs. Mare: two ovaries, fallopian tubes, mammary glands; one uterus, cervix, vagina. Stallion: two testes, epididymides, vas deferentia, seminal vesicles and bulbo-urethral glands; one penis, scrotum, prostate gland. **external g.** Organs outside body, eg testes. See descent of testes.
genome	The complete chain/s of heritable material (nucleic acids) which determines offspring's similarity to parent and which contains all genes for a species.
genotype	(geno- + Gr typos, type) Genetic makeup of an individual. Cf phenotype.
gentamicin	Antibiotic belonging to aminoglycoside group, qv. Used in infections of foals and adults often in combination with penicillin, qv. May cause kidney toxicity (nephrotoxicity). **g. sulphate** (trade names: Cidomycin, Garamycin) Drug to treat pseudomonas.
gentian	Light or yellowish-brown powder with characteristic odour and taste, from root of *Gentiana lutea*. Used to improve appetite. Dose: 8–30g. **g. violet** Antiseptic dye used alone or with antibiotic on wounds and proud flesh.
genu	(syn stifle) Joint between femur (thigh) and tarsus (gaskin). See stifle.
germ	(L germen) Microorganism capable of causing disease. See bacteria, fungi, virus. **wheat g.** Embryo of wheat containing tocopherol, thiamine, riboflavin and other vitamins. Cf bran. **g. layers** 3 types of body cells, originating in embryo. See embryology.
germicidal	(L germen, germ + caedere, to kill) Destructive to germs.
gestagen	Any hormone with progesterone-like activity. See also progesterone.
gestation	(L from gestate, to bear) Pregnancy; period of development of young inside uterus from fertilisation of ovum to birth.
gestational age	Length of pregnancy at time foetus is expelled by abortion or birth. Usually measured from last date of service but should be from ovulation following last mating. Can also be measured by weight and crown to rump length (see foetus). **g. length** Average in Thoroughbred: 340 days, range 320–60. Foals have lived after only 287 days' gestation and after as long as 419 days. Pony breeds have shorter **g.l.** (315–35 days) and colts longer **g.l.** than fillies. See abortion; birth; dystocia; position; posture; presentation; prematurity.

Abbr gamma glutamyltransferase, qv. **GGT**

Laboratory term for red blood cell which has lost its haemo- **ghost**
globin. See haemolytic jaundice.

Large saddle horse of Hungary developed by covering local **Gidran**
mares with English half-bred or Thoroughbred stallions; usually bay or chestnut. **G. Arabian** Hungarian breed developed
from the Arab Siglavy-Gidran, imported in 1816. S and E
European types have Arabian looks but the mid-European is
heavier. All types most often chestnut.

Inflamed gingiva (L gum of mouth). See gum. **gingivitis**

(L cingulus, Gr zoster) A surrounding structure, eg pelvic **g**. See **girdle**
pelvis.

Clear colourless liquid with pungent odour. Applied to warts **glacial acetic acid**
after protecting surrounding area with petroleum jelly. See
milk warts.

(L glans, acorn) Small organ or structure which produces flu- **gland**
ids, eg hormones, enzymes, mucus, milk, saliva. **endocrine g.**
One which secretes directly into blood or lymph (rather than
through duct) and is effective at a distance, eg pituitary.
exocrine g. One which secretes through duct towards outside
of body, eg salivary.

Endocrine	Exocrine
adrenal	gastric
liver	Lieberkuhn (intestinal)
ovary	mammary
pancreas (islets of	pancreas
Langerhans)	prostate
parathyroid	salivary
pituitary	sebaceous
thyroid	sweat
testes	liver (bile)

lymph g. (syn node) not a true **g.**; see lymphatic system.
Endocrine and exocrine **g.**s further classified by their type of
fluid, viz, apocrine, holocrine and merocrine. **apocrine g.** One
that throws off part of cells with secretion, eg mammary.
holocrine g. One in which cells forming secretion come away
with the fluid, eg sebaceous. **merocrine g.** One in which cells
forming secretion remain intact, eg salivary.

(syn farcy) Contagious, notifiable disease of horse and man **glanders**
(see veterinary rules). First described by Aristotle 300 years BC.

glanders	Causal organism: *Loefflerella mallei* (syns malleomyces or pfeifferella) discovered by Loeffler and Schutz in 1882. Disease restricted to Eastern Europe, Asia and North Africa (eradicated in North America and not present in Britain since 1925). Infection is spread by contaminated fodder or utensils. Organism enters blood through gut wall and is localised in skin and mucosal surfaces, especially in nostrils. Symptoms, in acute form: high fever, cough, nasal discharge, ulcers and nodules which spread rapidly on nasal mucosa, legs and abdomen. Death occurs in a few days. In chronic form signs depend on where lesions occur, eg if in lungs there is chronic cough, nosebleeds and difficult breathing. Nodules in nostrils ulcerate producing blood-stained nasal discharge. Lymph nodes between angles of the jaw swell. Affected horse may be ill for several months then appear to recover, but remain a carrier. Eventually it relapses and dies. Diagnosis: on mallein test or complement fixation test on blood and isolation of germ from ulcers. There is no specific treatment. **genital g.** See dourine. **pseudo-g.** See epizootic lymphangitis.
glandular	Of a gland.
glans	(L acorn, pl glandes) Small, gland-like body. **g. clitoridis/clitoris** Tissue at end of clitoris. **g. penis** (syn rose) Cap-shaped tip of penis.
glauber's salt	See sodium sulphate.
glaucoma	(Gr glaukoma, opaque lens) Condition of eye characterised by increased pressure inside eyeball. See eye, diseases of.
GLDH	Abbr glutamate dehydrogenase, qv. Also abbreviated GDH.
globin	Protein constituent of haemoglobin, qv.
globulin	(L globules, globule) Class of protein insoluble in water, soluble in saline. Several types: alpha 1 and 2, beta, gamma. Latter contains antibodies which form basis of immunity, qv.
globulinuria	(globulin + Gr ouron, urine) Abnormal presence of globulin in urine.
glomeruli	Pl of glomerulus.
glomerulonephritis	Inflamed kidney (nephritis) in which capillary loops in glomeruli are affected. See kidney, diseases of.
glomerulus	(L from glomus, ball; pl glomeruli) Cluster, eg of blood vessels, nerve fibres or tufts of capillaries in kidney (renal **g**).

(Gr glossa, tongue) Combining form meaning relationship to tongue. **gloss-/glosso-**

Inflamed tongue. **glossitis**

Of tongue and pharynx. **glossopharyngeal**

Abnormal clucking noise made by soft palate, qv. **gluck**

(Gr gleukos, sweetness) Combining form meaning relationship to sweetness. **gluco-**

One of several hormones secreted by adrenal cortex, affects body's metabolism, such as build-up of glycogen and blood sugar (process known as glyconeogenesis/gluconeogenesis). See cortisone, mineralocorticoid. **glucocorticoid**

(1) Carbohydrate in blood, being simple sugar produced by enzyme breakdown of starch etc. (2) Colourless crystals or white powder, up to 2kg sometimes given to Thoroughbreds night before race or up to 0.2kg to foals suffering from maladjustment. Can cause diarrhoea in adult horse. **g. tolerance test** Assess absorptive capacity of small intestine in cases of weight-loss. **glucose**

(GLDH, GDH) Enzyme predominantly in liver and kidney. Normal level less than 5 IU/l serum, but increases in liver pathology. **glutamate dehydrogenase**

(abbr Gsh-Px) Enzyme in red blood cells, normally more than 50 IU/ml. Low levels found in selenium deficiency. **glutathione peroxidase**

(Gr glykys, sweet + haima, blood) Presence of sugar in blood. See hypoglycaemia; hyperglycaemia. **glycaemia**

(L glycerinum) Syrupy liquid used as softener or solvent for drugs. Given through stomach tube or as enema to foals. See meconium retention. **glycerin**

(Gr glykys, sweet) Combining form: relationship to sugar. **glyco-**

(glyco- + Gr gennen, to produce; syn animal starch) Body's main carbohydrate-storing substance. Formed by (and stored mostly in) liver, which releases it as glucose when needed. Small amounts stored in muscles. **glycogen**

Formation of glycogen, qv. **glycogenesis**

Accumulation of glycogen and blood sugar. **glyconeogenesis/ gluconeogenesis**

glycoprotein Chemical compound; a protein with a carbohydrate. Found in mucus, cartilage, synovia, virus capsule (see virus).

glycosaminoglycan See polysulphated glycosaminoglycan.

glycosuria (glyco- + Gr ouron, urine) Abnormally large amount of glucose in urine; symptom of kidney disease, diabetes (rare in horses), Cushing's disease, qv.

gnat Flying insect. In Britain colloq for mosquito, elsewhere insect smaller than mosquito. Can spread diseases, eg swamp fever, by sucking blood of affected horse and feeding on another.

gnotobiota Sterile life free from germs, as in gnotobiotic foal, one taken by caesarean section and reared in environment free from microbes, for experimental study.

goitre Enlarged thyroid gland, qv.

gonad (L gonas from Gr gone, seed) Sex gland of male (testis) or female (ovary). Grows large in foetus between 100 and 280 days' gestation, then reduces by full term. See gestational length.

gonadotrophin Substance stimulating gonads. 3 varieties: (1) those of anterior pituitary; (2) of foetus (chorionic); (3) of pregnant mare serum. See follicle stimulating hormone, luteinising hormone, pregnant mare serum **g**. Cf steroids.

gone in the wind Colloq for any respiratory unsoundness. See wind.

goneiis/gonitis Inflamed stifle joint.

GOT Abbr glutamic oxaloacetic transaminase. See AST.

Gotland (syns Russ, Skogsbagge) Swedish moorland breed in demand as child's pony, though some still feral. Appear to suffer rare brain condition similar to cerebellar degeneration, qv.

GPT Abbr glutamic pyruvic transaminase. See ALT.

gr. Abbr grain. See weights and measures.

Graafian follicle (after Dutch anatomist Reijnier de Graaf, 1641–73) Follicle (qv) in ovary.

graft (1) To implant skin or other tissue. (2) The skin etc so used. See skin graft.

gram (Fr gramme) Basic unit of mass of metric system, equivalent to 15.432 grains. See weights and measures. **g.-negative bacteria** Those bacteria which, stained with dye, are decolourised by alchohol, eg *Escherichia coli*, *Klebsiella pneumoniae*, *Proteus vulgaris*. **g.-positive bacteria** Those that resist decolourisation by alcohol, eg *Clostridium tetani*, *Corynebacterium equi*. **g. stain** (after Hans Christian Joachim **G**.) Method used in laboratory to identify bacteria. Bacteria on slide are (1) stained with gentian violet or methyl violet dye, (2) immersed in iodine, (3) decolourised with alcohol, (4) re-stained with carbolfuchsin dye.

granulation (L granulatio) Formation of soft, fleshy mass (proud flesh) in base of wound; contains numerous blood vessels. See wound.

granule (L granulum) Particle. See white blood cell, inclusion body, virus.

granulocyte (L granularis, containing granules or grains + Gr kytos, hollow vessel) Cell containing granules eg eosinophil. See blood.

granulosa cell Epithelial cell lining ovarian follicle and growing into blood clot after ovulation to form yellow body, qv (see ovary, follicle). **g.c. tumour** Abnormal growth of **g.c.**s in ovary and formation of cysts containing blood-stained fluid. The affected ovary may be large, or small and inactive. Causes infertility. Treatment: surgical removal.

grass See food **g. rings** See hoof rings. **g. sickness** Fatal condition of major disturbance of alimentary canal (not confined to horses at grass). First reported in Scotland in 1911 and most common there and in N England but occasionally occurs in S England, N France, Ireland and possibly USA. 4 types: (1) Per-acute – horse may die within 24 hours without previous attack. Symptoms: depression, fast pulse, absence of gut movement, regurgitation of green, evil-smelling fluid down nostrils, profuse sweating and sometimes pain. (2) Acute – death in 24–48 hours. Symptoms: similar to those in (1) plus jaundice, muscle tremor. On rectal examination hard faeces can be felt in colon. (3) Sub-acute – death in 10–21 days. Symptoms: as (1) and (2) plus increased jaundice, muscle tremors near elbow and between hip and stifle (possibly staggering), variable appetite, rising haematrocrit. (4) Chronic – death from exhaustion after 21 days. Symptoms: firm faeces often turning to diarrhoea. Diagnosis: on symptoms, impacted masses in colon and haematrocrit rising from 45 to 60 or 70 per cent. On postmortem green fluid, distending stomach, dry faeces in the colon, abnormal change in nerve cells (possibly responsible for paralysed gut). Cause: unknown, possibly infection with virus.

grass   Treatment: unlikely to be effective, but saline IV and injections of neostigmine or physostigmine may help. Siphoning off fluid from stomach eases pain temporarily. Purgatives have little or no effect on impacted faeces. Chronic cases occasionally live if given enough nourishment by stomach tube, but they are seldom capable of hard work again. Control: horse should be isolated to reduce risk of spread, but as cause is unconfirmed control is difficult. Infection might be carried by migrating birds. Moredun Research Institute, Edinburgh takes affected animals for research.

gravel   Black track in sole of foot, leading upwards into wall of heel. May be due to stone penetrating sole, more probably result of abscess or degenerating horn. See foot, abscess of.

gravid   (L gravida, heavy, loaded) Pregnant. See gestation.

gravida   Pregnant individual. **g.** I/II/III etc. Describes first, second, third pregnancy etc. **primigravida** Mare pregnant for first time. **multigravida** In foal for second or successive time.

greasy heel   (syn scratches) See mud fever.

Greener   Humane killer. See euthanasia.

grey/dappled g.   See coat colouring. **g. matter** See brain. **g. roan** See coat colouring.

Griffin   Colloq Chinese pony.

griseofulvin   (trade names: Dufulvin, Equifulvin, Fulcin, Grisol-V, Grisovin, Norofulvin) White colourless bitter powder; antibiotic capable of destroying fungus in skin and effective against ringworm (cure and prevention).

Groningen   Dutch farm/saddle/carriage horse, dying out. Similar to, but heavier than, Gelderland.

growth   (1) Normal process of increase in size. Height measured in hands, 1 hand = 4in (approx 10cm). Most rapid in first 3 months of life, when gain is only slightly less than during whole of next 9 months. See foetus, hand and various breeds. (2) Abnormal formation of bone or tissue (syns tumour, neoplasm). Arises from normal cells but different in behaviour and structure (leads useless existence, does not arise in response to normal body reaction). It may grow without regard for surrounding structures and can destroy them by infiltration or pressure. Known causes include virus, irritation and hormones. Classification based on clinical behaviour of **g.** (1) Benign or simple (those which grow slowly and rarely recur after removal, do not form seedlings (metastases) and are serious only if they press on surrounding tissues or ulcerate and bleed). (2) malignant (grow rapidly, infiltrate locally and produce seedlings (metastases) in other parts of body, recur after removal and cause serious consequences by destroying normal tissue and organs). **G.** also described by its cells, eg epithelial or connective tissue. Epithelial **g.**s include papilloma (benign) and carcinoma (malignant). Connective tissue **g.**s include fibroma (benign) and fibrosarcoma (malignant). Bone tissue **g.**s include osteoma (benign) and osteosarcoma (malignant).

growth

Growth	Arises from	Character
adenocarcinoma	glands	malignant
adenoma	glands	benign
*carcinoma	an epithelial surface	malignant
fibroma	beneath skin	benign
fibroma	fibrous tissue	benign
fibrosarcoma	fibrous tissue	malignant
*granulosa cell tumour	ovary	benign
hemangioma	blood vessels	benign
hepatoma	liver	benign
interstitial cell tumour	testicle	benign
lymphoma	blood-forming tissues (lymph nodes)	malignant
(1) leukemic	raised white blood cell count	
(2) aleukemic	decreased white blood cell count	
lipoma	fat in abdomen	benign
melanoma	skin (esp.nr tail in greys)	benign
*melanosarcoma	skin	malignant
osteoma	bone	benign
osteosarcoma	bone	malignant
*papilloma (wart)	skin	benign
polyp (papilloma)	nasal passage, bladder	benign
*sarcoid (angleberry)	skin	**semi-malignant
*squamous cell carcinoma	skin, sinus	malignant
*teratoma	ovary/testis (see dermoid cyst)	benign

*relatively common
**grows rapidly, recurs after removal; but does not form seedlings

Region at end of long bone formed by cartilage cells dividing and becoming incorporated into bone, thereby increasing its length. Growth plates close at varying times up to age five, eg at ends of cannon bones by 6–9 months, ends of radius and tibia about 18 months.

growth plate

Abbr glutathione peroxidase, qv.

Gsh-Px

gubernaculum	(L helm) Structure which guides, eg **g.** testis. See descent of testes, rig, testis.
Gudbrandsdal	Hardy Norwegian horse/pony, sometimes dun with dorsal stripe.
gum	(L gummi; syn gingiva) (1) Membrane of upper and lower jaw which covers lower part of teeth. Regarded as part of buccal membranes (those of cheek) and their colour helps diagnose anaemia, internal haemorrhage (when they turn pale), disturbed blood system (purple) or shock (remain blanched after pressure of thumb removed). (2) Excretion of plants, some types used in drugs, eg tragacanth mucilage.
gurgling	See wind.
gut	Colloq for intestine, bowel, alimentary canal. See alimentary canal, catgut.
guttural	(Of throat) **g. pouches:** paired air-filled sacs between ear and throat continuous with eustachian tube. Present in only Equidae and hyrax (small hoofed animal in Africa and Asia). Opening into throat protected by cartilage flap which opens only during swallowing. Each pouch has capacity of approx 300ml and it may become distended by air (tympany, qv), pus (empyema, qv) or by blood following haemorrhage from internal carotoid artery. Haemorrhage usually due to fungal infection (**g. p.** mycosis). See mycelium.
gyn-/gynaeco-/gyne-/ gyno-	(Gr gyne, gynaikos, woman) Combining form meaning relationship to female sex.
gynaecology	Branch of medicine dealing with diseases and conditions of female genital tract.
gyrus	(L, Gr gyros, ring) Tortuous convolution of surface of brain. See brain cortex.

H

(Gr habros, graceful + nema, thread). See stomach worm.

habronema

(syn summer sores) See stomach worm.

habronemiasis

(1) To ride casually rather than in particular fashion. (2) Any horse used for riding, not a specific breed. Most popularly mixture of breeds such as cob, Thoroughbred, Anglo-Arab. British Show **H.**, Cob and Riding Horse Assn, 88 High St, Coleshill, W. Midlands B46 3BZ (01675 466211).

hack

(Fr haquenée) Harness horse: 14.3–15.2 h, or pony: 12–14.2 h. Descended from English trotting horses which had some Thoroughbred blood. Now characterised by particularly high-stepping trot. **H. Horse Soc**, Clump Cottage, Chitterne, Wilts BA12 0LL (01985 850906).

Hackney

Agglutination (clumping) of red blood cells by serum, as a result of an antibody/antigen reaction. **h. inhibition test** Basis of blood pregnancy test (see pregnancy test).

haemagglutination

Antibody (qv) that causes clumping of red blood cells.

haemagglutinin

(Gr haima, blood + Gr arthron, joint) Bleeding into joint or synovial cavity; follows injury. Joint fills, causing pain.

haemarthrosis

(haemato + Gr krinein, to separate) See packed cell volume.

haematocrit

(haematocyte + Gr ouron, urine) Presence of red blood cells in urine. Cf haematuria, haemoglobinuria. See stone; setfast.

haematocyturia

Science of blood.

haematology

See blood blister.

haematoma

Blood in urine (term less specific than haematocyturia, qv).

haematuria

Condition in which proportion of blood cells to plasma is greater than normal, ie above 50 per cent. Occurs, normally, after exercise and excitement; abnormally in dehydration, qv. See haematocrit.

haemoconcentration

Of movements concerned with blood circulation.

haemodynamic

Oxygen-carrying pigment of red blood cells formed in bone marrow. Consists of protein, globin combined with iron-containing

haemoglobin

haemoglobin pigment. Average **h.** in blood is 14g/dl; decreases in anaemia and haemolytic diseases.

haemoglobinuaria (haemoglobin + Gr ouron, urine + -ia) Presence of free haemoglobin in urine. Cf haematocyturia. See setfast; haemolytic jaundice.

haemolysin (haemo- + Gr lysis, dissolution) Naturally occurring substance which destroys red blood cells, causing haemolysis, eg in rare cases mare produces **h.** against red blood cells of her foetus. When foal is born it absorbs mare's **h.** from the first milk (colostrum) and suffers haemolytic jaundice, qv.

haemolysis Liberation of haemoglobin from red cells. Caused by the chemical haemolysin, by freezing, heating or contact with water. See haemolytic jaundice; jaundice.

haemolytic jaundice Disease of newborn foal caused by reaction between antibodies in dam's colostrum and foal's red cells. A few foetal red cells cross into mare's bloodstream and in rare instances, because of an inherited difference, they cause mare to produce antibodies; these are concentrated in the colostrum which foal swallows during its first feed; antibodies are absorbed through intestine lining into foal's bloodstream and destroy its red cells. Condition is result of inherited blood groups. Foetus is not affected until it is born because antibodies do not cross placenta. Symptoms vary. Acute cases develop within 36 hours of birth and jaundice is severe. Urine turns red and breathing and heart rate increase, especially on exertion. Foal dies in a matter of hours, unless treated. Other cases may not develop for 2–4 days and jaundice, although marked, does not cause severe symptoms until just before death. Diagnosis: on examination of blood, red cell count is below 3 million/cu mm, haemoglobin below 7g/100ml and haematrocrit below 20 per cent. Treatment: transfuse compatible blood to replace lost red cells. Prevention: mare's blood or colostrum can be tested for diagnosis in last two weeks of pregnancy. Foal should be muzzled in first 24–36 hours and fed donor colostrum and artificial milk. After 24 hours antibodies in mare's milk can no longer be absorbed by foal and it is safe to allow foal to suck from its dam. Once mare has been affected, she tends to suffer condition in subsequent pregnancies.

haemophilia (haemo- + Gr philein, to love) Disease characterised by inherited defect in blood cells. Rare, but reported in closely-related Thoroughbreds due to deficiency in coagulation factor 8. Probably sex-linked defect associated with sex chromosome X; **h.** carried by fillies and occurs only in colts. Symptoms: blood blisters in skin forming without apparent reason or on slightest knock. See chromosome; coagulation.

(haemo- + poiesis, formation) Forming of red blood cells in special tissues such as bone marrow. See red blood cell. — **haemopoiesis**

(haemo- + Gr rhegnynai, to burst forth; syn bleeding) Escape of blood normally contained in blood vessels, ie veins, arteries and capillaries. Occurs if these are broken by trauma, increased fragility of walls and/or increased blood pressure. **H.** may be external, eg in wound, or internal, eg in ulceration or rupture of vessel. (See birth **h.**) Blood may be from artery, vein or capillary. That from an artery is usually bright red and gushes out under pulsating pressure; from a vein it is darker and emerges in a steady flow. **H.** is stopped by natural mechanism of clotting (coagulation, qv) and can be helped by direct or indirect pressure (see tourniquet). **petechial h.** See bleeder; petechia. — **haemorrhage**

(haemo- + Gr sideros, iron) Form in which iron is stored. — **haemosiderin**

(haemo- + Gr stasis, halt) Cessation of bleeding. Adjective: haemostatic, as in the action of drug that stops bleeding. — **haemostasis**

Austrian mountain pony named after **H.** district. Origin obscure, now popular for pulling sleighs. Most often bay, chestnut or palomino-like with flaxen mane and tail. **H. Soc of GB**, 25 Hilltop Park, Rugby Road, Princethorpe, Warwicks CV23 9PW (01926 632516). **H. Registry of North America**, 14640 State Route 83, Coshocton, OH 43812 (614 829 2790). — **Haflinger/Hafflinger**

Usually horse with Arab or Thoroughbred on one side of pedigree, but can mean any cross-bred horse. — **half-bred**

(trade names: Fluothane, Halathane, Halothane) Liquid easily vaporised by extreme air/oxygen and used for general anaesthesia. Administered by open, semi-open or closed-circuit methods of inhalation. — **halothane**

White powder with slight odour. Drug given by stomach tube or in feed to kill whiteworms and seatworms. May also kill redworms and botfly larvae. — **haloxon**

4in (10cm) of horse's height. So-called because width of human **h.** (about 4in) can be used to gauge distance between ground and highest point of withers (qv). Smallest recent Equidae, known as miniature horse, is 4.3 **h** (19in or 48cm) and weighs 85lb (38.5kg). Falabella breed is about 7 **h** (28in or 70cm) and tallest, eg Shire, may reach 18 **h**. Forerunner of horse, Eohippus (55 million years ago), varied from 2.2 to 5 **h**. See evolution. — **hand**

One of best-known German breeds. Traces to Middle Ages when English Thoroughbreds were crossed with heavy types — **Hanoverian**

Hanoverian such as German Great horse. In 17th and 18th centuries breed modified to lighter cavalry type, which fell into 3 main groups: **H.**, Danish and Mecklenburg. Now popular for riding, especially dressage, though some claim **H.** is deteriorating due to apparent inability to breed true. **British H. Horse Soc**. Ecton Field Plantation, Sywell, Northants NN6 0BP (01604 492750).

haploid Cell containing single chromosomes (qv) as opposed to pairs. Cf diploid. Sex cells, eg spermatozoa and ova, are **h.**, containing 32 single chromosomes in the horse.

harvest mite (*Trombicula autumnalis*; colloq harvester, berry bug, orange tawney, red bug, chigger) Arthropod parasite belonging to family Trombiculidae. Has scarlet, red-orange or yellow velvety body. Adults and nymphs are free-living. Parasitic larvae hatch from eggs laid on ground. They cling to host and use saliva to digest outer layer of skin, to suck fluid. They attack head and legs of horse, causing itchy dermatitis, loss of hair and scabbing. Most common in autumn when larvae, whose natural hosts are rodents such as mice, crawl onto grazing horses. Diagnosis: on recovering larval mites in skin scrapings. Treatment: apply gamma benzene hexachloride (qv) to kill mites, then antiseptic lotion on sores. See mange.

HBLB abbr. Horserace Betting Levy Board, 52 Grosvenor Gardens, London, SW1W 0AU (0171 333 0043). The board has a veterinary committee which issues codes of practice on equine contagious diseases.

healing Process of making good an injury, particularly skin wound. **h. by 1st intention** Skin which unites without granulation (proud flesh). **h. by 2nd intention** Filling of wound with granulation tissue before skin cells (epithelium) grow over. See wound.

heart (L cor, Gr kardia) Muscular organ with 4 chambers which pumps blood through system of vessels – arteries, veins, capillaries. Weighs 3.5–6.8kg (8–15lb) and has walls of muscle (myocardium), lined on inside with membrane of epithelium (endocardium) and on outside (epicardium). **H.** is contained in tough sac (pericardium) and is divided into left and right. Each side has 2 chambers; the first (auricle or atrium) has relatively thin walls, the second (ventricle), below, has thicker walls. The left ventricle pumps blood to all parts of body so has thicker walls than the right, which pumps blood through lungs only. Between first and second chambers of both sides, there are valves (mitral on the left, tricuspid on right). These prevent blood returning to first chamber when the ventricles contract and force blood into aorta and pulmonary artery. These arteries have valves at their entrances; three cusps known as semilunar valves. They stop blood returning from arteries to the second chambers when heart relaxes and fills with blood from veins. See myocarditis; endocardium; pericarditis; aorta; aortic semilunar valves. **h., diseases of** Primary heart disease of humans is uncommon in horses; they rarely suffer coronary thrombosis or heart attack, nor is there evidence of angina. Secondary infection, from bacteria, virus or toxaemia is frequent. Conditions fall into following categories:

heart

1. Damaged heart muscle (myocardium) = myocarditis.
2. Damage to any one of 4 sets of valves = valvular endocarditis.
3. Haemorrhage from, or clot in, coronary arteries = coronary thrombosis.
4. Inflamed inner lining (endocardium) = endocarditis/outer lining (pericardium) = pericarditis.
5. Dilated chamber walls.
6. Rupture of wall of 1st chamber.
7. Abnormal increase in the thickness of the chamber wall = hypertrophy.

See myocarditis; pericarditis; thrombus; haemorrhage; endocarditis. **h. failure** Stopping or reducing of **h.** action. Caused by defect in organ, eg damaged valve, or by excessive strain, eg raised blood pressure in lungs due to broken wind condition. **h. impulse** Electrical activity which spreads through the **h.** muscle during each beat. Impulse starts at SA (sinoatrial) node and spreads into walls of first chamber, then to AV (atrioventricular) node. From there, travels into special bands of cells (bundle branches) to muscles of left and right second chambers (ventricles). Passage of impulse coincides with contraction of muscle and can be recorded in an electrocardiogram, qv. Abnormalities include ectopic beat (syns extrasystole, extra systolic beat, premature beat), one originating outside SA node. **h. murmur** Sound made by blood as it passes through **h.** May be set up by counter current (whirlpool effect). Classified according to pitch (low, high), quality (blowing, musical), area where most clearly heard (mitral, aortic, tricuspid) and place in relation to heart sounds (eg systolic or diastolic). May be benign result of condition which does not reduce **h.**'s efficiency, or pathological, when it indicates damage to heart valve. **ejection h.m.** One caused by forward-flowing blood being forced through relatively small opening. Intensity (volume) is graded from 1 (almost inaudible) to 6 (heard at a distance from chest). Grade 4 or over usually pathological. **h. muscle** (syn cardiac m.) One of 3 types of muscle. That which forms wall of **h.** chambers is not arranged in individual fibres, but is a sheet of muscle which has rhythmic properties. Cf striped muscle; smooth muscle. **h. rate** Normal adult: 35–40 beats per minute. May be slower at rest; increases in excitement,

heart | fever, anaemia. Foals at birth: 80–120 per minute; older foals: 60–80; yearlings: 40–60. **h. sounds** Movement of blood heard on auscultation with ear or stethoscope. Sounds divide into 2 phases, when muscle is contracting (systole) and relaxing (diastole). First sound (termed lubb) is low pitched and corresponds to muscle contracting and mitral and tricuspid valves closing. Second sound (termed dupp) has a higher pitch and occurs when semilunar valves close. Instruments such as phonocardiogram can record parts of these sounds which are inaudible to naked ear. Sounds are described according to where they are most clearly heard when stethoscope is used, eg mitral, aortic or tricuspid area. Abnormal sound usually termed a **h. murmur**, qv.

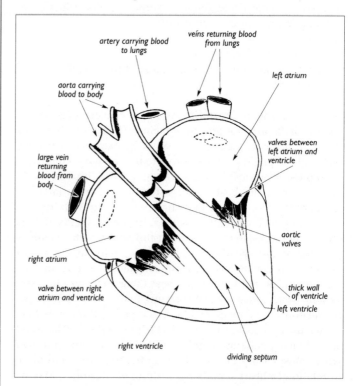

(left) **18** Heart from left side *(right)* **19** Right side of heart with walls of first and second chambers removed to show tricuspid valve

heat | (L calor, Gr therme) (1) Colloq for oestrus, qv. (2) Form of energy transferred by conduction, convection through air, or in electromagnetic waves by radiation. See physiotherapy; radiation. **h. exhaustion** Dangerous condition of extreme fatigue due to **h.** and/or exercise, eg in endurance races. See temperature; drycoat.

heaves | Type of abnormal breathing. See broken wind.

Hindmost part of foot. **contracted h.** See contracted **h. h. crack** | **heel**
See hoof crack. **greasy h.** (syn scratches) See mud fever. **run-under h.** (syn sloping **h.**) **h.** too far forward at angle more acute than toe, causing weakness. Leads to quarter cracks, bowed tendons, navicular disease, or deformed hoof. May be congenital or caused by neglect or improper shoeing. **sheared h.** Condition in which hoof is unbalanced at heel, displacing coronary band upwards and distorting frog and hoof wall. Result of uneven weight distribution so that one heel is lower. Coronary band of lower-heeled foot will be high; other side will have flared hoof wall at **h.** resulting in abnormal force to hoof wall (shearing force). May lead to tearing of laminae and sensitive structures. **straight/stumpy h.** One that is short and straight (**h.** angle higher than toe angle). Most often congenital and frequently associated with club foot but may result from injury, especially at coronary band.

Vertical measurement from ground to top of withers, qv. See hand. | **height**

Ulcer on cornea. See eye. | **helcoma**

(Gr helmins, worm) Parasitic worm. See tapeworm, stomach worm, strongyle, strongyloides. | **helminth**

See words beginning haem-. | **hem-**

(Gr hemi, half + plege, stroke) Paralysis of one side of body. **laryngeal h.** Paralysis of one side of larynx. See whistling, roaring. | **hemiplegia**

(hemi- + Gr sphaira, ball or globe) Half of spherical organ. **cerebral h.** See brain. | **hemisphere**

Occurs if plant, which contains an alkaloid, is eaten, though this is unlikely unless food is scarce. Symptoms: dilated pupils, weakness, staggering, loss of consciousness just before death. Treatment: purgatives, tannic acid and stimulants, eg strychnine or atropine. | **hemlock (Conium maculatum) poisoning**

Hybrid offspring of jenny donkey and male horse. Opp of mule. Since foetal size may be limited by dam's size, **h.** may be smaller than mule. | **henny**

Substance, formed by liver, which prevents blood clotting. Also, **H.** trade name for anticoagulant used when collecting blood samples. See blood tests. | **heparin**

(L hepaticus) Of the liver. | **hepatic**

hepatitis

Inflamed liver caused by bacterial, viral or parasitic infection, poisonous chemicals or plant toxins such as ragwort. **multifocal h.** In foals caused by *Bacillus piliformis* which infects gastric or liver lesions (may result from ingesting milk too high in steroids, eg from mare eating too much protein). Cf neonatal maladjustment syndrome. **serum h.** Usually fatal toxicity. Follows use of antiserum and characterised by jaundice, nervous signs, staggering and death. Thought due to virus or allergic reaction. See swamp fever; abortion, viral; tuberculosis; cirrhosis.

herbicide poisoning

May occur if horse allowed to graze next to field sprayed with weed-killer. Symptoms: loss of appetite, loss of weight, depression, muscular weakness. Postmorten findings: inflamed alimentary tract, liver/kidney changes and/or lung congestion.

hereditary

(L hereditas) Inherited. Established **h.** conditions include parrot jaw, HYPP, coat colouring. Suspected **h.** tendencies: navicular disease, temperament, cryptorchidism. See American Quarterhorse, rig, Welsh Mountain pony.

hermaphrodite

(Gr hermaphrodites) Individual with male and female tissue in sex organs. See intersex.

hernia

(L) Protrusion of abdominal (or other) contents (gut, organs) through opening in containing walls. May be inherited, congenital or caused by trauma. Consists of opening (ring) and pouch (sac) lined with peritoneum. **diaphragmatic h.** When abdominal contents pass through opening in diaphragm to chest. **scrotal h.** Abdominal contents pass into scrotum through inguinal canal. **strangulated h.** Contents of any type of **h.** squeezed by opening, causing pain and death if not relieved. **umbilical h.** Muscular ring (through which vessels pass to umbilical cord in foetus) does not close after birth and soft external swelling develops at 4–6 weeks. Can be reduced by pressing contents of sac back into abdomen. Cf umbilical abscess. Treatment: surgery to remove pouch and close ring. Essential for strangulated and diaphragmatic types though umbilical **h.** often disappears unaided by yearling stage. See inguinal.

herpesvirus

DNA virus infecting many species. **H.**s that infect horses are designated equine herpesviruses, qv. **h. vaccine** Vaccine (qv) to stimulate immunity against equine **h.** 1. Trade name: Pneumabort-K. Duvaxyn EHV1–4 protects against strains 1 and 4.

hexamine

Colourless odourless crystals, which taste at first sweet, then bitter. Given by mouth to acidify urine, to treat cystitis and infections of urinary tract.

Chemical symbol for mercury. **Hg**

(trade name Hexocil) Antiseptic used as skin wash. **hexetidine**

(colloq Garron) Largest of British mountain and moorland **Highland pony** types. Those on mainland up to 14.2 h, smaller on Scottish islands. Rhum Island ponies are probably oldest-established. Extremely strong breed used for pony trekking and carrying stags. Colours: black, brown, grey, dun and chestnut with flaxen mane and tail. Sometimes has black dorsal stripe. **H.P. Soc**, Beechwood, Elie, Fife, KY9 1DH (01333 330696).

(L a small thing) Part of organ where vessels and nerves enter, **hilus** eg on ovary, kidney.

Ball and socket joint formed by head of femur and acetabulum **hip** of pelvis. Joint is characterised by absence of external ligaments but contains round ligament, a short strong band attached to rim of acetabulum and notch in head of femur. **h. joint, dislocation of** Uncommon and can occur only if round ligament is ruptured. Symptoms include deformed angle of leg so that toe and stifle turn out and hock turns in. Treatment: anaesthetise, manipulate back into position, rest horse.

Ancient Gr for veterinary surgeon. **hippiatry** Veterinary med- **hippiatra** icine. Greeks based words on hippus (horse), showing their main veterinary interest was in the horse.

Combining form meaning relationship to horse. **hippo-**

(Gr horse madness; syn pad) Brown, yellowish, white or green- **hippomane** ish rubber-like structure in allantoic (placental) fluid of various animals. Develops in first 4 months of pregnancy and grows to form flat, oval, or rectangular object about 10cm x 5cm (4in x 5in), 1.5cm (thin) thick; made up of cells and salts; has no known biological function; traditionally believed to have mysterious powers. Often found on floor/ground after mare has foaled. Cf placenta.

(ancient Gr) Horse, as in Eohippus. See evolution. **hippus**

Substance produced from amino acid histidine when tissues **histamine** are damaged. Causes capillaries to dilate and become more permeable and water passes from blood into tissues, eg injection beneath skin causes area of oedema. **H.** also causes smooth muscle in uterus and lungs to contract and is released in anaphylactic reactions and allergies, eg in asthma it causes small air tubes to constrict.

histological | Of histology, eg **h. section** Small sample of tissue, usually mounted on slide, for studying under microscope.

histology | (Gr histo-, tissue + -logy) Detailed study of normal and abnormal microscopic tissues. Cf cytology.

Histoplasma farciminosus | Fungus which causes epizootic lymphangitis, qv. (Used to be called Cryptococcus or Blastomyces.)

Hobday | (after Sir Frederick **H.**, FRCVS; syns laryngeal ventriculectomy, ventricle stripping) Operation to relieve roaring/whistling caused by paralysed muscles controlling vocal and arytenoid cartilage of voice box (larynx). Usually performed under general anaesthesia, less commonly under sedation and local anaesthesia. Larynx is opened and a burr (round instrument covered with spikes) used to strip mucous membrane from inside cups formed by vocal cords. Part of cord may be removed. In healing, cords are pulled back against larynx walls so they no longer obstruct air passage. Horse is then mute. Often instead of, or combined with, 'tie-back' operation, qv.

hock | Joint in hind leg between gaskin (second thigh) and cannon bone, equivalent to human ankle. **capped h.** Soft swelling over point of **h.**, containing fluid in sac (bursa, qv) caused by bruising. Does not usually impair action.

holocrine | (holo- from Gr holos, entire + Gr. krinein, to separate) Type of gland (qv) in which entire secreting cell forms substance of gland, eg sebaceous gland.

Holstein | German horse used for driving and riding. Similar to Hanoverian but with little Thoroughbred blood. Believed to date from 13th century and to have been improved by imported Yorkshire coach horses (similar to Cleveland Bay but now virtually extinct). Most often brown. **American H. Assn** 222 E. Main St, Georgetown, KY 40324 (502 863 4239).

homatropine hydrobromide | Colourless crystalline odourless powder. Used in eye-drop solutions to dilate pupil. See mydriatic.

homeostasis | (homeo, combining form meaning unchanging + Gr stasis, standing) Tendency to stability, in normal body, eg blood levels of salts, sugar and protein.

homidium bromide | Dark purple bitter-tasting crystalline powder without smell. Used to treat some *Trypanosoma* spp infections. IM injection may cause local swelling.

homoeopathy | (Gr homois, like + pathos, disease). Therapy founded by

Samuel Hahnemann (1755–1843) in which drugs capable of causing disease in healthy animals are given in minute doses. This stimulates body's defences.

homoeopathy

(L ungula) Horny casing of foot, qv. **h. bound** See cracked heels. **h. crack** (syn sandcrack) Vertical split in **h.** wall classified according to location, eg toe, quarter, heel, etc. See sandcrack. **h. rings** (syn fever rings, grass rings, founder rings) Lines around outside hoof wall parallel to coronary band. Straight lines are considered normal and associated with changed environment, nutrition or body system. Wavy lines considered abnormal, especially if near heel, and often associated with disease, eg laminitis, hoof abscesses, thrush, ringbone, sidebone.

hoof

See influenza.

Hoppengarten cough

Of a hormone.

hormonal

(Gr hormaein, to set in motion, spur on) Chemical substance produced by gland or body organ and which travels in blood- or lymph stream to a distant part, on which it has an effect, eg follicle stimulating hormone (FSH) secreted by pituitary gland in head causes follicle to grow in ovary. **adrenocortical h.** One produced by part of adrenal cortex. **adrenocorticotrophic h.** One from anterior pituitary gland which acts on the adrenal cortex. **anterior pituitary h.** Secreted by anterior lobe of the pituitary gland. See gland; pituitary; sex; adrenaline; cortisol; oestrogen; follicle stimulating hormone; insulin; luteinising hormone; oxytocin; progesterone; prostaglandin; testosterone; thyroxine.

hormone

(L cornu) (1) Anatomical description for **h.**-shaped part, eg **h.** of uterus. (2) Hard cells which form hoof. See foot.

horn

Results from damage to sympathetic nervous system innervating the head. Symptoms include drooping of upper eyelid, protrusion of third eyelid, increased blood to mucous membranes of nose and eye, increased skin temperature over face and sweating, usually on the side of injury. Causes include damage to neck, infection of guttural pouch (qv), tumours, surgery in the region of carotid artery and vagus nerve. Condition may be temporary or permanent depending on cause.

Horner's syndrome

See Equus and various breeds. **American H. Protection Assn**, 1000 29th St NW, Washington, DC 20007 (202) 965–0500. **British H. Soc**, British Equestrian Centre, Stoneleigh, Warwickshire CV8 2LR (01203 696697). Cf pony. **h. fly** See tabanid fly. **h. sickness** See African horse sickness, Crofton

horse

horse	weed. **h. tails** (equisetum) Plant found on damp land which causes symptoms similar to bracken poisoning, qv.
host	(L hospes) Animal which harbours or nourishes a parasite, eg horse is **h.** of redworm.
hot-blooded	Colloq for any high-spirited horse, usually of Oriental origin, eg Thoroughbred. Cf cold-blooded, warm-blooded.
hot-spot	See scintigraphy.
hotting-up	Colloq for signs of 1st stage labour. See birth.
humane	With feelings befitting man, ie merciful. See blister. **h. killer/killing** See euthanasia.
humerus	(L, pl humeri) Long bone between shoulder joint and elbow joint (one either side of chest).
humour/humor	(L, a liquid) Term meaning oedematous swelling in body, particularly legs. See oedema. **aqueous h.** See eye.
Hungarian Shagya	Hardy horse similar to Arab but usually without dished face. Originated from Hungarian mares (similar to Przewalskis) crossed with Arab stallion named Shagya. Now used for riding and driving. About 14.2 h, most often grey.
hunter	Type rather than breed, the only essential being that it can stand a day's hunting. Divided into three groups for show purposes: heavyweight to carry 92kg (14st 7lb) or over, middleweight 82–92kg (13–14st 7lb); lightweight under 82kg(13st). **National Light Horse Breeding Soc (HIS)**, 96 High Street, Edenbridge, Kent, TN8 5AR, (01732 866277). **British Field Sports Soc**, 367 Kennington Rd,. London, SE11 4PT. (0171 582 5432).
hyaline	(Gr hyalos, glass) Glassy, transparent as in **h.** membrane of lungs of newborn foals suffering from convulsions. See neonatal maladjustment syndrome. **h.** cartilage.
hyaluronate	See sodium **h.**
hyaluronic acid	Substance in joint fluid and cartilage. Synthetic **h.a.** injected into joint, tendon sheath or vein to reduce joint or synovial inflammation.
hybrid	(L hybrida, mongrel) Animal or plant produced from parents of different strains, breeds or species. **h. equine pregnancy** Term used in embryo transfer, qv, between species. **h. vigour**

Improvement in offspring when unrelated strains or breeds crossed.

hybrid

See clay.

hydrated aluminium silicate

(Gr hydor, water) Combining form: of water or hydrogen.

hydra-

(hydro-, from Gr hydor, water + kephale, head) Abnormal accumulation of fluid in head. May be congenital or acquired. In either case, due to interference with drainage of cerebrospinal fluid. Rare in horses.

hydrocephalus

White crystalline odourless powder with slightly bitter taste. Increases excretion of sodium in urine; used as diuretic to treat oedema.

hydrochlorothiazide

(trade name: Ef-Cortesol) White crystalline odourless powder with bitter taste. Has the general actions and uses of a corticosteroid, qv. See allergy; inflammation; corticosteroids; cortisone.

hydrocortisone

Colourless odourless liquid with slightly acid taste; also known as 20 vol **h.p.** indicating volumes of oxygen obtained from one volume of solution; used as antiseptic and deodorant, to wash wounds, especially of feet because these are likely to be contaminated with anaerobic bacteria such as those causing lockjaw. Bleaches hair and other coloured organic matter.

hydrogen peroxide solution

Accumulation of fluid in pericardium (sac surrounding heart). Present in septicaemia, qv. See oedema.

hydropericardium

(hydro- + Gr phobos, fear) Fear of water, as in sign of rabies.

hydrophobia

(L Gr) Abnormal accumulation of fluid in membranes surrounding foetus.

hydrops amnii

Accumulation of fluid in pleural cavities, ie surrounding lungs. Caused by heart failure and septicaemia.

hydrothorax

Long-acting progesterone, qv.

hydroxymethyl-progesterone

(syn big knee, capped knee, carpitis, popped knee) Swelling, usually in bursa, eg on front of knee. Caused by a kick, falling on knees, hitting fence or, rarely, by kneeling, cowlike, when getting up. Severe case may be caused by broken carpal bone (hence carpitis). Treatment: remove cause, eg if horse paws at manger, place feed on ground unless soil is sandy (see colic),

hygroma

hygroma	drain fluid, inject corticosteroids, apply elastic bandages. Chronic injury may need surgery.
hyoid	(Gr hyoeides, u-shaped) Bone between vertical parts of lower jaw. Supports root of tongue, throat and voice box and is attached to skull by rods of cartilage. Sometimes fractured by trauma, causing difficult swallowing.
hyperaemia	(hyper- + Gr haima, blood) Excess blood in a part. See haemorrhage, inflammation.
hypercalcemia	(hyper-, above/more than normal + calcium + Gr haima, blood) Excess calcium in blood; above 11–15g/100ml blood serum.
hypercapnia	(hyper- + Gr kapnos, smoke) Excess of carbon dioxide in blood; normal: 40mm Hg pressure in arterial blood.
hyperextension	Over-extension of limb or joint. See stay apparatus.
hyperflexion	Overflexion, as in **h.** of limb. See contracted tendons.
hyperglycaemia	(hyper- + Gr glykys, sweet + haima, blood) Abnormally high level of sugar content in blood. Normal level: 3.5–5.9mmol/l blood. Cf hypoglycaemia.
hyperimmune serum	Solution of antibodies prepared from horse vaccinated to produce extremely high levels of antibody in blood. Serum is then taken and put into another individual to protect against infection, eg tetanus antitoxin, the antidote of lockjaw.
hyperkalaemic	Having excess potassium in blood. **h. periodic paralysis** (HYPP) muscle disease of, predominantly, Quarterhorses which causes uncontrolled muscle twitching, attacks of paralysis and sometimes death from cardiac arrest or respiratory failure. Caused by genetic defect and, from 1999, American Quarterhorse authorities test all foals tracing to stallion Impressive. Cf hypokalaemia.
hyperlipaemia/ hyperlipidaemia	Excess fat in blood. Condition seen in fat ponies which are stressed, eg heavily in foal and have sudden reduction in food intake. Can be fatal. Treatment includes inducing foaling, fluids, corticosteroids.
hyperparathyroidism	Increased amount of parathyroid hormone (parathormone) secreted by parathyroid glands; causes removal of calcium from bones, raising calcium level in blood. **primary h.** Caused by tumour of glands. **secondary h.** Caused by low levels of calcium in blood as a result of (1) low calcium or high phosphate diet, (2) failure to absorb calcium from intestine, (3) pregnancy

and lactation, (4) rickets (qv). Severe case may suffer loss of bone, which is replaced by fibrous tissue (osteitis fibrosa). See calcium and phosphorus, bone.

hyperparathyroidism

Excessive phosphates in blood. Normal level: 3–6g/100ml blood serum.

hyperphosphatemia

(hyper- + Gr plasis, formation) Abnormal multiplication of normal cells.

hyperplasia

Excessive salivation. See choke, grass sickness.

hypersalivation

Raised temperature. See temperature.

hyperthermia

(syn ex-ophthalmic goitre) Over-activity of thyroid gland and excessive uptake of iodine from blood. Too much thyroid-stimulating hormone (TSH) is produced and gland becomes enlarged and fibrous with an excess of colloid.

hyperthyroidism

(Gr hyper, above + trophe, nutrition) Overgrown organ/part due to increase in size of its cells. **h. pulmonary osteoarthropathy** See osteoarthropathy. Noun: hypertrophy, eg h. of heart muscle due to disease or increased work.

hypertrophic

Increased exchange of air in lungs due to deeper or faster breathing.

hyperventilation

(Gr hypo-, under or below + calcium + Gr haima, blood) Abnormally low levels of blood calcium.

hypocalcaemia

(hypo- + Gr chrome, colour) Decrease in haemoglobin content of red blood cells.

hypochromia

Genus of warble fly, qv.

Hypoderma

Beneath skin, eg **h.** injection.

hypodermic

Condition in which there is too little flexion in muscles and tendons supporting legs. Affects newborn foals; cause unknown. Pastern bone descends so that fetlock is close to, or on, ground, usually in all 4 legs. Treatment: bandage joints to give support and, possibly, give antibiotics. Cf hyperflexion.

hypoflexion of limbs

Abnormally low levels of gammaglobulin in blood. See immunity.

**hypogamma-
globulinaemia**

(hypo- + Gr glykys, sweet + haima, blood) Abnormally little glucose in blood. Occurs in newborn foals which are weak and ill-nourished; not usually associated with convulsions, as

hypoglycaemia

hypoglycaemia	would be case in adult horses. Cf hyperglycaemia.
hypokalemia	Abnormally low level of potassium in blood. Often occurs in chronic diarrhoea.
hypophysectomy	Removal or destruction of nerve supply of pituitary gland (syn hypophysis). Usually experimental.
hypoplasia	(hypo- + Gr plasis, formation) Incomplete or otherwise faulty development.
hyposodonty	Having long teeth. Sign of old age. Noted in study of equine evolution, to determine length and type of teeth and therefore type of food eaten and period when fossilised remains lived. Opp brachydonty. See evolution.
hypothermia	(hypo- + Gr therme, heat + -ia) Temperature (qv) below normal ie 38°C (100.4°F).
hypothyroidism	Any condition caused by inactivity of thyroid gland, when its uptake of iodine from blood is negligible.
hypotonia	Reduced activity or tone, eg of muscle in a wasting or congenital condition.
hypoventilation	Reduced air exchange in lungs as a result of shallow or slow breathing.
hypoxaemia	Low level of oxygen in blood; usually measured in pressure; normal 80–100mm Hg. See anoxaemia.
hypoxia	Low oxygen content. See anoxia.
HYPP	Abbr hyperkalaemic periodic paralysis, qv.
hysterectomy	(Gr hystera, uterus + ektome, excision) Surgical removal of uterus, rare in mares.
hysteroscopy	Visualisation of uterine lining with instrument known as hysteroscope (an endoscope).

I
Chemical symbol for iodine, qv.

IAP
Abbr intestinal alkaline phosphatase, qv.

Iceland/ic
Pony developed from Norwegian and Irish ponies taken to **I.** by first settlers. Extremely hardy with shaggy dun coat and usually about 12.2 h. Now used for riding or as pack pony but at one time settlers ate ponies' flesh and enjoyed encouraging stallions to fight. **I. Horse Soc of GB**, 12 Clare Court, North Berwick, East Lothian, EH39 4BZ (01620 893391).

ichthyosis
Condition in which skin becomes dry and rough as a result of excessive growth (hypertrophy) of horny layer. Cf drycoat.

ICSH
See interstitial cell stimulating hormone.

icteric
Of jaundice.

icterus
(L) Yellow discolouration of skin, tissues and organs. Adjective: icteric. See jaundice.

idio-
(Gr idios, own) Combining form meaning self or separate/distinct.

idiopathic
(idio- combining form, relationship to self) Of unknown cause.

idiosyncrasy
(idio- + Gr synkrasis, mixture) Habit peculiar to an individual; his/her unusual susceptibility to a drug, protein or substance. See allergy.

ileo-
Combining form, of or related to, ileum.

ileocaecal
Of ileum and caecum, particularly **i.** opening into caecum, at which impaction may lodge or ulcer form. **i. valve** Projection of mucous membrane; prevents food passing from caecum to ileum. See colic.

ileum
End part of small intestine opening into caecum. See alimentary canal.

ileus
(L, Gr eileos, from eilein, to roll up) Obstructed intestines due to lack of movement. **meconium i.** Stoppage due to first dung. See meconium retention. **paralytic i.** Paralysis of gut. See colic.

ilio-
Combining form, of or related to ilium or flank.

iliac thrombosis (syns thrombosis of posterior aorta or iliac arteries) Blood clot (see thrombus) which decreases blood supply to hind legs. May be caused by disease of artery, redworm larvae damaging artery, or by infection; most common in geldings following castration. Symptoms: lameness, painful spasm of muscles if exercised, sweating, anxiety. Affected leg will be cooler than opposite one and veins stand out less. No satisfactory treatment apart from rest.

ilium (pl ilia) One of 3 bones comprising pelvis (see ischium and pubis); consists of a wing, broad flat part to which gluteal muscles are attached, and shaft joined to ischium. Tuber coxae (point or angle of hip) and tuber sacrale (croup) are part of ilial wing.

immaturity Lack of maturity or development. Applied to whole or part of animal. **i. of behaviour** During period of learning. See behaviour. **i. of newborn** Foal which is weak, undersized and undernourished, born after 325 days' gestation (300–325 days usually termed premature). **sexual i.** Not having reached full sexual powers, before puberty. See maturity. **i. of skeleton** Before growth of bone has stopped. All bones have stopped growing by age 5 years but individual bones stop at various ages, eg cannon at about 12 months; forearm (radius) 24 months. Growth occurs at ends of bones (epiphyses). See growth plate.

immune (L immunis, safe) Protected against particular disease, eg by vaccination.

immunity (L immunitas) Exemption from something unpleasant. Individual resistant to infection said to possess **i.** (opp susceptibility). **I.** may be natural or acquired; active or passive. **acquired i.** Reaction of body following vaccination or contact with infection. **breed i.** Some breeds are more resistant to infection than others. **inherent i.** Inherited **i. natural i.** Body's resistance without external stimulation, eg skin, mucous membranes, secretions produced by cells and acidity of secretions all provide barriers to invasion by bacteria. **passive i.** Transference of **i.** by innoculation with serum from an immune individual to a susceptible one. **species i.** Certain diseases such as tuberculosis, anthrax, rabies are common to most species, but many diseases are species specific, eg human diphtheria does not affect horses.

immunology Science of immunity.

immunoglobulin Antibody, qv.

See colic.	**impaction**
Drug in tablet or other solid form for inserting beneath skin. Prepared so that drug leaves site at a steady rate over weeks or months. Most often used to give oestrogen and progesterone in treating infertility.	**implant**
(from L in, not + potentin, power) Lack of sexual power; in stallion lack of sexual drive (libido), ie mounting behaviour, pelvic thrust, erection of penis or ejaculation. **temporary i.** May occur if horse is ill or inexperienced. See behaviour.	**impotence**
Loss of appetite. Occurs with fever, colic. Early sign of ill-health. Cf anorexia.	**inappetence**
(L incidere, to cut into) Front tooth. See teeth.	**incisor**
Minute structure in cytoplasm or nucleus of cell, often containing virus, eg negri **i.b.** in cytoplasm of nerve cell in rabies; Cowdray A **i.b.** found in nuclei of lung and liver in herpesvirus 1 and adenovirus infections.	**inclusion body**
(L incontinentia) Unable to control urination or defecation. See enuresis.	**incontinent**
Uncontrolled movement. See cerebellar degeneration, encephalomyelitis, hyperkalaemic periodic paralysis, lockjaw, meningitis, wobbler syndrome, segmental myelitis.	**incoordination**
(L incubatio) Act of hatching. In laboratory, process by which viruses or bacteria are inoculated into special substances known as media. Germ then grows after being incubated at certain temperature (usually 38°C). **i. period** Time between infection and appearance of symptoms, eg glanders: 1–3 months or more, influenza: 1–5 days.	**incubation**
One of small bones of ear, qv.	**incus**
Failure to digest, ie poor digestion. See colic.	**indigestion**
Australian plant poisonous to horses. See birdsville disease.	**Indigofera dominii**
(L in, not + ducere, to lead) To cause. See oxytocin.	**induce**
Form of heat treatment. See physiotherapy.	**inductothermy**
(L infarctus) Death of tissue due to obstructed blood circulation. Occurs in small intestine due to lodging of blood clot that has broken away from aneurism (qv) caused by redworm infection.	**infarct**

infection | Nonspecific condition caused by bacteria, fungus, virus. Fever, dullness and disturbed functions in particular organs are diagnostic, eg lungs (pneumonia), kidneys (nephritis) and liver (hepatitis). **local i.** that in, eg, abscess, metritis (inflamed uterus). Type of **i.** can be diagnosed by examining white blood cell count and differential; bacterial **i.** causes marked increase in total white blood cells and/or an increase in polymorphonuclear leucocytes; viral **i.** causes increase in lymphocytes, (although some viruses, eg arteritis, cause a reduction in white cell count and a depression of lymphocytes); parasitic **i.** is characterised by an increase in eosinophils. (See blood tests.) If there is a discharge, or if fluid/tissue can be obtained by needle puncture or biopsy, the **i.** can be identified by laboratory growth.

infectious | Capable of being spread by infection. **i. anemia** See swamp fever. **i. equine bronchitis/cough** See influenza. **i. equine encephalomyelitis** See encephalomyelitis.

infective arthritis | See joint-ill.

infertility | (L in, not + fertilis, fruitful) Inability to conceive. In mare, may be due to fault in genital organs, eg underdeveloped ovaries or, more commonly, infection of uterus. In stallion may be due to immature behaviour which inhibits ejaculation or to poor-quality semen. Term relative to definition, eg mare said to be infertile if she does not conceive in given period; serious **i.** is when mare fails to breed in 2 or more consecutive stud seasons, stallion fails to impregnate 60 per cent of 40 mares (or fewer). Treatment: hormones, antibiotics, good management.

inflammation | Tissue reaction to injury. Symptoms: redness, heat (due to more blood vessels in area opening up), swelling (due to vessels becoming more permeable, so fluid passes into tissue spaces) and pain (due to stretched nerve endings). Blood vessels release white blood cells, antibacterial and antitoxic materials which clump bacteria together. White cells (phagocytes) invade area and, with amoeboid action, remove dead cells. Treatment: assist and control **i.** by applying heat (to draw blood to part) then cold (to draw it away). Phenylbutazone and cortisone reduce pain and swelling, antibiotics counteract any infection. See physiotherapy; oedema.

influenza | (syns flu, infectious equine bronchitis, Newmarket cough, Hoppengarten cough, infectious equine cough) Highly infectious disease caused by myxovirus, two main types known: A/equi 1 (Prague strain), A/equi 2 (Miami) and A/equi 2 (Kentucky 81). Symptoms: fever: 39–41°C (102.2°–105.8°F), watery nasal discharge, persistent hacking cough, shivering, loss of appetite, inflamed throat. Signs are present for about 48 hours, although some horses cough for several weeks after apparent recovery. Secondary bacterial infection is uncommon. Diagnosis: on symptoms and increasing levels of antibodies in blood between acute and convalescent stage. Culture of virus may be possible from nasal washings. See blood (seriological tests), virus. **i. vaccine** Solution which, when injected, gives immunity against **i**. **i.v.**s include Duvaxyn IE, Prevac, which contain inactivated **i.** virus. Recommended at 4–6 weeks, with boosters at 6 and 12 months, then annually, by intramuscular injection only. *influenza*

Energy rays between 7,700 and 120,000 angstroms. Used to heat foaling boxes. **infrared**

Pertaining to groin; inguinal region. **i. canal** Passageway between abdomen and scrotum, with internal **i.** ring at upper end, external **i.** ring at the lower end. See descent of testes; rig; hernia. **i. hernia** see hernia. **inguinal**

Drug or substance which is breathed in, eg benzoin for colds or infected sinus. **inhalant**

(L injectio) Act of forcing liquid into cavity or part of body. **hypodermic i.** One below skin; usually with syringe and needle. **intradermal i.** One into substance of skin. See also intravenous, intramuscular, subcutaneous. **injection**

Colloq to vaccinate. To introduce serum vaccines or infectious materials or vaccines into body; to implant microorganisms onto culture media in laboratory. **inoculate**

Member of class Insecta, which belongs to phylum Arthropoda, qv. Typical **i.** body has head, thorax and abdomen, three pairs of walking legs and one or two pairs of wings; parasites such as flea and louse have lost both pairs of wings. Those important in equine medicine: sub-class Apterygota (order Phthiraptera) – louse, qv; order Siphonaptera – see flea; order Diptera – see bot, tabanid fly, warble fly. **insect**

(L insectum, insect + caedere, to kill) Substance or drug which destroys insects, used eg in control of African horse sickness, qv. **i. poisoning** Symptoms: overactivity of gut causing salivation, abdominal pain, diarrhoea, possibly vomiting, muscle twitching, weight-loss and death from respiratory failure. **insecticide**

(L inseminatus, sown) Act of introducing semen into vagina or uterus. **artificial i.** By mechanical process or apparatus. **natural i.** By coitus. See artificial insemination, behaviour. **insemination**

insertion	(L from in, into + serere, to join) Non-mobile point where the muscle is attached to bone.
inspiration	(L inspirare from spirare, to breathe) Act of drawing air into lungs. If accompanied by roaring/whistling or rattling noise, wind unsoundness likely. See wind.
insufficiency	(L insufficientia) Inadequate, low levels, reduced function. **cardiac i.** Abnormal pumping of heart.
insufflation	(L in, into + sufflatio, a blowing up) Act of blowing powder, gas or air into cavity, eg **i.** of lungs in artificial respiration, qv.
insulin	Hormone of the pancreas produced by beta cells of islets of Langerhans. **I.** is secreted into blood in response to a rise in the amount of glucose in blood. **I.** reduces levels through pro moting storage of glucose in liver, muscles and elsewhere. See diabetes.
intensive	Of great force or intensity. Term applied to continuous and extensive care of sick foals, colic or post-operative cases. **i. care** More common term than 'critical care'.
interfering	(syn speedy cutting) Action in which horse strikes part of inside of one leg with inside of foot or shoe of opposite leg. Point of impact may be from coronary band to knee (carpus) of foreleg or up to hock of hind leg. See gait.
interferon	Protein formed by cells when stimulated by virus. Capable of conferring infection-resistance on other cells in same animal, or in another individual given **i.** May be natural or synthetic. See virus.
interleukin	Group of proteins from macrophages and lymphocytes which evoke immune or inflammatory response by lymphocytes.
internal fixation	See fixation.
intersex	Individual with some anatomical characteristics of opposite sex, so diagnosis of sex is confused. May have: (1) some reproductive organs of both sexes; (2) female and male sex chromosomes in same cells or in two different lines of cells; (3) inherited material (ie that in spermatozoa or ova) of different sexuality to that in body cells. **true i.** (syn hermaphrodite) One with gonads of both sexes, either a separate ovary and testis or combined ova-testis (psuedo-hermaphrodite has gonads of only one sex but has reproductive organs with some characteristics of opposite sex; individual may be classed as male or female depending on gonad present, eg male has large female

external genitalia but possesses testis). **freemartin** Sterile female with male characteristics. Condition common in cattle twins, not reported in horses. See chromosome.

intersex

Of or in interstice, small space in tissue or structure. **i. cell stimulating hormone** (ICSH of stallion equivalent to **FSH** of mare) Produced by anterior lobe of pituitary gland, one of pituitary gonadotrophin group of hormones. Acts on **i.** cells of testes causing them to produce male sex hormone testosterone, qv.

interstitial

(IAP) Isoenzyme of alkaline phosphatase. As name implies, enzyme found in intestine. Normal range less than 20 IU/l, increases in intestinal pathology.

intestinal alkaline phosphatase

(L inward, internal; Gr enteron) Colloq for whole of alimentary canal, qv.

intestines

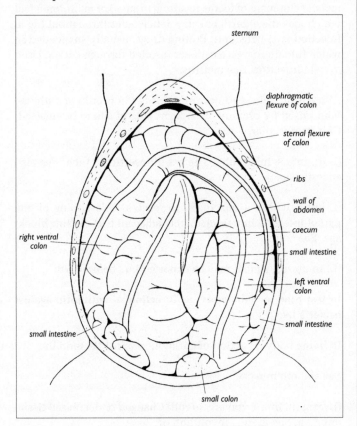

20 Intestines seen from below

(L within) Prefix meaning in. Opp extra-.

intra-

Into skin, eg injection.

intradermal

intramammary	Into mammary gland. **i. injection** Forcing of drug, usually antibiotic, through teat canal. Used to treat mastitis. May cause pain (canals of mare narrower than those of cow).
intramuscular/ly	(IM) Within muscle, eg site of drug injection; usually neck, hindquarters or brisket. Cf intravenous.
intranatal	During birth.
intraocular	(intra- + L oculus, eye) In the eye.
intraperitoneal	In the peritoneal cavity.
intratracheal	Into trachea (windpipe). See tube.
intrauterine	Into uterus. **i. growth retardation** (IUGR) Interruption of normal development of foetus resulting in small or malformed foal which may die at birth or carry deficiencies throughout life. **i. injection** (syn irrigation) Putting drugs, usually suspended in water, into uterus via a catheter inserted through cervix. Used to treat infection. See metritis.
intravenous/ly	(IV) Within vein, eg injection of drug via needle or catheter. Vein raised by pressing it on heart side of site to be injected. Cf intramuscular.
intubation	(L in, into + tuba, tube) The act of inserting a tube. See also anaesthesia.
intussusception	(L intus, within + suscipere, to receive) Telescoping of one part of intestine into immediately adjacent part causing blockage. See colic.
in utero	(L) In uterus, eg foal may be exported **i.u.**, before birth.
in vitro	In test tube, or laboratory, as in action of antibiotic against bacteria **i.v.**
in vivo	In living body, eg action of antibiotic against bacteria **i.v.**
involuntary muscle	See smooth muscle.
involution	(L from in, into + volvere, to roll) Changed or decreased tissue or organ. See uterus, involution of.
iodine	(chemical symbol: I) Blue-black plates with metallic lustre, distinct penetrating odour and acrid taste. Used in solution, externally, to treat ringworm. I_{131} Test dose of radioactive i. Its course in body can be followed with a geiger counter and

amount circulating measured in blood plasma. Used to test activity of thyroid gland, qv.	*iodine*
(Gr ion, going) An atom with a positive (cation) or negative (anion) charge of electricity.	**ion**
(irido- + Gr kyklos, circle + -itis) Inflamed iris and ciliary body of eye. See eye, diseases of: moon blindness.	**iridocyclitis**
Pigmented diaphragm in front of eye's lens with variable hole in centre (pupil) which regulates amount of light entering eye. See Albino, eye.	**iris**
Of Ireland. See veterinary surgeon. **I. breeds**: Connemara, qv; draught, qv; Thoroughbred, qv. **I. Hobby** Pony of Middle Ages, around 14 h. Believed to have had ambling gait and to have originated from Spanish jennet, qv.	**Irish**
Inflamed iris. See eye, diseases of.	**iritis**
Excessive **i.** is toxic. Symptoms: diarrhoea, drowsiness, shock and coma. Treatment: give milk of magnesia, milk of lime and treat for shock, qv. See poisons.	**iron poisoning**
(L in, into + radiare, to emit rays) See radiation.	**irradiation**
Abbr immune-stimulating complexes denoting special method of presenting antigen (immune-stimulating substances) to evoke an increased response over more traditional means of presentation. Therefore used to develop vaccine, qv.	**ISCOMS**
(Gr ischein, to suppress + haima, blood) Deficiency of blood to a part, eg to hindleg in iliac thrombosis, qv.	**ischemia**
One of 3 bones comprising pelvis (see ilium and pubis). Forms back of pelvic floor (front is pubis). See pelvis.	**ischium**
Volatile liquid used for general anaesthesia.	**isoflurane**
(isonicotinic acid hydrazide) Chemical used to treat bacterial microbes that enter body cells, such as *Rhodococcus equi*, the cause of pneumonia (qv) in foals. See tuberculosis.	**isoniazid**
Fluid in equal concentration with another, eg 0.9% sodium chloride (salt) is **i.** with fluid concentration of body cells. This means such a fluid can be injected without damaging cells; if applied to eye will not smart.	**isotonic**
A chemical element with a particular atomic mass. Radioactive	**isotope**

isotope　by an element possessing radioactivity. Used in medicine for nuclear imaging or scintigraphy, qv.

isoxsuprine hydrochloride　(trade names: Circulon, Navilox) Chemical with sympathomimetic (adrenergic, qv) action. Used as a vasodilator in treatment of laminitis (qv) and conditions where vascular insufficiency exists. May be administered orally or intramuscularly.

IV　Abbr intravenous/ly, qv.

ivermectin　(trade names: Eqvalen, Panomec) Anthelmintic (qv) drug used to treat and control gastrointestinal parasites including bot (qv) larvae and lungworms. Particularly effective because it kills larvae migrating through tissues as well as adults living in the intestines.

J

jack Male ass, qv.

janet Female mule, qv.

jaundice (Fr jaunisse, from jaune, yellow; syn icterus) Condition in which too much bile pigment circulates in blood and is deposited in tissues and organs. Yellow colour can then be seen in mucous membranes of mouth, eye and vagina. Due to: (1) excessive breakdown of red blood cells, liberating large quantities of haemoglobin from which bile pigment is formed, as in haemolytic disease of newborn foals, swamp fever; (2) damaged liver which cannot excrete haemoglobin brought to it as a result of normal destruction of red cells, as in poisoning with ragwort, chloroform, lead, arsenic, copper, phosphorus, carbon tetrachloride or infection with bacteria or virus; (3) obstructed bile ducts leading from liver, so that pigment seeps back into blood instead of being excreted into gut, as in whiteworm infection, impacted colic or growth. See hepatitis; haemolytic jaundice; colic; poisons; haemolysis; haemoglobin.

jaw One of 2 bony structures in head bearing teeth. **lower j.** Formed by mandibular bones and carrying lower incisor and molar teeth. **parrot j.** See parrot jaw. **upper j.** Formed by maxillary bones and carrying upper incisor and molar teeth. See skull; teeth.

jenny Female ass.

Jockey Club See Thoroughbred, veterinary rules.

joint (syn articulation) Union of 2 or more bones capped by cartilage or other tissue. **amphiarthrodial j.** Bones directly united by cartilage and ligaments and with limited movement, eg between vertebrae. **diarthrodial j.** Bones united by a capsule, with surfaces in a cavity containing fluid and having movement. J. usually has smooth surfaces of dense bone or cartilage, j. capsule with fibrous outer covering and inner lining which secretes j. oil (synovia). Ligaments may support j. by binding bones together. Movement of j. may be gliding, eg knee (carpus), angular, eg leg j.s which flex and extend. Equine j.s do not normally circumduct, adduct or abduct (these movements are typical of human arm). **j.-ill** (syns infective arthritis, navel ill, pyemia) Erosion of j. surfaces caused by microorganisms, streptococci, salmonella or *E. coli*. Found in foals up to 6 months and in older horses that have suffered a penetrating wound.

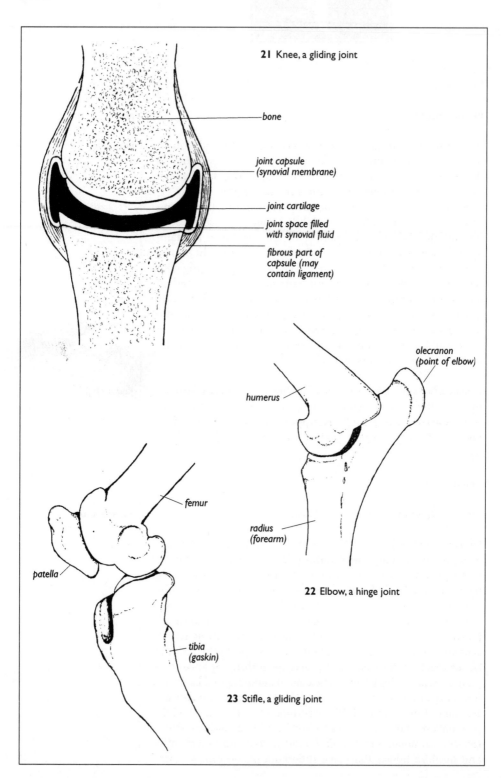

21 Knee, a gliding joint

bone

joint capsule
(synovial membrane)

joint cartilage

joint space filled
with synovial fluid

fibrous part of
capsule (may
contain ligament)

olecranon
(point of elbow)

humerus

radius
(forearm)

femur

patella

tibia
(gaskin)

22 Elbow, a hinge joint

23 Stifle, a gliding joint

Symptoms: painful swelling of j. especially knee, hock, stifle, hip and elbow, damaged surface either side of j. (probably causing lameness in later life), fever, anaemia, white blood cell count above 10,000 per cu mm, possibly abscess just inside navel. (Condition can be considered a local septicaemia, qv.) Cause: in foal, organism may enter body through mouth or navel (umbilicus) and become established if immunity is low (eg due to lack of colostrum). Diagnosis: on symptoms and finding pus cells in synovial fluid. Treatment: surgical removal of umbilical abscesses, inject antibiotics into j. and flush with sterile saline; disinfect to prevent organism spreading to other foals. **j. mouse/mice** Particles of bone which break off and lie free in j. cavity. Caused by trauma or arthritis. May be responsible for lameness. Diagnosed on X-ray and should be surgically removed. **synarthrodial j.** Bones united by fibrous tissue, bone or cartilage; no movement of j. cavity, eg skull bones, bones of pelvis. — *joint*

(L jugularis, jugulum, neck) Of neck, eg **j. vein,** one of 2 major veins in front of body. Each carries blood from head and lies in furrow on either side of neck. Site convenient for IV injection or collecting blood. — **jugular**

K	Chemical symbol for potassium.
kaolin	(syn China clay) White odourless and tasteless powder. Given by mouth to take up toxic substance (see poisoning) and form protective coating for mucous membranes. Also used as poultice, qv.
karyotype	Full set of chromosomes of a cell arranged in a standard order. Used when looking for chromosomal abnormalities and sexual defects such as individual lacking or possessing an extra sex chromosome eg XXX or XO instead of normal XX.
Kathiawari	Saddle horse named after peninsula on NW coast of India. Probably developed from Arab and Siwalik. Noted for its in-turning ears, tips of which almost touch.
Kentucky Saddle horse	See American Saddle horse.
keratin	Special type of insoluble protein, which contains sulphur. Main constituent of outer layer of skin, hair and horn. See eye, foot.
keratitis	Inflamed cornea of eye. See eye, diseases of.
keratoma	(Gr keras, horn + oma, suffix meaning tumour) Horny tumour in inner surfaces of wall of foot.
ketamine hydrochloride	(trade names: Ketaset, Vetalar) Drug which is used to produce short duration anaesthesia by intravenous or intramuscular injection.
ketoprofen	(trade name: Ketofen) Potent, non-narcotic, nonsteroidal anti-inflammatory drug with analgesic and antipyretic properties.
Kiang	One of 2 sub-species of ass. Lives in Tibetan mountains, in small herds and is very shy. See ass.
kidney	Organ which filters blood and forms urine, excreting waste products nitrogen, urea, acids and water. One on either side of aorta in upper part of abdomen. Right **k.** shaped as playing card heart; left **k.** bean-shaped. Each **k.** weighs about 680g (1^1/$_2$lb) (newborn foals about 170g (6oz); covered by thin fibrous capsule; consists of outer cortex containing glomeruli, qv, and inner medulla formed of collecting tubes which empty into

central pelvis, drained by ureter which carries urine to bladder. **K.** functions by filtering unwanted products from blood which passes through capillaries in glomerulus in close contact with thin-walled tube (loop of Henle and collecting tubule) that carries filtered fluid. Further exchange of salts, acid, water by contact of tubes with blood vessels produces urine, which passes to ureter. **k., diseases of** (1) Infection causing abscess. See sleepy foal disease, septicaemia of newborn foal. (2) Degeneration caused by bacterial toxins and metallic poisons. (3) Damage caused by massive quantities of haemoglobin in severe setfast (qv). (4) Haemorrhage due to back injury. (5) Stones, rare but may collect in **k.** See stone. Any inflammation of **k.** cells is termed nephritis. Nephrosis is rare condition in which **k.** is water-logged due to excess pressure if outflow of urine is blocked, eg by stone or congenital defect.

kidney

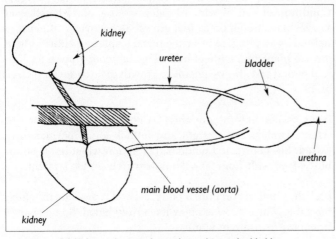

24 Kidneys, showing their relationship to the bladder

Aimless galloping, wasting, yawning and muscular spasm caused by poisoning from crotalaria plants (various types found in USA, Australia, S Africa).

Kimberley horse disease

Fast-disappearing Austrian/Bohemian breed, developed from Spanish jennet. Named after place in Czechoslovakia where bred at Imperial Stud. An ancestor of Lippizzaner; used as carriage horse and characterised by roman nose, heavy, arched neck and high action. Breeders aim for either black or white horse of 17/18 hands. Smaller **K.** now being bred to produce dressage horse.

Kladruber

Genus of gram-negative microorganisms (bacteria); with short rods and capsule, of tribe Escherichieae, family Enterobacteriaceae, order Eubacteriales. *K. pneumoniae* Subtypes I, II, V can be cause of infected genital organs and

klebsiella

klebsiella	spread by coitus. Occasionally responsible for abortion and septicaemia of newborn, qv. Treatment; antibiotics, especially neomycin; sexual rest. See abortion.
Klepper	Strong, long-lived pony of Baltic region. Often dun with black mane, tail and dorsal stripe.
Knabstrup	Danish spotted horse (with leopard, snowflake or blanket markings) similar to Frederiksborg in all but colour. Pure form almost extinct in Denmark but colouring has been passed on to many circus horses (cf Appaloosa).
knee	Colloq for carpal joint. True **k.** of horse is stifle. See carpal joint. **popped k.** See carpitis.
knock kneed	(syns medial deviation of carpal joints, carpal valgus) Condition of foal in which forelegs are too close together at knees. May straighten as foal grows. Severe cases sometimes helped by stapling, ie inserting metal staples on either side of growth plate, on inside of limb. This impedes growth for limited period and allows outside of growth plate to develop more quickly.
knuckling	(syns straight in front, upright) (1) Condition of young horse in which forelegs are straight and fetlock joints permanently flexed. See contracted tendons. (2) Action when horse stumbles. May result from fetlock joints which are too straight.
Konik	(Polish, small horse) Polish pony; several types, one of which resembles Tarpan; others may have Arab blood. Some change from grey to white in winter.

L

(L; pl labia) Lip, fleshy border, eg **l.** of vulva. **labium**

(L laboratorium, colloq lab) Place in which apparatus/machinery is used to investigate/experiment. Veterinarians should have **l.** or have access to one. **L.** tests used in clinical disease (abbreviations elucidated at foot of entry) **infection**: haematology, plasma viscosity, protein electrophoresis, fibrinogen, bacteriology, mycology, virology, serology; **intestinal parasitism**: haematology, protein electrophoresis, fibrinogen, IAP, faecal worm egg count, rectal biopsy; **liver abnormality**: AST, GLDH, LD, SAP, GGT, bilirubin, serum proteins and electrophoresis, BSP clearance, liver biopsy; **kidney abnormality**: urea, creatinine, serum proteins, urine analysis, electrolyte clearance ratios, bacteriology; **pancreatic abnormality**: GGT and serum amylase; **bone metabolism/parathyroid abnormality**: SAP, serum calcium and phosphate, urine phosphate clearance ratios; **intestinal abnormality**: SAP, IAP, protein electrophoresis, xylose and glucose absorption tests, peritoneal fluid cytology, rectal biopsy, faecal worm egg count and bacteriology, rotavirus assay, serum electrolytes, feed allergen tests; **pulmonary abnormality**: protein electrophoresis, fibrinogen, blood gas analysis, faecal lungworm larval examination, tracheal wash cytology, bacteriology, fungal allergen tests; **body fluid problems**: haematology, serum proteins and electrolytes, urine electrolyte clearance ratios, blood gas analysis; **skin disease**: scrapings, bacteriology, mycology, skin biopsy, feed allergen tests; **stallion reproductive abnormality**: genital bacteriology, semen analysis, testicular biopsy; **mare reproductive abnormality**: genital bacteriology, endometrial smear cytology, endometrial biopsy, plasma progestagens, serum eCG, oestrone sulphate, urinary oestrogens. **L.** tests in preventive medicine: **diarrhoea**: rectal/faecal bacteriology for salmonella, campylobacter, fluid faeces for rotavirus assay. **parasite control**: haematology, protein electrophoresis, faecal worm egg count, lungworm larval exam. **respiratory disease**: nasal/pharyngeal/tracheal wash bacteriology for *Streptococcus equi*, *Rhodococcus equi*. **ringworm**: skin scrapings. **venereal disease**: endometrial, clitoral/urethral, aerobic and microaerophilic bacteriology. Metabolic profiles performed at 36 hours old: haematology, proteins, serum IgG; in weanling and yearling: haematology, serum proteins and electrophoresis, fibrinogen, SAP, serum calcium and phosphate, urine phosphate clearance ratios; in horse in training: haematology, serum proteins and electrophoresis, fibrinogen, AST, CK, urine phosphate clearance ratios; in mature horse: haematology, serum proteins

laboratory

laboratory	and electrophoresis, fibrinogen, AST, CK, GLDH, SAP, IAP, GGT, urea, creatinine. **L.** tests as management aids – fitness: haematology, serum proteins, fibrinogen, AST, CK; pregnancy 45–95 days: serum eCG; more than 120 days: serum oestrone sulphate; more than 150 days: urinary oestrogens; luteal function; 19–23 days: plasma progestagens. Abbreviations: AST= aspartate aminotransferase (formerly SGOT – serum glutamic oxaloacetic transaminase); BSP=Bromsulphalein; CK=creatine kinase (formerly creatinine phosphokinase or CPK); eCG= equine chorionic gonadotrophin; GGT=gamma glutamyltransferase; GLDH=glutamate dehydrogenase; Gsh-Px= glutathione peroxidase; IAP=intestinal alkaline phosphatase; IgG=immunoglobulin gamma; LD=lactate dehydrogenase; MCH=mean corpuscular haemoglobin; MCHC=mean corpuscular haemoglobin concentration; SAP=serum alkaline phosphatase. See cross-matching, blood tests, dope test, filter, pregnancy tests.
labour	Part of foaling process divided into 1st, 2nd, and 3rd stage **l.** See birth.
laburnum poisoning	May occur if horse eats any part of plant, especially flowers and seeds which contain an alkaloid. See poisons.
labyrinth	(Gr labyrinthos) System of intercommunicating cavities or canals, eg in bone, qv or ear, qv.
laceration	(L laceratio) Wound, tear in skin. See wound.
lacrimal	(L lacrimalis, lacrima, tear) Of tears. **l. duct** Conveys tears from eyelids to discharge them close to nostrils. (Alternative spelling: lachrymal).
lactate	(1) To secrete milk from mammary glands, qv. (2) Salt of lactic acid. See birth; milk.
lactate dehydrogenase	(LD) Enzyme found in most tissues of body. Normal levels less than 400 IU/l in serum, increasing in muscle damage, heart muscle damage, pancreatitis and some types of liver damage. Five forms of LD (LD isoenzymes) in horse can be separated by electrophoresis: LD1 predominantly in red blood cells; LD2 in heart muscle; LD3 in most tissues; LD4 in intestines; LD5 in skeletal muscle and liver.
lactobacillus	Genus of bacterial family Lactobacillaceae. Gram-positive anaerobic bacillus. **L. acidophilus** Bacteria present in large gut concerned in digestion. Used for re-seeding gut during diarrhoea. Foals 5g twice daily in feed or as small drench, adults 50g daily.

Protein globulin in milk; normally passed by foal in urine during first 36 hours after birth.

lactoglobulin

(L dim of lamina, a thin layer) Thin leaf or plate of bone.

lamella

Disturbance in natural gait. Weight is unevenly distributed, in most cases so that horse can avoid as much pain as possible. **l., diagnosis of** Head and withers rise when painful foreleg meets ground; head is lowered as lame hind leg meets ground. Front limb lameness is best seen by watching head and withers; hind limb lameness by watching horse as it moves away – point of hip on side of lame leg rises as leg meets ground. Stride of affected hindleg is shortened. **L.** is best seen at walk or trot when severe cases readily detected, but slight **l.** may require considerable experience. After identifying lame leg, find site of pain by (1) palpation (pressure by fingers, or metal pincers over foot), (2) manipulation (flexing of joints and firm but forced retraction and extension of various parts of limb), (3) feeling for swellings and heat. Special techniques include radiography (X-ray), withdrawal and analysis of synovial fluid from joints, faradic stimulation of muscles (see physiotheraphy) and nerve block, qv. **l., cause of** Painful inflammatory reaction in part of limb. Origin may be (1) traumatic, as in sprains, strains, (2) infection, especially abscess in foot, local or general lymphangitis, (3) entry of foreign body, eg nail, thorn, etc in foot or higher in leg. Inflammation may affect joint surfaces and their capsules (arthritis and capsulitis) or ligaments that support joint; tendons (tendinitis) or sheaths (tenosynovitis) through which they pass; the lining of bones (periostitis); bones themselves (osteitis); lamina of pedal bone (laminitis), muscles (myositis) and bursae between muscle or tendon and bone (bursitis). Inflammation follows consistent pattern, ie escape of small quantities of blood and fluid, due to tearing of muscle, tendon, ligament, capsule, etc. followed by increased flow of blood to part, degree of swelling and pain. Fractures produce special inflammatory reaction resulting in formation of a callus, ie bridge of new bone uniting fractured parts. If fracture involves a major weight-bearing bone, eg cannon, femur or humerus, immobilisation of the ends may be impossible and healing cannot occur. In other bones, eg pastern, splint or sesamoid, union between fractured parts may be partial or complete. See carpitis, corn, curb, capped elbow, gravel, hock, navicular disease, osselet, ringbone, sandcrack, bucked shin, sidebone, bruised sole, spavin, bog spavin, splint, bowed tendon, windgall. **l., treatment of** Remove cause if possible, control the inflammatory process. Apply heat and cold alternately, massage, inject anti-inflammatory drugs. See physiotherapy. Rest is essential for most injuries although exercise may help muscle injuries.

lameness

lamina

(pl laminae) Velvety membrane or sheet containing fine leaf-like projections. **sensitive l.** Membrane lining pedal bone of foot and interlocking with insensitive l. (a similar membrane attached to hoof wall but unlike sensitive l. does not contain blood vessels). Together these structures bind hoof to bone. See laminitis, seedy toe, foot.

laminitis

(syn founder) Inflamed sensitive lamina of hoof, characterised by heat and pain causing lameness. Usually present in more than one foot. Occurs in acute and chronic forms, thought to be due to allergy (qv), to protein as a result of overfeeding with rich food and too little exercise, or to infection of uterus or disturbed alimentary canal causing toxaemia. Exact way condition develops is not known, possibly due to effect of histamine on blood vessels in membrane (lamina) lining pedal bone. Most common in horses fed grain or on rich pasture. Symptoms: acute pain, sweating, increased heart rate and respiration, sometimes raised temperature; standing with front feet stretched out with head low and back arched. Usually difficult to get horse to move and then gait is shuffling. Horses may lie down and have difficulty getting up. There is marked heat and pain on pressure on the hoof. Disease often leads to separation of hoof wall from sensitive lamina, horn crumbles (see seedy toe) and pedal bone may drop through sole. Cases that recover develop concave hoof walls with horizontal ridges. Treatment: antihistamine, anti-inflammatory and pain-relieving drugs, eg phenylbutazone, ACP to reduce blood pressure; reduced diet and rest. Standing and walking animal in cold water may help.

lampas

Swelling and hardening of mucous membrane lining hard palate of mouth, immediately behind upper incisors. Sometimes forms inflamed ridge but, contrary to usual belief, condition insignificant.

Lancefield classification

Division of haemolytic streptococci into groups A to N, based on precipitin test. Those in group C are important in equine diseases. See streptococci.

laparo-

(Gr lapara, flank) Combining form meaning relationship to flank also, less strictly, to abdomen.

laparoscopy

Use of endoscope to visualise abdominal organs and surfaces.

laparotomy

(laparo- + Gr tome, a cutting) Surgical incision through flank or abdomen as in caesarean section, qv. **exploratory l.** Opening of abdomen in colic or other condition to confirm diagnosis by direct examination of viscera.

(pl larvae) Young or immature stage in life history of insect or parasite, eg redworm. **migrating l.** Young parasite travelling through body. — **larva**

Of larynx (voice box) **l. hemiplegia** Paralysis of one side. **l. paralysis** Condition when muscles controlling arytenoid cartilage and vocal cord of larynx are paralysed, left side most often affected. Usually results in horse whistling/roaring. (See Fig 27, p200.) **l. prosthesis** Surgical placement of ligature to pull open larynx. See Hobday. — **laryngeal**

Inflamed larynx. See cough. — **laryngitis**

Instrument for viewing interior of larynx. See endoscope. (See Figs 25, 26 on p200.) — **laryngoscope**

(laryngo- + Gr tome, a cutting) Surgical incision of larynx. See Hobday. — **laryngotomy**

(pl larynges) See voice box; wind. — **larynx**

(light amplification by stimulation of emission of radiation). Beam of intense, nondispersing light mobilising concentrated heat and power at close range. Reduces swelling/inflammation and thought to enhance healing in soft tissue injuries. Some types ('hot' lasers) are used for their cutting ability in surgical procedures, eg on the eye. — **laser therapy**

Term used to describe condition in which virus lies dormant in tissues until reactivated by stress or other factors weeks, months or years after original infection. Herpesviruses tend to have this capability whereas influenza viruses do not. See also virus. — **latency of virus**

Anatomical reference, of or to a side (cf bilateral). **l. cartilages** Partly fibrous tissue, partly hyaline cartilage, attached to wings of pedal bone, forming bulbs of heel. **l. gait** See gait. — **lateral**

Heavy Russian horse developed from Zemaitukas, Oldenburg, Ardennes (Swedish) and Finnish draught. **L. harness horse** Heavyweight whose trotting ability is encouraged. — **Latvian**

(Fr) Irrigation or washing out of an organ or joint. **gastric l.** Used in poisoning or grain overload. **abdominal l.** Used in colic surgery to reduce contamination after opening intestine. — **lavage**

Mild purgative, eg liquid paraffin, glycerine. — **laxative**

Abbr lactate dehydrogenase, qv. Sometimes abbreviated LDH. — **LD**

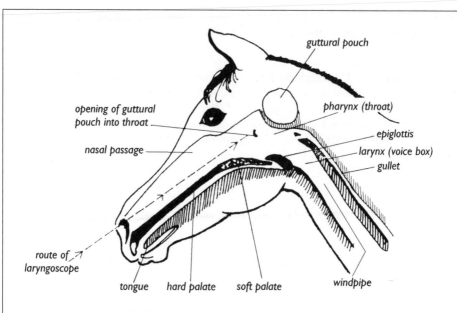

25 The way a laryngoscope is used to see voice box

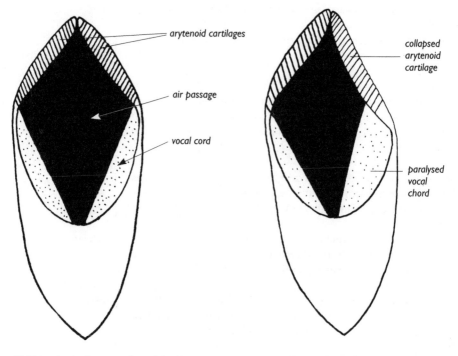

26 Normal voice box seen through laryngoscope

27 Voice box of a roarer or whistler

(1) Term used in electrocardiography to describe position of tracing, eg **l. one** (I) electrodes on left and right forelimbs, **l. two** (II) on right foreleg and left hind leg and **l. three** (III) on left foreleg and left hind leg. See electrocardiogram. (2) Chemical symbol Pb. Metallic element. **l. poisoning** Caused by chewing old paint or grazing pastures near **l.** works. Metal is absorbed from alimentary tract and passes to liver. From here it is excreted back to gut in bile and, via kidneys, to urine and in lactating mares, to the milk. It is also taken up by bones, heart, lungs, muscle and brain. Symptoms: convulsions, staggering, muscular spasms, dullness, abdominal pain and constipation, followed by diarrhoea, weightloss, swelling of limbs, gradual paralysis of hind legs, larynx and pharynx, causing shallow breathing or roaring. Tiny granules of **l. sulphide** may cause band of blue/black colour in gums. Diagnosis: on symptoms and **l.** in blood and faeces. At postmortem: typical smell on opening carcass, dirty grey/red muscles. Liver shows fatty degeneration. Poisoning is confirmed if there are more than 25 parts per million of **l.** in kidneys and 10 ppm in liver. Treatment: give saline purgatives, soluble sulphates, sodium sulphate, magnesium sulphate by mouth, calcium disodium versenate sub cut.	**lead**
Glass or transparent substance shaped to converge or scatter rays of light. See eye.	**lens**
Acute disease characterised by increasing haemolytic anaemia caused by *Leptospira pomona* and *L. icterohaemorrhagiae*. Symptoms: fever, fluctuating temperature, loss of appetite, depression, jaundice. Recovery may be followed by relapses. Diagnosis: on the examination of blood. Treatment: inject penicillin and streptomycin. See also eye, diseases of: moon blindness.	**leptospirosis**
(L laesio, laedere, to hurt) Pathological damage or abnormal condition of tissue. May be macroscopic (visible with naked eye) or microscopic.	**lesion**
(leuco- combining form meaning white from Gr leukos + kytos, cell) See white blood cell.	**leucocyte**
Increased number of leucocytes in blood (normal level: 5–10,000 per cu mm). Indicates infection.	**leucocytosis**
(leucocyte + Gr penis, poverty) Condition when white cells in blood fall below 5,000 per cu mm; may be caused by virus or radiation overdose. Cf leucocytosis.	**leucopenia**
(Gr leucos, white + haima, blood) A malignant disease of	**leukaemia**

leukaemia	blood-forming organs characterised by an abnormally high numbers of immature and mature white blood cells. See lymphosarcoma.
levamisole hydrochloride	Liquid drug to treat lungworm and gastroenteritis caused by parasites.
levo-	(L laevus, left) Combining form meaning towards the left (opp dextro-).
L-gamma glutamyltransferase	L denotes levo- as opposed to dextro-. See gamma glutamyltransferase.
LH	See luteinising hormone.
libido	Sexual drive. Increases in both sexes in natural breeding season, ie late spring and early summer. Can be artificially boosted with hormones or lighting. See behaviour; pituitary.
Lieberkuhn glands	(after German anatomist Johann **L.**) Glands in small intestine, producing digestive juice.
ligament	Band of fibrous tissue connecting bones or supporting organs.

Important ligaments

ligamentum nuchae	extends from poll to withers, helps to support head
round l. of hip joint	secures head of femur to pelvis
broad l. of uterus	suspends uterus from roof of abdomen
check l., superior and inferior	see stay apparatus
patella l.	three, anchor patella to tibia
suspensory l.	back of cannon over sesamoids to pastern
sesamoidean l.	see stay apparatus. See also annular l., nephrosplenic l.

ligation	(L ligatio) Application of ligature.
ligature	(L ligatura) Band, cord or fine thread for tying blood vessel. Cf stitch.
lignocaine hydrochloride	(trade name: Xylocaine + many others) White crystalline powder with slightly bitter taste, followed by local numbness. Used in general anaesthesia, with adrenaline as local anaesthetic

agent and in ointment to lubricate catheter for insertion into bladder or other sensitive area.

lignocaine hydrochloride

Heavy, late-maturing French saddle horse developed from English Thoroughbred. Dying out.

Limousin

(L lingualis from lingua, tongue) Relating to the tongue.

lingual

Fluid preparation which has oily, soapy or alcoholic base, applied externally with friction.

liniment

Oil from seeds of *Linum usitatissimum*. Yellowish-brown liquid with characteristic odour and bland taste. Used as laxative to treat impacted colic and occasionally tapeworms. Now largely replaced by other treatments. See danthron; colic.

linseed oil

Czechoslovakian coach horse.

Lipican

Fatty tumour. See growth.

lipoma

Proud-looking but tractable breed almost always grey, famous for dressage at Spanish Riding School, Vienna. Developed in Austria (stud founded 1580s) and later (1780s–World War II) at Baboloa Stud near Bana, N Hungary. **L.** developed from Kladruber, N Italian horse and, later, Arab. **L. Soc of GB**, Underhill Farm, Ludwell, Wilts SP7 0PW (01747 828639). **US L. Registry**, 13351 Chula Rd, Amelia, VA 23002 (804 561 4542).

Lipizzan/Lipizzaner

Transparent colourless, odourless and tasteless oily liquid. Bland laxative. See meconium retention, colic.

liquid paraffin

(litho- combining form, or relationship to, stone) Condition marked by calculi. See stone.

lithiasis

(Gr lithos, stone) Combining form: stone or calculus.

litho-

(litho- + Gr tome, a cutting) Surgical removal of stone from duct or organ. See stone.

lithotomy

Horse bred on same lines as Latvian (qv). Believed to date from 1870 when Zhmud Horse Breeding Soc was formed to cross this horse with Ardennes (Swedish).

Lithuanian heavy draught

(L jecur, Gr hepar) Largest gland in body capable of over 100 different functions; weighs about 5kg (11lb) in adult, lies in abdomen between diaphragm, stomach and intestines and is divided into right, middle and left lobe. It is supplied by arteries, veins, nerves and lymph channels and has bile duct which carries bile to duodenum. (Horse has no gall-bladder.) **L.** of

liver

liver newborn foal relatively large, with ratio to bodywt of 1:35 compared to 1:100 in adult. **L.** stores sugar in form of glycogen; converts amino acids to protein; stores fat and vitamin A; transforms substances into simpler or more complex ones, thus protecting body against poisons; copes with drugs and synthesises carbohydrate and fat; forms blood proteins, albumin and globulin; regulates blood's concentration of fat, sugar, amino acids and other nutrients, and produces bile including bilirubin, waste product formed in breakdown of haemoglobin. **L.** made up of minute cells arranged in sheets, between which blood circulates freely. Between adjacent sheets are tiny canals into which bile is secreted; these join together to deliver bile to intestine in common bile duct. Each **l.** cell therefore has contact with blood on one side and bile canals on the other. Section of **l.** examined under microscope shows cells arranged in lobules which form columns radiating towards central vein. This receives blood that has passed between the sheets of **l.** cells and carries it to the great veins of the heart. **l. biopsy** See biopsy. **l., diseases of** See abortion, viral; cirrhosis; jaundice; lead; ragwort; swamp fever; tuberculosis.

lobe (L lobus, Gr lobos) Defined portion of organ, eg anterior **l.** of pituitary.

lochia (Gr) Chocolate-coloured discharge from uterus after foaling, of blood and uterine secretions. Exercise helps evacuation.

lockjaw (syn tetanus) Horrific disease caused by *Clostridium tetani*, an anaerobic bacterium which lives in soil and body tissues (in abscesses, beneath scabs or in alimentary tract). Germ produces toxin which causes spasm of muscles (tetanic spasms). Symptoms: stiffness, rigid limbs and neck as flexor and extensor muscles contract at same time (spasm is brought on by noise or contact with skin), difficult jaw movement and swallowing, head thrust forward, ears pricked, tail raised and difficulty in getting up. Diagnosis: on signs gradually increasing in intensity, characteristic stance, spasm of 3rd eyelid when face is gently tapped with finger. Incubation period 5–21 days; foals particularly at risk in first 6 weeks because bacteria can enter through umbilicus. Older animals may be infected through wounds, especially on legs, which become contaminated with soil and dung. Treatment: see mephenesin. Prevention: antitetanic serum gives immunity for about 30 days. Vaccination with tetanus toxoid provides lasting immunity but needs booster injections. See tetanus toxoid.

loperamide hydrochloride (trade name: Imodium) Substance related to opiates which reduces activity of nerves stimulating the gut wall, thereby acting as a gut muscle relaxant. Used to control diarrhoea.

louse (L pediculus; pl lice) Skin parasite of phylum Arthropoda, class Insecta, order Phthiraptera. Some suck blood (sucking l.). Others chew (biting l.). They have small flat wingless bodies. Lice that live on horses: *Damalinia equi* (formerly known as *Bovicola equi* or *Trichodectes equi*; found in Australia and belong to sub-order Mallophaga, biting lice); *Haematopinus asini* (sub-order Siphunculata, sucking lice and, common in UK, sub-order Anoplura). Eggs are laid on skin, hatch in 20 days and are killed by dry heat. Sucking lice cause irritation and loss of hair. Diagnosis easy on warm days when parasites are active, particularly around mane and tail. Treatment: pyrethrum.

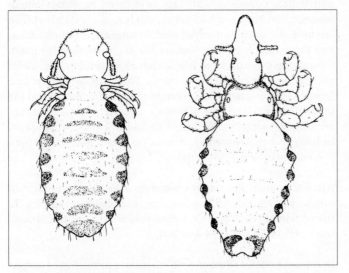

28 *(left)* Biting louse *(Damalinia equi)* and sucking louse *(Haematopinus asini)*

lucern poisoning Ingestion of plant can cause photosensitisation and liver disease associated with jaundice, dark urine and wasting. See poisons, liver.

lumbar Of the back. **l. vertebra** See skeleton.

lumen Cavity or channel inside a tube, eg l. of alimentary canal.

Lundy pony Hardy, thick-skinned animal which runs wild on **L.** island, in Bristol Channel, SW England. Thought to have developed from mainland's ponies. **L. P. Preservation Soc**. 33 Gregory's Tyning, Paulton, Bristol, BS18 5PW (01761 415073).

lung (L pulmo, Gr pneumon) One of 2 breathing organs in chest. It brings air into close contact with bloodstream for exchange of gases. As chest expands and contracts air is drawn down and up windpipe, into and out of l. Air passes through smaller *lung*   tubes (bronchi and bronchioles) into many millions of minute air sacs (alveoli). Capillaries in alveolar walls expose blood for exchange of oxygen and carbon dioxide. **L.** is divided into apical, cardiac and diaphragmatic lobes. See broken wind; percussion; pneumonia.

lungworm   Nematode parasite of the order Strongyloidea, family Metastrongylidae. Slender roundworm living in air passages of lungs where it lays eggs. These are coughed up and swallowed. **L.** is host-specific; type affecting horses and donkeys is *Dictyocaulus arnfeldi*, which has a direct life history and does not require intermediate host. Male is about 36mm (1¼in) long and female 60mm (2½in). The swallowed eggs pass out in faeces, where they hatch and are picked up by another host. The larvae bore through intestinal wall, to mesenteric lymph nodes, and enter lymph stream. Venous blood carries them to heart, through right ventricle, to lungs. Here they develop into adults and lay eggs, completing the cycle. They irritate and inflame bronchi (causing bronchitis, coughing and pneumonia) and the larvae cause diarrhoea. (Donkey can carry large numbers without showing symptoms, so should not graze with horses unless checked.) Treatment: ivermectin (qv), fenbendazole (qv), levamisole hydrochloride (qv).

Lusitano   Attractive, light Portuguese breed, possibly descended from Minho (qv). About 15 h, often grey and used in bullring. **L. Breed Soc of GB**, The Small House, Green End Rd, Radnage, Bucks HP14 5BY (01494 483683).

lutein   (L luteus, yellow) Hormone which causes formation of corpus luteum (yellow body) in ovary, qv.

luteinising hormone   (LH) Hormone produced by anterior lobe of pituitary gland. Acts on ovaries of mare causing rupture of ripe follicle (ovulation) and on testes of colt stimulating them to produce male sex hormone testosterone. **l.h. releasing factor** Hormone produced by hypothalamus of brain. It acts on pituitary gland causing it to produce **l.h.**

luxation   Dislocation usually referring to a joint. Subluxation: partial dislocation.

Lyme disease   First associated with Old Lyme, Connecticut and caused by *Borrelia burgdorferi*. Bacterium, which causes arthritis in humans and laminitis, skin sensitivity, fever, swollen joints and eye inflammation in horses, is spread by deer ticks (see tick). Treatment: antibiotics. Prevention: insecticide to kill first-stage ticks (larvae) which live on small rodents. Cotton wool impregnated with insecticide can be scattered and will be used by mice to build nests.

(L lympha, water) Transparent, slightly yellow liquid present in lymphatic vessels. See lymph gland. **lymph**

(lymph- + Gr aden, gland + -itis) Inflamed lymph nodes. See gland. **lymphadenitis**

(syn Monday morning leg) Inflamed lymphatic vessels and usually lymph nodes (lymphadenitis). Characterised by hot, painful swellings beneath skin, especially in legs. Caused by infection, which enters through skin, injury to lymph channels which become blocked, or overloading of lymph stream due to excess feed. There is chronic inflammation of vessel walls and abscesses may develop, discharging serum. Fibrous tissue may form beneath skin, causing chronic thickening. Specific diseases in which l. occurs are glanders, epizootic l., ulcerative l. See separate headings, also lymph gland. **lymphangitis**

System of thin-walled channels similar to veins, but without valves. Channels contain fluid consisting of water, protein, fat and small number of cells (lymphocytes). Channels start as blind-ended tubes in extremities, organs, muscles etc; by joining with others they form network, becoming larger nearer point where they enter bloodstream close to heart. They drain tissue fluid and are essential part of body's fluid balance, transport system (see blood) and defence mechanism (see immunity, lymphocyte). Lymph gland (node) is structure at intervals in lymph channels. Acts as filter and contains large number of lymphocytes. Gland is responsible for producing protective substances (antibodies) and preventing microbes spreading through body. Becomes swollen and inflamed (lymphadenitis) and may be seat of abscess when infection is at point of body it drains, eg pastern area may affect gland in groin (of hind leg) or axilla (foreleg). Glands can be felt if swollen: between branches of lower jaw (sub-maxillary), near ear (parotid), near throat (pharyngeal), in front of shoulder (pre-scapular) and inside thigh (femoral). Internally glands mostly affected by infection are those associated with drainage of lungs and intestine. See lymphangitis; sinusitis; strangles. **lymphatic system**

White blood cell with large nucleus produced from lymphoid tissue throughout body including thymus. Divided into two classes, B and T according to origin and function: B l.s responsible for producing antibodies (humoral immunity); and T for killing viruses and some other foreign cells (cell-mediated immunity). **lymphocyte**

Malignant tumour of lymphoid tissue. Like leukaemia (qv) it is a disease in which cells which normally fight infection get out of control, multiply rapidly and may invade other organs. Commonest form in horse is **alimentary l.**, where wall of bowel **lymphosarcoma**

lymphosarcoma	becomes infiltrated with lymphatic tumour cells. This causes improper food absorption, diarrhoea and weightloss. Seen sporadically: **cutaneous l.** and **thymic l.**, which produce lesions in skin and chest respectively.
lysis	(Gr a losing, setting free) Destruction or decomposition of cells, eg haemolysis, **l.** of red blood cells.

(pronounced mew) Abbr micron. See abbreviations, virus.	**μ**
Abbr Master of Arts.	**MA**
Large cell which develops in marrow-like white cells but then enters tissues. Important role in fighting infection and regulating inflammation.	**macrophage**
Metallic element, symbol Mg. **m. carbonate** and **m. oxide** White powders, heavy/light forms, given to foals as antacid, doses: 2–12g. **m. hydroxide** 2.5–5g as antacid in foals. **m. sulphate** (syn Epsom salts) Colourless odourless crystals with salty taste. Used as purgative. Unreliable action in horses. **m. trisilicate** White odourless tasteless powder. Used as absorbent and antacid to treat diarrhoea in foals, 1–6g.	**magnesium**
(Fr, L malum, ill) Disease. **m. de caderas** Weakening disease causing staggering. Occurs in horses, mules, sheep, goats and cattle in S America. Caused by *Trypanosoma equinum* and spread by tabanid and stable flies. **m. de coit** See dourine. **m. de zousfana** Algerian form of surra, qv.	**mal**
(mal Fr, from L malum, ill + adjustment) Failure to adapt. See neonatal **m.** syndrome.	**maladjustment**
(L malus, bad + formatio, a forming) Abnormal development. See cleft palate, conformation, parrot jaw.	**malformation**
(L malignans, acting maliciously) Disease or condition with tendency to become worse. **m. oedema** Acute infection of wounds caused by organisms of the soil, notably *Clostridium septicum* and *C. chauvoei*. Infection causes swellings (that contain air and froth which exude from wound), high fever, depression and death in 24–48 hours. Not common in horses. **m. tumour** Growth that spreads. See growth.	**malignant**
Extract of bacteria *Pseudomonas mallei* used to diagnose glanders, qv. Types: (1) 1ml of dilute **m.** injected under skin, body temperature recorded every 3 hours between 12–24 hours. Positive reaction indicated by plaque round site of injection and rise of temperature to 39.5°C (103.1°F). (2) 0.1ml of concentrated **m.** injected into lower eyelid. Positive reaction indicated by swelling 24–48 hours later.	**mallein/m. test**
(L hammer) See ear.	**malleus**

malposition (L malus, bad + positio, placement) Abnormal position of foetus. See dystocia.

Mammalia Division of vertebrates possessing hair and suckling young; includes horse. See evolution.

mammary glands (syns udder, bag) Two modified skin glands between mare's hindlegs on either side of midline. Each gland is a short flaccid cone consisting of a glandular mass or body and a teat (papilla) in which there are usually two small openings. Swell in last 4 weeks of pregnancy and may run milk before birth of foal. Abortion or death of one twin may trigger lactation. See birth; colostrum; running of milk.

Mangalarga Breed developed in Brazil, about 150 years ago, from a stallion imported from Portugal. Later improved with Andalusian blood. **M.** a is heavy variation of the Criollo found throughout S America.

mandible (from L mandere, to chew) Lower jaw bone, also termed mandibula (pl mandibulae).

mange Infective skin condition caused by mites of order Acarina. **chorioptic m.** (syns foot **m.**, itchy leg) Caused by *Chorioptes equi*, found in fetlock and pastern region; especially common on horses with long feathers, qv. Scabs appear, horse stamps its feet and rubs, scratches or bites affected region. Diagnosis: on parasites found in scab. Treatment: clip hairs from affected area and apply gamma benzene hexachloride. **demodectic m.** Scaly or pustular skin condition caused by *Demodex folliculorum*, a mite which lives in hair follicles or sebaceous glands of skin or in meibomian glands of eye. Infection is spread by contact. Treat with gamma benzene hexachloride. **psoroptic m.** Caused by *Psoroptes communis var equi*, mites which burrow into skin causing thick, heavy scabs. **sarcoptic m.** Caused by *Sarcoptes scabiei var equi*. Mites burrow under skin, causing thickened areas where females lay eggs. These hatch in 25 days and larvae stay in their burrows or make new ones at an angle. (Larvae moult and become nymphs which form further burrows.) Mites feed on tissue fluid and skin cells, causing small itchy red blisters. Hairs fall out leaving bald patches. Infection is by contact and infected bedding or grooming tools. Diagnosis: on recovery and identification of mite. Treatment: see gamma benzene hexachloride. Burn, or thoroughly disinfect bedding and grooming kit. Ivermectin might have some activity against chorioptes, psoroptes and sarcoptes.

Manipur Pony bred in **M.**, India. Reputed to date from 7th century, when used for polo. Probably has Mongolian and Arab blood (has

Arab-like flared nostrils). About 12 hands.

Manipur

Female of Equidae family. Term generally used when she is 4–5 years or when used for breeding (before that she is termed 'filly').

mare

(After Austrian physicians Pierre M. and Eugene B.) See osteoarthropathy.

Marie-Bamberger's disease

Mark on horse. (1) Shape and/or position of white hairs in darker coat. (2) Arrangement of hairs, eg whorl. (3) Anatomical **m.**, eg prophet's thumb mark (see depression). **m.**s include: blaze (down face, ie from between eyes to muzzle), sock (on pastern), star (centre of forehead), stocking (hock or knee down to hoof), flesh mark, wall eye, saddle or girth mark. **m. certificate** Paper containing diagrams of head, muzzle, left and right side of horse on which veterinarian draws horse's **m.**s to register foal, name yearling, etc. Also included in horse's passport.

marking

Red soft material in flat bones, yellow in central cavity of long bones (cannon, radius, etc). Consists of fat, blood vessels and blood-containing spaces (sinusoids). Red **m.** forms red blood cells (erythrocytes), a process known as erythropoiesis. Megaloblast is cell in wall of sinusoid which is forerunner of mature red cell; intermediate stages: early and late erythroblasts which possess nucleus and in which haemoglobin appears for first time; normoblast which contains full amount of haemoglobin, reticulocyte without nucleus, and finally red cell. Horse **m.** can be obtained for diagnosis by inserting special needle into **m.** cavity at point of hip (see pelvis). Yellow **m.** predominently fat.

marrow

Indian war horse of middle ages, now saddle horse similar to Kathiawari, qv.

Marwari

See physiotherapy.

massage

Inflamed mammary glands or udder. Caused by infection, especially with streptococcus. One or both glands become enlarged, firm and painful with cord-like swelling along abdomen as lymphatics become blocked. Diagnosis: on examination of milk for presence of pus cells and bacteria; condition must be distinguished from enlargements due to foal going off suck after weaning. Treatment: strip gland, insert ointment containing appropriate antibiotic such as penicillin and inject antibiotic. See weaning problems.

mastitis

(L manus, hand + stuprare, to rape) Self-manipulation of penis when horse rubs erect penis on underside of belly. Thought by

masturbation

masturbation   some to have adverse effect on training programme and increase risk of unsuccessful coitus. Treatment: some horsemen advocate use of pollution ring, ie ring of material and/or rubber/metal fitted on to sheath. This causes slight pain if horse tries to draw (achieve penile erection). Not a recommended practice.

Masuren   Polish name for Trakehner horses, some of which were taken from East Prussians after W W II.

matching   See blood tests, cross-matching.

mate   To put mare and stallion together for coitus. See behaviour.

mater   (lit mother) Anatomical term for a protecting membrane. See **dura m., pia m.**.

materia medica   Branch of medical science dealing with source, use and preparation of drugs.

maternal   (L, mater, mother) Of mother, eg **m.** instinct (see behaviour), **m.** bloodstream (see placenta).

mating   (Gr mate, companion) (1) Act of coitus or covering. (2) Selection of horses for breeding. See semen.

matrix   Material surrounding cells, as in bone and cartilage.

maturity   Age of attaining maximum development. **m. of bone** Indicates particular bone has completed its growth. **foetal m.** Length of gestation and ability of foal to live outside uterus. Between 300 and 325 days' gestation foal is premature, after that, immature until considered mature at 340 days (pony breeds mature around 325 days). **skeletal m.** All bones have stopped growing (at about 5 years). **sexual m.** Able to breed. See puberty.

maxilla   Irregularly shaped bone that forms upper jaw. See skull.

maxillary sinus   One of four pairs of air sinuses. Extends backwards to line in front of eye. Floor is formed by bony plates surrounding last three cheek teeth. It is divided into front and back compartment and communicates with frontal sinus through large oval opening. See skull.

MCH   Abbr mean corpuscular haemoglobin, ie average haemoglobin content of a red blood cell. Measured in picograms by dividing haemoglobin in g per dl blood by the number of red cells x 10^{12}/litre.

Abbr mean corpuscular haemoglobin concentration, ie average haemoglobin in g per dl blood divided by packed cell volume (normal range 30–38g/dl). **MCHC**

Abbr mean corpuscular volume (average volume of individual red blood cell) determined by packed cell volume divided by number of red cells in millions per cubic mm x 10 and expressed in cubic microns (normal range 38–50). **MCV**

(trade names: Telmin, Equivurm Plus) Drug for the treatment of intestinal parasites. Effective against large and small strongyles, roundworm, pinworm and lungworm. See also benzimidazole. **mebendazole**

Heavy, warm-blooded saddle horse. Evolved from heavier, cold-blooded, military **M**. **Mecklenburg**

(trade name: Arquel) Drug used for its inti-inflammatory, analgesic and antipyretic action. **meclofenamic acid**

(L, Gr mekonion) Faeces stored in colon, caecum and rectum of foetus and usually expelled only after birth. Brown, black or green, hard or soft pellets, with slimy covering. Voided during first 3 days of life and followed by yellow milk dung. May be passed in utero due to asphyxia or illness. Foal is then born with coat saturated with **m**. and amniotic fluid stained brown. See birth; neonatal maladjustment syndrome. **m. retention** (syns stoppage, ileus) Inability to void **m**. easily. Symptoms, in the first 3 days: rolling, straining, lying in awkward postures (head turned back, foreleg over head), refusing to suck, distended abdomen due to gas in intestine. Treatment: inject pain-relieving drugs, give enema (qv) and liquid paraffin (200–300ml) by stomach tube. **meconium**

(L medicina) Drug or remedy; science of healing. **clinical m.** Applied in practice rather than in laboratory or institute. **equine m.** That applied to horses. **experimental m.** Investigation of disease based on experiments. **forensic m.** That relating to legality. See dope test. **preventive m.** That which prevents disease. **proprietary m.** Drug or remedy manufactured under a trade name (see manufacturers' list at back of dictionary). **veterinary m.** Science and treatment of animal diseases. **medicine**

Innermost region of an organ eg **renal m**. centre of kidney. **adrenal m**. See adrenal. **medulla**

(Gr megas, big, great) Unit of measurement 1 million times basic unit, eg 1 mega of penicillin is 1 million times 1 unit. **mega-**

melanin	(Gr melas, black) Dark pigment of skin, hair, growth or eye. Grey horses may have deposits of **m.** in skin, especially under tail, size of walnut.
melanoma	See growth.
meiosis	(Gr) A halving of inherited material in sex cells (sperm and egg) so that new individual receives equal amount of material from each parent. Each cell in horse contains 64 chromosomes (diploid number); but each sex cell contains 32 chromosomes (haploid number). After fertilisation diploid number is restored in new individual (zygote). Cf mitosis. See chromosome.
membrane	Layer of tissue covering a surface or dividing a space. See also **mucous m.**
menaphthone sodium bisulphite	White crystalline odourless powder: synthetic water-soluble vitamin K. Essential for coagulation of blood, antidote to dicoumarol and rat poisons.
Mendel's law	(after Gregor Johann **M.**, 1822–84) Particular trait or characteristic passed to offspring from one or other parent by dominant or recessive unit of inheritance (gene), eg active temperament said to be more easily transmitted (dominant) than passive one. See behaviour, coat colouring, gene.
meningeal	Of meninges.
meninges	(Gr meninx, membrane) Three membranes enveloping brain and spinal cord, ie dura mater, arachnoid, pia mater.
meningitis	(Gr meninx, membrane + -itis) Inflamed outer lining of brain (meninges) caused by infection with bacteria, virus or protozoa. Symptoms: gross disturbance in behaviour, eg circling, convulsions, paralysis, loss of consciousness, pushing against objects. Usually associated with inflammation of brain itself. See encephalomyelitis, borna disease, dourine, septicaemia, surra.
mephenesin	Drug, used in human medicine, which Australian workers have found useful to lessen spasms in, eg, lockjaw.
mepivacaine hydrochloride	(trade name: Intra Epicaine) Potent local anaesthetic used to infiltrate skin wounds and in epidural anaesthesia and nerve blocks.
mepyramine maleate	White bitter-tasting odourless powder. Antihistamine and local anaesthetic drug used in allergic conditions and laminitis, lymphangitis and pulmonary oedema.

See red mercuric iodide.	**mercuric iodide**
Caused by eating cereals treated with mercurial compounds to prevent fungal growth. Symptoms: diarrhoea, shock, collapse and death. Chronic cases may develop inflamed mouth and kidneys. Treatment: corticosteroids and saline IV.	**mercury poisoning**
(mero- + Gr krinein, to separate) Partly secreting; gland in which cells remain intact and discharge secretion, as salivary and pancreatic glands. Cf apocrine, holocrine. See gland.	**merocrine**
Membraneous fold of peritoneum (qv) which suspends organs and alimentary canal from body wall. Adjective: mesenteric.	**mesentery**
(meso- + Gr derma, skin) Middle layer of 3 main layers (germ or germinal layers) of embryo, lies between ectoderm and endoderm; forms connective tissue, bone, cartilage, muscle, blood vessels, lymphatics, nervous tissue, epithelium of pleura, pericardium, peritoneum, kidney and sex organs. Cf ectoderm, endoderm.	**mesoderm**
(Gr metaballein, to change) General body changes in normal life; process by which energy is made available to body; affected by hormone thyroxine, qv. Cf anabolism, catabolism.	**metabolism**
Substance produced by metabolism.	**metabolite**
(Gr meta-, change/next + karpos, writst) Of metacarpus. **m. bones** Those forming front cannon and splint bones; the third **m.b.** (cannon) is strong, long bone taking weight; the second and fourth **m.b.**s are thin. See splint. Cf metatarsal.	**metacarpal**
Part of leg between carpus (knee) and phalanx (pastern), ie cannon bone.	**metacarpus**
(meta- + Gr morphosis, a shaping) Change of shape or structure, eg fatty **m.**, infiltration of fat into cells or tissues.	**metamorphosis**
(meta- + Gr phyein, to grow) Wider part of end of long bone, adjacent to epiphysis. See growth plate, bone.	**metaphysis**
(meta- + Gr stasis, stand; pl metastases) Spread of disease from one part to another, ie from a primary to a secondary focus. Characteristic of malignant tumours (in which secondary growths form in organs and tissues as a result of spread by blood or lymph streams); in bacterial infection (causing secondary abscesses, eg foal with abscess at umbilicus and others in liver, muscles, etc). See growth, joint-ill.	**metastasis**

metatarsal	Of metatarsus, area between hock and fetlock. **m. bones** 3 bones; hind cannon and inner and outer splint bones.
metatarsus	(meta- + Gr tarsus, tarsos) Area between hock and fetlock joint in hindleg.
metazoan	Organism belonging to phylum Metazoa. Has multicellular body and includes all animal life above single-cell protozoa.
methohexitone sodium	Short-acting barbiturate used for anaesthesia. Lasts 3–8 minutes after injection into vein. Used to cast horse before inserting tube into windpipe to give gaseous anaesthetic. See anaesthesia.
methylprednisolone acetate	(trade name: Depo-Medrone) Type of cortisone, qv.
Metis trotter	See Orlov.
metoclopramide hydrochloride	(trade name: Emequell) Drug used to stimulate upper digestive tract in cases of colic and chronic grass sickness.
metritis	(Gr metre, womb + -itis) Inflamed inner lining of uterus. If severe, characterised by vaginal discharge which may collect on tail hair, thighs and hocks. Caused by infection with bacteria, mainly streptococcus, *E. coli*, *Klebsiella pneumoniae*, staphylococcus, *Pseudomonas aeruginosa* or by fungus. Predisposing causes include abnormal entry of air into genital tract due to poor conformation of vulva, the after-effects of pregnancy and birth, dysfunction of hormonal glands. Treatment: irrigate uterus with sterile fluid, infuse antibiotics into uterus and inject IM, eliminate predisposing causes. See contagious equine **m.** (CEM); Caslick; endometritis.
metronidazole	(trade names: Metronex, Torgyl) White crystals or crystalline powder. Given by mouth or intravenously. Effective against gram-negative bacteria and anaerobes (qv).
mg	Abbr for milligram. See weights and measures.
micro-	(Gr mikros, small) (1) Combining form meaning small eg microphthalmia – congenital defect where eye(s) small and incomplete or absent. (2) In measuring, indicates a millionth, eg microgram, a millionth of a gram.
microbe	(micro- + Gr bios, life) Minute living organism, particularly one causing disease, eg bacteria, fungus, virus. Adjective: microbic.
microbiology	(micro- + Gr bios, life + -logy) Science of microorganisms, including bacteria, fungi, viruses.

Family of bacteria consisting of spherical cells, eg Staphylococcus, qv. **Micrococcaceae**

One of many minute subdivisions of mare's placenta which interlock with corresponding depressions in uterus, forming a unit where blood vessels of the maternal and foetal circulation come into close apposition. See placenta. **microcotyledon**

Abbr μ. Measurement of size 1 millionth of a metre, ie 1 thousandth of a millimetre. **micron**

(syn germ) Any microscopic living organism, usually a bacterium, fungus or virus and capable of causing infection. See bacteria, carbohydrate, fungus, virus. **microorganism**

(micro- + Gr skopein, to view) Instrument containing system of lenses; gives enlarged image of extremely small objects and reveals details of histological structures. **electron m.** One in which beam forms image on fluorescent screen. Used for magnification many times greater than light **m**. **microscope**

Genus of fungi causing ringworm. **microsporum**

(L micturire, to urinate) To urinate or (colloq) stale. See behaviour, urine sample. NB: the act of micturating is micturition. **micturate**

(Polish, medium) Native Polish pony similar to Konik. **Mierzyn**

(L lac) Fluid secretion of mammary glands forming natural food for foal. Cf colostrum. **m. warts** (syn equine cutaneous papillomatosis) Infectious disease of horses up to 3 years old. Numerous small warts appear on nose and lips; caused by virus, infectious only to horse family and with incubation period of about 2 months. **M.w.s** usually self-limiting and disappear in 1–3 months (see also growth). May ulcerate and bleed or recur if removed surgically. Can be treated by chemical cautery, eg silver nitrate or glacial acetic acid. **m. shake** Colloq IV bicarbonate (qv) solution given to horses in USA and Australia before racing. **milk**

Colloq big head, qv. **miller's disease**

One thousandth of a litre - symbol ml. **millilitre**

One of several hormones which is secreted by adrenal cortex; affects mineral (electrolyte) balance of blood and tissues. See glucocorticoid. **mineralocorticoid**

(syn Garrano) Popular, old-established Portuguese pony which **Minho**

Minho	probably influenced Alter, Lusitano and Galiceno breeds.
miniature horse	See hand, narcolepsy. **British M. H. Soc**, Howick Farm, The Haven, W. Sussex, RH14 9BQ (01403 822639). **American M. H. Registry**, 6748 N. Frostwood Pkwy, Peoria, IL 61615 (309 691 9661).
Ministry of Agriculture	See veterinary rules.
miosis	(Gr meiosis, diminution) Excessive contraction of pupil. See eye.
MIP test	(mare immunological pregnancy test) An assay detecting presence of eCG (equine chorionic gonadotrophin), qv, formerly called pregnant mare serum gonadotrophin (PMSG). Used between days 45 and 95 as pregnancy test.
mite	Colloq for tick (qv) and smaller relatives belonging to order Acarina, sub-order Trombidiformes (harvest **m.** and Demodex, qv) and Sarcoptiformes (see mange).
mitosis	Division of body cell (1st stage or prophase). Forms 2 cells, each containing identical amount of inherited material, ie in horse 64 chromosomes (diploid number). Cf meiosis. Fast-growing tumours show many cells in process of **m.**
mitral	Shaped like a mitre. **m.** valve (syn bicuspid valve) Valve guarding entrance between 1st and 2nd chamber on left side of heart. Consists of two cusps anchored to the ventricle wall by fibrous bands. See also heart.
molar	(L moles, mass) Tooth adapted for grinding. See teeth.
molybdenum	Metallic element, symbol Mo. **m. poisoning** May occur if horse grazes on plants which have taken up **m.** from contaminated soil. Symptoms: persistent diarrhoea any time up to 6 weeks after leaving pasture, weightloss, harsh staring coat and depigmentation of hair. Treatment: give copper sulphate daily. (More common in cattle than horses.)
Monday morning	Time when ill-health often discovered or starts, especially in Thoroughbreds which have been rested on Sunday. **M.m. disease** See setfast. **M.m. leg** See lymphangitis.
Mongolian	Old-established breed. Large number live semi-wild on poor land, others are bred at farms. Varies according to district but usually around 13 h with heavy head and small eyes. Has influenced Burmese, Turkoman and Manipur. Many **M.** ponies exported to Korea, Tibet and especially China, where they are

known as Griffins or Chinese ponies. May have bred with Przewalski, qv.	*Mongolian*
Combining form meaning one, from Gr monos, single.	**mono-**
Derived from a single cell or clone. **m. antibody** Antibody from one clone of plasma cells, producing product of specific type (normal immune response consists of hundreds of clones, each producing different antibodies). **m.a.** engineering used, eg, in vaccine against particular strains of influenza, qv.	**monoclonal**
Large white cell with oval, pale nucleus. See white cell.	**monocyte**
Individual with only one testis descended. See rig.	**monorchid**
Derived from a single ovum, eg identical twins, rare in horses. See twin.	**monovular**
(syn periodic ophthalmia) See eye, diseases of.	**moon blindness**
Ratio of healthy individuals to sick ones in a community, eg disease with high **m.** affects many individuals. See epidemic.	**morbidity**
American breed developed from one stallion, Justin **M.**, foaled in Massachusetts in 1789. He may have been type of American Quarterhorse or part Arab. Breed flourished and **M.** stud farm established. Breed is general purpose with quiet disposition and is often used in light harness. Was raced until ousted by faster trotter (the Standardbred) on which it had strong influence. Usually bay, brown, black or chestnut and around 14–15 h. See wobbler syndrome. **American M. Horse Assn,** PO Box 960, Shelburne, VT 05482 (802 985 4944). **British M. Horse Soc**, PO Box 155, Godalming, Surrey GU8 5YE (01483 861283). **Canadian M. Assn**, PO Box 286, Port Perry, Ontario LNL 1A3 (905 985 1691).	**Morgan**
Angular S. American Criollo (qv) living in mountains of Brazil and Peru.	**Morochuco/ Morochuquo**
(L morphine, morphinum) Main (and most active) alkaloid of opium. Colourless shiny crystals with bitter taste. Used as analgesic.	**morphine**
See chromosome.	**mosaicism**
Bloodsucking insect of family Culicidae. See gnat.	**mosquito**
May occur if horse eats mouldy plants or hay. Symptoms: frequent urination, nervousness, inflamed mouth, excessive salivation,	**mould poisoning**

mould poisoning	incoordination, paralysis, depression, weakness, jaundice and, in severe cases, death from internal haemorrhages.
mount	To get on. See behaviour, male sexual; artificial vagina.
mouth	Opening into alimentary canal. Houses teeth, gums, tongue. **m., injuries of** (1) Abrasions, caused by bit of bridle. May affect gums and angle of lips. (2) Wounds of cheek caused by kick, barbed wire, etc. (3) Fracture of one or both branches of lower jaw (from kick). (4) Abscess in the roots of molar teeth. (5) Tearing of root (frenulum) of tongue by rough handling. Treatment depends on nature of injury. If from bit, horse should be rested; if wounds or fracture, surgery; if abrasions, astringent lotions.
MRCVS	Abbr Member of the Royal College of Veterinary Surgeons, qv.
MRI	Abbr magnetic resonance imaging. Technique for viewing soft tissues based on their behaviour when exposed to magnetic force.
mucin	Chief constituent of mucus, produced by small glands in lining of air passages, alimentary tract, etc. Adjective: mucinous.
mucoid	Resembling mucus.
mucosa	(L mucus) See mucous membrane.
mucous	Of mucus. **m. membrane** Thin layer of cells consisting of epithelium and **m.** glands. Generally used to mean those **m.m.**s most easily seen, eg of eyelid, mouth, gums, vagina. **injected m.m.** Membrane in which blood vessels stand out abnormally. Sign of infection. See cyanosis.
mucus	Slimy secretion which lubricates mucous membranes; contains mucin, inorganic salts, cells. Produced in excess in inflammation of mucous membranes, eg catarrh.
mud fever	(syns rainscald, dermatophilosis, mycotic dermatitis, heel bug, greasy heel) Skin infection caused by *Dermatophilus congolensis* which enters skin when horses are saturated by prolonged rain, are in poor condition and/or stand for long periods under trees. Hair becomes matted and tufted, forming scabs and causing loss of hair over back, belly and lower limbs, coronet and bulbs of heel. Scabs reveal greyish-green pus and raw area when removed. Diagnosis: on laboratory examination of smears. Treatment: antibiotic ointment. Cf acne; ringworm; Queensland itch.

Offspring of male ass and female horse. Female **m.** is a janet. **M.** is usually infertile. See chromosome. **m. foot** Congenital defect in which horse has contracted heels (qv) and large frog, ie similar to normal foot of **m. British M. Soc**, Hope Mount Farm, Alstonfield, Derbys DE6 2FR (01335 310353).

mule

Combining form, many/much, eg **multiparous** Mare which has had 2 or more pregnancies.

multi-

Veterinary surgeon of Mesopotamian people. Distinguished from medical and witch doctor as early as 1800 BC. If his patient died, he had to pay owner more than quarter of animal's value.

munai-su

See heart murmur.

murmur

(syn flesh) Collection of fibres with ability to contract and exert a force. 3 types: striped, smooth and cardiac (heart). Striped **m.** is voluntary and found in muscles of legs etc. Smooth **m.** is involuntary and found in alimentary canal, uterus, walls of arteries etc. Cardiac **m.** of heart is characterised by capacity to contract rhythmically. **m. and tendon, abnormal conditions of** (1) Rupture of strong tendon (peroneus tertius) attached to back of femur and inserted on to cannon. It acts mechanically to flex hock when stifle joint is flexed. When ruptured, stifle flexes, but hock does not. Caused by over-extension of hock joint. Symptoms: limpness below hock, as if fracture has occurred. Horse can bear weight and shows relatively little pain. When it walks there is a dimpling in Achilles tendon. Treatment: rest for several weeks. (2) Rupture of gastrocnemius **m.** Has its origin on back of femur and its insertion through a tendon to point of hock (tuber calcis). Its action is to extend hock and flex stifle joint. A small bursa lies on front of its insertion on front of hock and another is interposed between it and superficial flexor tendon. Symptoms: dropping of hock joint at an excessive angle. If on both sides, horse appears to be squatting and cannot straighten hind limbs. (3) Myositis. Inflamed **m.** due to strain, virus infection, setfast. (4) Ossifying myopathy. Laying down of scar tissue in **m.**, usually in hindquarters or back of thigh, after injury. Adhesions limit action of **m.**s and cause lameness. Often seen in American Quarterhorse, qv. Symptoms: lameness, especially noticeable when walking; scar can be felt as an area of firmness. Treatment: remove fibrous lump surgically. (5) Tendinitis. Sprain of tendon, most common behind front cannon, ie deep and/or superficial flexor tendon.

muscle
(Table of Muscles, see p223–7)

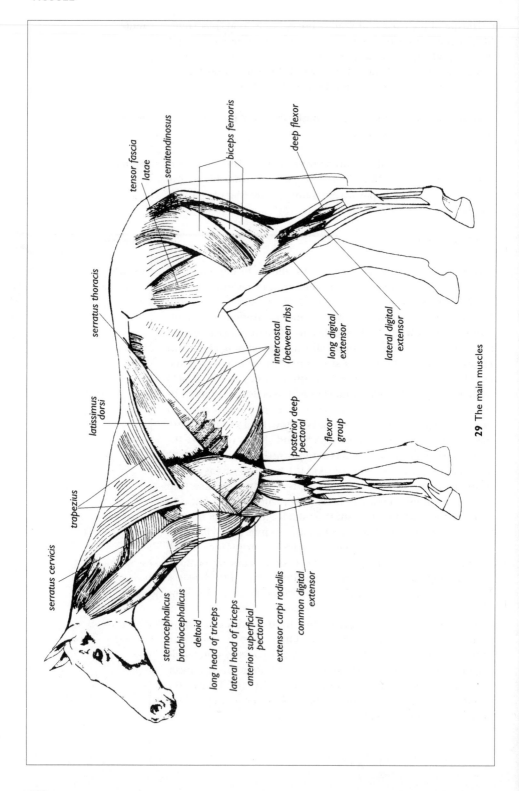

29 The main muscles

TABLE OF MUSCLES

Part	Muscle	Action
lips and cheek	orbicularis oris	close eyelids
	levator nasolabialis	raise upper lip and nostril
	levator labii superioris proprius	raise upper lip
	zygomaticus	pull back angle of mouth
	incisivus superior	depress upper lip
	incisivus inferior	raise lower lip
	depressor labii inferioris	depress and pull back lower lip
	buccinator	flatten cheek
nostril	levator nasolabialis	lift nostrils and lips
	dilatator naris lateralis	dilate nostrils
	transversus nasi	dilate nostrils
	lateralis nasi	dilate nostrils
eyelids	orbicularis oculi	close eyelids
	corrugator supercilii	raise upper lid
	malaris	depress lower lid
	levator palpebrae superioris	raise upper lid
lower jaw (mandible)	masseter	close mouth
	temporalis	close mouth
	pterygoideus medialis	close and move mouth from side to side
	pterygoideus lateralis	move jaw forward and from side to side
	occipito mandibularis	open mouth
	digastricus	open mouth and, when jaws are closed, assist in swallowing
hyoid	mylo-hyoideus	raise floor of mouth, tongue and hyoid bone
	stylo-hyoideus	draw back tongue and raise larynx in act of swallowing
	occipito-hyoideus	move hyoid bone during swallowing
	genio-hyoideus	draw hyoid bone and tongue forward
	kerato-hyoideus	raise hyoid bone and larynx
	hyoideus transversus	raise root of tongue
neck	brachiocephalicus	move head and neck, and pull forward; sprain causes lameness
	sternocephalicus	move head and neck
	sterno-thyrohyoideus	assist in swallowing and sucking movements
	omo-hyoideus	move hyoid bone and root of tongue
	scalenus	move neck and first rib

Part	Muscle	Action
neck	cervicalis ascendens	extend neck
	rectus capitis ventralis major	flex or turn head
	rectus capitis ventralis minor	flex head
	rectus capitis lateralis	flex head
	longus colli	flex head
	intertransversalis colli	turn neck to side
	splenius	extend neck or turn to side
	longissimus capitis et atlantis	extend neck or turn to side
	complexus	extend head and neck or turn to side
	multifidus cervicis	extend head and neck or turn to side
	obliquus capitis posterior	rotate head
	obliquus capitis anterior	extend head or turn to side
	rectus capitis dorsalis major	extend head
	rectus capitis dorsalis minor	extend head
back	longissimus costarum	largest and longest muscle of body; extends back or turns to one side
	multifidus dorsi	extend back or turn to one side
	intertransversalis lumborum	hold back rigid or turn to one side
	coccygeus	press tail down or turn to one side
	sacro-coccygeus dorsalis	raise tail and/or turn to side
	sacro-coccygeus lateralis	raise tail and/or turn to side
	sacro-coccygeus ventralis	press tail down
chest	serratus dorsalis anterior	assist in breathing (inspiration)
	serratus dorsalis posterior	assist in breathing (expiration)
	longissimus costarum	assist in breathing (expiration)
	levator costarum	assist in breathing (inspiration)
	external intercostals	assist breathing
	internal intercostals	assist breathing
	retractor costae	move last rib
	rectus thoracis	assist breathing
	transverse thoracis	assist breathing (inspiration)
	diaphragm (qv)	principal muscle of breathing (inspiration)
abdomen	obliquus abdominis extemus	compress abdominal cavity to assist in defecation, birth, breathing (expiration)
	obliquus abdominis internus	compress abdominal cavity to assist in defecation, birth, breathing (expiration)

Part	Muscle	Action
abdomen	rectus abdominis	compress abdominal cavity to assist in defecation, birth, breathing (expiration)
	transversus abdominis	compress abdominal cavity to assist in defecation, birth, breathing (expiration)
	cremaster	pull up testis from scrotum
forelimb (1) shoulder	trapezius	raise shoulder blade (scapula)
	rhomboideus	raise and pull shoulder blade forward
	latissimus dorsi	flex shoulder joint
	brachiocephalicus	extend shoulder and elbow joint; see **m.** of neck
	superficial pectoral	advance and adduct leg
	deep pectoral	pull limb back
	serratus ventralis	support chest between two shoulder blades
	deltoideus	flex shoulder joint and abduct leg
	supraspinatus	extend shoulder joint; bursa present between **m.** and shoulder joint
	infraspinatus	abduct leg
	teres minor	flex shoulder joint and abduct leg
	subscapularis	adduct humerus bone
	teres major	flex shoulder joint and adduct leg
	coraco brachialis	flex shoulder joint and adduct leg
	capsularis	flex shoulder joint
(2) arm	biceps brachii	flex elbow joint, bursa present between tendon of biceps brachii and humerus bone
	brachialis	flex elbow joint
	tensor fasciae antibrachii	extend elbow joint
	triceps brachii	
	(a) long head	extend elbow and flex shoulder joints
	(b) lateral head	extend elbow joint
	(c) medial head	extend elbow joint
	anconeus	extend elbow joint
(3) forearm	extensor carpi radialis	extend knee and flex elbow joints; the tendon of **m.** possesses synovial sheath from 4in above to middle of knee (see hygroma)

Part	Muscle	Action
(3) forearm	common digital extensor	extend toe and knee and flex elbow. Tendon of **m.** has sheath extending from above knee to upper part of cannon, bursa between fetlock joint
	lateral digital extensor	extend toe and knee. **m.** possesses synovial sheath over knee and bursa at front of fetlock
	extensor carpi obliquus	extend knee joint. **m.** has synovial sheath over knee
	flexor carpi radialis	flex knee and extend elbow. **m.** has synovial sheath from 3in above knee to cannon
	flexor carpi ulnaris	flex knee and extend elbow joint
	ulnaris lateralis	flex knee and extend elbow joint
	superficial digital flexor	flex toe and extend elbow; tendon of **m.** has synovial sheath from above knee to middle third of cannon; and between lower end of cannon to middle of second phalanx
	superior check ligament	supports superficial flexor tendon above knee
	deep digital flexor	flex toe, knee, extend elbow; tendon of **m.** has synovial sheath in common with superficial digital flexor, qv; bursa (navicular) between tendon and navicular bone behind pedal bone
	interosseus medius	see suspensory ligament
hindlimb (1) back	psoas minor	flex pelvis on back
	psoas major	flex hip joint; rotate thigh outwards
	iliacus	flex hip joint; rotate thigh outwards
	quadratus lumborum	flex pelvis on back
	tensor fasciae latae	flex hip and extend stifle joint
(2) hindquarters	gluteus superficialis	flex hip joint and abduct limb
	gluteus medius	extend hip joint, abduct limb; concerned in actions of rearing, kicking and galloping; bursa (trochanteric) placed between tendon of **m.** and trochanter of femur bone; see bursitis
	gluteus profundus	abduct thigh

Part	Muscle	Action
(3) thigh	biceps femoris	extend limb as in rearing, kicking and galloping; bursa between **m.** and large and small trochanter
	semitendinosus	extend hip and hock joints
	semimembranosus	extend hip joint and adduct leg
	sartorius	flex hip joint and adduct leg
	gracilis	adduct leg
	pectineus	adduct leg and flex hip joint
	adductor	adduct limb and extend hip joint
	quadratos femoris	extend hip joint and adduct thigh
	obturator externus	adduct thigh
	obturator internus	rotate femur outward
	gemellus	rotate femur outward
	quadriceps femoris	extend stifle and flex hip
	(a) rectus femoris	
	(b) vastus lateralis	
	(c) vastus medialis	
	(d) vastus intermedius	
(4) second thigh (gaskin)	long digital extensor	extend toe and flex hock
	lateral digital extensor	extend toe and flex hock
	peroneus tertius (entirely tendinous)	mechanically to flex hock when stifle is flexed
	tibialis anterior	flex the hock joint; bursa placed between tendon of **m.** and medial ligament of hock
	gastrocnemius	extend hock and flex stifle; bursa between tendon of **m.** and point of hock; tendon known as Achilles
	superficial digital flexor	flex toe and extend hock; bursa placed under joint; tendon of **m.** behind hock
	deep digital flexor	flex toe and extend hock; synovial sheath round tendon of **m.** behind hock
	popliteus	flex stifle

Mustang (from Spanish mestengo, stranger; syn Bronco) Intelligent breed of great stamina, about 14 h and often dun. Descended from first horses on American continent for thousands of years, those brought by Spaniards invading Mexico in early 1500s. American Indians stole or bargained for many of Spaniards' horses but were careless, or ignorant, about breeding and horses degenerated into today's Cayuse. In 1971 law was enacted to protect and manage free-roaming horses and burros (qv) on public lands in 10 W States. By continuing to cull old/sick animals and via adopt-a-horse programme, US Dept of the Interior (Bureau of Land Management) aims to reduce number to 30,000. **American M. and Burro Assn,** PO Box 788, Lincoln, CA 95648 (916 633 9271).

MVB Abbr Bachelor of Veterinary Medicine.

MVetMed/MVM Abbrs Master of Veterinary Medicine.

MVSc Abbr Master Veterinary Science. See veterinary surgeon.

mycelium Mass of thread-like processes (hyphae) constituting fungus. Grows on lining of guttural pouch and subsequently invades it. Occurs in horses of all ages, mostly mature, and usually on one side. Caused by the fungus *Aspergillus* spp. **M.** affects tissues below pouch lining including nerves, blood vessels and bone. Symptoms include spontaneous and profuse bleeding down nostril on the affected side, facial paralysis and dysphagia, qv. An aneurysm on the external carotid artery may form and this can rupture causing fatal bleeding. Condition thought more likely where horses are in unventilated barns and fed spore-ridden hay. Spontaneous nosebleed may occur after nasal discharge down one nostril for several weeks. Nosebleeding is not precipitated by exercise and therefore differs from the common nosebleed of racehorse (see exercise induced pulmonary haemorrhage). Amount of blood varies from trickle to several litres. The sufferer may survive a number of haemorrhages before one is fatal. Other signs include Horner's syndrome (qv), laryngeal hemiplegia (qv), head tilt, head shaking and interference in gait. Diagnosis: endoscopic inspection of guttural pouch. Treatment: place catheter and flush the pouch with fungicide. In severe cases surgery of carotid may be necessary. See also bleeder.

mycoplasma Genus of bacteria sometimes causing respiratory infection. Difficult to isolate culture.

mycosis (myco- combining form, fungus + osis) Any fungal disease, eg ringworm. See guttural pouch.

See mud fever. **m. lymphangitis** See epizootic lymphangitis. | **mycotic dermatitis**

Extreme dilation of pupil. See eye. Adjective: mydriatic, eg mydriatic agent or drug which causes pupil of eye to dilate. Cf myotic. | **mydriasis**

(Gr myelos, marrow + graphein, to write) Radiography of spinal canal after injection of an opaque substance to highlight spinal cord and surrounding vertebral canal. Used to diagnose cervical/spinal injuries of wobbler syndrome (qv) and ataxia, qv. | **myelography**

(myelos, marrow + pathos, disease) Functional disturbance and pathology of spinal cord, with possible incoordination and ataxia, qv. May be result of viral disease (see virus) or protozoal infection. See encephalomyelitis. | **myelopathy**

(Gr mys, muscle) Combining form, of/related to muscle. | **myo-/my-**

(myo- + Gr kardia, heart) Inflamed heart muscle (myocardium). Occurs in bacterial infection, eg strangles, or viral infection with herpes, arteritis or influenza virus. Symptoms: reduced stamina and output of heart with rapid, irregular beat, abnormalities on electrocardiogram, collapse and sudden death. Diagnosis: on examination of electrocardiogram, qv. Postmortem findings vary with stage of condition; if acute there are diseased cells in heart muscle, if of long standing, heart muscle may be interspersed with fibrous (scar) tissue. Treatment: eliminate infection, rest, give digitalis. | **myocarditis**

Oxygen-carrying pigment of striped (qv) muscle. | **myoglobin**

Myoglobin (qv) in urine. See setfast. | **myoglobinuria**

(myo- + Gr metre, uterus) Smooth muscle lining uterus. Sensitive, especially during pregnancy, to hormone oxytocin, which causes it to contract. See biopsy, metritis. | **myometrium**

The most abundant protein of muscle which, with actin, is responsible for muscle contraction. | **myosin**

Inflamed muscle; caused by injury, sprain or infection. See blood blister, influenza, setfast. | **myositis**

Agent or drug which causes pupil to contract. Cf mydriasis. | **myotic**

Group of viruses including influenza. See virus. | **myxovirus**

N

nagana   Disease of horses, camels, pigs, dogs and monkeys. Occurs in some parts of Africa. Caused by *Trypanosoma brucei* transmitted by tsetse fly, tabanid fly and stable fly. Trypanosomes live in blood and lymphatic systems, breeding by longitudinal division. They are sucked in by a biting fly and develop in the insect's gut and salivary glands. When infected fly bites an animal, nodule develops at site. This becomes larger and trypanosomes multiply, causing fever and swollen lymph glands. A series of crises and remissions occurs (parasite is in blood only during active stages). Essential features of trypanosomiasis: intermittent fever; anaemia; enlarged lymph glands, liver and spleen; progressive emaciation and sometimes drowsiness. Treatment: see diminazene aceturate, homidium bromide, quinapyramine salts and suramin.

nandrolone phenylpropionate   (trade name: Nandrolin) Drug with actions similar to male sex hormone testosterone but not as potent. Causes body to retain nitrogen, phosphorus and calcium and helps build muscle and improve appetite. Used in wasting conditions, fractures, excess bone reaction after injury, eg splint. Overdosage may cause temporarily smaller testes and virilisation in mares.

narcolepsy   (Gr narke, numbness + lepsis, taking hold, seizure) Uncontrollable desire for sleep or sudden attacks of sleep occurring at intervals, eg in foals with cerebral damage. Called also Gelineau's syndrome, paroxysmal sleep, sleep epilepsy. Familial pattern of **n.** in some miniature horses in USA.

nasal   Of the nose. **n. cavity** Passage through length of skull, divided into right and left halves (by septum nasi). See wind, sinusitis. **n. passages** Air passages of head, divided by **n.** septum and ethmoid turbinate bone.

nasogastric   From nostril to stomach. **n. tube** used to administer medication, fluids or oil. Can be indwelling ie stitched or taped in place for some time, especially in foals unable to suck.

nasolacrimal duct   Tube between eye and nostril, through which tears drain. May become blocked causing tears to overflow down face. See eye, diseases of.

natal   (L natus, birth) Of birth, qv.

natamycin   (trade name: Mycophyt) Antibiotic used to treat ringworm and other fungal infections.

Of a nation. **N. Foaling Bank** Private enterprise which tries to match orphaned foals with mares who have lost foals. Meretown Stud, Newport, Salop TF10 8BX (01952 811234). **N. Stud**, Newmarket, Suffolk CB8 0XE (01638 663464).

national

Popular, versatile breed around 15 hands, based on Arab, Criollo or Spanish horses.

Native Mexican

See umbilicus.

navel

(L navicula, boat) Boat-shaped bone behind coffin bone. **n. disease** (syns navicular bursitis, bursitis podotrochlearis) Inflammation of bursa, deep flexor tendon and **n.** bone. Bone and tendon develop adhesions which cause pain and lameness. Upright pasterns likely to increase concussion and make horses more susceptible to **n.d.** Symptoms: history of intermittent lameness which decreases on rest and after work (horse warms up); standing with affected toe pointed; shuffling gait, especially if both forefeet affected. Diagnosis: on symptoms, X-ray (**n.** bone seen to have ragged edge and areas of rarefied bone) and nerve block. Treatment: inject bursa with corticosteroids or hyaluronic acid. Only neurectomy (qv) will give permanent relief.

navicular

(syn Italian) Horse developed around Naples, from Spanish stock in 16th and 17th centuries. Now extinct in true form, but said to have been long-lived, late-maturing. Similar to Spanish Jennet, qv.

Neapolitan

(1) Anatomical term meaning constricted portion, eg **n.** of uterus. (2) Part between head and thorax; differs according to breed, but ewe-**n.** (qv) usually considered a fault (see Turkoman). Sexually mature male develops thicker, more crested **n.** than gelding or female.

neck

(Gr nekrosis, deadness) Death of cells or groups of cells. **focal n.** That affecting liver of foetus infected with herpesvirus.

necrosis

Affected by necrosis.

necrotic

Examination of body to determine cause of death. See post-mortem.

necropsy

Worm of class Nematoda. See filaria, redworm, stomach worm, whiteworm.

nematode

(trade names: Dermobion, Neobiotic, Neostat) White or yellow-white odourless powder produced from *Streptomyces fradiae*. Antibiotic poorly absorbed from alimentary tract and active

neomycin sulphate

neomycin sulphate | against gram-negative and some gram-positive bacteria. Used in diarrhoea, joint-ill in foals (injected into joints), in uterine infections and locally in dermatitis.

neonatal | (Gr neos-, new + L natus, born) Of newborn. **n. maladjustment syndrome** (syns NMS, barker, wanderer, dummy, respiratory distress, shaker foal, convulsive foal) Condition of newborn foal characterised by grossly disturbed behaviour including convulsions, loss of suck reflex, muscle spasms, incessant chewing, wandering, coma, subnormal temperature, increased acidity of blood, low blood oxygen and abnormally high breathing rate sometimes accompanied by barking noise. Symptoms appear in first 24 hours. Cause is unknown but damaged brain, lungs and heart (due to pressure during birth) or disturbed foetal development most likely. Treatment: good general nursing (see newborn foal), sedatives, anticonvulsant drugs, oxygen inhalation, intravenous sodium bicarbonate, corticosteroids and feeding by stomach tube – see nasogastric tube. Foal may deteriorate and die or recover without apparent after-effects.

neonate | Newly born, foal in first month or so of life.

neoplasm | (neo + Gr plasma, formation) New, abnormal growth. See growth.

neoplastic | Of tumour or growth.

neostygmine methylsulphate | Colourless crystals or white powder with bitter taste and no smell; has action similar to physostigmine qv, counters enzymes that destroy acetylcholine and therefore promotes effects similar to parasympathetic (qv) nerve stimulation. Used in grass sickness.

nephritis | (Gr nephros, kidney + -itis) Inflamed kidney(s) caused by bacterial infection, toxins, poisons such as mercury, arsenic, oxalates and certain drugs. Diagnosed on finding protein in urine (proteinuria). See kidney, sleepy foal disease.

nephro- | (Gr nephros, kidney) Combining form: kidney.

nephron | (Gr nephros, kidney + on) Anatomical and functional unit of the kidney (qv).

nephrosis | See kidney, diseases of.

nephrosplenic ligament | Ligament between kidney and spleen, important in some cases of colic where large bowel becomes trapped over ligament. Treat by rolling or laparotomy.

Colloq for pathway which conveys messages to and from brain and spinal cord, controlling purposeful and automatic actions of body and its parts. See autonomic nervous system. **n. cell** (syn neuron) Basic unit of nervous system; cell containing nucleus and one or more processes – dendrite (like branching of a tree) or axon (long, slender fibre). Axon carries nervous impulses which may be passed to other cells across junction known as synapse. See nervous system. **n. block** (syn block) An injection of anaesthetic along course of **n.** causing loss of sensation to area it supplies. Used to help stitching of wounds, minor surgery, or in diagnosis. **infra-orbital n. b.** anaesthetic injected where **n.** enters or leaves infra-orbital canal of skull, ie 3cm (approx 1in) below outer angle of eye and just below facial crest; or midway between nasal notch and front end of facial crest. Used for surgery of maxillary sinus, upper incisor and cheek teeth or nostrils and upper lip. **mandibular alveolar n. b.** One at entry to mandibular canal, on inside of lower jaw. Used for surgery of lower jaw, lower molars, incisors and lower lip. **supra-orbital n. b.** One blocking branch of 5th cranial **n.**, usually where it travels out of bony bridge over eye. Used in surgery of upper eyelid. **n.b. of legs** Used to diagnose lameness or repair wounds in area supplied by blocked **n.** (If pain is in foot, **n.** supplying foot is blocked and horse goes sound while anaesthetic lasts. If horse is still lame, the pain is above **n.b.**) (1) **median n.b.** At inside of elbow joint. Used with blocks of ulnar and musculocutaneous **n.** to diagnose lameness in knee joint (carpus) or for minor surgery. (2) **ulna n.b.** anaesthetic injected 10cm (approx 4in) above accessory carpal bone. Used for minor surgery of outside front of knee. (3) **musculocutaneous n.b.** One between distal ends of biceps and brachialis muscles. (See muscles, table of.) Used with blocks of median and ulna **n.s.** (4) **tibial n.b.** About 10cm (4in) above point of hock on inside of digital flexor muscle. Desensitises inside back of hock. (5) **volar and planter n.b.** Used to diagnose lameness or stitch wounds below knee or hock. Volar **n.s** are branches of median **n.** Throughout cannon region they lie either side of deep flexor tendon behind the artery and vein. Each volar **n.** divides into 3 branches at fetlock (on a level with sesamoid bones), 1 and 2 supply front of fetlock, pastern and coronary regions, the corium, lateral cartilages and corono-pedal joint capsule, 3 (the posterior digital nerve, largest branch) supplies deeper structures of foot, including navicular bone. Plantar **n.s** in hind limb originate from tibial **n.** and are distributed in a similar way. Volar and planter **n.s** can be blocked high or low, eg wound across front of fetlock can be treated by injecting 5 ml of local anaesthetic over nerves on both sides of flexor tendons (volar or planter **n.s**). After about 15 minutes area is insensitive and wound can be cleaned and stitched. Area will remain insensitive for up

nerve

TABLE OF NERVES

Nerve		Function
CRANIAL (12 PAIRS):		
I	olfactory	smell
II	optic	sight
III	oculomotor	eye movement
IV	trochlear	eye movement
V	trigeminal	sensation eyelids, face, soft palate mouth, gums, teeth, tongue
VI	abducens	eye movement
VII	facial	sense of taste, sensation of area round ear, movement of lips
VIII	vestibulocochlear	hearing and balance
IX	glossopharyngeal	sensation and movement of soft palate and tongue
X	vagus	controls certain actions of larynx, heart and lungs
XI	spinal accessory	movement of neck muscles
XII	hypoglossal	movement of tongue
SPINAL (42 PAIRS)		
(a) 8 cervical (neck)	1st to 5th	supply sensation to skin over ear, poll and neck; control muscular movements in these areas
	6th	sensation and movement to lower part of neck and front of shoulder; contributes to phrenic **n.**
	7th and 8th	contribute to phrenic **n.** and brachial plexus
phrenic		movement of diaphragm
brachial plexus: formed from last 3 cervical and first 2 thoracic **n.**s		sensation and movement of forelimb, branches include: **median n., suprascapular n., brachial n. and ulnar n.**
(b) 18 thoracic (chest)	1st to 18th	sensation of skin over chest and movement of muscles causing breathing motion of chest wall (rib cage)
(c) 6 lumbar (back)	1st to 6th	control muscle and skin of loins and croup
	1st, 2nd, 3rd	sensation and movement of belly muscles, external genitalia
	4th, 5th, 6th	form lumbosacral plexus
	lumbosacral plexus formed by 4th, 5th, 6th lumbar **n.**s	supplies sensation and control of movement to hind limb, branches include: **femoral n., obturator n., gluteal n., sciatic n., peroneal n.** and **tibial n.**
(d) 5 sacral (croup)	1st to 5th	sensation and movement to base of tail, perineum, anus, penis/vulva
(e) 5 coccygeal (tail)	1st to 5th	sensation and movement of tail

to 1 hour (depending on type of anaesthetic). **posterior digital n.b.** Limited to diagnosis of navicular lameness. Anaesthetic is injected over **n.** in middle of pastern in grooves between deep flexor tendon and 1st phalanx (pastern bone).

nerve

Arrangement of nerve cells (qv) and their fibres (axons) which transmit nervous impulses from one part of body to another, in definite pathways through the spinal cord and/or brain. **central n.s.** (CNS) Concentration of nervous tissue in head and spinal cord. **peripheral n.s.** (PNS) Part of **n.s.** outside CNS. **N.s.** is based on reflex arc in which two or more nerve cells (neurons) conduct nervous impulse from point of stimulation to structures of action, eg muscle acting to remove part away from needle. Stimulus initiates nervous impulse (sensory) which passes along a nerve connected to CNS; this sparks off a further impulse (motor) that passes outwards to muscle. Nerve cells in CNS form pathways which intercept or control reflex arc by conducting messages up and down spinal cord. In this way the higher centres of nervous activity in brain are made aware of happenings in all parts of body, at a conscious or unconscious level: eg (1) horse that overcomes instinct to withdraw its leg from a painful stimulus exerts conscious or voluntary (and higher) control; (2) when horse increases its breathing rate at exercise, chest muscles are responding to nervous impulses started by body cells sensitive to changes in blood levels of oxygen and carbon dioxide. These impulses reach breathing centre of brain which controls rhythmic rate and depth of breathing and alters rate and/or depth to compensate for changed gaseous concentration in blood. Cf autonomic nervous system.

nervous system

(urticaria) Form of allergic dermatitis caused by plant pollens or other protein antigens (see allergy). Weals develop on neck, flanks and quarters, varying from small spots to large areas. Hairs stand up and soft swelling beneath pits on pressure. May be painful but fluid may drain to dependent parts such as muzzle, abdomen or legs. Swelling of head is common in severe cases. Condition develops rapidly and usually disappears spontaneously, but can be controlled with antihistamine drugs, eg cortisone. See dog's mercury.

nettle rash

(L neuralis, Gr neuron, nerve) Of a nerve.

neural

Cutting of a nerve to abolish sense of pain (eg back (posterior) digital nerve at level of sesamoid bones). This removes sensation to navicular bone, allowing horse with navicular disease to go sound. Disadvantage is that loss of sensation removes protective reflexes, allowing injury. May cause stumbling and shedding of hoof.

neurectomy

neuron | (Gr neuron, nerve) Nerve cell, qv.

neurotoxin | Poison which affects nerves causing paralysis or tetany eg botulism and tetanus toxins.

neutralisation test | Laboratory test for antibody/antigen reaction (qv) between toxin and antitoxin.

neutropenia | (neutrophil + Gr penia, poverty) Decrease in number of neutrophilic white cells in blood. See blood.

neutrophilia | Increase in number of neutrophils (leukocytes stainable by neutral dyes) in blood; sign of infection.

newborn | Foal in first week of life. **n. foal, congenital abnormalities of:**

Condition	Synonyms	Predominant Signs
uroperitoneum	ruptured bladder	straining; reduced urine flow, abdominal distension (signs appear from 2nd or 3rd day)
hyperflexion of limbs	contracted tendons; contracted forelimbs	knuckling over
hypoflexion of limbs		slack ligaments; reduced muscle tone
cleft palate, hare lip		regurgitation of milk
parrot jaw	undershot jaw	
microphthalmia	button eyes	small or absent eye(s)
umbilical urachal fistula	pervious urachus, patent urachus	wet cord stump
hernia		failure of umbilical and/or inguinal ring to close

n. foal, diseases of | Groups: (1) Infective conditions characterised by fever, lethargy and weakened suck reflex. (2) Non-infective conditions characterised by gross disturbance in behaviour. (3) Congenital abnormalities. (4) Immunological conditions characterised by reaction between maternal and foetal tissues. See septicaemia (group 1); neonatal maladjustment syndrome, prematurity, meconium retention (group 2); haemolytic jaundice (group 4). **n. foal immaturity** (syn dysmaturity) Foal born after 325 days' gestation, showing all appearances of prematurity, qv. **n. foal, nursing** (1) Restrain foal gently and help it stand. (2) Feed through stomach tube or by bottle. See food. (3) Raise surrounding temperature if foal's rectal temperature falls below 37.2°C. (approx 99°F). Use hot-air blowers, heat lamps, rugs, washable electric blankets. In severe cases stable temperature should rise to 26.6°C. (approx 78°F). (4) Remove meconium by enema and give liquid paraffin in food. (5) Place convulsive and comatose foals on rugs or soft material to avoid damage to head. (6) Powder areas where bedsores are most likely, ie point of hip, outside of stifle and elbows. (7) Turn foal from side to side to help blood circulation. See National Foaling Bank.

n. foal, diseases of

New Forest pony

Tough sure-footed breed that has roamed **N.F.** district of S England for centuries (mentioned in Domesday Book, 1085). Attempts to improve breed include one by Queen Victoria, whose Arab stallion Zorah lived 8 years in the forest. **N.F.** is now fairly static type and breeds true. Its natural home is densely populated compared with those of other native breeds, and it is a traffic-proof and popular child's pony when broken. Seems able to eat acorns without serious ill-effects (see oak poisoning). Usually up to 14.2 h and grey, bay or brown. No piebald, skewbald or blue-eyed creams acceptable. **N.F. Pony and Cattle Breeding Soc**, Beacon Cottage, Burley, Hants BH24 4EW (01425 402272). See tabanid fly.

Newmarket cough

See influenza.

nicotinamide

White crystalline odourless powder with bitter taste. For actions and uses see nicotinic acid.

nicotinic acid

(syn vitamin B_3) White or creamy-white odourless acid-tasting crystals or powder; widely distributed in food. With nicotinamide, part of enzyme system.

nictitating membrane

(syn third eyelid) See eyelid.

nightshade poisoning

Rare, as all members of family Henbane (deadly **n.** (syn belladonna), thornapple, woody **n.**, garden **n.**, wild tobacco) unlikely to be eaten because they taste bitter. Symptoms: central nervous depression, salivation, inflamed gut with diarrhoea and colic.

nitrate/nitrite poisoning

Caused by eating artificial manures, plants and weed which take up **n.** eg oat, wheat and rye hay, barley, sugar beet. Symptoms: abdominal pain, diarrhoea, muscular weakness, incoordination, convulsions, difficult breathing, coma (seen as bluish mucous membranes) and death. Less severe cases may be listless and abort. Diagnosis: on symptoms and dark, chocolate-coloured blood.

nitrofurantoin

Odourless yellow powder with bitter taste. Antibiotic used to treat urinary or kidney infections but pH of urine must be below 8 as activity of drug greatly reduced by alkaline urine.

nitrofurazone	Antibiotic used in skin and urinary tract infections. Actions similar to nitrofurantoin, qv.
node	(L nodus, knot) Swelling. See gland.
Nonius	Hungarian breed developed from Anglo-Norman stallion named **N**. Usually quiet-tempered, often dark bay. Two types: large, up to 17 h used for agriculture; small, around 15.2 h.
noradrenaline	See norepinephrine. **n. acid tartrate** White crystalline odourless bitter-tasting powder; main substance released by medulla of adrenal gland when sympathetic nerves are stimulated. Causes rise in blood pressure. Less active than adrenaline, qv.
norepinephrine	A naturally-occurring amine (catecholamine, qv). A hormone released by special nerve cells and adrenal medulla. See adrenaline.
Northland	Little-known Norwegian breed. About 13 hands, usually dark-coloured.
normochromic	Having normal colour, eg normal haemoglobin content of red cells.
nose	(L nasus, Gr rhis) Part of face beneath eye level and above muzzle; includes nostrils. **roman n.** Convex profile, eg in Kladruber.
nostril	(syn naris, pl nares) Entrance to air passage of head; skin and mucous membrane supported by ring of cartilage. **false n.** Blind sac in upper part of **n. true n.** Direct entrance to nasal cavity (air passage).
notifiable diseases	See veterinary rules.
NSAID	Abbr nonsteroidal anti-inflammatory drug eg phenylbutazone ('bute'), flunixin meglumine.
nuclear	Of a nucleus. **n. scintigraphy** See scintigraphy.
nucleus	(L dim. of nux, nut, pl nuclei) Small body in cell, containing inherited material (chromosomes, genes) which controls cell function. See DNA.
Numinbah horse sickness	See crofton weed.
nutrition	See food.

(Gr nystagmos, drowsiness, deriving from nystazein, to nod) Involuntary rapid movement of eyeball. Occurs under anaesthesia or in brain damage or injury.

nystagmus

Yellow or light-brown powder with characteristic odour. Antibiotic active against wide range of fungi and yeasts. Poorly absorbed from alimentary canal. Used in powder, cream or ointment to treat ringworm, also to treat uterine infection following fungal abortion.

nystatin

O

oak poisoning | (from common **o**.s of Britain, *Quercus robur* and *Q. petracea*) Occurs if horse eats leaves or acorns (see New Forest pony). Symptoms, some days later: dullness, loss of appetite, constipation, sometimes followed by diarrhoea containing blood, excessive urination, pale mucous membranes and watery discharge from eyes. At postmortem: inflamed gut and stomach. Treatment: give liquid paraffin.

obstipation | (L obstipatio) Severe impaction (constipation).

obturator | (L) Disc which closes an opening. **o. foramen** Opening in floor of pelvis formed by ischium and pubis. See Fig 30 (p250).

occiput | Area at base of skull formed by occipital bone. Projects above as poll. Adjective: occipital.

OCD | See osteochondritis dissecans.

oedema | (syns edema, filling, filled leg, plaque) Abnormal accumulation of fluid outside cells. It collects in spaces below skin, causing soft swellings that leave a pit on pressure. Due to: (1) more permeable blood vessels (ie they allow water and protein to pass freely), caused by toxins, allergy, infection; (2) abnormal decrease in protein in blood, eg in malnutrition or wasting diseases; (3) obstruction of blood returning to heart in veins; (4) heart disease causing increased blood pressure in veins; (5) kidney disease causing increased blood pressure and improper filtering of blood; (6) too much food, especially that high in protein; (7) inflammation from any cause, including sprain; (8) obstruction of lymph flow due to overloading of vessels, eg in **o**. of belly, close to udder at foaling time. **pulmonary o.** Fluid in lung due to capillaries damaged by toxins, allergy or circulatory failure. Common in virus infection and fatal neonatal maladjustment syndrome.

oesophagus | (syns esophagus, gullet) Muscular tube from throat to stomach (about 150cm or 60in). Sited on left of lower part of neck. Extends through chest and diaphragm to open into stomach through a weak sphincter (ring of muscle), which prevents regurgitation of food except in rare cases. See vomit.

oestradiol | Naturally occurring oestrogen, qv.

Oestridae | Family of insects belonging to sub-order Cyclorrhapha, containing bot, qv, and warble, qv.

Naturally occurring oestrogen, qv.   **oestriol**

Hormone of steroid group. Natural **o.**s include oestradiol, oestrone, oestriol, equilin, equilenin; secreted by ovary, placenta, adrenal cortex and testes. In mare, responsible for behaviour and changes in sex cycle (see oestrous cycle). **synthetic o.** See stilboestrol.   **oestrogen**

Naturally occurring oestrogen, qv.   **oestrone**

(syn estrous cycle) Sexual cycle of mare. Alternating periods of sexual activity, ie oestrus (when mare accepts stallion) and dioestrus (when she rejects him). Typical oestrus lasts 5 days, dioestrus 15 days. Cycle varies, being a regular 20 days probably only in spring and summer. It is controlled by pituitary gland through secretion of hormones FSH (follicle stimulating hormone) and LH (luteinising hormone). During oestrus, follicle develops in ovary, which ruptures, shedding egg into fallopian tube. Ovary secretes hormone oestrogen which causes oestrous behaviour and changes in genital tract including outpouring of mucus. Oestrus ends when egg is shed (ovulation) and a yellow body is formed (under influence of LH). Yellow body secretes progesterone which causes dioestrus and prepares uterus for fertilised egg which arrives from fallopian tube six days after fertilisation. If fertilisation does not occur, the yellow body ceases to function about day 15 and thereby stimulates pituitary to produce more FSH and cycle starts again. Life of yellow body is probably ended by prostaglandin secreted by uterus. Successful mating requires that stallion serves mare about 12 hours before ovulation, which usually occurs about 24 hours prior to end of oestrus.   **oestrous cycle**

State of being in heat, ie in an oestrous (receptive) state.   **oestrus**

(L unguentum) Semi-solid preparation for external use and with fatty base, such as lanolin.   **ointment**

Early-maturing German breed of about 17 h. Has influenced Lithuanian, Latvian and Friesian breeds and now has some Thoroughbred blood. See cerebellar degeneration; warm-blooded.   **Oldenburg**

(Gr olekranon) Bony point of elbow (ulna bone). See dropped elbow.   **olecranon**

(L fat skin; pl omenta) Fold, near stomach, of the membrane (peritoneum) lining abdomen.   **omentum**

(trade name: Losec) Drug to prevent or treat ulcers of stomach   **omeprazole**

omeprazole *(italic)* and duodenum. Has powerful action of preventing secretion of acid by the gastric lining.

onager (*Equus hemionus onager*) One of 2 sub-species of Asiatic wild ass. Lives in herds in Afghanistan and Iran and was probably ass of the Bible. See ass.

Onchocerca See filaria.

ophthalmia (syn ophthalmitis) Inflammation of eye/s.

ophthalmic (from Gr ophthalmos, eye) Of the eye/s.

ophthalmoscope Instrument containing mirrors and light source. Used to see inside eye and retina.

opisthotonos Drawing back of head due to muscle spasms, as in brain injury. See bracken poisoning.

opportunistic Microorganism which causes disease only because of pre-existing condition such as other infection or immune suppression.

oral Of the mouth or by mouth, eg medication.

orchitis (Gr orchis, testicle + itis) Inflammation of a testis, normally as a result of infection or trauma.

Oribatid mite (colloq beetle mite) Species of family Oribatidae belonging to class Arachnida. Small blind dark-coloured mite which lives in soil where it digests organic matter. It carries the intermediate form (cysticercus) of tapeworm, qv.

Orlov (after Count Alexis **O.**) Russian (qv) breed founded when Count **O.** crossed Arab stallion with Dutch mare in 1770s. Thoroughbred, Mecklenburg and Danish blood introduced and breed is renowned for Arab-like head and trotting ability. Up to 17 h and sometimes termed **O.** trotter. **O.**/Standardbred cross (syn Metis trotter) may be faster than **O.** trotter. **O.** Rostopschiner is good saddle horse.

orthopaedic (Gr orthos, straight + pais, child) relating to function of skeletal system.

osselet New bone growth in lateral fetlock associated with lateral digital extensor tendon on front of pastern bone. Causes joint inflammation and enlargement, pain on flexion and lameness. Diagnosis: on X-ray and symptoms. Treatment: rest, anti-inflammatory therapy, intra-articular medication or irradiation. See degenerative joint disease.

Inflamed bone. Most common cause is trauma, qv. See **pedal o.**, periostitis.

osteitis/ostitis

(Gr osteon, bone + arthron, joint + itis, inflammation) See degenerative joint disease.

osteoarthritis

Any disease of bones and joints. **hypertrophic pulmonary o.** Previously known as Marie-Bamberger's disease. Formation of new, irregular bone on surface of each leg bone, often with lung disease. Symptoms include cough, difficult breathing. Result of infection, new growth, eg tumour or idiopathic (self-generated or unknown) cause. Treatment: antibiotics, anti-inflammatory drugs. Often fatal, spontaneous remission in some cases, response to therapy in others (eg if infection is cause).

osteoarthropathy

(Gr osteon, bone + chondros, cartilage + itis, inflammation) Conditions associated with defective development of bone from cartilage resulting in inflammation in affected joints. Often loose fragments of cartilage and/or bone present in joint, usually stifle, hock, fetlock, shoulder. Treatment: surgery, intra-articular medication with hyaluronic acid or cortisone.

osteochondritis/osis

Infection of bone marrow tissue and neighbouring bone. May occur after compound fracture (see fracture) or if site of surgery is infected. Symptoms: forming of cavities which discharge pus, pain, swelling, lameness and in severe cases, fever. Diagnosis: on symptoms, X-rays and increasing white blood cell count (leucocytosis).

osteomyelitis

Abnormal development of bone from surface of joint, often a result of degenerative joint disease, qv. Referred to as an osselet if on front of fetlock joint. May break off to float in joint. Cf joint mouse/mice.

osteophyte

Abnormal rarefaction of bone. See big head.

osteoporosis

One of pair of female glands; typically bean-shaped, varying from 4–8cm (1¹/₂in–3in) long and weighing about 18g (²/₃oz). It is attached to broad ligament suspending uterus and enclosed in a capsule with an opening (ovulation fossa) through which egg passes at ovulation. O. consists of network of fibrous tissue in which numerous fluid sacs (follicles) develop; in each follicle is an egg. Follicle grows and eventually ruptures (ovulates), shedding egg into fallopian tube. Bleeding occurs into cavity of ruptured follicle and a yellow body (corpus luteum) is formed. See oestrous cycle.

ovary

over-reaching	Action in which hind foot steps on heel of the forefoot on same side. Fault lessened by careful shoeing. Cf cross-firing, forging. See gait.
oviduct	See fallopian tube.
ovulation	The shedding of an ovum. See follicle stimulating hormone.
ovum	(L; pl ova; syn egg) Female gamete containing hereditary material. At birth, ovary contains about 30,000 ova; after sexual maturity they develop in Graafian follicles; during heat periods one or two are released (ovulation) to enter fallopian tube for fertilisation. **O.** is one of the largest cells of body, 120–180 thousandths of a millimetre (or 120–180μ). It contains mass of cytoplasm surrounded by cell membrane (vitelline membrane) and a thick, transparent membrane (zona pellucida). During development chromosome numbers are reduced by half to haploid number (see chromosome). Egg survives only about 12–24 hours after ovulation unless fertilised. Unfertilised egg stays in fallopian tube and slowly disintegrates, but fertilised egg passes into uterus.
oxybendazole	(trade names: Equidin, Equitac). Drug to treat intestinal parasites of the horse. Effective against large and small strongyles, roundworms and pinworms. See benzimidazole.
oxyfenbendazole	Drug to treat intestinal parasites of the horse. Effective against large and small strongyles, roundworm, pinworm and stomach worm. See benzimidazole; anthelmintic.
oxygen	Colourless odourless gas, given by inhalation, (1) with other gases during anaesthesia, (2) to foals suffering from low blood oxygen, (3) to resuscitate foals. See neonatal maladjustment syndrome.
oxyphenbutazone	Chemical excreted in urine if horse given phenylbutazone, qv.
oxytetracycline hydrochloride/ dihydrate	(trade names: Duphacycline, Embacycline, Engemycin, Terramycin) Yellow odourless bitter-tasting crystalline powder. Antibiotic with actions and uses similar to tetracycline hydrochloride, qv.
oxytocin	(trade names: Oxytocin-S, Oxytocin Leo) Hormone formed by posterior lobe of pituitary gland. Causes contraction of uterus, completion of 3rd stage labour, running of milk before and during birth and possibly the let-down of milk when foal is sucking. Sometimes given to induce foaling. Synthetic **o.** used after foaling to restrict uterine bleeding. See birth; pituitary.

Symbol for phosphorus.	**P**
See gait.	**pace**
Sino-atrial (SA) node from which impulse causing heartbeat originates. See heart impulse.	**pacemaker, cardiac**
(Gr pachy, thick + derma, skin) Abnormal thickening of skin, qv. Inexplicable condition in which horse loses hair over large parts of body and skin becomes thick, dry and scaly.	**pachyderm**
(syns pcv, haematocrit) Percentage volume of red blood cells to whole blood measured by centrifuging (spinning) column of blood containing anticoagulant for 10 minutes, so that cells separate from plasma. Normal values 35–50 per cent according to age, conditioning. Level rises with fitness, on excitement and in pathological conditions such as acute colic, grass sickness and dehydration. It falls in anaemia, haemolytic jaundice, infections, especially those associated with fever, and severe haemorrhage. **Pcv** measured in very small (capillary) tube and spun for 5 minutes is termed microhaematocrit. See blood tests.	**packed cell volume**
Form of Anglo-Arab established in Iran from English Thoroughbred, Arab and Plateau Persian.	**Pahlavan**
(L poena, dolor; Gr algos, odyne) Sensation produced by stimulation of specialised nerve-endings; most plentiful in skin and membrane (eg peritoneum) lining body, body cavities, joints, etc. Symptoms: sweating, pawing ground, anxious expression, possibly rolling (see meconium retention; colic) or lameness. **p.-killing drugs** Buscopan, pethidine, phenyl butazone, flunixin meglumine, butorphanol.	**pain**
Horse developed from American Quarterhorse and Thoroughbred. Popular for its patchy colouring, similar to Pinto, qv. **American P. Horse Assn**, PO Box 961023, Fort Worth, TX 76161-0023 (817 439 3400).	**Paint**
Partition separating mouth and nasal cavities. Divided into hard **p.** (in front) and soft **p.** behind. Foals sometimes born with openings in, or complete lack of, **p.** (cleft **p.**). See soft palate.	**palate**
Original golden horse of the West; colour rather than breed.	**palomino**

palomino | Societies promoting **p.** allow all shades of gold, from pale blond to almost chestnut. Mane and tail should be cream and only markings allowed are white, on legs and face. Many foals born with blue eyes which darken with maturity, blue eyes not accepted in adult. Pinto, draught, albino and pony blood barred, otherwise any breed can be used to produce **p.** colouring. Probably of Spanish origin with Arab and Barb blood. May take name from Spaniard Juan de **P.**, who was given a **p.** by Hernan Cortez (conqueror of Mexico). **P. Horse Breeders of America**, 15253 E Skelly Dr, Tulsa, OK 74116-2637 (918 438 1234). **British P. Soc**, Penrhiwllan, Llandysul, Wales SA44 5NZ (01239 851387). Cf Haflinger; Highland pony; coat colouring.

palpation | (L palpatio) Act of feeling with hand, eg **p.** of foal's abdomen in order to detect tympany or fluid. **p. of ovaries** See rectal examination.

palpebra | (L, pl palpebrae) Eyelid, qv. Adjective: palpebral.

pancreas | (L from Gr pan, all + kreas, flesh; pl pancreata) Digestive gland in abdomen. It secretes substances which pass through duct to duodenum and help digest food. Also secretes hormone (insulin) which is absorbed into bloodstream and controls level of blood sugar. See diabetes. Adjective: pancreatic.

pancreatitis | Inflamed pancreas.

pancuronium bromide | (trade name: Pavulon) Substance which blocks nervous control of muscles resulting in paralysis. Used in anaesthesia. See tubocurarine.

Pange | A popular cross between native Baltic mares and a trotter stallion.

pannus | (L, a piece of cloth) (1) Condition where cornea invaded by granulation tissue and blood vessels. (2) Thickening of inflamed joint lining, forming pad-like enlargement.

papilla | (L, pl papillae) Anatomical term meaning small, nipple-shaped projection or elevation, eg teats of mammary glands, openings of salivary glands onto oral mucosa.

papilloma | See growth.

papillomatosis | Syn milk warts, qv.

para- | (Gr pare, beyond) Prefix meaning besides or near.

(para- + Gr kentesis, puncture) Surgical puncture of cavity to draw off fluid, eg from abdomen (**p.** abdominis) of newborn foal with ruptured bladder. See bladder, rupture of.

paracentesis

See liquid paraffin.

paraffin

Little known worm parasite, about 4cm long, found in tissue beneath areas of raised skin, usually on shoulders and hindquarters. Life-cycle not fully documented. Cf filaria, see Budyonovsky.

Parafilaria multipapillosa

(para + Gr lyein, to loosen) Loss of use of a part due to injury or disease of nerve or brain. **facial p.** Common condition caused by injured facial nerve as it rounds back of lower jaw. Symptoms: drooping of upper eyelid and ear, nostrils and lips pulled to one side, drooping of lower lip. Usually occurs on one side; if on both (bilateral), it is more serious. Treatment: feed with soft mashes or, if severe, by stomach tube. Partial recovery may occur but horse may be left with permanent disability. **obturator p.** May occur after fracture of pelvis or at foaling. Symptoms: inability to move hindlimb due to paralysis of muscles obturator externus, pectineus adductor and gracilis. **pharyngeal p.** Associated with guttural pouch mycosis, qv, and botulism. Results in inability to swallow, with food material present at nostrils. **pudendal nerve p.** Due to infection or fracture of pelvis injuring nerve which supplies retractor muscles of penis, so that it hangs limply from sheath. **radial p.** See dropped elbow. **supras-capula nerve p.** (syn sweeny) Symptoms: wasting of muscles on shoulder, possibly lameness. Wasting is usually permanent but some recovery of muscle function is normal. Treatment: inject corticosteroids immediately after injury, use faradic stimulation. **tail p.** Tail root hangs limp and is not raised during defecating or staling; anus and surrounding skin may also be paralysed. Caused by fractured sacrum or injured tail (coccygeal) vertebrae. See Hobday, wobbler syndrome, stringhalt, wind, physiotherapy, corticosteroids, muscle, hyperkalaemic periodic **p.**

paralysis

(Gr parasites) Animal living on or in another and at host's expense. Those which affect horses: **external** (ectoparasites) – tick, qv, harvest mite, qv, mites causing sarcoptic mange, chorioptic mange, psoroptic mange, and demodectic mange (all see mange), louse, qv; **internal** (endoparasites) – tapeworm, qv, fluke, qv, redworm, qv, lungworm, qv, stomach worm, qv, whiteworm, qv, seatworm, qv, filiaria, qv, *Parafilaria multipapillosa*, warble fly maggot (see warble fly), botfly maggot (see bot), Babesia (see biliary fever).

parasite

parasitic	(Gr parasitikos) Of, or caused by, parasite. **p. mange** Colloq for sarcoptic mange. Notifiable disease. See mange, sarcoptic.
parasiticide	(L parasitus, parasite + caedere, to kill) Drug or chemical used externally to destroy parasites on skin.
parasitology	(Gr parasites, parasite + -logy) The science of parasites and parasitism.
parasympathetic nervous system	Part of the autonomic nervous system, qv. Nerves which originate from the brain and spinal cord. **p. nerve-endings** These supply blood vessels, glands, intestines and eye.
parasympathomimetic	Agent or drug which mimics action of parasympathetic nerve, eg carbachol.
parathyroid	(1) Beside thyroid gland. (2) One of 4 small glands, near thyroid. See hyperparathyroidism.
paravertebral	By vertebral column. Used in connection with anaesthesia.
parenteral	Given by injection rather than by mouth. **p. nutrition** nourishment via intravenous drip.
paresis	(Gr paresis, relaxation) Slight paralysis. See paralysis, wobbler syndrome.
parotid	(para- + Gr ous, ear) Situated near ear, eg **p.** gland.
parotitis	Inflamed parotid gland.
parrot jaw	(syn undershot jaw) Short lower jaw. Inherited condition, results in overgrown front teeth and end molars, due to lack of wear from teeth in opposite jaw. Older horses may suffer malnutrition.
parturition	(L parturitio) Act of foaling. See birth.
pars	Anatomical term meaning division or portion of area, organ or structure.
Paso Fino	(Sp, fine step; syn Chongo) Tough but attractive and gentle pony established on island of Puerto Rico, off S America, about 400 years ago. Descended from Spanish Conquistadors' horses. Has natural gait similar to the Peruvian Paso, qv. **P.F. Horse Assn**, 101 N Collins St, Plant City, FL 33566 (813 719 7777).
passive transfer	(of immunity) The direct transfer of antibodies and other

factors which enhance immunity eg foals receive antibodies from dam via colostrum. **p.t.** also possible via serum or plasma intravenously, compared with acquired immunity from vaccination or infection.

Part of leg between fetlock and coronet, formed by 1st phalanx. See ringbone. **split p.** Colloq for fracture of 1st phalanx. Crack usually starts near midline proximally and extends in any direction (but is rarely entire length of bone) or bone may be in small fragments (comminuted fracture). Causes acute lameness. Horse may pull up sound and go lame on way home; usually sweats and shows distress. Diagnosis: on signs and X-ray. Treatment: rest in box on peat or woodshavings for 2–3 months then exercise gently 2–3 months. Bandage or plaster cast support may be necessary. If pieces of bone are separated, fix with internal screws. Complete recovery is usual unless arthritis sets in. **p. joint** Formed by 1st and 2nd phalangeal bones (pastern and coronary bones). Joint capsule bulges when distended by excess synovia at coronary band.

pastern

Disease caused by infection with pasteurella bacteria. Uncommon in horses but may cause acute fever and infectious disease of respiratory tract, usually during long sea or road journey.

pasteurellosis

Large sesamoid bone articulating with femur and forming part of stifle joint. **upward fixation of p.** Locking of hindleg. Symptoms: hindleg locks briefly when extended, sometimes with repeated catching of **p.** when walking. Cause: poor conformation of central (medial) ridge (trochlea) of femur. Condition may be inherited or caused by loss of condition and poor musculature; often affects both hindlegs. Treatment: relieve pain by pushing **p.** to inside and down. Medial **p.** ligament can be cut to produce permanent cure.

patella

(L patens, open) Open. See ductus arteriosus. **p. bladder** See bladder, rupture of.

patent

(Gr pathos, disease) Combining form, relationship to disease.

patho-

(patho- + Gr gennan, to produce) Disease-producing microorganism, ie bacterium, fungus, virus.

pathogen

Way in which disease process develops in body.

pathogenesis

Resulting in disease.

pathogenic

An organism's ability to produce disease.

pathogenicity

pathognomonic	(patho- + Gr gnomonikos, fit to give judgment) Characteristic of certain disease, eg spasm of third eyelid in lockjaw, qv.
pathology	Science of disease as it affects body structures, tissues and organs. See postmortem.
pCO₂	(PCO₂) Symbol for carbon dioxide gas partial pressure (tension). Usually measured in millimetres of mercury. It represents pressure exerted by CO_2 in a space (eg lungs) or fluid (eg blood). It is partial if other gases (eg oxygen) are present; and together they form a total pressure which is usually atmospheric.
PCV or p.c.v.	Abbr packed cell volume, qv.
pedal	(L pedalis/pes, foot) Of the foot. **p. bone** (pronounced peedal, syns coffin bone, 3rd phalanx) Bone inside hoof. See foot. **p. osteitis/ostitis** Inflamed **p.** bone causing pain and lameness. Diagnosis: on X-ray examination. Treatment: rest, shoeing with pad underneath sole, possible neurectomy. Outlook: unfavourable. See quittor; ringbone.
pediculosis	Infested with lice. See louse.
peduncle	Stem-like part, eg base of wart. Many brain parts have a **p.**
pelvis	Group of bones forming ring with sacrum (croup area of spine) above, ilia at sides and pubic and ischial bones, below.

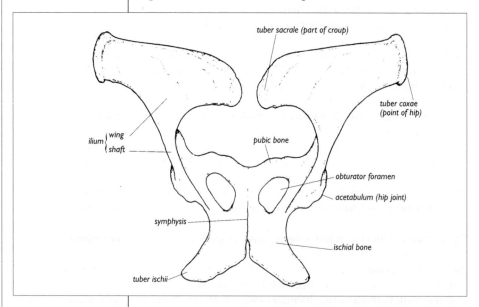

30 Pelvis, seen from above

Cup-like area of ischium fits around head of femur, forming hip joint. Bones form area of attachment for muscles and ligaments which control movement of back and hind legs. Pelvic ring/girdle houses rectum, vagina and urethra in the mare; accessory glands and part of urethra in the stallion. Its diameter is about 24cm (approx 9½in) in the mare and 18cm (approx 7in) in stallion. **p., fracture of** Relatively common, particularly shaft of ilium. Caused by trauma, eg in fall or during galloping. Symptoms depend on site of fracture: tuber coxae – moderate lameness with point of hip on fractured side flatter than normal; shaft – severe lameness with refusal to take weight on affected leg; symphysis – severe lameness affecting both hind legs. Diagnosis: on physical signs and on rectal palpation which detects grating of bones (crepitation). Treatment: rest 3–6 months on peat or similar bedding. Slings may be necessary in severe cases. **renal p.** Funnel-shaped cavity in kidney at kidney duct (ureter).

penicillin Powerful antibiotic. See benzamine **p.**, benzylpenicillin and procaine **p.**

penicillinase Enzyme-like substance which reacts against penicillin; produced by certain bacteria, eg staphylococcus.

penis Male organ of coitus composed mainly of erectile tissue with common duct for semen and urine and with one end free, in prepuce, ending in glans penis. The whole is similar to human **p.** (rather than bull's **p.**) and has to become engorged with blood to become erect (see behaviour). At rest it is entirely enclosed in sheath (lubricated by smegma).

pentobarbitone sodium (trade name: Pentoject) White odourless slightly bitter-tasting granules or crystals. Short-acting barbiturate with a more rapid effect than phenobarbitone. Used as anticonvulsant in newborn foals and anaesthetic during surgery on young foals. See anaesthesia; neonatal maladjustment syndrome.

pepsin (L pepsinum, from Gr pepsis, digestion) Enzyme of gastric (stomach) juice which acts on proteins of food, converting them into simpler substances. See digestion.

peracute (L peracutus) Excessively acute, eg a disease.

Percheron Draught breed developed in La Perche district of France about 150 years ago. Now popular in many countries. Has very heavy body on short, comparatively featherless legs. May be up to 17 hands and black or grey only. **British P. Horse Soc**, Lodge Farm, Beccles, Suffolk, NR34 8HG (01502 714502). **P. Horse Assn of America**, Box 141, Fredericktown, OH 43019 (614 694 3602).

percussion   (L percussio) Act of striking part with short sharp blow to sound part beneath. **p. of chest** Can distinguish between hollow and solid part of lung. Two fingers are placed between each rib in rotation and lightly tapped with two fingers of opposite hand. With slack wrists this produces resonant sound where there is air in lung beneath. Chalk line can be drawn joining points where resonance becomes a dullness. Horse is then trotted and procedure repeated. In broken wind (emphysema) new chalk line will be well behind first one. Chalk marks on healthy horse will not move back as far. **P.** can identify consolidated (airless) areas of lung in pneumonia.

performance   Term used colloquially to describe end point of athletic prowess. Depends ultimately on power of muscles acting on optimal conformation of skeleton to produce ability. Conformation differs with athletic purpose, eg racehorse compared with Standardbred (trotter or pacer). Muscle also plays part in conformation, eg sprinter (bulkier muscles) compared with stayer (longer muscles). Power of muscle to propel bones and joints depends on adequate oxygen and immediately available energy sources such as glycogen, fatty acids and enzymes of energy (ATP and ADP). Supply of these depends on adequate bloodflow, based on efficiency of heart and circulation. All tissues need oxygen. Ability of lungs to replenish blood's oxygen and expel its waste gas (carbon dioxide) is crucial. Athletic **p.** depends therefore on a series of functions. **loss of p.** Failure to meet proven or anticipated potential. May result from disease affecting the chain of functions described. Viruses (most notably equine herpesvirus, qv) lead to structural damage of the lungs (bronchiolitis, qv, pulmonary haemorrhage, qv). Injury to skeleton/muscles, causing lameness and poor mental attitude, especially in colts, also contributes to loss of **p.**

peri-   (Gr) Prefix meaning around, eg **periarticular**, around joint; pericardium (see pericarditis).

periarteritis   (Gr peri- + arteria, artery + -itis) Inflamed external coat of artery and surrounding tissues.

periarticular   (peri + L articulus, joint) Around a joint, eg **p.** tissue refers to structures outside joint capsule.

pericarditis   (pericardium + -itis) Inflamed membraneous sac (pericardium) surrounding heart. Caused by infection with *Streptococcus equi, Streptococcus pyogenes* and other bacteria or, in newborn foal, by injury during birth; often accompanied by septicaemia, pneumonia or pleurisy. Symptoms: pain, shallow fast breathing, fever, increased heart rate.

Diagnosis: on hearing grating or rubbing in heart area. Treatment: rest, antibiotics. See auscultation; birth; heart.	*pericarditis*
(peri- + Gr kardia, heart) Fibrous sac which surrounds heart and is joined to membrane (epicardium) covering outside of heart.	**pericardium**
(peri- + L natus, birth) Occurring shortly before or immediately after birth. **p. mortality** Death from about 2 weeks before birth is due, to 1 week afterwards.	**perinatal**
Of the perineum.	**perineal**
(Gr perineos) Area between anus and scrotum/vulva. Adjective: perineal.	**perineum**
See eye, diseases of: moon blindness.	**periodic ophthalmia**
Special tissue which covers all bones of body and has bone-forming capacity. See periostitis.	**periosteum**
Inflamed membrane (periosteum) covering surface of bone, caused by sprain, blow or infection. Symptoms: pain, swelling and heat. See ringbone, osselet, bone, bucked shin, spavin, splint.	**periostitis**
Belonging to Perissodactyla, ie odd-toed.	**perissodactyl**
(Gr perissos, odd + daktylos, finger) Order of ungulates with odd number of toes; includes the horse and rhinoceros. See evolution.	**Perissodactyla**
(peri- + Gr stalsis, contraction) Movements of alimentary canal which propel food along muscular wall. See alimentary canal, borborygmus, colic. Adjective: peristaltic.	**peristalsis**
(L, G peritonaion from per, around + teinein, to stretch) Smooth, glistening membrane lining abdomen and its contents; helps one part of gut slide easily on another. Adjective: peritoneal.	**peritoneum**
Inflamed peritoneum, qv. Caused by infection with bacteria, migrating redworm larvae, clot (thrombus), blocked arteries which supply gut, foreign bodies penetrating gut wall. Symptoms: fever, reluctance to move, grunting, looking round at flanks, raised white blood cell count (as condition progresses, count usually falls). **P.** may cause portions of intestine to stick together or to abdominal wall. Treatment: antibiotics while primary cause is identified. See adhesion,	**peritonitis**

peritonitis	blood tests. If due to larvae or clot, corticosteroids indicated.
per rectum	Through rectum, as in administration of drugs by enema, or examination **p.r.**
Peruvian Paso	Horse loved for its lateral gaits which, although smart and high-stepping, give a wonderfully smooth ride. Inherent gaits are pace, marching paso and normal paso, although undisciplined horse may break into trot or canter. Gaits may have caused tendency towards long pasterns, long hindlegs, sometimes with sickle hocks, and flexible leg and spinal joints. Thought to have descended from Andalusians used by Spanish cavalry to conquer Peru. Later there was probably Arab influence. Cf Paso Fino. See gait. **P.P. Horse Registry of N America**, 3077 Wiljan Court, Santa Rosa, CA 95407 (707 579 4394).
pervious urachus	Condition when urine drips from umbilical stump of newborn foal. Happens if urachus (duct between bladder and placenta) does not close immediately after birth. Condition may be cured by antibiotics, but surgery necessary if it persists.
pessary	(L pessarium) Cone-shaped tablet of antibiotic or other drug for inserting into uterus. Used after difficult foaling or to treat infection. See infertility.
petechia	(L, pl petechiae) Abnormal, round spot of blood to be seen under mucous membrane. Cf ecchymosis. See purpura haemorrhagica.
pethidine/ p. hydrochloride	Odourless colourless crystals or white crystalline powder with bitter taste. Relieves pain from smooth muscle, eg of alimentary canal. Effects last 3–4 hours; used in colic, meconium retention and with tranquillisers to sedate.
pevidine/iodine solution	(trade name: Saniphor) Brown solution used as antiseptic to treat minor wounds and abrasions.
PG	See prostaglandin.
PGF₂ alpha	Prostaglandin (qv) of uterus.
pH	Symbol for measurement of alkalinity/acidity of body fluids: **pH** 7 is neutral; above 7 alkaline and below 7 acid. Normal **pH** of blood: about 7.40.
phago-	(Gr phegein, to eat) Combining form meaning eating or engulfing.

Cell that devours and destroys (amoeba-like) microorganisms or other cells and foreign particles. May be fixed, eg cell of reticuloendothelial system (qv) or free, eg white blood cell. **P.** action is phagocytosis. See T-cell.	**phagocyte**
The first, second and third phalanges (or pastern, coronary and pedal bones) forming extremity of leg. See foot.	**phalangeal bones**
Pl of phalanx.	**phalanges**
(Gr a line of soldiers; pl phalanges) One of 3 bones below fetlock joint. Adjective: phalangeal. See foot.	**phalanx**
(L pharyngeus) Of the pharynx (throat).	**pharyngeal**
Inflamed pharynx. See strangles, influenza, virus, tongue swallowing.	**pharyngitis**
White odourless powder or crystals with slightly bitter taste. Used to treat biliary fever and other Babesia infections, in particular *B. caballi*.	**phenamidine isethionate**
Study of how drugs alone and in combination affect the body. Cf pharmacokinetics.	**pharmacodynamics**
Study of absorption, distribution, metabolism and excretion of drugs, ie how body affects drugs. Cf pharmacodynamics.	**pharmacokinetics**
Throat. See Fig 25, p200.	**pharynx**
White odourless slightly bitter-tasting powder. Barbiturate drug with effect varying from mild sedation to full anaesthesia, depending on the dosage and route of administration. **p. poisoning** Treat with artificial respiration and bemegride or picrotoxin. See pentobarbitone sodium, thiopentone.	**phenobarbitone**
Colourless or pink needle-shaped crystals with characteristic odour. Potent bactericide but, because it tends to penetrate skin and other tissues, its use as antiseptic has declined.	**phenol**
See BSP.	**phenoltetrabromphthalein**
Group of drugs previously used for anthelmintic (qv) effect but now as tranquillisers, eg chlorpromazine. In equine medicine group largely replaced by detomidine (qv). See urine.	**phenothiazines**
(Gr phainein, to show, + typos, type) Characteristics of an animal; result of its inherited material (DNA genes) but not	**phenotype**

phenotype   necessarily transmitted to progeny. The visible or discernible expression of genotype, qv.

phenylbutazone   (syn bute; trade names: Equipalazone, Pro-Dynam) Fine creamy-white crystalline odourless powder with slightly bitter taste. Used to treat painful conditions including arthritis, torn muscle and wounds, splint, ringbone, bucked shin. Response to **p.** varies greatly; if no improvement in 3–7 days it should be stopped. If successful, withdrawal of **p.** may allow reappearance of symptoms. Excreted from body as oxyphenbutazone. **P.**, no longer used in humans because of slight stomach ulcer and blood disorder risk, may be banned in equine medicine in EU except Britain. (EU countries consider horse a food-producing animal, so drug residue may cause illness in consumer.)

phenytoin   (trade name: Epanutin) White odourless powder made into solution to control convulsions, especially in foal (see neonatal maladjustment syndrome).

pheromone   Substance or hormone secreted by one animal and which alters behaviour of another, eg **p.** in mare's urine, when she is in oestrus, excites stallion, who exhibits flehmen posture, qv.

PHF   Abbr Potomac horse fever, qv.

phlebitis   (Gr phleps, phlebos, vein + itis, inflammation) Inflamed vein or veins.

phonocardiogram   (phono-, combining form, sound from Gr phone, voice + Gr kardia, heart + gramma, a writing) Graph of heart sounds using phonocardiograph connected to microphone on chest.

phosphorus   (symbol **P.**) (1) See calcium and **P.** (2) Can cause poisoning (sources: rat poisons and organophosphorus drugs). Symptoms: those of irritant poisons, ie abdominal pain, relief, then more pain, jaundice and nervous symptoms followed by convulsions, coma and death. Postmortem findings include inflamed mucous membranes of stomach and intestines, fatty degeneration of liver, jaundice and a smell of **p.** on opening abdomen. Diagnosis: chemical analysis of gut contents. Treatment: reduce shock with corticosteroids, heart stimulants and intravenous glucose.

photosensitisation   Sunlight sensitivity. Occurs in unpigmented areas, eg white heels, face markings. Symptoms: inflamed skin and, especially on face, sores which ooze serum. Allergy or drugs (eg phenothiazine) may predispose to **p.** Equine sunscreen lotions available.

(L phrenicus, Gr phen, mind) (1) Of the mind. (2) Of the diaphragm, eg **p.** nerve.

phrenic

(or phthalylsulfathiazole) White or yellowish-white odourless crystals or powder, with slightly bitter taste. A sulphonamide (qv) drug. Not absorbed from alimentary canal and used to treat diarrhoea in foals. See sulphanilamide.

phthalylsulphathiazole

(L, Gr phylon, race) Main division of animal or vegetable kingdom. Horses belong to **p.** Chordata which includes fish, birds, reptiles, amphibians and mammals. See evolution.

phylum

(Gr physis, nature + logy) Study of the metabolic function of tissues, organs and organisms.

physiology

Person specialising in physiotherapy.

physiotherapist

(physis + Gr therapeia, cure) Diagnosis and treatment using agents such as light, heat, cold. **cold therapy** Popular treatment for sprains, particularly those of deep and superficial digital flexor tendons of forelegs. Cold water from a hosepipe is played over injured parts for up to half an hour twice a day. Cold-water bandages are used but need constant changing. Bandages soaked in cooling lotions, generally based on lead acetate and zinc sulphate solution, are also used. Horse can be stood in bucket or boot and cracked ice packed around leg, more ice being added as original melts. **heat therapy** Includes poultices, electrically heated boots, short-wave diathermy, inductothermy and microwave diathermy. Poultices can be made from bran or linseed, kaolin, etc. Heat from boot or poultice does not penetrate deeply so high energy waves can be used. Horse should stand on rubber mat placed on dry floor. In short-wave diathermy a flexible piece of metal between two pieces of rubber forms a pad. A lead connects it to a generator and it is kept off skin by perforated felt pad. It has been calculated that temperature of muscle 5cm (2in) below skin can be raised by 5 or 6°F. Inductothermy is used to treat tendons, ligaments, muscles, splints and bucked shins. Output of machine has to be varied as horse is not consistent in amount of heat it can tolerate. Microwave diathermy units are portable, so horse can be treated in own stable. Ultrasonic therapy gives pulsated heat; one 'on' period to four 'off' periods. The micromassage produced is particularly useful in muscle injuries. Faradism produces rhythmical muscular contractions. Power is from dry batteries which eliminates risk from mains electricity and allows machine to be used anywhere. Electrical contact is through indifferent electrode pad. Skin over saddle area is wetted and a plastic sponge moistened in water laid across back just behind

physiotherapy

physiotherapy

withers. A leather pad, fitted underneath with two plates, is strapped over sponge. The two metal plates are connected to a single plug to which one lead of machine is fitted. The mobile electrode consists of chain and two sponges in chamois leather, to which the second lead is attached. Area to be treated is again wetted and substance, eg tragacanth mucilage, used to maintain good contact. Useful to diagnose site of injury – when painful muscles are contracted, patient is restless or moves away from mobile pad. Treatment 20–30 minutes; number of contractions 100–130 a minute, daily or every other day. Swimming allows horse to exercise without strain on legs and whirlpool baths are used to jet warm water onto horse, sometimes with magnesium sulphate added. In whirlpool boots, cold or warm water is added until it covers knee. Air is forced through a number of holes in the boot at level of fetlock by means of a compressor. Water temperature rises during treatment so ice is added when cold therapy used. Massage and manipulation are difficult as horse is so large.

physostigmine salicylate

Alkaloid from calabar bean of W Africa. Colourless odourless crystals with slightly bitter taste. Produces effects similar to parasympathetic nerve stimulation by preventing destruction of acetylcholine. Causes increased peristalsis, diarrhoea, constricts finer air tubes. Large doses cause muscle twitching. Used in eye to reduce pressure and counteract action of atropine.

phytoferol

See tocopheryl acetate.

pia mater

(L tender mother) Innermost of 3 membranes known as meninges and covering brain and spinal cord. Cf dura mater.

pica

See appetite, depraved.

picrotoxin

White or off-white crystalline odourless powder with very bitter taste. Powerful stimulant of brain, increases frequency and depth of respiration, raises blood pressure. Used to counteract barbiturate poisoning.

piebald

See coat colouring. **British Skewbald and P. Assn**, 54 Burnt House Rd, Turves, Cambs PE7 2DP (01354 840157).

pilocarpine nitrate

Alkaloid from leaves of pilocarpus plant. Colourless or white crystals with faintly bitter taste; action similar to effects of parasympathetic nerves. See autonomic nervous system. Used in eye drops, or as injection to treat impacted colic, but should be used with caution.

(Sp pintado, painted) Type with patchy colouring, popular with American Indians for its natural camouflage. Similar horses were drawn on walls of Egyptian tombs 3,000 years ago. Piebald **P.** termed Overo, skewbald is Tobiano. Either may have blue eyes. Developed from wide range of types and recognised as breed in 1960s. **P. Horse Assn**, 1900 Samuels Avenue, Fort Worth, TX 76102 (817 336 7842). Cf Paint. — **Pinto**

Draught breed first developed in Pinzgau district of Austria; said to trace to Friesian, but now dying out. Usually roan with short, compact, featherless legs. Often crossed with S German Cold Blood. — **Pinzgauer**

(adipate, citrate, hydrate, or phosphate) White crystalline or granular odourless powders with a slightly acid taste. Anthelmintic effective against seatworm and whiteworm at all stages in the gut; acts by paralysing worms. Wide safety margin in overdose. — **piperazine salts**

(syn babesiosis) **equine p**. See biliary fever. — **piroplasmosis**

Colloq any member of Equidae used in mining. In Britain, National Coal Board phased out use of **p.p.** but private mine owners, eg in S Wales, still use Welsh Mountain, qv, as **p.p.**. See Dales. — **pit pony**

Destruction of brain and spinal cord by thrust of blunt instrument, usually after shooting. See euthanasia. — **pithing**

Endocrine (ductless) gland connected to base of brain. About 2.5cm (1in) long in adult, with two parts (lobes): anterior (front) and posterior (back). Controlled by (1) releasing factors from hypothalamus (part of brain) and (2) its own hormones, ie those it produces which work on distant glands. When these react by liberating another hormone, **p.** cuts down its own secretion. Activity increases with amount of light filtering through eyes (it produces more of the sex hormones, which is why horses are more sexually active in summer). **p. injection** Clear colourless liquid with faint odour obtained from posterior lobe of **p.** gland. Has actions similar to oxytocin, qv. Also raises blood pressure, reduces excretion of urine (an antidiuretic) and raises levels of blood sugar. Used to treat inertia of uterus during birth or involution of uterus afterwards (see uterus). Oxytocin is generally preferred. — **pituitary**

Produced by posterior lobe	Acts on
oxytocin	smooth muscle of uterus
antidiuretic hormone	kidney
prolactic hormone	mammary glands

pituitary	**Produced by anterior lobe** (syn conductor of orchestra)	**Acts on**
	follicle stimulating hormone (FSH)	ovaries
	luteinising hormone (LH)	ovaries
	adrenocorticotrophic 　　hormone (ACTH)	adrenal gland
	thyrotropic hormone	thyroid gland
	interstitial cell stimulating hormone (ICSH)	interstitial cells of testes (causing production of 　testosterone)

placenta   (L a flat cake; syns chorioallantois, allantochorion) Membrane or organ developed by foetus to nourish it and transport waste material by close contact with mare's uterus. Formed in first 15 days of foetal life by fusion of 2 embryonic membranes, the chorion and allantois. By day 90 it is attached (implanted) to uterine wall. There is insufficient room in uterus for 2 placentae and carrying twins is difficult for mare (usually stunted or aborted if conceived, see twin). Material passes from foetal to maternal bloodstream via capillaries that lie close together. Gases and materials pass by diffusion or by selective action of cells. They must pass 6 layers: (1) maternal capillary wall; (2) subcutaneous tissue; (3) epithelium, qv, then similar layers in placenta; (4) epithelium; (5) connective tissue; (6) capillary wall. This separation of bloodstreams of foetus and mare makes equine **p.** epitheliochorial type. (Compare with human **p.** (haemochorial) which erodes maternal uterus and leaves 3 layers.) Mare's uterus retains all its tissue and does not bleed or lose many cells when **p.** is removed, ie it is non-deciduate. **P.** communicates with foetus by blood vessels of umbilical cord. This also contains the urachus, a duct from bladder through which urine passes and is stored as allantoic fluid, qv. **P.** is about 10mm (½in) thick and is thinnest at part adjacent to cervix. It ruptures, releasing allantoic fluid (breaking water) at start of 2nd stage labour. Diseases of **p.** include infection with bacteria, fungus and probably virus, causing inflammation (placentitis). These cause abortion or interfere with growth and nourishment of foetus. In twins capillaries and larger blood vessels may fuse, allowing bloodstreams to mix. **P.** normally weighs 2–5kg (4.5–11lb) at full term and is expelled (about 30 minutes) after foaling. See abortion; afterbirth; hippomane; Cf yolk sac **p.**

placental   Of the placenta.

planter   Of sole of foot.

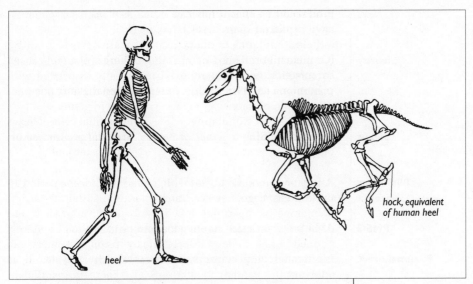

hock, equivalent of human heel

heel

31 The difference between plantigrade (walking on sole of foot) and digitigrade (raised on toes)

(L plants, sole + -gradus, walking) Characterised by walking on full sole of foot, eg man. Cf digitigrade. See evolution.	**plantigrade**
Patch or raised area. See nettle rash.	**plaque**
(Gr anything formed or moulded) Fluid part of blood in which cells are suspended. Distinguished from serum by presence of fibrinogen.	**plasma**
Calcium sulphate reduced to fine powder by driving off most of water. Used to make casts and cover bandages to immobilise part, eg fractured leg.	**plaster of Paris**
(1) Lightweight shoe, normally aluminium and about 85g (3oz). Fitted when Thoroughbred races. Cf shoe. (2) Colloq for media on which bacteria are grown in laboratory, eg blood agar **p**. (3) Flat, thin layer, eg of bone. See growth **p**.	**plate**
Light but hardy type. Bred by tribesmen roaming from Persian Gulf to Zagros Mountains.	**Plateau Persian**
Oval or round disc-like cell in blood, concerned in clotting. See coagulation, blood.	**platelet**
(Gr platys, broad + Gr helmins, worm) Phylum of flatworm including Cestoda and Trematoda. See tapeworm, fluke.	**Platyhelminthes**
(Gr side, rib; pl pleurae) Outer covering of lungs. It is	**pleura**

pleura   moistened so that lungs can move and encloses potential cavity (pleural space). Adjective: pleural.

pleurisy   (Gr pleuritis) Inflamed outer lining of lungs (pleurae) caused by infection with bacteria or virus; usually associated with pneumonia and pericarditis. Symptoms are those of pneumonia, qv.

plexus   (L braid) Joining together of nerves. **brachial p.** See nerves, table of.

Pliohippus   Ancestor of modern horses which lived in Pliocene period 10 million years ago. See evolution.

PMSG   Abbr pregnant mare serum gonadotrophin, qv.

Pneumabort-K   Inactivated herpesvirus vaccine containing suitable oil as adjuvant.

pneumo-   Combining form, of or related to lungs, breath or air, from Gr pneumon, lung.

pneumonia   (syn pneumonitis) Inflamed lung tissue (as opposed to air tubes). Commonly associated with inflamed air tubes (bronchitis) and caused by infection with bacteria, virus, fungus, migrating parasitic larvae (see whiteworm; lungworm), inhalation of injurious particles or chemicals, allergic reaction. Symptoms: increased rate and depth of respiration, fever and coughing, especially in bronchitis and bronchiolitis (inflamed bronchioles). Abnormal sound, eg moist râle or high-pitched tone, may be heard on auscultation (qv) if bronchitis present. Areas of dullness can be detected if air sacs are obliterated by inflammatory reaction (see percussion). Treatment: antibiotics and/or removal of precipitating cause. **summer p.** Condition of foals under 6 months. Caused by *Rhodococcus equi* (*Corynebacterium equi*) organism inhaled or swallowed. Symptoms: abscesses in lymph glands and lung tissue, high temperature, distressed breathing, thick discharge from nostrils, areas of dullness and râles on auscultation of chest. There may be wasting, and condition often fatal. Successful treatment possible using erythromycin (qv) and rifampicin (qv). **tuberculosis p.** Rare condition caused by *Mycobacterium tuberculosis* organism. Symptoms: increased cells in lung (not comparable with tuberculosis in humans). **virus p.** Caused by herpes and adeno viruses which inflame supporting tissues of alveoli and bronchioles. See also snotty nose.

pneumothorax   Accumulation of air in pleural cavity as a result of injured chest wall or ruptured lung.

Air abnormally present in vagina due to failure of vulva to seal entrance. See Caslick; Pouret; uterus, infection of. — **pneumovagina**

Symbol for oxygen gas partial pressure (tension). Usually measured in millimetres of mercury. It represents pressure exerted by O_2 in a space (eg lungs) or fluid (eg 90–100mm of mercury in arterial blood). It is partial if other gases (eg carbon dioxide) are present. Together they form total pressure which is usually atmospheric. See anoxia, neonatal maladjustment syndrome. — **PO_2**

Many meanings. In equine anatomy usually a projection. **p. of hip** (syn tuber coxae) See pelvis. **p. of hock** (syn tuber calcis) See tarsal bones. — **point**

Substances which harm body externally or internally and which can kill or interfere with function. Various amounts produce toxic effects; what is harmful in one circumstance may be harmless in another, eg food may be toxic if fed in excessive amounts or under unsuitable conditions. **inorganic p.** Lead, mercury, arsenic, phosphorus, salts. **organic p.** Carbon compounds, chloroform, carbon tetrachloride, ether, organic acids, alkaloids, glycosides, phytotoxins. Apart from substances which burn (strong acids and alkalis) most **p.** must be absorbed into blood to be toxic; they enter body by ingestion, inhalation, absorption through skin or injection. The liver detoxifies them and is therefore damaged or inflamed in most poisoning. Diagnosis: (1) diarrhoea, abdominal pain – due to metals and their salts (eg arsenic, copper, iron, strong acid or alkali, chlorates, phosphorus) and anthelmintics (eg carbon tetrachloride, phenol, turpentine); (2) convulsions – ammonium salts, lead, silver nitrate, phenol, opium, strychnine, ethylene glycol; (3) coma – bromide, carbon monoxide, zinc phosphide, barbiturate, anaesthetic, sedative, atropine, phenol, turpentine; (4) muscular incoordination – ammonium salts, nitrate, lead, phenothiazine, nicotine, turpentine, oxylate; (5) dilation of pupils – atropine, hyacine, nicotine, aconite; (6) constriction of pupils – opium derivatives, physostigmine, pilocarpine; (7) distressed breathing – carbon monoxide, cyanide, nitrates, zinc phosphide, strychnine, yew, nitrite; (8) sensitisation – phenothiazine, dimadidium bromide, grasses, buckwheat; (9) blood in urine – chlorate, copper, kale, rape, bracken, lupin. See also aconite, ragwort, rodent killer, rhododendron, selenium, sugar-beet poisoning, walking disease. (Leaflet on poisonous plants and trees available from British Horse Society; see horse.) — **poisons**

Anglo-Arab widely and carefully bred in Poland. **P. Arab** Breed kept at a high standard by the Poles, a nation long — **Polish Anglo-Arab**

Polish Anglo-Arab	renowned for horse breeding. Oldest Arab stud in Poland dates from 1500s and fresh stock has often been imported from Arabia. Arab studs in the USA have been founded with **P.** horses. See Arab. **P. Half-Bred** Type often produced with Trakehner blood.
poll	·Highest point of head, just behind ears. **p. evil** Infection of **p.** area (occipital bursa) with bacteria, often Brucella spp. Painful swelling appears on one or both sides of neck just below **p.** Treatment: drain through needle and inject antibiotics. Surgery may be necessary in severe cases. See filaria, occiput.
pollution ring	See masturbation.
polo pony	Type rather than breed, term 'pony' being used loosely as animals used for polo may be up to 16 hands. Performance during the game, ie speed and agility, are only criteria. Many ponies have Thoroughbred blood or trace to Manipur (qv) ponies of Assam, India, where polo was popular in the 7th century. **P. p. Welfare Ctte,** Fairview Cottage, Wicks Green, Berks RG42 5PF (01344 860976).
poly-	Combining form many/much from Gr polys, many.
polycythemia	(poly- + Gr kytos, cell + haima, blood) Excess of red blood cells. See haemoconcentration.
polydipsia	(poly- + Gr dipsa, thirst) Excessive thirst and drinking. Associated with diarrhoea, excessive staling (polyuria) and diabetes mellitus. Follows saline medicine. See diarrhoea, behaviour.
polymixin(s)	Antibiotic substances obtained from *Bacillus polymyxa.* **p. B sulphate** Used to treat uterine infection. Creamy white powder which absorbs moisture and is effective against proteus and pseudomonas infections. Used locally, eg to irrigate uterus or in ointment to treat mastitis.
polymorph	(abbr polymorphoneuclear leucocyte) White blood cell, nucleus of which has several lobes. See also blood tests, haematology (5).
polyp	(Gr polypous, a morbid outgrowth; pl polypi) Growth from mucous membrane, occasionally found in nose or throat causing horse to make breathing noise (see wind). May also occur in bladder and vagina. See growth.
polypropylene	See wound.

(trade name: Adequan) Chemical substance similar to that present in cartilage. Used in treatment of damaged joints and those suffering from degenerative joint disease. — **polysulphated glycosaminoglycan**

(poly- + Gr ouron, urine + -ia) Passage of large volume of urine, excessive staling. See diabetes. — **polyuria**

(L bridge) Tissue connecting two parts of an organ. See brain. — **pons**

Any member of *Equus caballus* (qv) beneath 14.2 h. Some breeds take **p.** (rather than horse) even if above 14.2, eg Camargue. **P.** seems more susceptible than horse to sweet itch, laminitis. It rarely conceives twins, even when researchers try to induce them, cf Thoroughbred. **National P. Soc**, 102 High Street, Alton, Hants, GU34 1EN (01420 88333). **British Show P. Soc**, 124 Green End Rd., Sawtry, Cambs CB6 2TB (01353 699430). See separate breeds, eg Dales; Dartmoor; Exmoor; Highland; New Forest; Welsh Mountain. **p. of the Americas** (syn POA) Type developed in 1950s from Arab and American breeds, Appaloosa and Quarterhorse. Up to about 13.2 h. Sometimes has Appaloosa-type colouring. **POA Club**, 5240 Elmwood Ave. Indianapolis, IN 46203. — **pony**

See carpitis. — **popped knee**

Of an entrance, eg to liver. — **portal**

(L positio) Relationship of foal's spine to that of mare during delivery, eg **dorsal p.** Spine uppermost (normal). During last third of pregnancy foetus is upside down (head towards cervix) in uterus. Normally it revolves during 1st stage labour, so is born in **dorsal p. ventral p.** Foal upside down. Cf presentation; posture. See birth; dystocia. — **position**

Anatomical for hind part or surface (opp. anterior). — **posterior**

(L after death) **p. examination** (PME) Study of carcass to discover or confirm cause of death. Usual method is a midline incision to expose suspect areas and/or take tissue samples. These are put in preservative, eg formalin, for laboratory testing. **P.** especially important on foetuses (to check for virus abortion), on sudden deaths and cases of suspected infectious disease. Usually required by underwriters if horse is insured. — **postmortem**

Occurring after birth. — **postnatal**

(L postura) Alignment of foal's legs and neck during delivery or in utero, eg flexed or extended. Cf position, presentation. See birth. — **posture**

Potomac horse fever	(PHF) First recognised 1979 along **P.** River, Maryland. Causal agent, *Ehrlichia risticii*, named in 1984. This microbe is classed a bacterium but is smaller than most bacteria and larger than most viruses. It must be in host cell to reproduce (like virus) but is sensitive to antibiotics (like bacterium). Similar (rickettsial) microbes spread by insect, eg fly/tick, but vector in **P.h.f.** not yet identified. Symptoms: fever, depression, colic, laminitis, sometimes severe diarrhoea. Diagnosis on organism antibodies raised x 4 in blood taken 10–14 days after first sample. Treatment: give oxytetracycline in mild cases (risk of salmonellosis in stressed horses). Prevention: vaccinate.
poultice	(L puls, pap; Gr kataplasma; syn cataplasm) Hot or cold substance applied to a part to alter its temperature or draw dirt, maggot or pus from area. See boil, physiotherapy, warble fly.
pound	(L pondus, weight) Unit of mass of avoirdupois system. See weights and measures.
Pouret	(after Edouard **P.**, French veterinarian.) Operation to reconstruct vulva and posterior vagina to improve conformation and reduce the risk of infection of vagina and cervix. Normally performed with mare standing and under epidural anaesthesia.
pox	Skin eruptions which go through characteristic changes starting as small red spots and developing into blisters or vesicles. These burst, leaving ulcer, on which scab forms; eventually this falls off. May occur on skin or mucous membranes. See coital exanthema, acne.
precipitation	Antigen/antibody reaction in which particles which clump together are smaller than those in agglutination reaction. Used in laboratory to test for presence of antitoxin in blood serum.
prednisolone	(trade names: Pred Forte, Predsol) White or off-white crystalline, odourless, bitter-tasting powder. Actions similar to cortisone acetate, qv. Injected into and around joints. Given orally in cases of COPD.
pregnancy	State of being pregnant. **p. hormone** See progesterone. **p. tests/diagnosis** (1) Rectal palpation, ie putting arm into the rectum to feel uterus through rectal wall. Usually 40 days after last mating (and at intervals up to birth) but sometimes detection possible from 19 days. (2) Ultrasound (qv) scanning at 14–20 days. Foetal sac evident as black spot on screen. Must be differentiated from cyst by shape and growth.

Presence of foetus and heartbeat detectable by 28 days. (3) Blood tests measure (a) PMSG (pregnant mare serum gonadotrophin) at 45–100 days using immunological assay, either (i) haemoglutination inhibition or (ii) agar gel diffusion (b) oestrogens in mare serum from 120 days to birth. (4) Urine tests detect oestrogens from day 150 to birth (cuboni test).

pregnancy

(L praegnans, with child; syn gravid) Condition of having foetus in body after ovum has been fertilised by spermatazoon. Marked by interrupted oestrous cycle, calmer disposition (possibly), steady enlargement of abdomen, development of mammary glands. See also gestation. **p. mare serum gonadotrophin** (PMSG) Mixture of follicle stimulating hormone (FSH) and luteinising hormone (LH) in **p.** mare from day 40–90. Can be measured in blood plasma (see blood tests) and given to mare as serum gonadotrophin, qv. See echography.

pregnant

(L praematurus, early ripe) Foal born before it is mature.

premature

Condition of weakness in foals born from 300–325 days' gestation (see gestational age). Symptoms: low weight, delay in standing for first time (over 2 hours after birth), reduced strength of suck and ability to maintain sucking position, emaciation, dehydration, tendency to suffer from diarrhoea and susceptibility to infection. Treatment: see newborn foal.

prematurity

Term commonly used in breeding hunters. Horse awarded **p.** (for conformation not racing performance) said to stand at **p.** of £x. French National Stud (Le Haras du Pin, Orne) runs **p.s.** service with Percherons and trotters.

premium stallion

(L praepotens) Having more power (than fellow parent) to transmit characteristics. See gene.

prepotent

(syn sheath) Double fold of skin which contains and covers non-erect penis. Contains glands which secrete smegma, qv.

prepuce

(L praesentatio) The way foal is presented to birth passage; direction of spine. **anterior p.** Head first (normal). **posterior p.** Hindquarters first. **transverse p.** Lying across birth passage. Cf position, posture. See birth.

presentation

Equine influenza vaccine, inactivated. **P.T. Plus** Combined equine influenza and tetanus vaccine, inactivated. Manufacturer: Hoechst Roussel Vet Ltd.

Prevac Plus

White crystalline odourless slightly bitter-tasting powder. Anticonvulsant used on newborn foals. See neonatal maladjustment syndrome.

primidone

267

primigravida	(L prima, first + gravida, pregnant) Individual pregnant for first time, ie maiden mare.
probiotic	Formula containing live protected microorganisms which occur naturally in the gut. Given to restore gut flora in cases of diarrhoea and other alimentary disturbances.
procaine hydrochloride	Colourless, odourless, crystalline powder with bitter taste, followed by local numbness (acts as anaesthetic). Effect increased when used with adrenaline to delay absorption. Used in solutions from 0.5–5 per cent for operations such as removing warts, stitching wounds, stitching vulva. **p. penicillin** (trade names: Depocillin, Depopen, Duphapen, Econopen) White crystalline powder. Antibiotic released slowly, forms a depot when injected.
process	(L processus) (1) Prominence or projection, eg of bone. See point. (2) Series of happenings, eg birth **p.**
progesterone	(syn pregnancy hormone) (1) Hormone secreted by ovaries, placenta and adrenal glands; prepares uterus to receive fertilised egg and necessary for implantation of foetus and maintenance of pregnancy; antagonistic towards oestrogen and associated with dioestrus (state of rejection). Together with oestrogen promotes growth of mammary glands towards the end of pregnancy and inhibits production of luteinising hormone and follicle stimulating hormone (see pituitary gland). (2) **synthetic p.** White odourless crystalline powder; made into tablet for implanting in mare in an attempt to prevent abortion. Usual implant, 0.25–1g, now thought to have little effect. See oestrous cycle.
progestins	Hormones secreted by yellow body (corpus luteum); 95% consist of progesterone, qv.
prognosis	(Gr prognosis, foreknowledge) Forecast of probable end of disease, ie prospect of recovery.
prolactin	Female hormone produced by posterior lobe of pituitary gland. Acts on mammary glands causing them to develop and produce milk.
prolapse	(L prolapsus from pro, before + labi, to fall) Passing outwards of part of organ through a natural opening or tear. **p. of uterus** See uterus, prolapse of.
promazine hydrochloride	White crystalline odourless bitter-tasting powder. Has actions similar to chlorpromazine hydrochloride (qv) but less potent and toxic. Used as tranquilliser.

White or cream-coloured odourless bitter-tasting powder. Antagonises histamine; has actions and uses similar to mepyramine maleate, qv. See antihistamine. **promethazine hydrochloride**

First stage in mitosis, qv, and meiosis, qv. **prophase**

See depression. **prophet's thumb mark**

(Gr prophylassein, to keep guard before) Preventive treatment. See vaccine. Adjective: prophylactic. **prophylaxis**

Drug with relaxant effect on smooth muscle and a mild tranquillising action. Used for relief of choke, colic, dystocia. Can cause temporary staggering and prolonged lying down if injected too rapidly. **proquamezine fumerate**

(PG) Natural hormone-like substance first described in 1930 by Lieb and Kurzrok. Isolated and named in 1934. Many types (in body tissues and fluids) which act on, eg, blood pressure, gut action, breathing, nervous system, inflammation. Inhibited by aspirin and anti-inflammatory drugs. **P.** secreted by uterus, PGF_2 alpha, causes yellow body (corpus luteum) to stop working, so that mare comes into season. Synthetic preparations can be used to cause mares to show heat; effective only if active yellow body present in ovary. Also used to induce foaling but less effective than oxytocin, qv. **prostaglandin**

(Gr prostates, one who stands before) Gland in the male which stretches across neck of bladder, beginning of urethra and below rectum. It consists of 2 lobes connected by an isthmus. Opens into urethra by about 20 ducts which convey a milky secretion with characteristic odour. Secretion, like those of other accessory glands (seminal vesicles and bulbo-urethral glands), nourishes and carries sperm, qv. **prostate gland**

(Gr a putting to) Replacement of part by artificial substitute, eg modified Hobday operation. Prosthetic legs have been fitted. **prosthesis**

(Gr protos, first) Complex organic compound containing nitrogen; widely distributed in plants and animals; combination of amino acids and derivatives. **simple p.**s Albumin, globulin, glutelin, alcohol-solubles, albuminoids, histones and protamines. **conjugated p.**s Nucleoproteins, glycoproteins, phosphoproteins, haemoglobins, lecithoproteins, lipoproteins. **derived p.**s Metaproteins, coagulated **p.**s proteoses, peptones and peptides, eg albumin, casein, legumin, fibrin. **P.** in blood consists of albumin and globulin in the ratio of about 0.8:1.0. Albumin maintains osmotic balance, **protein**

protein | ie it enables bloodstream to retain fluid; globulin is made up of alpha 1, alpha 2 and beta 1, produced in liver and forming part of hormones, bile pigment, mucus and blood-clotting mechanism. Beta 2 and gamma globulins formed from special cells lining blood spaces of liver and spleen and are part of antibody system. **p.-binding** Method of assaying levels of cortisone and other hormones in blood. See blood tests. **p. hydrolysate** Clear brown liquid with strong meaty taste. Product of digested first-class animal **p.** plus dextrose. Given to newborn foals suffering from malnutrition, dehydration or diarrhoea.

proteinuria | (protein + Gr ouron, urine) Presence of protein in urine. Symptom of disease in the kidneys or bladder. See nephritis, cystitis.

prothrombin | (pro- + Gr thrombos, clot + -in, chemical suffix) Glycoprotein in blood plasma and converted to thrombin, also called coagulation factor II. See coagulation.

protoplasm | Vital substance of living cells composed of proteins, carbohydrates and inorganic salts. See cell.

Protozoa | Phylum of organisms with one-cell bodies, ie unicellular (opp metazoa). Life histories vary. Members important in equine medicine include *Trypanosoma brucei* (see nagana), *T. evansi* (see surra), *T. equinum* (see mal de caderas), *T. equiperdum* (see dourine), *Babesia equi* and *B. caballi* (see biliary fever). Singular: protozoon.

protozoan | Organism belonging to phylum Protozoa.

protozoon | (pl protozoa) A single-cell organism.

proud flesh | See wound.

proximal | (L proximus, next) Nearest (opp distal).

pruritus | (L from prurire, to itch) Condition characterised by itching or scratching. Symptom of skin infested with lice or mange mites. **anal p.** Itching caused by seatworm. See seatworm, mange, louse.

Przewalski | (*Equus przevalskii*, after Russian colonel) Wild horse, discovered in Mongolian wilderness, not seen there since 1968. Looks like stocky pony about 12 h with thick dun coat, tufted tail and erect mane. Has large head, small eyes and ears and horse-like (rather than boxy) hoofs. **P.** Stud Book kept by Prague Zoo. **P.** has 66 chromosomes, qv. **Foundation for the**

P. Horse, University of Georgia, Athens, GA 30602-2771 (706 542 0976). See Mongolian.

Przewalski

Combining form, false, from Gr pseudes, false. **p.**-glanders See epizootic lymphangitis.

pseudo-

Group of gram-negative bacteria. See bacterial diseases, amikacin sulfate.

pseudomonas

(Gr pterygodes, like a wing) Shaped like a wing, eg shoulder blade (scapula).

pterygoid

(Gr ptosis, fall) (1) Prolapse of part or organ. (2) Drooping of upper eyelid caused by injured third cranial (oculomotor) nerve, by conjunctivitis or painful condition of eyeball. Usually affects only one eyelid. See eye; nerves, table of.

ptosis

(Gr ptyalon, spittle) Enzyme in saliva, which converts starch to maltose.

ptyalin

(L pubertas) Age of full sexual powers, about 2 years in fillies, 3 in colts, earlier in exceptional cases. Defined as the time when mature spermatozoa first appear in ejaculate of young male, and when ovulation first occurs in young female.

puberty

Of or near the pubis. See pelvis.

pubic

Smallest of 3 bones of pelvis (with ischium and ilium). Forms back part of pelvic floor and of obturator foramen; known as pelvic brim. See pelvis.

pubis

Of lungs. **p. haemorrhage** See exercise-induced **p.h.**. **p. hypertrophic osteoarthropathy** See Marie-Bamberger's disease. **p. semilunar valve** 1 of 3 cusps forming valve at exit of right ventricle and entrance to **p.** artery. Prevents blood returning from artery to ventricle (see aortic semilunar valve).

pulmonary

(L pulpa, flesh) Soft tissue, eg **p.** of tooth (see teeth).

pulp

(L pulsus, stroke) Beat of artery coinciding with heartbeat; felt by placing ends of fingers against artery, (1) on lower jaw, midway between angle of jaw and front teeth, or (2) on inside of the foreleg, just in front of the elbow. See heartrate. **p. rhythm** Normally regular but irregular in some heart conditions (atrial fibrillation, partial block, sinus arrhythmia). **p. quality** Refers to strength of beat. Strong in health, weak if heart is failing.

pulse

pupil (L pupilla, girl) Opening at centre of iris of eye. Dilated by drugs such as atropine. See eye.

purgative (syn cathartic) Drug which causes evacuation of intestinal contents (1) by increasing volume of non-absorbable matter, (2) by irritating intestine, increasing its movements (peristalsis) and (3) by direct stimulation of nerves (parasympathetic) supplying gut. **irritant p.** One that stimulates intestine. **p. overdose** Symptoms: severe diarrhoea, collapse and occasionally death. Treatment: give demulcent, eg kaolin. **saline p.** Acts by increasing fluid in gut.

purging See diarrhoea.

purpura haemorrhagica (L purple) Acute non-contagious disease characterised by bleeding into mucous membranes and extensive soft swellings beneath skin. Usually follows acute infectious disease of upper respiratory tract, strangles, or stress of travelling. Cause: unknown. Damage to walls of small blood vessels results in plasma and blood leaking into surrounding tissues. Symptoms: face, muzzle or other parts of body develop extensive cold, painless swellings which pit on pressure, mucous membranes of nose and mouth contain blood, temperature is unchanged, heart rate rises. May last 1–2 weeks, majority die from blood loss and secondary bacterial infection. Diagnosis: on symptoms (must be distinguished from equine viral arteritis, swamp fever and dourine), fall in red cell count and haemoglobin level. Treatment: inject antihistamine and corticosteroid drugs; transfuse blood, give calcium. Postmortem reveals haemorrhages (see petechia, ecchymosis) throughout body, congested organs and intestinal wall.

purulent (L purulentus) Containing pus.

pus Inflammatory product consisting of cells, fluid and bacteria. See abscess.

put down Colloq to destroy. See euthanasia.

pyemia (Gr pyon, pus + haima, blood) Septicaemia in which numerous abscesses occur in different parts of body. See joint-ill.

pyramidal disease See buttress foot.

pyrantel tartrate (trade name: Strongid-P) Anthelmintic (qv) effective against large and small strongyles (redworms), pinworms and large roundworms (whiteworms).

One of group of synthetic compounds (pyrethroids); kills ectoparasites and repels insects. | **pyrethrum**

Fever. See temperature. | **pyrexia**

Component of vitamin B. | **pyridoxine**

(trade name: Daraprim) Antimalarial drug used in horses to treat equine protozoal myeloencephalitis. | **pyrimethamine**

q.d.	Abbr L quaque die, every day. Used especially in prescriptions. **Q.** also used with h (hora, hour) eg **q.** 8h.
q.i.d.	Abbr quater in die, 4 times per day.
quadri-	(L quattuor, four) Prefix meaning four or quarter/ed, eg quadriplegia, paralysis of four limbs.
quadruped	(quadri- + L pes, foot) Four-footed animal, eg horse.
quagga	Type of Burchell's zebra with brownish body and stripes limited to legs, which roamed Africa until hunted to extinction late 1800s. Through careful selection of Burchell's zebra which most resemble extinct strain, herd of **q.** is being recreated around Cape Town. See zebra.
quarantine	(Ital quarantine) Period horse is isolated to avoid risk of spreading infectious disease.
quarter crack	(syn hoof crack) See hoof.
quarterhorse	See American quarterhorse.
Queensland itch	(syns allergic dermatitis, sweet itch) Disease causing itchy skin and common in Australia. Fly bites cause allergy, producing lesions round tail, rump and on withers. Itching is intense and oozing sores develop. Treatment: antihistamine drugs and protection from bites by making stable insect-proof.
quid	To chew grass or hay into mass (bolus) ready for swallowing, then drop it. Result of injured throat or associated structures, neglected, overgrown teeth or partial paralysis of swallowing mechanism.
quinapyramine	(chloride or sulphate) White, cream or pale-yellow odourless bitter-tasting powder. Active against *Trypanosoma* spp such as *T. equinum* (see mal de caderas). Dose: 4.4mg/kg bodywt sub cut. Overdose causes trembling, salivation, collapse, but recovery is usually swift. Local reactions common and dose should be divided and given at 2 or 3 sites.
quinidine sulphate	White needle-like odourless bitter-tasting crystals. Slows heart rate. Used to treat atrial fibrillation (qv). Overdose causes diarrhoea and severe depressive illness leading to collapse and death.

Odourless creamy-white to canary-yellow crystals with bitter taste. Used to treat biliary fever. Single injection will cure within 24 hours if disease is treated early. Signs of reaction, which may occur 10–15 minutes after injection: restlessness, muscular spasms, salivation and defecation. These may continue for a few hours, but are rarely serious and can be controlled with adrenaline or atropine. Because of risk of sensitisation, 2 weeks–3 months should be allowed before second treatment. | **quinuronium sulphate**

Necrosis of lateral cartilage of foot due to infection, with severe lameness and discharge of pus. Treatment: antibiotics, possibly surgery to remove affected cartilage. | **quittor**

R.	Abbr Roentgen. See radiation.
Ra	Abbr radium, qv.
rabies	(L rabere, to rage) Fatal virus infection of central nervous system. Rare in horses but can affect any warm-blooded animal (including man). Symptoms: madness, biting other animals (which spreads the disease), chewing skin, fear of water, salivation, falling, rolling and eventually paralysis and death. Notifiable disease, as is Aujeszky's disease (pseudo **r.**). Where **r.** is endemic, vaccination of domestic animals including horses should be considered.
rack	See gait.
rad	Abbr radiation absorbed dose. Measure of radiation, qv.
radial	(L. radialis) Of the radius. **r. paralysis** See dropped elbow.
radiation	(L radiatio; syn irridation) Use of radioactive elements which emit rays. One form of diagnostic imaging (see veterinary). High-energy rays (eg X-ray) can penetrate skin and are used to diagnose broken bones (especially useful in hairline fractures, eg of pedal bone) and bony growths. Alpha, beta and gamma rays can be produced from radium (Ra) salts. Alpha rays have low penetrating power, beta rays slightly more and gamma rays are approx same strength as X-rays. (Can be used to reduce inflammatory process, eg in arthritic joint, and treat skin diseases, by killing damaged or cancerous cells.) Ultraviolet rays have powerful germ-killing properties and are especially useful in diagnosing ringworm. International unit (IU) of **r.** is Roentgen (**R.**). 0–25 **R.** is unlikely to injure; more than 25 **R.** can cause burns and reduce red and white cells in blood (anaemia and leukopenia); more than 400 **R.** can kill.
radio-	(L radius, spoke, ray) Combining form meaning relationship to radius or rays.
radiocarpal	Of the radius and carpus, eg **r.** joint. See knee.
radiograph	(radio- + Gr graphein, to write) Photograph taken with X-ray equipment.
radioiodine	Radioactive isotope of iodine, usually $I._{131}$ used in thyroid function test. See iodine.

(RIA) Technique to measure very small quantities of antigen or antibody, hormones or other substances based on immune reaction and monitored by radioactively labelled antigen. — **radioimmunoassay**

(abbr Ra after its radiant appearance) Rare metal. Its rays can be used in radiation, qv. — **radium**

(L spoke (of wheel); pl radii) Larger of 2 bones of forearm (cf ulna) between elbow joint (above) and knee (below). Lower end includes growth plate, qv. — **radius**

Radioactive gas of radium. **r. seeds** Particles which emit gamma rays and can be put into plaster to treat cancerous or bony growths. — **radon**

Occurs when pasture is scarce and horse eats **r.** (*Senecio jacobaea*, or other members of family: marsh **r.**, Oxford **r.**, groundsel). Plants should not be cut or pulled then left on pasture. Symptoms: dullness, rapid pulse and breathing, weakness, constipation, jaundice and death in a few days or several weeks. Slow build-up of poison causes wasting, jaundiced mucous membranes, nervous symptoms characterised by yawning, drowsiness and staggering. At postmortem: enlarged, hardened (cirrhotic) liver, fluid in abdomen and lungs, spots of blood on small intestines, heart. Diagnosis: on liver biopsy and blood tests showing liver dysfunction. There is no known treatment. — **ragwort poisoning**

See mud fever. — **rainscald**

(Fr râle, rattle) Abnormal harsh or soft breathing sound, depending on whether fluid is present in air passages. See auscultation, pneumonia. — **râle**

Small structure given off by larger one. **r. of jaw** Branch of lower jaw. — **ramus**

See royal. — **RNA**

(trade name: Zantac) Used to treat gastric and duodenal ulcers by mouth or IM injection. Reduces gastric acid production by blocking acid-secreting receptors. — **ranitidine**

Colloq for spots on the skin. See nettle rash, ringworm, acne, dermatitis. — **rash**

Speed, frequency or measure of events. **basal metabolic r.** Amount of oxygen used by body at rest. **breathing (respiratory) r.** Number of breaths in 1 minute. **death r.** Number of deaths — **rate**

rate	resulting from disease or particular circumstances. **dose r.** amount of drug given per kg bodyweight per unit time. **erythrocyte sedimentation r.** (ESR) Time taken for red blood cells to settle when blood containing anticoagulant is allowed to stand. Expressed as percentage fall in a given time, usually 1 hour. Increased in infectious diseases, eg swamp fever; slowed in states of dehydration, eg diarrhoea. **fertility r.** See fertility. **heart r.** Number of beats per minute. See breathing; blood tests, haematology (7); heart.
ratio	Quantity of substance in relation to another. **a./g. (albumin/globulin) r.** Relation of albumin to globulin in blood serum, normally approx 1:0.7, reversed in liver disease to 0.5:1. **calcium/phosphorus r.** See calcium and phosphorus. **nutritive r.** That between protein, fats and carbohydrates in feed. See blood tests, food.
rat killer poisoning	See rodent killer poisoning.
RBC/r.b.c.	See red blood cell.
RCVS	Abbr Royal College of Veterinary Surgeons, qv.
reagent	Any material used in chemical or biological reaction.
receptor	Sensory nerve-ending which responds to stimulus. See nerve cell.
recombinant	Cell with combination of genes not found together in either parent. **r.. vaccine** One engineered by joining parts of genome (qv) from two distinct viruses. See vaccine.
rectovaginal fistula	Abnormal opening between rectum and vagina, caused by foreleg of foal puncturing vagina during delivery. See birth, hazards of; dystocia.
rectum	Last part of large intestine. See alimentary canal.
recumbent	Lying down. Horse rarely **r.** for long (see behaviour); if it is, sores may develop. See decubitus; newborn foal, nursing.
red blood cell	(syns erythrocyte, RBC) Cell of blood, 4–5μ diameter. Produced in bone marrow and unusual as it has no nucleus. Contains pigment (haemoglobin) and carries oxygen from lungs to all parts of body. See blood.
red mercuric iodide	Scarlet odourless tasteless highly irritant powder. Solution: **r.m.i.** dissolved in equal weight potassium iodide and water. Repeated use of 1% solution is mild counter-irritant. See blister.

redworm (syn strongyle) Nematode parasite (roundworm) of order Strongyloidea, family Strongylidae. Several genera, viz,

Strongylus vulgaris	14–16mm
Strongylus equinus	6–35mm
Strongylus edentatus	23–28mm
Tridontophorus (4 spp)	6–25mm
Trichonema spp,	4–17mm
Posteriostomum and	
Gyalocephalus spp	

Lengths refer to males; females are smaller. All are parasites of large intestines (colon and caecum). Life history: female in intestine lays eggs which pass out with dung onto pasture; 1st larvae hatch, feed on bacteria and moult to become 2nd larvae; further moults lead to infective larvae. These are swallowed by new host. Inside host, habits differ by species, eg larvae of *Trichonema* spp enter wall of large intestine and develop inside nodules, then return to cavity of large intestine. Larvae of *S. equinus* penetrate walls of caecum and colon and hibernate in nodules beneath peritoneum. After further development for about 11 days, 4th-stage larvae leave nodules and migrate to liver, where they stay 6–7 weeks. They return to intestine through pancreas and peritoneal cavity, where they develop further, then again travel to gut about 120 days after infection; larvae of *S. edentatus* cause nodules in mesenteries and wall of large intestine. Larvae of *S. vulgaris* enter blood vessels supplying small intestine and cause an aneurysm (qv) where the vessels branch from main aorta. *S. vulgaris* has longest life cycle, ingestion of larvae to appearance of adults in large intestines taking 6–12 months. **R.** damage can be divided into that caused by adults and that by migrating larvae. Adults suck blood from intestine walls and cause anaemia, ulceration, haemorrhage, colic or diarrhoea. They can rupture intestines, especially in young horse, if present in large numbers. Larvae cause peritonitis, ulcerative enteritis, aneurysms, colic, liver disease, wasting and can migrate to heart, damaging valves. Treatment: workers are trying to perfect a vaccine, using irradiated **r.** larvae; until this is available horses at grass should be wormed regularly (see dichlorvos, mebendazole, phenothiazine, pyrantel tartrate, thiabendazole, ivermectin). Larvae are infective only when on grass, so stabled horses are not at risk unless allowed to graze contaminated pasture.

reflex (L reflexus) Automatic nervous reaction to a stimulus at some point of body. **r. arc** See arc.

(re + L fluxus flow) Backwards flow especially of fluid from stomach. Seen in colic associated with obstruction of the small *reflux* | intestine. Facilitated by passage of stomach tube. If spontaneous, ie occurs without stomach tube, severe problem likely.

regurgitation | (re- + L gurgitare, to flood) Backward flow. **aortic r./mitral r.** Blood flows backwards against main stream due to faulty heart valves. See also grass sickness, vomit.

renal | (L renalis) Of the kidney, qv.

reproduction | (L re, again + productio, production) Process of conception, gestation and birth of foal. See behaviour, embryology, birth.

resistance | (L resistentia) Horse's ability to withstand pathogenic microorganisms. Partly due to immunity, partly to natural defence mechanisms of body, eg white blood cells.

resonance | (L resonantia) Noise produced by percussion (qv) of cavity.

resorb | To absorb again. Used especially about early pregnancy loss: foetal tissues are resorbed into maternal tissues rather than expelled. Cf abortion.

respiration | See breath.

respiratory distress | (syn difficult breathing) See also neonatal maladjustment syndrome.

retained sole | See sole.

reticulo-endothelial system | Network of cells lining liver and bone marrow which engulf harmful substances. Cells are named phagocytes; their ingesting action, phagocytosis.

retro- | Prefix meaning backward or behind, eg retropharyngeal, at back of pharynx; retrobulbar, behind eye (qv) or pons (qv).

rhabdomyolysis | (Gr rhabdos, rod + myo, muscle + lysis, dissolution). See setfast.

Rhenish | Draught horse from Rhine area of Germany. Usually 16 h, most often sorrel with little feathering.

rhinitis | Inflamed mucous membranes of nose. See snotty nose, catarrh. Cf sinusitis.

rhinopneumonitis | Virus now called equine herpesvirus 1. See virus.

rhinovirus | One of the picornaviruses associated with respiratory disease, usually with another virus or viruses. Exposure can be detected by rise in antibody titre using complement fixation test.

Previously called *Corynebacterium equi*, qv. Organism (natural habitat soil) which causes pneumonia in foals. See pneumonia. **Rhodococcus equi**

Caused by eating **r.** (Ericaceae family). Symptoms: attempts to vomit, salivation, colic, shallow breathing, weakness, staggering, collapse and death after several days. Little, if any, evidence of inflammation at postmortem. No specific treatment. **rhododendron poisoning**

(L, Gr rhonchos, a snoring sound) Dry, coarse râle. See râle. **rhonchus**

(L rhythmus, Gr rhythmos) Regular beat or recurrence. **gallop r.** Heartbeat with accentuated extra sound, so that 3 sounds can be likened to noise of hoofbeats at fast pace. Best heard after exercise. See heart sounds. **rhythm**

Long, curved bone. **R.**s form walls of chest and are arranged in pairs. Each articulates with thoracic vertebra (above) and a cartilage attached to sternum (below). Most breeds have 18 pairs. Cf Arab. **rib**

(syn vitamin B$_2$) Orange-yellow crystalline powder with slight odour and bitter taste. Forms part of enzyme system necessary for oxidation of carbohydrates, amino acids and other products of metabolism. Important for red cell production and health of eye and capillaries. Storage organs: liver, heart, kidneys. Deficiency unlikely as **r.** widely distributed in foodstuffs. Moon blindness may be prevented, but not cured, by adding 40mg per day to feed. See eye, diseases of: moon blindness. **riboflavin**

Disease of young horses characterised by lack of calcium in bones. Symptoms: stiffness, lameness, enlargement of growth plates (qv) resulting in firm, painful swellings on inside and outside of fetlock, knee and hock joints. In extreme cases – rare in horses – there may be bow-leggedness. Treatment: give vitamin D and correct any calcium/phosphorus imbalance. See calcium and phosphorus. **rickets**

A genus of microorganism of tribe Rickettsieae. **R.** are rod-shaped or round and live in cytoplasm or in gut of lice, fleas, ticks or mites. These hosts then transmit Rickettsial disease when they bite man or animal. See Potomac horse fever. **Rickettsia**

Antibiotic isolated from *Streptomyces mediterranei*. Useful to treat tuberculosis and *Rhodococcus equi* infections. See also pneumonia. **rifampicin**

(syns cryptorchid, ridgling) Colloq for state when one testis has not descended into scrotum; may be retained in inguinal canal (high testis) or in abdomen (intra-abdominal **r.**). Can also mean **rig**

rig | rarer state when neither testis has descended (double or bilateral **r.**). Condition may be inherited; likely to cause aggressive behaviour. Treatment: castrate under general anaesthesia, removing retained testis through inguinal canal, qv, abdomen or flank. **false r.** Gelding which behaves like colt, eg when first put with mare/mares. Mounting behaviour usually wears off after a week or so. See Welsh Mountain; inguinal.

rigidity | (L rigidus, stiff) Stiffness. See rigor mortis, neonatal maladjustment syndrome, convulsions, lockjaw.

rigor mortis | (L) Stiffening of body after death. Due to chemical changes which shorten and harden muscle tissues. Occurs 1–7 hours after death, varying with temperature (heat accelerates process, cold delays it) and cause of death (faster in conditions such as lockjaw). After a period of **r.m.** bacterial fermentation in tissues causes body to become limp.

ring | Circular ridge in horn of hoof due to change of season, level of nutrition or laminitis, qv. See foot.

ringbone | Growth of new bone (exostosis) on first, second or third phalanx due to inflamed bone lining (periostitis). Caused by trauma, underlying bone disease, nutritional deficiency or infection. **R.** classified as high (at lower end of 1st phalanx or top of 2nd); low (lower end of 2nd phalanx or top of 3rd); articular (involving joint surface of pastern or coronopedal joint); or peri-articular (at distance from joint, not involving surface). Symptoms: pain, swelling and usually lameness. Diagnosis: on X-ray examination. Treatment: inject corticosteroids, rest horse and, in extreme cases, cut nerve supply or fuse joint (arthrodesis, qv).

Ringer's solution | (after Sydney **R.**, English physiologist) Sterile solution of salt (sodium chloride), potassium and calcium chloride. Can be given to replace electrolyte (qv) loss.

ringworm | (syns dermatomycosis, mycotic dermatitis) Condition caused by fungal invasion of skin cells and hair fibres. (No type of worm is involved.) Occurs in all countries; more common in winter and where horses are stabled. Common causal organisms are: *Trichophyton equinum*, *T. mentagrophytes*, *Microsporum gypseum* and *M. equinum*. Spread by direct contact or infected bedding, saddlery, grooming kit, blankets or human clothing. Stables are difficult to disinfect because fungus spores can live for years. Fungi attack skin which oozes serum and forms scabs of matted hair. These peel off, leaving red, moist areas. Infection spreads outwards and tends to form circles. These may amalgamate so that large areas are affected.

Lesions are common on girth area, flanks and neck and tend to be deeper on young horses. Diagnosis: on examination of skin scrapings for fungus, which can be seen under microscope or grown on culture. Some fungal infections can be diagnosed by exposing skin or hairs to a fluorescent light (see radiation). Treatment: apply weak solution of iodine, salicylic acid or proprietary fungicide spray, ointment or lotion. Give griseofulvin by mouth. Control: **r.** not a health menace and has little economic consequence apart from the Jockey Club ruling (Thoroughbreds) that affected horses must not go to race meetings. — *ringworm*

See swamp fever. — **river bottom disease**

Abbr ribonucleic acid, several types of which function in cytoplasm of cells. **RNA** and protein provide the means by which the genetic code, DNA (qv), is expressed in the body. See chromosome. — **RNA**

See coat colouring. — **roan**

(syn laryngeal hemiplegia) Abnormal noise made by horse breathing in. See wind; Hobday. — **roaring**

Rare condition when horse is affected by rodenticide. (1) ANTU (alphanaphthylthiourea), causes oedema of lungs and sac around heart. No treatment known. (2) Castrix, causes convulsions. (3) Fluoracetate, causes heart failure. (4) Red squill, causes convulsions and heart failure; chronic cases develop gastritis and enteritis. (5) Warfarin, interferes with production of prothrombin in liver and prolongs clotting time of blood. Symptoms: lameness due to haemorrhage, diarrhoea, often blood-stained, multiple haemorrhages throughout body. Treatment: give vitamin K, 5mg/kg bodywt. — **rodent killer poisoning**

Turning or revolving. Sometimes horse indulges in **r.** in effort to shift trapped/twisted intestine. See nephrosplenic ligament, colic, behaviour. — **rolling**

(trade name: Sedivet) Drug which produces sedation and tolerance of pain by stimulating central nervous system. Used to facilitate handling and minor surgery. — **romifidine**

Colloq enlarged state of glans penis, qv. — **rose**

(L rostralis from rostrum, beak) Towards the head or front. — **rostral**

Parasite of class Nematoda with six orders. Those important in equine medicine: Strongyloidea (redworm, qv, lungworm, qv, — **roundworm**

roundworm   stomach worm, qv); Ascaroidea (whiteworm, qv); Filarioidea (filaria, qv); Spiruroidea (stomach worm).

rotavirus   RNA virus causing diarrhoea (qv) in foals. Named after its wheel-like appearance. Diarrhoea associated with loss of suck and sometimes colic. Many cases recover spontaneously. Virus, taken in through mouth, very resistant and survives for long periods in stables and pasture.

royal   Of/worthy of a king/queen. **R. Animal Nursing Auxiliary** (RANA) Lay assistant who has passed exam set by RCVS. **R. College of Veterinary Surgeons** Opened 8 April 1791 as Veterinary College of London. Granted Royal Charter 8 March 1844. First president of College: Hugh, second Duke of Northumberland. Address: Belgravia House, 62–64 Horseferry Road, London SW1P 2AF (0171 222 2001). See soundness, veterinary surgeon. **R. Netherlands Draught horse** See Dutch Draught.

rubefacient   (L ruber, red + facere, to make) Drug or substance that increases blood flow to part. See blister.

rules   See veterinary rules.

rump   Colloq for buttocks or gluteal region.

run-down   (syn suspensory sprain) Dropped fetlock due to damaged suspensory ligament.

running   Flowing. **r. of milk** Colloq for premature secretion by mammary glands. Mare may run first milk (colostrum) as early as 3 weeks before foaling, or if she aborts. See birth, colostrum, gland, oxytocin. **r. walk** See gait.

run under heel   See heel.

rupture   Tear or break. See bladder, rupture of; cord, rupture of; birth; vomit.

Russian   Of Russia. **R. Saddle** syn Orlov Rostopschiner, qv. **R. Steppe** Extremely tough type, either ewe-necked pony similar to Przewalski, or horse descended from English Thoroughbred cross. See Beetewk, Budyonovsky, Latvian, Zemaituka/s. **R. Horse Soc**, Priam Lodge Stables, Burgh Heath Rd, Epsom KT17 4NN (01372 722080).

S

Extremely hardy pony which runs on **S.I.**, 150 miles off Nova Scotia, E Canada. Ponies have been there about 300 years, they may have swum ashore from shipwrecks or been imported to feed wreck survivors. They live on coarse grass and seaweed. The inhospitable island, about 30 x 9 miles, probably supports a few hundred ponies, but their number fluctuates greatly depending on severity of winters.

Sable Island

(L saccus, Gr sakkos) Pouch. **allantoic s.** That part of placenta which contains fluid. Colloq for scrotum.

sac

(L sacred) Single bone formed from 5 vertebrae fused together. It is triangular and forms joint with pelvis (sacro-iliac articulation). Articulation may be dislodged causing lameness. Spinal processes above form croup. Adjective: sacral.

sacrum

(L sagitta, arrow) (1) Straight. (2) Parallel to or along median (midline) plane of body or limb.

saggital

(Hypericum species) Plant which causes photosensitisation, qv.

Saint John's wort

Pain-relieving drug which may irritate the intestinal lining causing haemorrhage and diarrhoea. Used to treat arthritis in preference to cortisone.

salicylate

(L sat, salt) Containing salt. **normal s.** 0.9% sodium chloride in water, ie approx 1 teaspoonful to 600ml (approx 1 pint).

saline

(L) Clear, alkaline fluid discharge into mouth by salivary glands. Contains a digestive enzyme and moistens food ready for swallowing.

saliva

Inflamed fallopian tube, qv.

salpingitis

(Gr a tube, pl salpinges) Tube, particularly of ear or of uterus (syn fallopian tube, qv). Inflammation of **s.**: salpingitis.

salpinx

Genus of aerobic gram-negative bacteria. Classified by serology for differing protein content, which is antigenically distinct. **S. abortive-equine** (syn *S. abortus-equi*) Organism causing abortion and septicaemia. Once common but less so now. Causes abortion (in seventh or eight month of pregnancy), retained placenta and infection of uterus (metritis). Foals develop septicaemia (see septicaemia of the newborn) and joint-ill (qv) during first few days of life. **S. enteritidis** Occasionally causes

salmonella

salmonella   salmonellosis in horses. **S. typhimurium** Most common cause of salmonellosis (qv) in horses.

salmonellosis   Infection with a salmonella bacterium, in horses often *Salmonella typhimurium*. Causes acute enteritis or less typically joint-ill, qv. Symptoms: high fever, dullness, blood-stained diarrhoea and death, usually in 24–48 hours. May reach epidemic proportions on a farm. Spreads through pasture, feeding stuffs and drinking water contaminated with faecal material. Diagnosis: on recovery of organism from faeces. At postmortem there is extensive haemorrhage in wall of alimentary canal and enlarged lymph nodes. Treatment: chloramphenicol, nitrofurazone, neomycin. Infectious to humans so strict hygiene should be enforced.

salt   See sodium chloride.

sandcrack   (syn toe, quarter or heel crack) Crack in wall of hoof from ground surface upwards; or starting at coronary band and extending downwards. Often several together. Caused by lack of foot care, injury to coronary band, weakening of wall from excessive drying, poor conformation. May result in lameness. Treatment: smooth horn above or below crack and to either side; use shoe with clips to support wall either side of crack. May need to use screws and plate or patch across crack to reduce movement.

sanguineous   Of blood; bloody.

SAP   Abbr serum alkaline phosphatase, usually termed merely AP or alkaline phosphatase unless confusion with another type of AP, eg intestinal (IAP), possible. See alkaline phosphatase.

sarco-   (Gr sarx, sarkos, flesh) Combining form meaning relationship to flesh.

Sarcocystis   Protozoan, qv, different types of which cause diseases including equine protozoal myeloencephalitis.

sarcoid   (syn equine sarcoid) Tumour which occurs on skin. May appear on leg, head, shoulder, breast or flanks. Resembles simple wart at first but subsequently grows rapidly and ulcerates. On removal it tends to recur and may bleed. May be troublesome when mating if situated near genitalia, or when foal sucks if close to udder. Treatment: cryosurgery/surgery but radioactivity may be necessary to prevent recurrence. BCG, qv, used by injection into sarcoids near eyes. Cream containing cytotoxic drugs used on alternate days sometimes effective.

See mange.	**sarcoptic**
(pl sarcomas or sarcomata) A tumour of closely packed cells, often highly malignant. See growth.	**sarcoma**
Pony of Italian island of Sardinia, about 13.2 h. Roams free until broken for riding/driving.	**Sardinian**
Crust or hard covering of sore on the skin. See ringworm, dermatitis.	**scab**
Type of diagnostic imaging. See echography; veterinary.	**scanning**
(pl scapulae) See shoulder blade.	**scapula**
(Gr eschara, scab on a wound caused by burning) Fibrous line in skin after healing of wound, qv.	**scar**
Heavy artillery or cart horse of German **S.** province.	**Schleswig/er**
(Gr skirrhos) Firm swelling of fibrous connective tissue. **s. cord** Infected spermatic cord, eg with staphylococcus, after castration. Symptoms: swelling in region of wound, stiffness (due to pain). Treatment: surgical removal and antibiotics.	**scirrhus**
Method of diagnosing local disturbance in function of bones or internal organs by injection of radioactive substances. Substances are taken up by inflamed or damaged part and the image they form is photographed by special camera. Photographs or graphs interpreted according to nature of damage and tissues involved. Intense activity is known as a 'hot spot'. See veterinary re diagnostic imaging.	**scintigraphy**
(L, Gr skleros, hard, pl sclerae) White of eye; tough, outer covering of eyeball. See eye. Adjective: scleral. Scleral inflammation: scleritis. See eye, diseases of.	**sclera**
Substance which hardens tissues, eg sodium oleate, sodium morrhuate (used to treat fractured sesamoid bones). Others helpful in cases of soft palate or distended (varicose) vein.	**sclerosing agent**
(Gr skoliosis, curvation) Rare crooked spine in newborn foals. May be associated with leg deformities but simple cases recover.	**scoliosis**
Of Scotland. See grass sickness. **S. breeds** See Clydesdale; Eriskay; Highland pony; Shetland pony.	**Scottish**
See diarrhoea.	**scour**

scratches	Syn greasy heel. See mud fever.
scrotum	Fold of skin or sac containing testes. Problems include scrotal hernia. See hernia.
seatworm	(syn *Oxyuris equi*) Nematode (roundworm parasite) of order Ascaroidea, family Oxyuridae, which lives in caecum and colon. Male is 9–12mm (just under $^1/_2$in) long, female is 40–150mm (approx $1^1/_2$–6in). Life cycle: female passes to anus, where she lays eggs, which stick to skin; larvae develop in eggs, which then drop off host and are later eaten with food or drink. After further development larvae grow into adults, completing the cycle. They may irritate anus, causing horse to rub against objects. Treatment: see piperazine salts.
sebaceous	(L sebaceus) Secreting greasy substance, eg **s. gland** Gland in skin which secretes oily matter called sebum. Overactive **s.g.**s may cause seborrhoea, qv.
seborrhoea	(L sebum, suet + Gr rhoia, flow) Excessive discharge of grease from glands (sebaceous) of skin; may develop into infection. Most common in heels (see mud fever). Treatment: ensure clean bedding, wash area and apply astringent lotion.
second thigh	See gaskin.
secretion	(L secretio) A gland's production of substances such as hormone, digestive fluid.
sedative	Drug which lessens activity of brain, reducing excitement, eg barbiturate.
sedimentation	Deposit of particles on standing (settling out) or using centrifugal (spinning down) machine. See blood tests.
seed	Colloq for spermatozoa, qv.
seedy toe	A separation of wall and sole at toe by soft, granular, cheese-like material surrounded by pale yellow horn. Usually infective agent is *Candida albicans* but condition may be related to chronic laminitis. Filthy stabling predisposes feet to yeast infection. Debridement (removal) of infected material and abnormal hoof wall and sole is necessary. Often associated with brittle feet.
segmental myelitis	Nervous disease characterised by hindleg incoordination, crossing-over (qv). Cause: inflamed segments of spinal cord. Horse usually deteriorates until euthanasia is necessary.

(symbol Se) Essential trace element required by horses in their diets. Constituent of vitamin E. **s. poisoning** (syns blind staggers, alkali disease) Important in N America and W Canada. Has been reported in Ireland. Source: **s.** content of soil and certain plants, eg astragulas (vetch), stanlea (prince's bloom), oonopsis (golden weed) and xylorrhiza (woody aster). These contain 2–6,000 parts per million of **s.**, but horses usually avoid them unless food is scarce. Symptoms are acute, subacute or chronic. Acute poisoning – death occurs within a few hours, preceded by rapid and weak pulse, difficult breathing, bloat and colic. Postmortem findings are haemorrhages and serum in abdominal cavity (ascites). Subacute poisoning (blind staggers) – weight loss, staring coat, listlessness, staggering, impaired sight, abdominal pain, salivation and inability to swallow, finally paralysis and death. At postmortem: chronic degeneration in all organs, particularly liver. Chronic poisoning (alkali disease) – loss of hair from mane and tail, rough coat, dullness, emaciation, anaemia, depraved appetite. Rings appear on hoof and in severe cases there may be complete separation and shedding of hoof. No known treatment. See gamma glutamyltransferase. **s. deficiency** Occurs in certain places eg New Zealand and causes white muscle disease.

selenium

(L seed) Thick whitish secretion of stallion's testes and accessory sex glands. Average ejaculum:

semen

volume of **s.**	40–120ml
number of sperm	100–150 million per cu mm
abnormal sperm (coiled tails/protoplasmic drops)	about 16 per cent
pH (acidity/alkalinity)	about 7.330

seminal plasma

specific gravity	1.012
ergothioneine	7.6mg/100ml
citric acid	26mg/100ml
fructose	15mg/100ml
phosphorus	17mg/100ml
lactic acid	12mg/100ml
urea	3mg/100ml

It has been estimated that a minimum 500 million sperm per ejaculum are necessary for fertilisation and that the average content is 4–18 billion (American billion, ie 1,000 million).

See aortic **s.v.**, pulmonary **s.v.**

semilunar valves

seminal | Of semen (qv) or seed. **s. vesicles** Two long sacs lying either side of top of bladder and opening by ducts into urethra. 15–20cm (6–8in) long in stallion but much shorter in gelding. They form part of accessory glands and provide nourishing fluid in which spermatozoa travel at ejaculation.

sense/sensation | (L sensus, sentire, to perceive) Feeling conveyed by (afferent) nerves, eg of warmth, cold, pain. See arc.

sensitisation | State of body or cells induced by specific substance. See allergy, anaphylaxis, immunity, photosensitisation.

sepsis | (Gr decay) Infection of blood or tissues. **puerperal s.** That after foaling due to septic material absorbed from the uterus/birth passage.

septicaemia | (septic + Gr haima, blood + -ia) Presence of bacteria in blood. **s. of the newborn** Includes conditions such as sleepy foal disease, joint-ill, pneumonia, diarrhoea and meningitis, ie bacterial infections caused by streptococci, staphylococci, *E. coli*, *Actinobacillus equuli* (formerly *viscosum equi*, *Shigella equirulis*), *Klebsiella pneumoniae*. Similar conditions may be caused by virus, qv. Symptoms vary with main site of infection, eg if brain, it causes convulsions; if joints, lameness and painful swelling; if alimentary tract, diarrhoea; if lungs, rapid breathing. Characteristic signs are fever, gradual loss of suck reflex and strength to approach mare, inability to stand unaided, coma and convulsions. Dehydration (shown in sinking of eyeballs into sockets) is especially associated with diarrhoea and affected foals exude aromatic smell. Signs first show between birth and 3 days, although joint-ill may appear up to third month (see joint-ill). Diagnosis: on laboratory examination of faeces, blood, urine and other body fluids (see paracentesis abdominis and occipital puncture). Treatment: maximum antibiotic drug effective against particular organism. Pathology varies with infecting bacteria. *Actinobacillus equuli* (which causes sleepy foal disease) produces abscesses in kidney, adrenal glands, lungs and brain. *E. coli* causes pneumonia and inflamed alimentary tract. Streptococci cause pleurisy. Adjective: septicaemic.

septum | (L, pl septa) Any dividing wall, eg that between nostrils (**s. nasi** or nasal **s.**).

sequestrum | Detached piece of bone which degenerates because blood no longer supplies it. Result of injury or infection. Should be surgically removed.

serology | The study of immune substances, usually antibodies, in blood serum or other body fluid.

Any membrane which is serous (of or resembling serum) but term used particularly for outer surface of abdominal organs.

serosa

(pl sera) Clear liquid which separates from red blood clot, ie whole blood minus cells and fibrinogen. See blood. **s. glutamic oxaloacetic transaminase** (SGOT) Former name for aspartate aminotransferase, qv. **s. glutamic pyruvic transaminase** (SGPT) Former name for alanine aminotransferase, qv. See laboratory tests. **s. gonadotrophin** (trade names: Folligon, PMS) Dry, sterile preparation of follicle stimulating hormone obtained from **s.** of pregnant mares. Stimulates growth of follicles in many species, but results in mares are disappointing. Cf pregnant mare **s.** gonadotrophin. **s. hepatitis** See hepatitis.

serum

Small bones inserted into tendons where pressure occurs. **proximal s.b.** Two small bones behind fetlock joint attached to cannon bone and pastern bone by ligaments. Each is shaped like three-sided pyramid and forms back of fetlock joint, beneath deep flexor tendon. **distal s.** (syn navicular bone) Flat, elongated bone behind joint formed by 2nd and 3rd phalanges (coronopedal joint). **s.b., fracture of** Caused by trauma; results in lameness. Diagnosis: on X-ray examination. See sclerosing agent.

sesamoid bones

Inflamed sesamoid bones (suspensory ligament and distal sesamoidean ligaments may also be affected). Caused by strain, nutritional disturbance and trauma. Symptoms: pain and swelling around back of fetlock joint and, in severe cases, lameness. Diagnosis: on X-ray examination. Disproportion of one sesamoid bone best seen from point several paces behind horse, first on one side, then other.

sesamoiditis

(syns azoturia, Monday morning disease, paralytic myoglobinuria, tying up) Painful condition of large muscle masses with degeneration of fibres. Occurs in horses on highly nutritious diets, eg racehorses and brood mares. Onset follows exercise especially after period of rest, as at weekends. Cause: thought to be rapid use of glycogen laid down by liver during idleness. When horse works, production of lactic acid exceeds its removal and destroys muscle fibres (rhabdomyolysis). The pigment myoglobin is liberated, colouring urine red. Some individuals seem particularly susceptible. Symptoms: profuse sweating, stiffness, reluctance to move, hard and painful muscles, particularly in back and hindquarters, restlessness, rapid respiration and pulse, raised temperature and sometimes difficult passing of port-coloured urine. Symptoms develop several hours, or immediately, after exercise. Most horses recover in matter of hours if rested, but some lie down, cannot get up and die. Diagnosis: on characteristic symptoms, confirmed by

setfast

setfast — urine colour and rise in AST and CK enzymes in blood (see blood tests). Treatment: do not exercise horse, give anti-inflammatory drugs, corticosteroids and pain reliever. When recovered, reduce grain ration, give regular exercise and if attacks recur, give salicylates. Dantrolene sodium can be given to help return to exercise. Pathology: kidney damage, extensive pale discolouration of large muscle masses, giving cooked appearance. See anti-inflammatory; carbohydrate; corticosteroid; metabolism; muscle; temperature.

seton (Fr seton, L seta, bristle) Strip of silk or linen drawn through wound to help drainage, as in infection of frontal sinus. See sinusitis.

sex (L sexus) Distinction between male and female based on genitalia, qv. See chromosome; intersex. **female s. hormones** Oestrogens: oestradiol, oestrone, oestriol, equilin, equilenin. Progestogens: progesterone, ethinyltestosterone. Responsible for female **s.** characteristics, oestrous cycle and maintenance of pregnancy. **male s. hormones** Androgens: testosterone, androstenediol, androsterone, androstenidione found in testes (and ovaries), adrenal cortex and in placenta of mare. Responsible for male **s.** characters and libido. **other s. hormones** Follicle stimulating hormone (FSH), luteinising hormone (LH), pregnant mare serum gonadotrophin (PMSG).

SGOT Abbr serum glutamic oxaloacetic transaminase, now termed aspartate aminotransferase, qv.

shaft Main part of long bone. See bone.

shaker foal Syndrome caused by *Clostridium botulinum*. See botulism, neonatal maladjustment syndrome.

sheath Structure enclosing and protecting another. **artificial s.** See condom. **s. of penis** Colloq for prepuce, qv. See masturbation. **synovial s.** One secreting synovial fluid which lubricates contained part (eg tendon), reducing friction. Main **s.s.**s are those of deep and superficial digital flexor tendons of front and hindlegs; and tendons of common digital extensor, extensors carpi radialis and obliquus, lateral and long digital extensors, tibialis anterior and ulnaris lateralis.

shelly foot (syn brittle foot) See foot; seedy toe.

Shetland pony Probably strongest member of Equidae in relation to its size. (Limited by stud book rules to 10.3 h but averages less.) May have originated in **S.** Isles of Scotland, where now bred. Good child's pony, usually long-lived. Seems to have some immunity to grass sickness. Most colours including piebald and skew-bald. Minimum values placed on **S.** for export (see veterinary rules) to combat export for slaughter. **S. Pony Stud Book Soc**, 6 King's Place, Perth, PH2 8AD (01738 623471). **American S. Pony Club**, 6748 N. Frostwood Pkwy, Peoria, IL 61615 (309 691 9661).

Shetland pony

See sleepy foal disease.

shigellosis

Front of cannon bone. See bucked **s.**; periostitis.

shin

Largest English draught horse, usually over 17 hands. Takes name from the shires, eg Lincolnshire, Cambridgeshire, where traditionally bred. Bays and browns most common and all colours have white around legs. **S. Horse Soc**, East of England Showground, Peterborough PE2 6XE (01733 234451).

Shire

Involuntary quivering of muscles of hindlegs and tail; forelegs occasionally affected. Cause unknown, but may be damaged nerves supplying hindleg. Best seen on flexing hindleg and pulling it to side; as leg returns to ground it will shake and tail is elevated and quivers. Should not be confused with **s.** of shoulders and forelegs due to nervousness, eg before race. Foals normally shiver during first 2 hours of life to maintain body temperature.

shivering

Condition of failure in blood circulation characterised by pale mucous membranes, clammy skin, decreased blood pressure, feeble rapid pulse, slow breathing and eventual unconsciousness. Caused by surgery, severe injury, reaction to injected drugs (anaphylaxis), haemorrhage, acute allergy or infection. Treatment: give large amounts of intravenous fluid initially, then more slowly over next few hours (normal saline, antibiotics, corticosteroids); ensure adequate ventilation (possibly oxygen direct into windpipe or through mask); treat underlying cause of **s.** and use good general nursing.

shock

Piece of iron or aluminium fitted to circumference of foot to protect it. Used on most ridden horses (should be removed from hind feet if horse is turned out with others). **S.** consists of toe, quarter and heel, usually with groove (fullering) in surface which meets ground. Groove contains about 3 or 4 nail holes on each side (branch). **s. boil** See capped elbow. **bar s.** One with full or half bar across heels to increase pressure on frog. **egg-bar s.** oval shoe to provide support behind heels for collapsed foot or tendon injury. **half-rim s.** One which raises side of foot worn down when horse puts too much weight on it. **tip s.** One which covers only toe, throwing weight on heels and frog. **surgical s.** One which reduces injury through faulty

shoe

shoe   action, eg roller toe **s.** which, fitted on hind foot, tempers bruising if horse over-reaches (catches forefoot). Cf plate. See blacksmith.

shoeing   (syn farriery) Art of applying horseshoes. Good **s.** can lessen faults, eg contracted heels, tendency to develop corns. See blacksmith.

shoulder blade   (scapula) Flat bone on side of chest with muscles of shoulder and forearm attached; forms joint with humerus bone. See skeleton.

sidebones   False bones caused by hardening of cartilages of pedal bone. See quittor.

side-effect   Unintended happening or result of giving drug, eg tranquilliser may cause **s.-e.** of incoordination. See donkey.

siderocyte   Red blood cell containing non-haemoglobin iron. Presence of large number suggests swamp fever, qv.

sign   (L signum) Evidence of abnormality/disease seen by person tending horse, rather than reported to him second-hand (a symptom).

silver   (L argentum) Soft white metal. **s. nitrate** Colourless bitter-tasting odourless crystals. Used in weak solution as astringent or antiseptic; in eye lotion to treat ulcers; in concentrated form on warts or proud flesh to reduce bleeding. **s. n. poisoning** Occurs in overdose. Symptoms: abdominal pain, diarrhoea and possibly convulsions, paralysis and death from shock. **s. weed** (*Potentilla anserina*) Has high tannin content. May cause death if large amount eaten.

sinus   (L a hollow) Body space containing blood or air. **s. arrhythmia** See arrhythmia. **s. of head** Cavity connected directly or indirectly to nasal cavity. 4 pairs: maxillary, frontal, sphenopalatine and ethmoidal. Functions: to lighten head (which if solid would be too heavy for horse to carry), to provide space for roots of teeth. Sometimes site of infection (see sinusitis).

sinusitis   Infected air sinuses of head, causing pain, thick discharge (usually from only 1 nostril) and swollen lymph node between angles of lower jaw. Discharge may be evil-smelling if bone of skull is diseased. Cause: bacterial infection (most common), trauma causing broken bone, or growth (rare). Treatment: antibiotics and/or surgery (opening sinus from the outside, flushing and causing free drainage into nasal passage).

Pony originally from **S.** (Himalayan foothills) but now all over India. Up to about 13.2 h, narrow and poor-looking but hardy.
Siwalik

(from Gr, dried mummy, body) Body's framework of bones, all cartilage in embryo, gradually hardening throughout life until brittle in old age. Contains average of 210 bones: 37 in skull (qv), 2 branches of lower jaw, 54 vertebrae (7 cervical, 18 thoracic, 6 lumbar, 5 sacral), 15–21 coccygeal (tail), 36 ribs (some breeds, eg Arab, sometimes have 37 or 38), 1 sternum, 40 forelimb, 40 hind limb (including pelvis). See bone; cartilage; and individual bones. See Fig 32.
skeleton
(illus page 296)

See coat colouring. **British S. and Piebald Assn** See piebald.
skewbald

(syn cutis) Outer covering of body. Consists of epidermis (4 layers) and dermis (2 layers) containing hair follicles, sweat glands and sebaceous glands. It is 3.8mm thick on average, and 6.2mm thick where mane and tail emerge. **s., diseases of** Dermatitis, ringworm, external parasites (louse, tick, harvest mite), acne, baldness (alopecia), cracked heels, mud fever, warble fly, photosensitisation, sores, eg from poorly fitting saddlery, Queensland itch.
skin

Bones of head – 37 in all including 3 in each ear (auditory ossicles). Divided into cranium (which surrounds brain) and face. Those of cranium (10): occipital, sphenoid, ethmoid and intraparietal (single bones) and parietals, frontals and temporals (paired). Bones of face (21): vomer, mandible and hyoid (single) and maxilla, incisive, palatine, pterygoid, nasal, lacrimal, zygomatic (or malar) upper and lower turbinates (paired) bones. Lower jaw is formed by mandible which has 2 branches (rami).
skull

Break in third carpal bone (in knee joint) or third tarsal bone (in hock joint) in which bone is split so that a slab becomes detached in front of joint. Treat by surgical removal or screwing together. See also carpal bones, fracture of.
slab fracture

See behaviour.
sleep

(syn shigellosis) Fatal disease of the newborn foal caused by *Actinobacillus equuli* (*Shigella equirulis*). Infection may start in utero or may enter through the mouth or navel after birth. Symptoms include fever, sleepiness, rapid breathing and loss of strength to get up and suck. Death may occur within 24 hours, but some foals live several days. At postmortem kidneys, adrenal glands, brain and possibly joints contain abscesses. See also septicaemia of the newborn.
sleepy foal disease

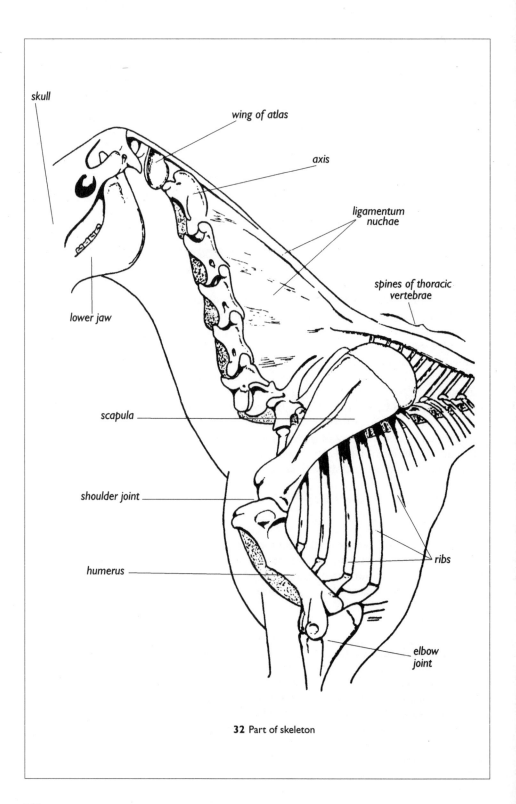

skull

wing of atlas

axis

ligamentum
nuchae

spines of thoracic
vertebrae

lower jaw

scapula

shoulder joint

humerus

ribs

elbow
joint

32 Part of skeleton

(syn run-under heels) See heels. **sloping heels**

Breaking away of dead matter from surface of body; necrotic area. **slough**

(Gr smegma, soap) Thick, cheesy, evil-smelling secretion in sheath of penis. See penis, prepuce. **smegma**

(syn involuntary muscle) One of 3 types of muscle; that not under voluntary control and found in walls of such organs as bladder, uterus and alimentary tract. Cf striped muscle, heart muscle. **smooth muscle**

Can kill, eg if from rattlesnake. Usually occurs on legs or head (when horse lowers head to investigate). Causes swelling around site and possibly nosebleed. Treatment: insert tubes in nostrils if bite on face (to prevent nostrils swelling shut). Depending on type of **s.b.**, calm horse and keep it still (to avoid spreading venom), send for help immediately; or cut open fang wounds, draw off venom and give antibiotics to prevent secondary infection. **s. venom** Used in some anticoagulants. **snake bite**

Sudden expulsion of air through nostrils (horse cannot normally breathe through mouth). May be due to excessive dust, inflamed mucous membranes infected with influenza virus, cerebral irritation through tumour, infection or haemorrhage. See neonatal maladjustment syndrome. **sneeze**

(syns equine viral rhinopneumonitis, cold, catarrh, stable cough) Mild disease of upper respiratory tract caused by equine herpesvirus 1 (qv). Cf influenza. **snotty nose**

Hard granules, white or coloured with indicator to show when their capacity for absorbing carbon dioxide is exhausted. Used in anaesthetic breathing circuits to absorb carbon dioxide. See anaesthesia. **soda lime**

An alkaline metallic element. **s. acid citrate** White odourless salty-tasting powder. Used to prevent clotting of blood for transfusion. 1.7–2 per cent with 2.5 per cent dextrose in 120 ml water will prevent clotting of about 420 ml blood. See anticoagulant. **s. acid phosphate** Colourless crystals or white crystaline powder with acid, saline taste. Used to treat low phosphate conditions. **s. bicarbonate** White opaque odourless crystals, with saline taste. Given by mouth to treat excess staling; intravenously in 5 per cent solution, to foals suffering from convulsions or diarrhoea. See polyuria; neonatal maladjustment syndrome. **s. calcium edetate** (trade name: Calcium Disodium Versenate) White tasteless powder with **sodium**

sodium slight odour. Used IV to treat poisoning by lead and other heavy metals, eg mercury. **s. chloride** (1) Common salt of the body. Imbalance will show as pale, livid red or purple mucous membranes of gums, cheeks and eyes. (2) Colourless odourless crystals with salty taste. Used to treat colic or as purgative. **s. citrate** White odourless crystals or powder. Used in solution as anticoagulant. Solution 2.5–3.8 per cent prevents clotting of blood for laboratory study. **s. cromoglycate** (trade name: Cromovet) Drug acting on mast cells that produce histamine, which constricts smooth muscles. Drug therefore used to prevent asthmatic attacks. See broken wind. **s. fusidate** See fusidic acid. **s. glycarsamate** Odourless tasteless creamy-white crystalline powder. Given to treat redworm infestation (best after soft food, eg bran mash). Should not be given if intestines are inflamed. **s. hyaluronate** (trade names: Hyalovet, Hylartil, Hyonate) Used to treat noninfectious inflammatory disease of joints **s. morrhuate** Salt of morrhuic acid. See sclerosing agent. **s. oleate** See sclerosing agent. **s. salicylate** (syn aspirin) Colourless odourless salty-tasting crystals or powder. Reduces temperature by depressing heat-regulating centre of brain. See also acetylsalicylic acid. **s. sulphate** (syn glauber's salt) Colourless to light-brown odourless bitter-tasting crystals. Acts as laxative. Should be given by stomach tube with large volume of water. **s. thiosulphate** Colourless odourless crystals with salty taste. Given to reduce flatulence and fermentation in stomach/intestines, also to treat poisoning by arsenic, mercury and some other metals.

soft palate Membrane of muscle which separates mouth from pharynx except when swallowing. Continuation of hard palate (mouth) with upper surface forming end of nasal cavities. Undersurface forms back of throat (seen in man as uvula). Sides of **s.p.** merge with walls of pharynx and contain tonsils, which are not compact, as in man, but consist of a series of lymphoid tissues and mucous glands. Average length of **s.p.** is 15cm (6in) and its shape probably explains why horses cannot normally breathe through the mouth. Muscles of **s.p.** are the palatines, levator palati and tensor palati. Their action is to shorten, tense and raise the **s.p.** during swallowing. Nerves supplying palate are from the trigeminus, vagus and glossopharyngeal cranial nerves. Symptoms of **s.p.** condition (when **s.p.** interferes with breathing) include gurgling, roaring or whistling at exercise (see wind). Treatments include injection of sclerosing agent (qv), cautery, reducing size of **s.p.** by surgery. All measures have limited value. Cause unknown but may be virus infection affecting nerve supply to **s.p.** muscles.

sole (L solea, sandal) Undersurface of foot (hoof). Usually concave and non-weight-bearing. **dropped/flat s.** (syn pumiced foot)

One which has lost its concavity and is susceptible to bruising. *sole*
retained s. (syn false sole) Abnormally thick sole of hoof which does not flake away, desirable for horses on rocky terrain as it protects foot. In stabled horses it can promote thrush and abscesses beneath sole.

(L soporificus) Drug or substance which induces sleep. **soporific**

Colloq (1) any lesion on skin or mucous membrane; (2) feeling **sore** of stiffness. **s. shin** See bucked shin. **summer s.** See stomach worm.

Native pony of Spain, usually dun with dorsal stripe. Similar **Sorraia** to Przewalski and Tarpan.

(L sonus) (1) Colloq fit/healthy/not lame. (2) Energy waves of **sound** frequency between 8,000 and 20,000 cycles per second (Hz). (3) Normal or abnormal noise heard in body, eg murmur, râle, borborygmus, roaring. See also equine sounds, percussion, stethoscope, wind.

State of health or fitness to carry out particular function, eg **soundness** sound for racing, breeding, etc (recent move to avoid use of word 'sound'). **s. examination** Methods used by veterinarian to ascertain state of horse at a given time, eg before it changes hands or is insured. Royal College of Veterinary Surgeons and British Veterinary Association recommendations on examining horse for a buyer are as follows:

Stage 1: preliminary examination
    2: trotting up
    3: strenuous exercise
    4: a period of rest
    5: second trot and foot examination

Stage 1: Preliminary examination. This is best conducted in stable...note animal's general appearance and condition. Veterinarian should develop habit of examining horse methodically part by part, so there is no chance of inadvertently overlooking any part. Teeth should be examined, age assessed...resting heart should be auscultated for comparison with its action after exercise. Eyes should be examined with an ophthalmoscope. Veterinarian should run hand over animal's body and legs to ensure he has not missed abnormalities or lesions. Horse should be turned right around in stable and each foot picked up and examined and leg joints flexed to detect pain or limitation of movement. Horse should then be brought outside and inspected from all sides in daylight.
Stage 2: Trotting up. Animal should be walked and trotted on

soundness | hard, level ground...Horse should be walked 20 yards away from veterinarian, turned and walked back. Horse should then be trotted back...If animal is not fit to be exerted...or if it is lame when trotted, examination should not be continued...

Stage 3: Strenuous exercise...age, condition and fitness should be considered. Animal should be given sufficient exercise: (1) to make it breathe deeply and rapidly so that any unusual breathing sounds may be heard; (2) to increase action of heart so abnormalities may be more easily detected; (3) to tire animal so that strains or injuries may be revealed by stiffness or lameness after period of rest. Riding horse should be ridden at canter 5–10 minutes and pass close to veterinarian so that he can hear horse's breathing. Speed should then be increased to controlled gallop, again passing close to veterinarian until he indicates it should be pulled up. He can then auscultate heart and observe rate and depth of breathing. More exercise can then be given if necessary. Untrained animals and those too young or too small to be ridden can be lunged, which should be stated on certificate. [Racehorses are normally galloped past vet for about 6 furlongs, then pulled up and immediately trotted back to him.] Horse is then returned to stable.

Stage 4: A period of rest. The horse should be allowed to stand quietly in stable for at least half an hour...attention by groom defeats object of rest period. During this time vet should observe breathing and check heartbeat as it settles. He should write down name, colour, breed, sex, age and markings needed for animal's identification and also any conditions of disease or injury observed so far.

Stage 5: Second trot and foot examination. Horse should be brought out and walked and trotted as before. It is then turned round sharply, first one way then the other and made to step back a few paces. If there is doubt about condition of feet, animal's shoes must be removed. Owner's permission should be obtained and it should be agreed his farrier replaces shoes.

Presenting facts and opinion in form of a certificate

Certificates should be as brief as possible but should clearly record any signs of 'disease, injury or physical abnormality' detected during examination. If any abnormality is omitted, the vet may later be accused of having carelessly failed to see it. Specialised techniques such as endoscopy, radiography or ultrasonography which are used should be recorded and findings reported separately. Special examinations such as rectal examination for pregnancy or breeding purposes or examination of colts for stallion duties should be recorded separately. Opinion should be formed on basis of above findings and potential use of horse. Certificate should say: 'On the balance of probabilities the conditions set out above are/are not (delete clearly as appropriate) likely to prejudice this animal's use for ...'.

Certificates are available from British Veterinary Association. Blood may be taken for storage for future testing for nonsteroidal anti-inflammatory drugs. **Vices:** are objectionable habits, but concern vet only if they might affect animal's physical condition. Vices seen or evident during examination should be recorded on certificate. **Height:** exact height of a horse or pony is not the concern of the examining vet and is included on certificate only to aid identification. **Warranty:** any warranty governing animal's height, freedom from vices, non-administration of drugs prior to examination, or existing ability or performance, should be sought in writing from seller as these matters are not the responsibility of vet.

soundness

(syn Noric) Heavy harness breed, probably with Haflinger blood. Originally concentrated around Salzburg, Austria, now also common in S Germany.

South German Cold Blood

Of Spain. **S. Andalusian** See Andalusian. **S. Jennet** Horse of Middle Ages developed from heavy Spanish horse, Barb, Arab, Persian and Turkish. Docile with showy action, including ambling gait. Extinct in pure form. Ancestor of Kladruber and others.

Spanish

(L spasmus, Gr spasmos) Violent, involuntary contraction of muscle or group of muscles giving pain. **s. of alimentary canal** See colic. **tetanic s.** See lockjaw.

spasm

Condition of hock joint or surrounding area. **bone s.** Inflamed bone (ostitis) or covering of bone (periostitis) of upper end of cannon and inside of third and central small bones of hock, associated with arthritis. **jack s.** Bone s. of large proportions. **bog s.** Enlarged joint capsule of hock. **occult s.** Typical hock lameness, without any visible X-ray or clinical changes. Cause: trauma; conformation (sickle or cow hocks); dietary deficiency or imbalance. Symptoms of hock lameness: shortened stride; excessive wear on toe. Exercise usually improves condition but may worsen severe cases. Diagnosis: on X-ray; nerve block (of posterior tibial and deep peroneal nerves). **s. test** Flex hock for minute or two, then trot. Increased lameness, especially in first few steps, indicates faulty hock. Treatment: corticosteroids, short-wave therapy and for bone s. surgical removal of part of cunean tendon, qv. Cf thoroughpin.

spavin

Division of animals or plants subordinate to a genus. **S.** of domestic horse is *Equus caballus*, qv.

species

Sample of body fluid, faeces or tissue. Usually collected for laboratory examination. See artificial vagina; blood tests; dope test; mud fever; ringworm.

specimen

speculum   (L mirror) Hollow metal tube used for internal examinations, usually of vagina and cervix.

speedy-cutting   See interfering.

sperm   Abbr spermatozoa (pl), spermatozoon (singular). See semen. **s. duct** See vas deferens.

spermatic cord   Cord containing structures carried by testis in its descent from abdominal cavity to scrotum, ie spermatic artery and veins, lymphatics, nerve, vas deferens, internal cremaster muscle and fold of peritoneum (tunica vaginalis).

spermato-/spermo-   Combining form from Gr sperma/spermatos, seed.

spermatocyte   Immature spermatozoon.

spermatozoon   (pl spermatozoa, from spermato + Gr zoon, animal; syns sperm, seed) Male cell (gamete) consisting of head, mid-piece and tail. Contains hereditary material of stallion. Mature **s.** contains half number (haploid) of chromosomes of body cell. See semen, genome.

Sphaerophorus   In former classifications, genus of anaerobic bacteria, rod-shaped but also growing long filaments. **S. necrophorus** A cause of thrush, qv.

sphincter   (L, Gr sphinkter, that which binds tight). Ring-like band of muscle fibres that constricts or closes natural opening, eg anus.

spinal   (L spinalis) Of spine. **s. column** See vertebral column. **s. cord** See cord.

Spiti   Native pony of India named after mountainous **S.** area, where it thrives on little food in low temperatures. Most often grey and about 12.2 hands.

splint   Slender bone, one either side of cannon bone. They represent second and fourth metacarpal and metatarsal bones, remnants from animal which had 3 toes on each forefoot (see evolution). Each **s.** consists of shaft, large upper end or head and small lower end or button. Shaft and head are closely bound to cannon bone by ligaments, the button sticks out and can be felt beneath skin. **S.** also colloq for condition of the bone, usually the one on inside of cannon bone of foreleg; 3 types of **s.**: (1) fractured shaft causing a callus; (2) inflamed binding ligament; (3) inflamed covering of cannon bone (periostitis). Cause: a knock as when one foreleg strikes the other; faulty nutrition, eg deficiency of calcium, vitamin A or D; faulty conformation.

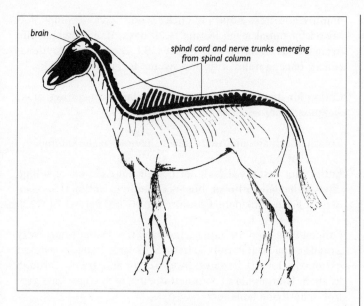

33 Spinal column

Symptoms: lameness and heat, firm swelling over area. Diagnosis: on symptoms and X-ray. Treatment: rest, surgical removal of the bone, corticosteroid injections, irradiation.

splint

See pastern.

split pastern

(spondylo- combining form, of/relationship to a vertebra from Gr spondylos, vertebra + -itis, inflammation) Inflamed vertebra/e.

spondylitis

Small area, maybe with central core, on skin or mucous membrane. See acne, ringworm. Having **s.s**: spotted. See Appaloosa, Knabstrup.

spot

Abbr species.

spp

(syn strain) Abnormal stretching of a part causing torn fibres of ligaments, tendons, muscle, joint capsule, tendon sheaths and membrane lining outer surface of bones (periostium). Results in bleeding and typical inflammatory reaction, with heat, swelling and pain. Heals with fibrous or scar tissue (see inflammation). Severity is directly related to the number of fibres torn.

sprain

(*Stomoxis calcitrans*) Common insect belonging to phylum Arthropoda. Resembles housefly but distinguishable by long, stout sucking tube (proboscis). Adult about 7mm (approx ¹/₄in) long and darker than housefly. **S.f.** usually lays eggs in horse

stable fly

stable fly	manure and bites horses to suck blood. Larva develops, followed by pupal stage lasting 6–20 days, though whole life cycle can be completed in 14 days. **S.f.** can transmit trypanasomes, encephalomyelitis and swamp fever. Cf tabanid fly.
staggers	Colloq for incoordination. See cerebellar degeneration, grass sickness, meningitis, wobbler syndrome.
stale	Colloq to urinate, micturate. See behaviour, urine sample.
stallion	Entire (not castrated) male, or colt. If not used for breeding, often called 'an entire' or 'horse'. Cf gelding. **National S. Assn**, School Farm, Pickmere, Cheshire WA16 6RD (01565 733222).
Standardbred	Official type used for harness racing, either trotter (diagonally gaited) or pacer (laterally gaited). **S.** is large, long-legged and extremely tough. It dates from 1870s and traces through English Thoroughbred foundation sire, Messenger. See gait; trot, whorlbone lameness.
stapes	(L stirrup) One of small bones of ear, qv.
staphylo-	Combining form meaning resemblance to bunch of grapes, eg staphylococcus. See bacteria.
staphylococcal dermatitis	See acne.
stasis	(Gr stasis, a standing still) Stoppage in flow of blood or other fluid.
stay apparatus	System of ligaments in all legs. Helps support horse while standing, reduces concussion in action and prevents over-extension of fetlock, pastern and coronopedal joints. **s.a. of foreleg** Top to bottom: (1) serratus ventralis muscle, from ribs to shoulder blade (scapula); (2) biceps brachii tendon, from point of shoulder to radius and tendon of extensor carpi radialis – this muscle originates on front of humerus bone and inserts on front upper part of cannon bone (metacarpal tuberosity); (3) long head of triceps muscle, from back of shoulder blade to point of elbow (olecranon); (4) superior check ligament, from back of radius and fuses with tendon of superficial digital flexor muscle, above knee joint; (5) superficial flexor tendon (muscle originates behind humerus and radius and inserts through its tendon on back of first and second phalanges); (6) inferior check ligament, from back ligament of knee joint to deep flexor tendon; (7) deep digital flexor muscle, from back of humerus and inner surface of elbow to third phalanx (pedal bone); (8) intersesamoidean ligament,

binds 2 sesamoid bones of fetlock, forming groove for flexor tendons; (9) collateral sesamoidean ligaments, bind sesamoid bones to cannon and first phalanx (pastern bone); (10) suspensory (or interosseous) ligament, from back of cannon bone and lower row of knee (carpal) bones; lies on back of cannon bone and divides into 2 branches: one attaches to sesamoid bones on either side of fetlock joint, the other runs downward and forward to front of first phalanx. Both join tendon of a common digital extensor muscle; (11) distal sesamoidean ligaments, join sesamoid bones of fetlock to first and second phalanges. **s.a. of hindleg** System similar to foreleg, except without superior check ligament: (1) tensor fascia lata, from point of hip to patella (knee cap) and outside of stifle joint; (2) gastrocnemius muscle, from femur bone to bone forming hock (tuber calcis); (3) peroneus tertius muscle, from lower end of femur to upper end of cannon bone and front of hock joint; (4) deep digital flexor, from back and upper part of tibia to pedal bone; (5) tarsal check ligament, from ligaments behind hock to tendon of deep digital flexor

stay apparatus

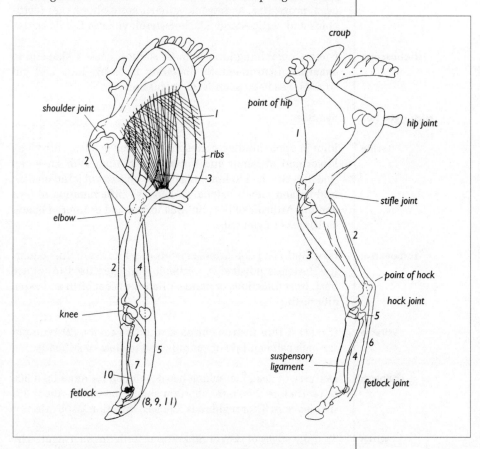

(left) **34** Stay apparatus of foreleg (for explanation of numbers, see text)
(right) **35** Stay apparatus of hindleg

stay apparatus	muscle, just below hock joint; (6) superficial digital flexor muscles, from back of femur to hock and upper end of second phalanx and lower end of first phalanx. Cf suspensory apparatus.
stenosis	(Gr) Narrowing of duct or opening, eg **aortic s.** Narrowing of opening into aorta from heart.
sterile	(L sterilis) (1) Infertile; barren. (2) Free from microorganisms. See infertility.
sterilisation	Destruction of microorganisms by heat, eg steam under pressure, at 120°C, (248°F) for 15 minutes; dry heat at 360°–380°C (680°–684°F) for 3 hours; chemical compounds.
sternum	See breast bone.
steroids	Important biological substances of body; based on system of 4 carbon rings joined in a characteristic way; include oestrogens, progestins, androgens, adrenal cortex hormones (corticoids and corticosteroids), cholesterol, vitamin D, bile acids.
stethoscope	(stetho- combining form from Gr stethos, chest + skopein, to examine) Instrument for listening to heart, lung and gut sounds. See heart sounds, cf percussion.
stick-tight flea	See flea.
stifle	Joint in upper hindleg, corresponds to human knee. Formed by lower end of femur and upper end of tibia with knee cap (patella) attached to front. Ligaments on front of joint: medial, middle and lateral patella. Cf knee. **s., inflammation of** (syn gonitis) Arthritis of the joint due to infected or injured bones, cartilages or ligaments.
stilboestrol	(syn diethyl **s.**) Colourless crystals or white crystalline odourless tasteless powder. A synthetic oestrogen used to induce heat, treat infections of uterus, dilate cervix at birth and expel afterbirth.
stilette	(Fr) (1) A thin instrument used to probe cavity. (2) Wire put through catheter (qv) or cannula (qv) to clear or stiffen it.
stillbirth	Delivery of dead foal which has developed for more than 300 days. (Before this, term abortion should be used.) About 2% incidence in Thoroughbreds. Causes: infection, asphyxia.
stitch	To unite edges of skin or other tissue with thread, catgut, wire or nylon threaded through needle. See wound, Caslick. Cf ligature, tape suture.

(L stomachus, Gr stomachos) Muscular bag inside rib cage. **stomach**
Digests food by secreting digestive (gastric) juices. Small in
horse (see alimentary canal). **s. tube** Rubber or plastic tube
used for passing fluid into stomach. Inserted up one nostril
and, after horse swallows, end pushed gently down gullet to
about chest, ie not into stomach. Varies in diameter according
to horse (about 1cm (approx ⅖in) for foals, 3cm (approx 1in) for
adults). Can be open-ended or blunt with opening on side.
Used to feed foal (see neonatal maladjustment syndrome, food
by **s.t.**) or to give liquid drugs. **s. worm** (1) *Trichostrongylus
axei*, nematode (roundworm) parasite of order Strongyloidea.
Only roundworm not host-specific; found in **s.** of horse,
donkey, pig, sheep and goat. Causes thickened, inflamed
s. and possibly unthriftiness. Treatment: see thiabendazole,
phenothiazine. (2) *Habronema muscae, H. microstoma,
H. megastoma*, small nematode (roundworm) parasites
8–20mm (approx ⅓in –¾in) long, of order Spiruroidea, found
in **s.** Eggs pass out in faeces and are eaten by fly maggot. This
enters either wounds or horse's feed and finds its way to **s.**
Larvae may cause itchy, fibrous walnut-sized nodules in skin.
Nodules ulcerate and weep (condition known as summer sores,
bursatti or habronemiasis and, in Australia, as swamp cancer).
In **s.**, adult worm lays eggs, thus completing life cycle.
Habronema megastoma found in tumours, eg in **s.** wall.

(pl stomatitides; syn aphtha) Small white blister. See also **stomatitis**
vesicular stomatitis.

(syn calculus, pl calculi) Accumulation of salts the size of a **stone**
grain to size of a melon. Can occur in kidney (renal calculus),
bladder (cystolith), ureter (ureterolith) or intestines
(enterolith). In intestines **s.** may start forming when host
increases secretions to minimise irritant effect of foreign body,
eg pebble. See colic, sand. Enteroliths occur most often in
Arabs and particularly in dry, sandy areas. All types of **s.** more
common in geldings than in mares. **S.** either rough,
yellow/brown composed of calcium carbonate, or smooth and
white, mainly phosphate. If **s.** is not dislodged by flushing/oil-
ing of urinary/gastrointestinal system, surgery or euthanasia
may be necessary.

See sprain. **strain**

(L strangulare) Infectious disease characterised by swollen **strangles**
throat. Occurs in all countries, especially in groups of horses,
eg draught, Welsh Mountain ponies. Young horses particularly
susceptible and about 2 per cent of cases die. Cause:
Streptococcus equi bacteria, specific to condition (should not
be confused with *Strep. pyogenes var equi*). Spread by eating

strangles   or inhaling infected droplets. Organism can live in an empty stable for about 6 weeks. Symptoms (after 4–8 days incubation): fever to 41°C, abscesses in lymph glands around throat which burst after about 10 days; watery nasal discharge becoming thick pus, inflamed eyes, lack of appetite, moist cough. Infection may spread to other organs (**bastard s.**) eg abscesses in lungs, brain, liver, muscles. Carrier state exists.

streptococcal   Of streptococcus. See bacteria.

Streptococcus   Gram-negative bacterium. **S. equi** Cause of strangles, qv; produces strong haemolytic toxin. In laboratory, grows as honey-like drop on blood agar, from pus or nasal discharge of infected case. **S. pyogenes var equi** (syns *S. zooepidemicus*, beta haemolytic **s.**, BHS). Ubiquitous germ which infects nasal passages, uterus, wound and any tissues damaged or made susceptible by virus infection, trauma or other cause of reduced resistance. May follow herpes infection of lungs and air passages or damage to uterus during foaling. (Does not cause epidemics as does *S. equi*, therefore syn zooepidemicus is a misnomer.)

streptococci   Gram-positive bacteria, shaped as minute beads and occurring in strings of varying length and also sometimes in pairs (diplococci).

streptomycin   Antibiotic of aminoglycoside group. Produced by bacteria *Streptomyces griseus*. Effective against gram-negative and acid-fast bacteria.

stress fracture   Minute break in bone, eg cannon, due to concussion. Less common in other bones. **S.f.**s difficult to diagnose even on careful X-ray. Causes inflamed membrane around bone (periostitis). See bucked shin.

stridor   Harsh, high-pitched respiratory sound, eg in spasm of voice box. May occur during removal of intratracheal tube at end of anaesthesia.

stringhalt   Involuntary snatching up of hindleg and flexing of hock when walking. May affect both hindlegs. Cause unknown, but probably injured nerves. Considered an unsoundness and usually worsens, but some cases occur and disappear spontaneously. Treatment: remove tendon of lateral digital extensor muscle as it crosses outside of hock joint.

striped   Lined. **s. horse** See zebra. **s. muscle** One of 3 types of muscle; that concerned with voluntary actions, eg movement of legs, head, neck and back. Muscle fibres have irregular lines. Cf smooth muscle; heart muscle; sphincter.

See redworm.

strongyle

See threadworm.

strongyloides

Stimulant from *Strychnos nux-vomica* seed. **s. poisoning** Usually fatal. Symptoms: restlessness, muscle twitching, stiffness followed by convulsions, extended legs and curved neck between periods of relaxation. Diagnosis on recovery of **s.** from stomach. Treatment: potassium permanganate by stomach tube; anaesthetic.

strychnine

(Gr styptikos) Drug or substance which stops bleeding by astringent action eg silver nitrate, qv.

styptic

Combining form meaning underneath.

sub-

Between acute and chronic.

sub-acute

Area of bone, less solid than normal, immediately below joint cartilage forming cavity which is spherical or mushroom-shaped.

subchondral bone cyst

(Abbrs sub cut/sub cu) Situated or occurring beneath skin, eg **s.** injection of drug.

subcutaneous

Below mandible, eg **s.** swelling in strangles.

submandibular

(trade name: Antepsin) Drug to protect lining of stomach and small intestines in cases of ulceration.

sucralfate

Draught horse, which takes name from English county of **S.** Always chestnut, usually docile and with featherless legs. Dates back to 1500s. **S. Horse Soc**, The Market Hill, Woodbridge, Suffolk IP12 4LU (01394 380643).

Suffolk/S. Punch

Caused by eating fresh, unwilted **s.b.** tops which contain oxalic acid. Horses particularly susceptible and suffer paralysis, restlessness, cold limbs, salivation and inability to swallow. Treatment: inject 0.2g of pilocarpine and feed artificially until swallowing power returns. See stomach tube; food by stomach tube.

sugar beet poisoning

(trade name: Negasunt) Colourless odourless crystals of white crystalline powder with slightly bitter taste. Sulphonamide drug active against streptococci and, to lesser extent, other microorganisms. Used to treat septicaemia, pneumonia and local infections. Useful as the wound powder, reducing the production of excessive granulation (proud flesh).

sulphanilamide

sulphonamide Type of anti-infection drug, eg sulphanilamide. Overdose may cause loss of appetite, weak pulse, debility, diarrhoea, jaundice, kidney dysfunction. Treatment: normal saline IV or through stomach tube.

sulphur poisoning May occur after exposure to the gas. Symptoms: diarrhoea, dullness, weak and rapid pulse, pale mucous membranes. Treatment ineffective if symptoms have developed. See also poisons.

summer sores (syn habronemiasis) See stomach worm.

suppuration (L sub, under + puris, pus) Forming and oozing of pus.

suprarenal (L supra-, above + ren, kidney) Above kidney.

suramin White powder with no smell and slightly bitter taste. Used to treat trypanosome infections.

surfactant Chemical substance (phospholipid) in lung. Reduces surface tension of air-sac lining, enabling sac to remain expanded. If absent or destroyed, air-sac deflates (atelectasis). See broken wind.

surgery (1) Colloq for centre where surgical operations are performed or patients received for diagnosis and treatment (cf veterinary hospital). (2) Operation for repair, alteration, reconstruction or removal of part or parts. Performed by surgeon under sterile conditions and local or general anaesthesia. **bowel s.** Of gut, as in twists. **cosmetic s.** Improves or alters appearance. **dental s.** Of teeth. **ophthalmic s.** Of eye/e. **orthopaedic s.** Of bones, joints. **plastic s.** Changes part by transplanting or moving skin or other tissue.

COMMON SURGERY OF HORSES:
Caslick, Hobday, Pouret, castration, hernia, ruptured bladder of foal, knee chip, joint mice, fractured sesamoid, sinus infection, stringhalt, contracted tendons, dislocated patella, aberrant growth of tooth, internal fixing of fracture (by screws, plates), growth (wart) removal, twisted gut, caesarean section. See also anaesthesia.

surra (in Algeria: mal de zousfana) Disease of horses and dogs in India and Africa, especially the Sudan. Caused by *Trypanosoma evansi*, spread by stable fly and tabanid (horse) fly. See suramin.

suspensory Of suspension, holding up. **s. apparatus** Part of the stay apparatus (qv) that supports fetlock and prevents it touching ground. Includes: (1) suspensory ligament, (2) sesamoid bones of fetlock joint, (3) intersesamoidean ligament, (4) distal sesamoidean ligament (superficial, middle and deep), (5) short sesamoidean ligament. **s. ligament** (syns interosseous tendon, superior sesamoidean ligament) Broad, elasticised band of fibrous tissue behind, and attached to, cannon bone. Runs between lower row of carpal bones (in hind limb: tarsal bones) and sesamoid bones of fetlock. A branch continues across pastern bone to join extensor tendon inserted into front of pedal bone (see stay apparatus). **s. ligament sprain** Most common at insertion into the sesamoid bones and at attachment to the cannon. Symptoms: swelling, oedema, pain and sometimes lameness. Treatment: rest, corticosteroid injections, irradiation.

suspensory

(L, a seam) (1) Type of fibrous joint especially that of skull. (2) Surgical stitch or series of stitches. See wound. Cf tape suture.

suture

(trade names: Anectine, Scoline) White crystalline odourless saline-tasting powder. Given intravenously to relax muscle and may cause respiratory paralysis. Used in anaesthesia.

suxamethonium bromide/s. chloride

Wire or stick with end covered by tuft of sterilised cotton. Used to collect material for study in laboratory. **cervical s.** That put through speculum to cervix. See uterus, infection of.

swab

Marshland; natural habitat of some breeds, eg Camargue. **s. cancer** See stomach worm. **s. fever** (syns infectious equine anaemia, river bottom disease, EIA) Contagious disease caused by virus, characterised by chronic illness alternating with acute attacks of fever, anaemia and debilitation. Occurs in USA, Canada, Europe, occasionally in British Isles. Affects only horses; most in an outbreak area will be affected, with death rate about 50 per cent. Full recovery rare and convalescent animals remain carriers, greatly increasing danger of spread. All breeds and ages susceptible. Virus destroyed by sunlight but persists several months in urine, faeces, dried blood and serum. Infection spread by biting flies, contaminated needles, etc. Virus present in body for many years prevents re-infection but is source of infection to other horses through secretions and excretions. Causes damage to walls of small blood vessels and inflammatory changes in most organs, particularly liver; also massive destruction of red blood cells. Symptoms (after 2–4 weeks' incubation): depression, weakness, incoordination, marked loss of body condition, fever rising to 41°C (106°F), jaundice, oedema of abdomen, haemorrhages in mucosa of mouth, tongue and eye, increased heart rate. After acute phase there is temporary recovery, then relapses coincide with periods of stress. Diagnosis: on identifying virus in laboratory (see

swamp

swamp	Coggins test). There may be small haemorrhages on tongue associated with clinical symptoms and increase in sedimentation rate of blood. Treatment: none available. Control: euthanase carriers, eliminate biting insects (helped by draining marshy areas), sterilise surgical instruments. Notifiable disease.
sweat	Salty fluid secreted by **s.** glands in skin on stimulation of sympathetic nerves or release of adrenaline. Evaporation of **s.** from skin causes cooling of body. Increased in exercise, hot surroundings, excitement, painful conditions, eg colic. **lack of s.** (syn anhidrosis) See drycoat.
Swedish	Strong, compact horse for agricultural work or riding. Developed from various breeds including Anglo-Norman and Hanoverian. **S. Ardennes** See Ardennes. **North S.** Cross between **S.** and Gudbrandsdal or Oldenburg. Breeding association formed about 1900.
sweeny	Colloq for wasting (atrophy) of shoulder muscles (supraspinatus and infraspinatus) due to damaged nerve supply (suprascapular nerve). See paralysis.
sweet itch	See Queensland itch.
swimming	See physiotherapy.
symbol	Written sign, usually used to save space. Those used by veterinarians include:

Ω	about
=	equals
♀	female
<5	less than 5
♂	male
>5	more than 5
±	plus or minus, eg 10±3=7–13

sympathetic nervous system	Part of autonomic nervous system, qv. Nerves which originate from spinal cord and supply blood vessels, secretory glands, hairs and smooth muscle of intestines. They stimulate increased bloodflow, glandular secretions, sweating and intestinal movement. (See parasympathetic nervous system.)
sympathomimetic	(sympathetic + Gr mimetikos, imitative) A mimicking of effects of those produced by stimulation of the sympathetic nervous system; an agent producing such effects, eg adrenaline, dopamine, noradrenaline. A **s.** produces increased rate and force of contraction of the heart, increased wakefulness, rate

and volume of respiration, increased oxygen consumption, release of glucose from liver and muscle, increase of blood concentrations of glucose and free fatty acids, increase in bloodflow to skin and mucous membranes, increased blood pressure and relaxation of smooth muscle around tubes of respiratory airways and intestinal tract. See also catecholamine; clenbuterol; dopamine; noradrenaline; adrenaline.

sympathomimetic

Reported evidence of disease. Cf sign.

symptom

(Gr symptomatikos) Of nature of a symptom.

symptomatic

(Gr synapsis, a conjunction, connection) Place of contact between 2 nerve cells, where nervous impulse is transmitted from cell to cell. See nerve cell.

synapse

(Gr concurrence) Set of symptoms which characterise a disease, eg neonatal maladjustment **s.**

syndrome

(L, Gr syn, with + oon, egg) Transparent, sticky fluid secreted by part of joint (synovial membrane). Present in, and helps lubricate, joints and synovial structures such as bursae and tendon sheaths.

synovia

Inflamed synovial membrane. See arthritis.

synovitis

(L syrinxe, Gr syrinx) Glass or plastic instrument used, with needle, to inject liquid drug or other fluid or withdraw same; colloq plunger-in-cylinder device to dose horses by mouth with, eg, worming paste.

syringe

(Gr systema, a complex or organised whole) Set of parts which function together, eg nervous system. See parasympathetic nervous **s.**

system

Relating to whole body.

systemic

(Gr a drawing together) Period of contraction of heart chambers when blood is pumped into the aorta and pulmonary artery. **extra s.** A beat which does not originate from usual point. See electrocardiogram.

systole

Occurring during contraction of heart chambers. **s. murmur** See heart sounds.

systolic

tabanid fly Large bloodsucking fly belonging to family Tabanidae of phylum Arthropoda; commonest British species: *Chrysozona pluvialis* (cloak or horse fly). Erroneously called gad fly (because it annoys animals causing them to gad about) but name is reserved for warble fly, qv. Other genera of **t.f.** found in different regions, eg *Chrysozona caecutiens* widespread in England, *C. quadrata* common in New Forest and south of England, *Tabanus montanus* common in hilly areas and *T. suditicus* (females of which may be 2.5cm (1in) long and emit a deep hum when flying) chiefly in Scotland. **T.f.** has powerful wings and large, irridescent, multicoloured eyes. It lays eggs on leaves of aquatic plants, on stones near water or on damp ground; larvae hatch, drop into water and feed on small aquatic animals; larval stage lasts 2–3 months, then larvae leave water and pupate on dry ground. Adults emerge during July and August for brief period of activity and mating. **T.f.** bites host after host, so spreads trypanosomes (qv) and viruses of VEE and swamp fever (infectious anaemia).

tachycardia (Gr tachys, swift + kardia, heart) Excessively fast heartbeat, qv.

tail (L cauda, Gr oura) End of spinal column from back of croup. Covered in short, furry hair in foal, develops into fall of hair past hocks in most adults (see American Saddle horse, Camargue, donkey). **t. rubbing** May be symptom of sweet itch or seatworms. **t. swishing** Common after defecation/urination (see behaviour), also considered sign of ill-temper (eg in race). **t. (coccygeal) vertebrae** Vary in number, averaging 18.

tape suture Stitch made of linen, used for tying umbilical cord if this bleeds profusely after birth, but not recommended as routine procedure. Sometimes used to tie the skin together after an abdominal operation.

tapeworm Internal parasite belonging to class Cestoidea with elongated, flat body without cavities or alimentary canal. The two genera of **t.** affecting horses (Anoplocephala and Paranoplocephala spp) belong to order Cyclophyllidea, family Anoplocephalidae. They are distinguished from other orders by having neither a protrudable part (rostellum) nor hook (scolex) on head. *Anoplocephala magna* – up to 80cm (31in) long and 2cm (³/₄in) wide, lives in small intestine. *A. perfoliata* – up to 8cm (3in) long and 3–4mm (¹/₆in) wide with small head infests small and large intestines. *Paranoplocephala mamillana* – 6–60mm (¹/₄–2¹/₃in) long and 4–6 mm (¹/₈–¹/₄in) wide, lives in small intestine. Each type has number of segments containing male and female reproductive organs. Eggs are self-fertilised or cross-fertilised by male gametes from other segments and stored in uterus of segment, which breaks off and passes out in faeces. An intermediate host, eg oribatid mite, feeds on eggs which develop into cysticercoids (bladderworms). These have an outer cuticle, inner germinal layer and central cavity filled with fluid, with head turned inwards. When mite with cysticercoid is swallowed by horse, cysticercoid ruptures, releasing head, so **t.** has gone full cycle. Light infestations do not produce symptoms but cause ulcers in intestine. Large numbers cause digestive disturbances, shaggy coat and anaemia and have been known to cause colic and rupture the caecum. Diagnosis: on finding **t.** eggs in faeces (by microscopic examination).

tapeworm

Breed centred on town of Tarbes in Pyrenees. Descended from local horses but after Arab and Thoroughbred influence it is virtually Anglo-Arab. Most often chestnut or brown, around 15 h.

Tarbenian

Wild horse of Poland. True type became extinct about 150 years ago; descended from horse of prehistoric times and influenced breeds including Spanish Sorraia and ponies on Greek island of Skyros. Was usually grey or dun with dorsal stripe and stripes on upper forelegs; coat colour sometimes changed to white in winter; mane had bushy hogged look; ears and nostrils large. **T.** bred from relatives of wild **T.** now thrives in Poland where it is known as Konik (qv). **American T. Assn**, 1658 Coleman Ave, Macon, GA 31201 (912 741 2062).

Tarpan

(L tarsalis) Of bones of tarsus. **t. bones** Small bones of hock joint (usually 6, occasionally 7). Arranged in 2 rows (proximal and distal). Proximal row: tibial bone, with 2 oblique ridges which articulate with tibia; fibular **t.** bone, largest bone of hock, forms tuber calcis (point of hock); central **t.** bone between tibial **t.** and third **t.** bone. Distal row: first and second **t.** bones, articulate with metatarsal bones (cannon and splints); third **t.** bone, between central **t.** and metatarsal bone (cannon); fourth **t.** bone articulates with fibular **t.** and other **t.** bones.

tarsal

(Gr tarsos, wickerwork frame) (1) Hock or spavin area. (2) Framework of eyelid.

tarsus

(L tartarum, Gr tartaron) Build-up of scaly deposit on teeth. Can be filed off during dental examination.

tartar

(L gustus) (1) Sensation transmitted to brain via taste buds, mainly in tip of tongue. Horse who continually licks human hand may **t.** salty dried sweat and be suffering from salt deficiency. (2) Colloq for action of stallion or teaser when he nudges/licks mare's vulva.

taste

Taylorella equigenitalis (after Cambridge venereologist Dr C. E. D. Taylor) Causative organism of contagious equine metritis, qv.

TB/Tb Abbr (1) Thoroughbred, qv. (2) tuberculosis, qv.

T-cell Type of lymphocyte, qv, so-named because it matures in the thymus, qv. **T-c.**s important in defence against viruses which get inside body's cells making them harder for antibodies to attack. **T-c.**s fall into 3 categories: T-killer (which recognise and attack infected cells); T-helper (which assist in phagocytosis, qv); T-suppressor (which help coordinate actions of killers and helpers with B-cells, see lymphocyte).

tear (L lacrimae, Gr dakrya) Watery, slightly saline, alkaline secretion of lacrimal glands which moistens conjunctiva. See eye.

teaser Entire horse (see vasectomy) used to find out if mare will accept stallion. **T.** encouraged to nibble mare across trying (teasing) board. If she is in oestrus she will lean towards him and wink vulva, if not she will be hostile and may kick (board should prevent injury to **t.**). **T.** common in breeding of Thoroughbred, less so in other breeds.

teat Nipple of mammary gland. See mammary glands.

teeth (pl of tooth) Structures in upper and lower jaws for grasping and chewing food. Normally 40 in adults – 12 front (incisor), 24 cheek (molar) and 4 tusks (canine). May also be up to 4 rudimentary wolf **t.** **T.** consist of a crown above gum, a neck embraced by gum, a root embedded in bony cavity (alveolus) of jaw. Each tooth has 5 surfaces: an upper chewing, an outer, presenting to lips or cheek, an inner presenting to tongue, plus two sides next to adjacent **t.** All except old **t.** contain a cavity open at top of root and containing pulp which nourishes hard structures of **t.** (dentine, enamel and cement). **t., growth of** Process of extending deeper and gradually outwards. Limit of jaw reached at about 7 years, when roots are formed and movement is outwards only. Rate of growth and outward movement parallels rate of surface wear. Entire tooth length lasts about 34 years, then horse would suffer malnutrition. **front (incisor) t.** 2 central **f.t.** in upper and lower jaws at birth; joined by 2 more **(lateral f.t.)** at 4 weeks; and a further 2 **(corner f.t.)** at 10 months. Centrals replaced by permanent **f.t.** at $2^1/_2$ years, laterals at $3^1/_2$ years, corners at $4^1/_2$ years. **cheek (molar) t.** (syn grinders) First 3 (temporary or milk **t.**) present at birth, on each side, upper and lower jaws. 1st and 2nd shed at $2^1/_2$ years, 3rd at $3^1/_2$ years. They are pushed up and replaced by permanent **t.** and remain for short time as caps. Second 3 **c.t.** develop without milk **t.** (premolars). 4th cheek tooth in use by 12 months,

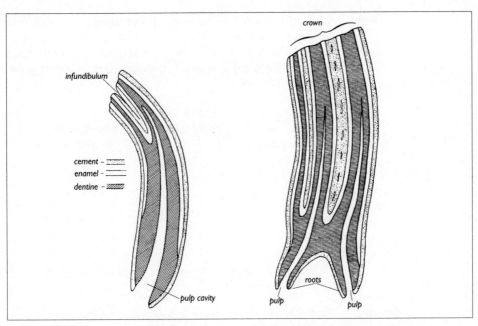

36 Section through front tooth **37** Section through back (molar) tooth

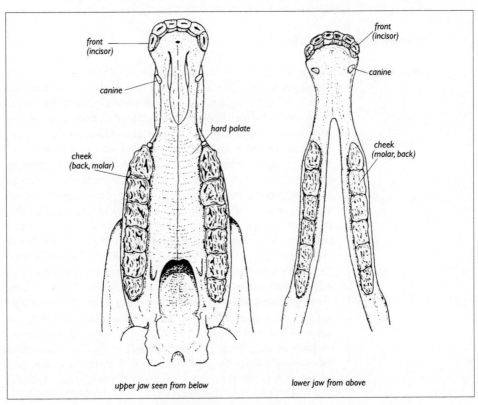

upper jaw seen from below lower jaw from above

38 Teeth in full mouth, ie 6 years or over

teeth 5th by 2 years, 6th by 4½ years. **tusk (canine)** 1 on each side of upper and lower jaw by 4 years old in male (absent in female). Horse's age can be estimated by noting which **t.** have erupted, which are in wear and amount of wear at grinding surfaces (see bishop).

TABLE OF TEETH

Approx. age through gums	Front teeth			Cheek teeth					
	1	2	3	1	2	3	4	5	6
Birth	°								
4 weeks	°	°		°	°	°			
9 months	°	°	°	°	°	°	1		
1½ years	°	°	°	°	°	°	1	1	
2½ years	1	°	°	1	1	°	1	1	
3½ years	1	1	°	1	1	1	1	1	
4½ years	1	1	1	1	1	1	1	1	1

° = a temporary, first or milk tooth 1 = a permanent or 2nd tooth

telemetry (from Gr metron, measure) Transference of signals by radio, so that they can be recorded at distance, eg horse can be fitted with a transmitter (usually strapped to back) and let loose or ridden so that electrocardiogram (qv) can be recorded at a distance.

temperament See behaviour.

temperature Measurement of heat. **t.** of healthy horse: 38°C (100.4°F), usually taken per rectum (rectal **t.**) which is slightly lower than core **t.** in conditions of diarrhoeic or dry faeces (when rectum is ballooned with air). **body or core t.** True **t.** of body, ie in centre. Measured only under experimental conditions by placing thermometer in oesophagus. **skin t.** Raised in any condition, local or general, when horse is afraid, in pain or body needs to lose heat, eg colic, first stage labour, inflammation, such as sprained tendon. Body has 4 ways of losing heat: convection (air blowing over skin), conduction (skin in contact with saddle, straw etc), evaporation (involving fluid, eg sweat on skin) and radiation. Skin is main route of heat loss, though urine, faeces and lungs (evaporation) play small part. **raised t.** (hyperthermia) Occurs in infectious disease, after exercise, in some poisoning and in painful conditions, eg colic. Extreme post-exercise **r.t.**, the result of dehydration (qv) should be reduced as quickly as possible by placing cool cloth on head, giving cool water by stomach tube (qv) or via enema (qv). Cold water should not be used on body as may cause symptoms of setfast, qv. See antipyretic. **sub-normal t.** (hypothermia) common in foals (see neonatal maladjustment syndrome), also occurs in coma, chronic wasting and some poisoning. **T.** can be raised by reducing heat loss, eg with clothing or heated stable. See weights and measures.

Inflamed tendon. See sprain; bowed tendon.

(L tendo, Gr tenon) (1) Fibrous cord which attaches muscle to bone (prominent below carpus and hock where horse has no muscles). See contracted tendons. (2) Colloq for injured deep and/or superficial flexor **t.** of forelimb. **t. splitting** Operation devised in Scandinavia to enhance healing of injured tendon, eg superficial flexor tendon. See bowed **t.**

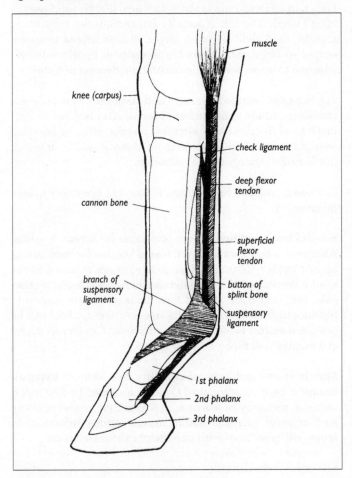

39 Tendons of foreleg

(syn Plantation Walking Horse) Good, all-purpose breed, originally developed to carry farmers of S States over plantations at comfortable running walk (see gaits). Foundation sire was Black Allan, a Standardbred trotter, foaled in 1880s and taken to Tennessee. Usually has long mane and tail and may adopt dog-like stance, ie forelegs together, hindlegs together and behind (instead of underneath) quarters. **T.W. Horse Assn**, Box 286, Lewisburg, TN 37091 (615 359 1574).

tenosynovitis/ tenovaginitis	Inflamed tendon sheath, usually after fibres of tendon have been ruptured or as result of infection.
tension	(L tensio, Gr tonos) (1) Stretching or being stretched. (2) Pressure of gas measured in millimetres of mercury. See pO_2, pCO_2.
testis	(syn testicle, pl testes) One of 2 reproductive glands of male; produces spermatozoa and male sex hormone testosterone. Each **t.** in adult stallion is about 13 x 5cm (5 x 2in) and weighs 300g (10oz). The left is usually larger than the right to 21 months, then right becomes larger. Size is related to sperm output so large testes desirable in stallion. Epididymis (qv) attached to upper border. See castration, descent of testes.
testosterone	Sex hormone secreted by testes and responsible for male sex characters, libido and descent of testes. Also isolated or synthetic **t.**, white crystalline odourless powder, given by injection or subcutaneous implant to promote libido of stallion or teaser. (trade name: Androject). Cf castration.
tests	(L testum, crucible) See Coggins **t.**, blood **t.**, laboratory **t.**, also pregnancy **t.**
tetanus	See lockjaw. **t. antitoxin** Gives protection for approx 3 weeks. Also used to treat lockjaw, qv. **t. toxoid** Vaccine for immunising against lockjaw (tetanus). Given in 2 injections at least 4 weeks apart followed by 3rd a year later and thereafter at 5-yearly intervals. Pregnant mare should have booster in 11th month to produce high level of antibodies in colostrum, qv. Foal will be protected against lockjaw for about 6 weeks. Can be vaccinated at 3 months, 1–2 ml by deep IM injection.
tetany	Muscle spasm and hyper-excitability. See lockjaw. **hypocalcaemic t.** (syn **lactational t.**) Condition caused by low blood calcium, normally in mares with foal at foot subject to stress such as travel. Characterised by muscle rigidity, reluctance to move, stiffness. Treat with parenteral calcium solution.
tetrachloromethane	See carbon tetrachloride.
tetracosactrin acetate	(trade name: Synacthen [short-acting], Synacthen depot [long-acting]) Synthetic compound with actions of ACTH (adreno-corticotrophic hormone), qv. Used in short-acting form as test for adrenocortical sufficiency in newborn foal (**t.a.** is injected and neutrophil:lymphocyte ratio examined, then measured again at 120 minutes when ratio should widen significantly in normal full-term foal. Ratio does not increase in premature foal because adrenal cortex is functioning improperly.) Long-acting (depot) preparation available to treat premature foal.

(trade name: Achromycin) Yellow crystalline odourless powder with bitter taste. Antibiotic effective against gram-negative bacteria, eg streptococci, staphylococci. Given as pessary in uterus, by IV injection or in ointments. Used to treat strangles, sinusitis, infected wounds, frog thrush, joint-ill, pneumonia. See septicaemia. **T.**s Group of antibiotics including oxytetracycline, doxycycline.
**tetracycline/
t. hydrochloride**

(pl thalami; L, Gr thalamos, inner chamber) Part of brain, qv.
thalamus

Caused by rat poisons. See rodent killer poisoning, poisons.
thallium poisoning

The science and art of healing and treatment of disease.
therapeutics

(Gr therapeia, service to the sick) Treatment of disease. See therapeutics.
therapy

(Gr therion, beast + gennan, to produce + logy, study of) Branch of veterinary medicine dealing with reproduction and infertility in male and female.
theriogenology

Way in which body achieves a balance between heat produced and heat lost. See temperature.
thermoregulation

Drug to treat intestinal parasites. See benzimidazole.
thiabendazole

See aneurine hydrochloride.
thiamine hydrochloride

Part of hindleg between hip and stifle. **second t.** See gaskin.
thigh

(trade names: Intraval sodium, Pentothal, Thiovet) Yellowish-white powder with characteristic odour and bitter taste. Has tendency to absorb moisture if exposed to air. Used in anaesthesia as knock-down dose to induce sufficient unconsciousness to insert tube into windpipe (see anaesthesia). Used alone, may cause incoordination during recovery.
thiopentone sodium

(L sitis, Gr dipsa) The craving for a drink. Increases in hot weather, when in hard work and if salt intake is high. Excessive **t.** symptom of diarrhoea (especially in foals), kidney disease involving excess of urine and diabetes insipidus. (Colic case may swill water through mouth without drinking.)
thirst

Of thorax, qv. **t. vertebra** One of vertebrae of withers region. Usually 18, sometimes 19. Articulates with rib and has well developed spinous process (upper tip) which may fracture if horse falls over backwards.
thoracic

thorax	(Gr, pl thoraces) Body between withers/shoulder and diaphragm (internal organ approx beneath last rib).
Thoroughbred	(Arabic Kehilan, pure all through; sometimes abbreviated TB) Breed most countries use for Flat and jump racing. Has been developed over more than 250 years; its athletic form is exploited and it commands far higher prices than other breeds. Every T. traces to one of 3 Oriental sires: the Byerley Turk (imported in 1860s), Darley Arabian (about 1700) and Godolphin Arabian/Barb (about 1730), but their close descendants, Herod, Eclipse and Matchem respectively, are better known. Though most T.s have lost obvious Arab characteristics (eg dished profile) breed has inherited and improved Arab speed (see wobbler syndrome). As racing puts great stress on body structures and T. is raced before it has finished growing, breed has reputation for unsoundness. T. more likely than other breeds to conceive twins. Fit T. stores more of its red blood cells in spleen than other breeds. Average height at week old: 104cm (41in), average girth: 90cm (35in) (see also growth). Adult T. usually 15.1.–16.3 h. In N hemisphere official birth-date of every T. is 1 Jan (in S hemisphere, 1 Aug). Arbitrary date outside Flat-racing season was chosen for easy administration but imposes unnatural breeding season, generally accepted as 15 February to 15 July (see fertility rate). **T. Breeders' Assn**, Stanstead House, The Avenue, Newmarket, Suffolk, CB8 9AA. (01638) 661321. **T. Owners and Breeders' Assn**, PO Box 4367, Lexington, KY 40544 (606) 276–2291. Most countries which race the T. have breeders' assn – contact local turf club or jockey club for referral.
thoroughpin	Inflamed tendon sheath which encloses deep digital flexor tendon as it passes behind hock. Soft swelling appears approx level with point of hock and extends from one side to the other beneath the tendons (gastrocnemius and superficial flexor) that cross over point of hock. Treat by draining fluid through needle and injecting corticosteroids or hyaluronic acid. Often recurs, but seldom causes lameness. Cf spavin.
threadworm	*Strongyloides westeri* Very small fine worm found in intestines of foals world-wide. T. has complicated life cycle: mare passes worm larvae in milk to foal when it is a few days old, larvae develop rapidly and adults lay eggs which pass out in faeces by age 10 days. Eggs develop within 24 hours to infective third-stage larvae which re-infect foal or other foals. May cause diarrhoea or more severe symptoms although most infected foals are symptom-free. Infection may be treated with ivermectin, qv, thiabendazole, qv, fenbendazole, qv.
thrill	Tremor or vibration felt on body above (usually abnormal)

condition, eg friction of air in mucus-filled air passage or turbulence in bloodflow due to badly damaged heart valve. *thrill*

(syn pharynx) Area at back of tongue. Contains soft palate, glottis, epiglottis, openings to larynx (voice box), eustachian tubes and nasal cavities. See wind. **throat**

Of a blood clot. **thrombotic**

(Gr, pl thrombi) Blood clot in artery or vein. Acts as plug, restricting bloodflow. Usually due to rough vessel lining, caused by bacterial infection, trauma or migrating redworm larvae. Most common sites: mesenteric artery where it leaves aorta to the gut; aorta where it divides into iliac arteries which pass to hindlegs. See iliac thrombosis. **thrombus**

(syn canker) Degenerative condition in which microorganisms infect frog, causing black, evil-smelling erosion. In severe cases erosion may reach sensitive laminae below. Caused by standing in soiled bedding and lack of attention to foot. Symptoms include lameness and contracted heels. Treatment: ensure bedding is kept clean, cut away rotting frog and apply chloramphenicol and gentian violet or dilute formalin solution. **thrush**

Gland in chest. Source of blood lymphocytes. Particularly large and active in foal and concerned with immunity. **thymus**

Ductless (endocrine) gland either side of voice box (larynx). Made up of vesicles (small balloon-like sacs) filled with colloid (sticky protein material which in **t.** gland contains the iodine-containing protein thyroglobulin, part of which is thyroxine, qv). Lack of thyroxine causes hypothyrodism (goitre and cretinism) and is common in yearlings eating food with antithyroxine effect, eg kale. **T.** gland over-reacts, becomes fibrous, and vesicles fill with colloid which is difficult to convert into thyroglobulin. Gland swells and can be felt by placing thumb and forefinger either side of larynx. See iodine. **t. extract** Cream-coloured powder with faint meat-like odour and taste, obtained from **t.** gland. Given by mouth, but slow to take effect. Maximum activity from a single dose may take 10 days to develop and the effects persist more than 14 days, therefore danger of overdosage by accumulation. Used to promote libido. Dose 1–2mg/kg bodywt. **t. stimulating hormone** (syns TSH, thyrotrophic hormone) Produced by front (anterior) lobe of pituitary gland. Acts on **t.** gland, causing it to produce colloid. **thyroid**

Hormone produced by thyroid gland. Circulates in blood and when at certain level pituitary gland reduces its production of thyrotrophic hormone. Has many important effects: raises basal **thyroxine**

thyroxine	metabolic rate (BMR), helps liver to change glycogen into glucose; promotes absorption of glucose from gut, accelerates heart rate and calcium removal from bones.
thumps	'Hiccups' associated with spasm of diaphragm, sometimes seen after strenuous exercise.
Tibetan	Pony descended from Mongolian and Chinese breeds, often dun.
tibia	(L pipe/flute) Long bone between stifle joint (above) and hock joint (below). Forms second thigh (gaskin).
ticarcillin	(trade name: Timentin) Antibiotic with a broad spectrum of activity. Used as injection with clavulate (which extends its spectrum of activity) against gram-positive and gram-negative bacteria.
tick	Arthropod insect belonging to class Arachnida, order Acarina. Important in human and veterinary medicine because many types are parasitic and transmit disease. They live on skin and suck blood and, in large numbers, cause anaemia and loss of condition. Infestation in ears can affect balance and cause symptoms similar to wobbler syndrome qv. Can transmit infectious diseases including spirochaetosis (*Spirochaeta theileri*), biliary fever (*Babesia equi* and *B. cabelli*), the virus of equine encephalomyelitis (Western and Venezuelan types), swamp fever. Those affecting horses belong to family Ixodidae, the hard **t**. Male has chitinous shield over back; female's shield covers only small portion. Female lays small, rough, dark brown eggs in one batch under stone or in sheltered spot, then dies. Larvae hatch and crawl on to grass or shrubs from which they fasten on to host. After feeding, larva moults and becomes

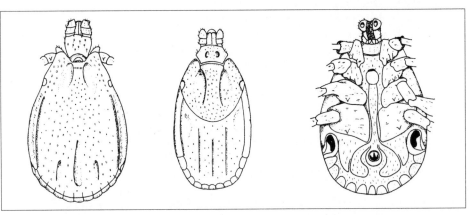

40 Male *(left)* and female tick – *Rhipicephalus appendiculatus* – from above

41 Male tick *(right)* (genus Damacentor)

nymph; nymph becomes an imago; male and female copulate and, after feeding, female drops off host to lay eggs; males may stay on host for many months. **T.** classed as 1-, 2-, or 3-host depending on number of hosts it needs during life cycle. It is sensitive to change in temperature or moisture; some survive only in warm regions, others most active in cold, dry climates and not usually host-specific.

    tick

Important members of family:

Ixodes	*I. dammini*: deer tick in/around Connecticut, transmits Lyme disease
	I. ricinus: castor bean tick
	I. canisuya: British dog tick
Boophilus	*B. annulatus*: North American tick
	B. decoloratus: Blue tick in South Africa, transmits spirochaetosis of horses
Margaropus	*M. winthemi*: Argentine tick, also in South Africa
Hyalomma	*H. aegyptium*: bont-leg tick, in Africa, Asia and S Europe
Rhipicephalus	*R. appendiculatus*: brown tick, in South Africa
	R. evertsi: red tick, common in South Africa transmits, equine piroplasmosis
	R. Bunsa: common in South Africa
Dermacentor	*D. reticulatus*: in Asia and S Europe, transmits biliary fever
	D. andersoni: transmits encephalomyelitis and Rocky Mountain spotted fever

Treatment: dislodge **t.** from horse with t. remover (Canac Pet Products 01373 864775) or by applying heat (eg hot match head) to insect's back. This will cause it to disengage mouth parts and drop off. (If it is picked off, mouth parts may be left in skin, to set up infection.) See dicophane; gamma benzene hexachloride.

Abbr L ter in die, 3 times per day. Used on prescriptions.

    t.i.d.

Hard-working harness or saddle pony of New Zealand and Australia. All colours, including mixtures similar to Appaloosa, qv.

    Timor

(L tingere, to wet, to moisten) Solution of drug in alcohol, eg **t.** of chloroform and morphine (syn chlorodyne), used to treat colic, especially of newborn foal.

    tincture

(1) Pointed body part, eg **t.** of tongue. Cf point. (2) Small metal plate used to shoe foal with slightly contracted tendons or deformed, upright feet. Cf plate, shoe.

    tip

tipped vulva   Poor conformation in which vulval lips form concave line beneath anus. See Caslick, Pouret.

tissue   (Fr tissu) Collection of specialised cells, eg fat (adipose) **t.t. culture** Cells from kidney or other organs grown in laboratory specially for cultivation of virus. **t. fluid** Water, salts and dissolved gases which pass through capillary walls to bathe body cells. See dehydration; oedema.

titre   Measurement of antibodies (developed against a particular organism) in blood serum. See virus.

tocopheryl acetate   (trade names: Tocovite, Vitenium) Pale yellow odourless liquid. (Alpha-tocopheral is one form of vitamin E.) Essential to cell metabolism. Found in green foods and germ of cereals. Appears to be interrelated with selenium, qv.

toe   Colloq end of limb, ie front of hoof. See base-wide, evolution, tip.

tongue   (L lingua, Fr glossa) Muscular, moveable pad of flesh on floor of mouth. Used extensively when grazing, to help teeth gather food. May be injured by rough edges on teeth or by bit of bridle (which should be on, not underneath **t.**). **t., swallowing** Colloq for abnormal gurgling noise made at fast paces. Some claim strapping down of **t.** stops gurgling and eases breathing, which is doubtful. Cf wind.

tonic   (Gr tonikos) Colloq for medicine believed to restore health and vigour, eg beer, stout or manufactured. **t.** mixed in feed may put on weight and improve coat condition.

topical   (Gr topikos) Associated with a surface as in use of ointment or powder.

tourniquet   Rope, rubber band, or other device to compress blood vessels, control bleeding, eg after injury, during surgery. Must be placed at a point between heart and site of bleeding. Should not be applied longer than 30 minutes unless circumstances exceptional. Cf Esmarch bandage; twitch.

toxaemia   (toxin + Gr haima, blood + -ia) Spread of toxin from focus of infection via bloodstream.

toxin   (Gr toxidon, arrow [poison] from toxikos, bow) Poison or substance produced by bacteria, eg *Clostridium tetani*, cause of lockjaw, qv. See poisons.

toxoid   See tetanus toxoid.

See windpipe.	**trachea**
(tracheo- + Gr tome, a cutting) Opening into windpipe so that tube can be inserted. See tube.	**tracheostomy**
(L tractus) Passageway, eg urinary t., alimentary t. or canal.	**tract**
Suspending agent for medicines and a base for drugs in tablets and pills. See gum.	**tragacanth mucilage**
Breed developed in Trakehnen, E Prussia by King Frederick II 250 years ago. Royal stud became part of Russia in World War II, other farms were taken over by Poland. T. adapted from cavalry, to work horse to today's eventer. See Masuren. **American T. Assn**, 1520 W. Church St, Newark, OH 43055 (614 344 1111). **T. Breeders' Fraternity**, Highwell Stud, Houghton Bank, Co. Durham DL2 2UQ (01325 775148). **Canadian T. Soc**, Box 1270, New Hamburg, Ontario NOB 2GO (519 662 3209).	**Trakehner**
(L tranqillus, calm) Drug which allays fear and anxiety. Given to horses to make them more tranquil and therefore easier to handle.	**tranquilliser**
See immunity, passive.	**transfer**
To give blood or blood product eg plasma into vein. See haemolytic jaundice.	**transfuse**
To take organ or part and use it in another horse (only in experiments) or in another part of donor, eg part of extensor tendon can be used to strengthen bowed tendon of foreleg. Cf skin graft.	**transplant**
(trans- + L sudare, to sweat) Fluid which passes through membrane as result of inflammation.	**transudate**
Wound, injury or severe shock (adjective: traumatic). **birth t.** Injury to foal, usually chest, as it emerges through mare's pelvis. See birth.	**trauma**
Mechanically controlled moving surface designed to take weight of a horse. Horse walks, trots, etc. depending on speed of t. Used in study of exercise physiology (qv). T. enables investigation of horse in action within confined space or laboratory. May also be used to train a horse and study its action with cinematography.	**treadmill**
(L trephina) Instrument for boring hole in sinus. See sinusitis.	**trephine**

triamcinolone	(trade name: Kenalog) White odourless powder; synthetic cortisone with actions and uses similar to cortisone acetate, qv.
Trichophyton	See ringworm.
tricuspid valve	(syn right atrioventricular valve) Set of valves with 3 cusps guarding opening between first and second chambers on right side of heart. Cusps are attached to fibrous ring which forms atrioventricular (AV) opening. Free edges of cusps contain fibrous cords (chordae tendineae), the other ends of which are attached to wall of second chamber. Valve prevents blood regurgitating from second chamber to first. Valve may be infected with bacteria or redworm larvae, causing incompetence and back flow of blood during heart contraction (leaking valve). See endocarditis; mitral valve; heart.
trimethoprim	(trade names: Duphatrim, Equitrim, Tribrissen, Trivectrin, Uniprim) Drug used with sulphadiazine or sulfadoxine to treat bacterial diarrhoea in foals and infections of adult horses.
trocar	(Fr trois quarts) Pointed instrument used with cannula (hollow tube) which fits around stilette.
trochanter	(Gr) Bony projection, eg parts of femur: major, minor and third **t.** Adjective: trochanteric.
trochanteric bursitis	See whorlbone lameness.
trot	See gait. **US Trotting Assn**, 750 Michigan Ave. Columbus, OH 43215 (614 224 2291).
Trypanosoma	(Gr trypanon, borer + soma, body) Genus of protozoan parasite in blood of man and animals, including horse. Most live part of lifecycle in insects, eg tabanid fly. **T. equinum** See mal de caderas. **T. equiperdum** See dourine. **T. evansi** See surra.
trypanosome	Organism of genus Trypanosoma. See dourine.
trypsin	(Gr tryein, to rub + pepsin) Enzyme secreted by pancreas.
TSH	Abbr thyroid stimulating hormone, qv.
tube	(L tubus) (1) Round, hollow pipe, eg air **t.** (any air passage). (2) Pipe of rubber or similar, used in treatment, eg stomach **t.** (qv). Cf speculum. **intratracheal (or endotracheal) t.** One into windpipe (trachea). (3) Colloq. to operate on windpipe, inserting small **t.** (tracheotomy). Seen from outside as 3cm (approx 1in) hole in neck beneath throat, covered with metal mesh to prevent objects being drawn in with air. Performed to counteract

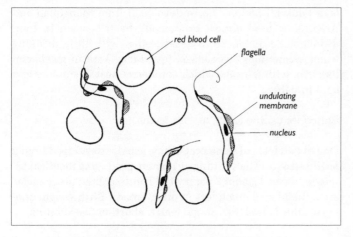

42 Trypanosoma evansi in blood. See surra

obstructed wind, ie when horse cannot get sufficient air into lungs at fast paces, via nostrils and throat (pharynx). Horse will drown if tubed part of neck is submerged.

tube

Pointed part, eg **t. coxae**. See pelvis.

tuber

Liquid containing extracts from Mycobacterium spp (from birds or mammals). **t. test** The liquid is injected into skin (intradermal injection) to test reaction 48 hours afterwards. See tuberculosis.

tuberculin

(Tb) Disease rare in horses due to limited exposure to infection and apparent resistance; caused by *Mycobacterium tuberculosis* or *M. bovis*. *M. avium* may result in fusion of neck vertebrae, causing stiff neck and inability to get head down to graze. Pneumonia may develop, destroying air spaces and increasing breathing rate, with wasting and fluctuating temperature. *M. avium* causes miliary (widespread minute) abscesses of gut associated with wasting, inappetence and death. Treat with isoniazid, qv. **t. pneumonia** See pneumonia.

tuberculosis

(trade name: Jexin) Substance derived from the plant alkaloid curare, used in anaesthesia to produce relaxation (paralysis) of muscles.

tubocurarine chloride

See growth.

tumour

Fast, light breed virtually extinct in original form even in Turkey, but known in England around 1700 when several were imported. White and Yellow **T.** both raced in England. According to some authorities, Byerley **T.** was an Arab. See Thoroughbred.

Turk

Turkoman	(syn Pouseki) Slender horse developed from Mongolian and Arab. Now bred almost exclusively by tribesmen in Iran. Ridden long distances in desert, often with little drinking water. Sometimes ewe-necked (qv). Many kept in racehorse-like trim with felt rugs which counteract heat in summer and cold in winter.
tush/tusk	Colloq for canine tooth, qv. See teeth.
twin	One of two foals of same pregnancy, usually developed from 2 fertilised ova. (The splitting of 1 ovum, producing identical **t.**s, rare in horses.) About 7 per cent of Thoroughbred pregnancies are **t.**; incidence much less in other breeds. Birth weight one- to two-thirds less than single foal. **t. abortion** See abortion.
twist	(syn volvulus) Colloq for torsion of part of alimentary tract, usually small intestine. May be complete, with tube tied in knot, or partial, involving membrane (mesentery) suspending gut. Results in strangulated blood supply and acute gut damage. Symptoms: as colic (qv) and unless treated surgically, death. At surgery **t.** can be counter-rotated and necrosis (qv) resected (cut away). Cause unknown but may follow damage by redworm larvae.
twitch	(1) Reflex action, particularly flashing of third eyelid (nictitating membrane) and muscle tremor, both symptoms of lockjaw (tetanus). (2) Length of cord or similar, looped at top of rod, usually about 30cm (12in) long. Used to restrain horse by gathering flesh, usually upper lip, into loop and twisting rod until skin is pinched. It has been suggested this causes release of endorphins (qv). May increase blood pressure so should be used with caution on pregnant or recently foaled mare.
tying-up	Mild form of setfast, qv. May also be result of pulled muscle (myositis), ie tearing of fibres causing inflammation and pain. Diagnosis: signs, blood tests for raised enzymes (AST and CK). Treatment: Anti-inflammatories such as phenylbutazone, salicylates, faradism (see physiotherapy) .
tympany	(Gr tympanias) (1) Colloq for cavity or sac distended with gas or air (tympanites), eg abdomen, guttural pouch. (2) A bell-like sound. Cf percussion. Adjective: tympanitic. See colic.
Tyzzer's disease	Bacterial infection caused by *Bacillus piliformis* resulting in fatal liver disease in foals 9 days to 6 weeks old. Some foals die unexpectedly, others develop jaundice, depression, neurological signs before death.

U

See mammary glands.

(L ulcus) Eroded, inflamed area on mucous membrane especially mouth, small intestine, stomach (gastric **u.**). Latter found increasingly in foals and racehorses. Symptoms in foals include salivation, teeth grinding, weightloss, colic. In adults associated with weightloss, poor appetite. Diagnose by signs and gastroscopy, qv. Treat with ranitidine, cimetidine. See also coital exanthema.

Enteritis (qv) caused by ulcers in lining of alimentary tract due to redworm larvae. Cf aneurysm. **u. lymphangitis**. Rare, occasionally fatal contagious disease characterised by swollen lower legs; caused by *Corynebacterium pseudo-tuberculosis*. Infection enters leg wounds and spreads to lymphatic vessels where abscesses develop. Symptoms: swelling and pain around pastern with nodules beneath skin. These rupture, discharging creamy-green pus and leaving ulcers with ragged edges. They heal in 1–2 weeks but fresh crops occur. (Should not be confused with glanders.) Diagnosis: on laboratory examination of pus. Treatment: antibiotics, especially penicillin. Control: good stable hygiene. See also lymphangitis.

Smaller of 2 bones of forearm, upper part of which forms point of elbow (olecranon). Cf radius.

Means of diagnosing conditions of deep structures of body by recording reflections of echoes produced by pulses of ultrasound waves. See echography, physiotherapy.

Radiant energy with a frequency greater than 20,000 cycles per second (abbr Hz). Sound frequency is between 8,000 and 20,000 Hz.

(L umbilicalis) Of the umbilicus. **u. abscess** Focus of pus at navel (umbilicus), usually in remnant of vein which in foetal life carried blood from placenta to liver. May become infected when **u.** cord breaks after birth. Swelling is much harder than a hernia (qv) or may not show externally. Can harbour germ causing lockjaw, qv, joint-ill, qv.

(syn navel) Point of attachment in foetus. At birth cord breaks about 3cm (1¹/₄in) from abdominal wall, forming stump which shrivels. Abdominal opening (umbilical ring), through which urachus and blood vessels passed in foetal life, closes during

umbilicus	first week. Failure to close allows abdominal contents to push through ring of opening. See hernia.
uni-	Prefix meaning one eg unilateral, one-sided.
urachus	(Gr ourachos) Tube connecting foetal bladder with allantois (placenta). Cf pervious **u.**
uraemia	Abnormal increase in urea content of blood (above 8 mmol/litre). Occurs in kidney disease or after kidney damage by toxins or bacteria, eg sleepy foal disease. See septicaemia.
urea	Nitrogenous waste formed by breakdown of excess amino acids by liver. Excreted in urine.
ureter	One of two tubes which drain urine from kidneys to bladder. See kidney.
ureterolith	See stone.
urethra, male	Long tube from urinary bladder to glans penis. Passes backward on floor of pelvis, turns round brim of pelvis and comes forward as part of penis. Therefore divided into pelvic and extra-pelvic parts. See stone. **u., female** Duct which conveys urine from bladder to outside. About 7cm ($3^3/_4$in) long and 2.5cm (1in) wide, though capable of dilation.
urethritis	Inflamed urethra.
urinary	Of urine.
urinate	(syns micturate, stale) To void urinary bladder. See behaviour, cystitis.
urine	Fluid of water and soluble substances formed by kidneys and excreted after collecting in bladder. Adult horse may pass 2–10 litres (0.4–2.2gal) per day, depending on water intake, amount of sweating and fluid content of faeces. Colour depends on substances known as urochromes. High volume of **u.** dilutes them, so that fluid is pale; conversely, dark **u.** is due to concentration. Equine **u.** normally pale to brown, but red or black in setfast and red after phenothiazine intake. Cloudy **u.** is due to calcium carbonate crystals. Odour comes from volatile acids and breakdown of urea, producing ammonia. Specific gravity depends on volume, average 1.050. U. is usually alkaline (pH 7–9) but changes if left to stand and varies with diet (high-concentrate rations may cause slightly acidic **u.**). It normally has high mucin content. Abnormal substances in **u.** include: protein, sugar, red and white blood cells, haemoglobin, myoglobin,

bilirubin. **u. sample** Small amount of **u.** collected: (1) to aid diagnosis of conditions such as cystitis; (2) to discover any drug content. Horse may not urinate for an hour or more after exercise, but can be encouraged to do so if attendant whistles or shakes up straw bedding; **u.s.** must be collected in sterile container if analysis is to be accurate. See cystitis; dope test; phenylbutazone.   *urine*

(uro- , combining form, of urine + Gr chroma, colour) Pigment in urine, qv.   **urochrome**

(uro- + Gr lithos, stone) Urinary calculus. See stone.   **urolith**

Allergic skin reaction characterised by small lumps, plaques or rings of raised skin (oedema). See nettle rash.   **urticaria**

(L uterinus) Of the uterus. **u. inertia** See uterus.   **uterine**

Muscular, Y-shaped organ in female. Horns of **u.** are about 25cm (10in) long; body 20cm (8in) long. Horns are connected to fallopian tubes and body is separated from vagina by neck (cervix). Body and horns are suspended from abdominal wall by membrane, the broad ligament of **u.** See Fig 17 (p153). Uterine wall has 3 layers: outer serous coat of peritoneum, middle, muscular coat and the inner mucous membrane (endometrium) containing glands. **u., inertia of** Weak uterine contractions during 2nd stage labour, causing delay in delivery. Cause: not established, possibly an imbalance of hormones, ie oxytocin, oestrogen and progesterone. Treatment: oxytocin and/or oestrogen. See birth. **u., infection of** Colloq any nonspecific infection. Commonly caused by streptococci, *E. coli, Pseudomonas aeruginosa* and klebsiella. Symptoms: thick discharge from cervix. May result in permanent infertility if not cleared. Diagnosis: on laboratory examination of discharge and, possibly, uterine biopsy (see biopsy). Cervical or uterine swab should be taken from mare before covering, to ensure she is free of infection. See metritis, endometritis. **u., involution of** Return of **u.** to non-pregnant size after foaling. See afterbirth, retention of; birth. **u., prolapse of** Protrusion of **u.** through vagina. Inner lining is exposed as organ hangs between vulval lips. Occurs in mares of all ages after foaling or, more rarely, abortion. Cause: unknown, but presumably result of slack ligaments retaining **u.** Treatment: mare should be kept standing and organ supported in clean sheet wetted with saline solution (teaspoonful of salt per pint of water). Replace **u.** by massaging at edge and squeezing gently towards vulva; when partially returned, complete process by working arm and clenched fist into vagina. Replacement helped by injecting muscle relaxant to abolish straining, and oxytocin to   **uterus** *urine* contract **u.** Tape sutures (qv) can be inserted across lips of vulva. Give anti-tetanus serum. If **u.** is not badly damaged and is replaced within about an hour, mare will breed normally after recovery. Complications include rupture of **u.** and pro-lapse of intestines, haemorrhage from uterine artery, infection of **u.** and laminitis. **u., rupture of** Tear in **u.** wall. May occur during 2nd stage labour or as result of prolapse. Signs include mare's reluctance to proceed with 2nd stage. Treatment: surgi-cal repair under general anaesthesia. Difficult to diagnose and mare often dies from peritonitis.

uveitis Inflammation of uveal tract, part of eye, qv. **anterior u.** Inflammation of structures in front part of eye, can be caused by trauma or infection. If recurrent may result in blindness.

To inject vaccine to stimulate immunity. **vaccinate**

(L vaccinus) Solution containing live, altered (attenuated) or killed microorganisms (bacteria, virus) or part of microorganism which stimulates immunity to a particular microbe when injected or administered by mouth. Solution may or may not have carrying agent known as adjuvant. Dead **v.**s used on horses include: *Brucella abortus,* influenza (contains several strains) and tetanus, prepared from *Clostridium tetani* (inactivated). Live **v.**s include: African horse sickness (several strains), encephalomyelitis (Western, Eastern and Venezuelan types) and equine herpesvirus 1. **vaccine**

(pl vaginae) Passage from neck of uterus (cervix) to vulva and about 20cm (8in) long. Walls normally touch but at mating, or if speculum is inserted, air can be sucked in to distend organ into large cavity. See Fig 17 (p153). Cf artificial **v.** **vagina**

Of the vagina. **v. bruising** May occur during birth, causing type of blood blister (haematoma) which can be seen just inside the vulval lips. This swelling may burst, releasing blood. Cf birth haemorrhage. **vaginal**

Inflamed vagina. May be caused by infection introduced at coitus, foaling or when mare takes air into vagina due to poor conformation. See Caslick, Pouret. Cf metritis. **vaginitis**

See nerves, table of. **vagus**

(from L valvae, folding doors) Fold of membrane which regulates flow of a body fluid, eg heart **v.** See heart. **valve**

Inflamed heart lining especially tricuspid, mitral, or pulmonary and aortic semilunar valves. Caused by infection with bacteria, eg *Streptococcus equi* or *Strep. pyogenes var equi*, resulting from damage by redworm larvae. May accompany inflamed heart lining (endocardium). Thickenings and cauliflower-like growths appear on edges of valves, causing incompetence (failure to close properly, allowing backflow of blood and reduced pumping capacity of heart). Symptoms depend on heart's ability to contract more strongly to overcome defect; if it compensates there are no symptoms, if not there is decreased stamina, distress after exercise, filling of legs and/or sheath. Diagnosis: on signs, anaemia, increased white blood cell count (see blood tests) and hearing a heart murmur, qv. **valvular endocarditis**

vascular	Full of vessels or related to blood vessels.
vas	(pl vasa) Tube or vessel. **v. deferens** (pl **v.** deferentia; syn ductus deferens, sperm duct) Duct which carries spermatozoa from each testis to urethra. It is 15–20 cm (6–8 in) long and together ducts form ejaculatory duct of penis. See Fig 8 (p106).
vasectomy	(vas + Gr ektome, excision) Severence of vas deferentia. See teaser.
vasoconstriction	Reduced calibre of blood vessels, lessens bloodflow; caused by action of sympathetic nervous system or substance, eg adrenaline, which mimics nervous stimulation. May be local, as in skin during cold weather to reduce heat-loss, or general, as in reaction to exercise or excitement, resulting in raised blood pressure. Drug or substance that causes **v.** is known as vasoconstrictor.
vasodilation	Dilated blood vessels, causing increased bloodflow to part. See inflammation.
vasopressin	(syn pitressin) Hormone secreted by back lobe of pituitary. Name is misnomer because it has little effect on the vascular system. Decreases the amount of water excreted by the kidneys, cf diuretic.
vector	(L one who carries, from vehere, to carry) Carrier, usually an arthropod, which transfers infective agents from one host to another, eg tick carries organisms causing biliary fever.
vecuronium bromide	(trade name: Norcuron) Substance used to relax muscle during anaesthesia.
VEE	Abbr. Venezuelan equine encephalomyelitis. See encephalomyelitis.
vein	(L vena) Part of blood circulatory system. Carries de-oxygenated blood (except pulmonary **v.**s) from capillaries of organs and muscles to heart. **V.**s are thin-walled, non-muscular, relatively large-calibre tubes containing valves which help prevent backflow. In general, arranged like arteries (see arteries, table of). Largest **v.** is vena cava. **jugular v.**s One on either side of neck in jugular furrow, convey blood from head to anterior vena cava. **anterior vena cava** (syns AVC, superior vena cava, SVC) Returns blood from head, neck, forelegs and chest to heart. **posterior vena cava** (syns PVC, inferior vena cava, IVC) Returns blood from abdomen, pelvis, hindlegs and hindquarters to right, 1st chamber of heart. Lies close to aorta in roof of abdomen and passes through diaphragm. **portal v.** Collects

blood from gut, pancreas and spleen, returning it to liver where it is distributed among cells and then carried by **hepatic v.** to posterior vena cava. **pulmonary v.**s 7 or 8 **v.**s which return blood from lungs to left side of heart. **cardiac v.**s Collect blood from heart muscle and open into coronary sinus (a **v.**) which discharges into right atrium (first chamber) of heart.

vein

See vein.

vena cava

(L venereus) Any infection passed on via coitus, eg klebsiella.

venereal

See encephalomyelitis.

Venezuelan equine encephalomyelitis

(L venosus) Of a vein, eg **v.** blood.

venous

(L ventralis) Position which is below, ie towards belly or under-surface.

ventral

Small cavity, eg one of lower heart chambers. See heart. **v. stripping** Removal of membrane lining pocket behind vocal cord, so that vocal cord sticks to wall, preventing whistling, roaring etc. See Hobday, wind.

ventricle

A tiny blood vessel that joins capillary bed with vein.

venula/venule

(L vermis, worm + ous) Related to worms. **v. arteritis** Inflammation of artery due to migrating worm larvae. See redworm.

verminous

One of 51–57 bones of spinal column. See cord; skeleton.

vertebra

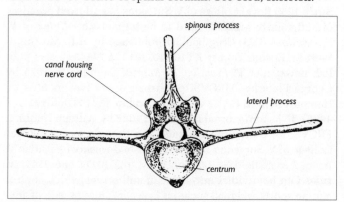

43 A back (lumbar) vertebra

(syn spinal column) Bones articulating in a line from head to tail and which house spinal cord. Numbers: 7 neck (cervical) vertebrae, 18 withers region (thoracic), 6 back (lumbar), 5 croup (sacral), 15–21 tail (coccygeal). See cord; Fig 33 (p303).

vertebral column

vesicant | A blistering agent. See blister.

vesicle | (L vesicula, dim of vesica, any sac or bladder for a secretion) Bladder or sac containing liquid, eg seminal **v.**, qv.

vesicular | Of vesicle/s. **v. exanthema** See coital exanthema. **v. stomatitis** Infectious disease caused by virus and characterised by blisters on mouth and feet. Indiana and New Jersey strains of virus have been isolated from horses, donkeys, cattle and pigs. Saliva and blister fluid are highly infective and biting flies probably spread disease which has occurred in USA and Mexico. Blisters appear on tongue, lips and lining of mouth; there is mild fever, salivation and loss of appetite. Similar to foot and mouth disease, which does not occur in horses. Recovery is spontaneous and no treatment required.

vessel | Channel for carrying fluid, eg blood or lymph.

vestibule | Anatomical term for space at entrance to an opening, eg part of vagina just inside vulva.

Vestland | See Fjord.

veterinary | (L veterinarius) Of animals and their diseases. **v. clinics:** *Equine Practice Book* published four times per year by W.B. Saunders Co, W. Washington Square, Philadelphia, PA 19105. *V. Data Sheet Compendium* Drug list published by National Office of Animal Health (0181 367 3131). **v. ethology** See ethology. **European Assn of V. Diagnostic Imaging** c/o Richard Ewers, Mostyn St, Leicester LE3 6DT. **v. hospital** Treatment centre. Since 1965 Royal College of **V.** Surgeons has allowed premises of sufficiently high standard to be termed **v.h.** *Index of V. Specialities* (IVS) Drug booklet published by A.E. Morgan, 9 West St, Epsom, Surrey KT18 7RL (01372 741411); also publish newspaper *V. Practice. V. Journal* Founded in 1875 by George Fleming, MRCVS, published every two months by Harcourt Brace & Co, 24 Oval Rd, London NW1 7DX (0171 267 4466). *V. Record* Journal founded in 1888 by William Hunting, FRCVS, an Edinburgh graduate and President of the Royal College of **V.** Surgeons 1894–5. Published weekly by British **V.** Assn, 7 Mansfield St, London W1M 0AT (0171 636 6541). **v. rules** Can be divided into those of authorities which control equine sports, of breed societies (see particular breed), of government bodies and (recommendations) of **v.** bodies. See also soundness. Sports bodies include: **The Jockey Club** (controls racing in Britain and publishes **v.r.** annually in March), 42 Portman Square, London W1H 0EN (0171 486 4921); **The Jockey Club** (controls racing in New York and influences horseracing boards of other States): 40 East 52nd St, New York,

NY 10022; (212) 371–5970. See also Thoroughbred. **British Horse Society** (and its division, **British Show Jumping Assn**), see horse. Government bodies issuing **v.r.** include: in Britain, **Ministry of Agriculture** (State Veterinary Service), Hook Rise South, Tolworth, Surrey KT6 7NF. (0181 330 4411). **v.r.** covering import, export and infectious diseases of horses are available from HM Stationery Office, 49 High Holborn, London WC1V 6HB (0171 873 0011). **Equine notifiable diseases** (those of which the Ministry must be informed) are: African horse sickness qv, contagious equine metritis qv, dourine qv, epizootic lymphangitis qv, equine infectious anaemia (see swamp fever), equine viral encephalomyelitis (see encephalomyelitis), glanders (farcy) qv, anthrax qv, Aujeszky's disease (see rabies) and rabies. Ministry can restrict movement of horses to reduce spread of diseases in other animals (eg foot and mouth). Breed societies, particularly those whose members travel for sporting events or breeding, issue recommendations (see Thoroughbred, hunter, polo pony, horse) on quarantine, travel etc designed to reduce spread of disease.

veterinary

(syns veterinarian, vet, probably from L vetus, old or veterinae, old hack) Anyone whose name is on register of Royal College of Veterinary Surgeons (qv) or equivalent body (in USA **v.s.** is licensed by State). In Britain **v.s.** qualifies, usually after 5 years, at one of 6 universities (Bristol, Cambridge, Edinburgh, Glasgow, Liverpool, London), entitling him/her to initials MRCVS (Member of Royal College). Students graduating from Dublin who want MRCVS status must apply to Royal College (due to EU regulations). Each university awards different degree, viz: Bachelor of Veterinary Science (BVSc–Bristol, Liverpool); Bachelor of Veterinary Medicine (Vet MB–Cambridge); Bachelor of Veterinary Medicine and Surgery (BVMS–Edinburgh, Glasgow); Bachelor of Veterinary Medicine (BVetMed–London); Bachelor of Veterinary Medicine (MVB–Dublin). Higher qualifications are masters' degrees and doctorates, eg Master in Veterinary Medicine (MVM–Cambridge and Dublin); Master of Veterinary Science (MVSc–Liverpool); Master of Veterinary Surgery (MVS–Glasgow); Master of Philosophy (MPhil–London); Doctor of Veterinary Science (DVSc–Liverpool); Doctor of Veterinary Medicine (DVetMed–London); Doctor of Veterinary Medicine (DVM–Glasgow); Doctor of Veterinary Medicine and Surgery (DVM&S–Edinburgh); Doctor of Philosophy (PhD); Master of Science (MSc); Doctor of Science (DSc). (Initials of other higher degrees are BV, DEO, DESM, Dr, DV, FR, MB, MV, VetMB, VM.) Fellowship of the Royal College (FRCVS) is gained by thesis, additional exam, by contribution to learning or by election. Vets also work in general practice, in teaching/research for Ministry of Agriculture etc. Sports fixtures appoint **v.s.** and Royal College approves vets to inspect riding schools.

veterinary surgeon

vice   Act of atypical, usually unpleasant, behaviour. Either declarable at most sales (eg weaving); aggressive towards humans (eg biting, kicking); or developed against restraint, eg bucking. V.s usually declarable: crib-biting, weaving, wind-sucking, shivering. (Hobday or other wind operation or state of being a rig should be stated.) Any of these conditions can affect soundness, qv. Other habits considered a **v.** include rearing, bolting, jibbing or shying. These may have developed as a result of fear, faulty hearing or vision or they may be a sign of ill-temper or playfulness.

viral   Of, or caused by, a virus. **v. arteritis** See equine **v.** arteritis. **v. abortion** See abortion.

viremia   Presence of virus in blood.

virology   Study of viruses.

virulence   (L virulentia, from virus, poison) Microorganisms' ability to cause disease, especially acute or fatal one.

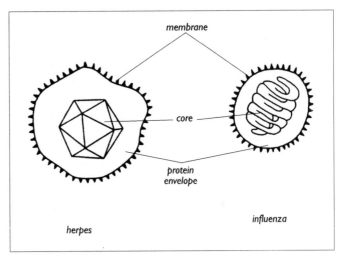

44 Herpesvirus and influenza virus, illustrating different shapes of nucleic acid core

virus   Extremely small living particles which infect and cause disease in man, animals and plants. Unlike bacteria, they are not visible with standard microscopes; they reproduce only in living cells and they can pass through filters which trap bacteria. **v. abortion** See abortion. **v., classification of** Depends on size (measured in millimicrons-mμ), shape and chemical make-up. Group 1 contains ribonucleic acid (RNA); group 2 contains deoxyriboneucleic acid (DNA). Group 1: (a) myxovirus (80–120mμ) A/equi 1 and A/equi 2 – equine flu; (b) picornavirus

(20–35mμ) parainfluenza 3 – acute respiratory infection; (c) reovirus (about 70mμ) – diarrhoea, African horse sickness; (d) arborvirus (20-50mμ) – Arthropod-borne virus – encephalomyelitis. Group 2: (a) equine herpesvirus (EHV–1, syns rhinopneumonitis, equine abortion virus – about 150mμ) sub-types: Ky-D strain, isolated in Kentucky, USA 1952; army 183 strain and Japanese isolate H-45 strain – snotty nose); EHV-3, syn coital exanthema; EHV-4. (b) adenovirus (60–90mμ) – pneumonia; (c) papillomavirus (about 50mμ) – warts. **v. diseases, diagnosis of** 2 methods: (1) By culture of **v.** in tissue. Sheets of cells grown in special media are innoculated with suspect material, such as nasal swabs from horses with influenza symptoms. The **v.** grows in cells, causing characteristic changes. (2) By blood examination. Serum is tested for presence of antibodies against a particular **v.** The concentration of antibodies is measured in terms of titre (qv). In a **v.** disease the concentration of antibodies rises from acute phase to convalescent stage, 2–4 weeks later. Increase of antibodies is diagnostic of disease because they are specific for the **v.** To test, it is necessary to have a captive **v.** (influenza **v.** strains A/equi 1 and 2 are known and serum can be tested for them – it is impossible to test against an unknown strain.) See complement fixation test and haemagglutination. **v.-immunity after infection** Recovery from most **v.** diseases is followed by strong immunity, though notable exceptions are equine herpesvirus 1 and, to a lesser extent, influenza. Immunity is based on production of antibodies which neutralise **v. v.-interference phenomenon** Animals innoculated with one **v.** may become resistant to innoculation with another. This interference is not fully understood but may be associated with production of interferon, qv. This appears to be liberated by cells during a **v.** infection and to prevent further infection by that **v.** or any other which may enter cells. **v., laboratory study of** viral particles can be separated from bacteria or other matter with filters. (A relatively large **v.**, influenza, is only a tenth the size of a staphylococcus bacterium.) A microscope can be used (1) to see changes in organs affected by **v.**, (2) to detect inclusion bodies, qv, and (3) to see changes in tissue culture, qv. An electron microscope (magnification: 1–200,000 diameters) is widely used to study **v. V.** can be cultivated in minced rabbit kidney and serum; on membranes of chick embryo and in its yolk sac; or in tissue culture, qv. **V.** cannot be isolated without suitable cells and the use of antibiotics to prevent growth of contaminating bacteria. **v., latency of** See latency of virus. **v., resistance of** Most **v.**s are destroyed by heat and oxidising agents but are resistant to: dryness, low temperature, glycerin and weak concentrations of phenol (0.5 per cent). They can be conserved for some time in glycerin at 0°C. **v., spread of** Similar to spread of bacteria, ie by direct contact, droplet inhalation, ingestion or injection by biting insects or contaminated needles, etc.

viscera — Organs, alimentary canal and other contents of abdomen, qv.

vision — (L visio, videre, to see) Act or sense of sight. See eye.

vitamin — (from L vita, life) Organic substance necessary for normal metabolism. **v. A** See concentrated **v. A** solution. **v. B** See aneurine hydrochloride. **v. B$_{12}$** (cyanocobalamin) Cobalt-containing substance produced in liver and gut. Dark red crystals essential for protein metabolism and therefore for growth and reproduction. Deficiencies can cause anaemia but unlikely in horses. Dose: 2 micrograms/kg body wt. **v. C** See ascorbic acid. **v. D** See concentrated **v. D** solution. **v. E** Essential **v.**, deficiency of which is associated with white muscle disease (see selenium). Helps to avoid harmful effects of free oxygen radicals that accumulate in certain diseases.

vitreous — (L vitreus, glassy) Transparent. **v. humour** Jelly-like fluid in back chamber of eye. Cf glaucoma.

vitro/vivo — See in vitro, in vivo.

viviparous — (L vivus, alive + parere, to produce) That which produces offspring which has been nourished by a special organ (placenta), eg mare.

VMD — Abbr Doctor Veterinary Medicine (Stockholm and Pennsylvania Universities).

vocal — Of voice. **v. cord** One of two string-like cords in voice box (larynx) which enable horse to whinny, neigh etc. See equine sounds, Hobday, wind.

voice box — (syn larynx) Short, connecting tube between throat and windpipe; regulates air intake, protects against inhaling dust and is site of voice. Composed of cartilages: 3 single (cricoid, thyroid and epiglottis) and 1 paired (arytenoid). See wind; Figs 25–7 (p200).

volemia — Blood volume. **hyper-v.** Abnormally high volume of circulating blood. **hypo-v.** Abnormally low volume.

volume — Measure of quantity. **blood v.** Total blood in body, approx 1 tenth of total weight, eg foal: 3–4 litres; adult: 30–40 litres. **packed cell v.** See haematocrit, blood tests. **stroke v.** Amount of blood pumped by heart at each beat. **tidal v.** Amount of gas passing into or out of lungs during one breath.

volvulus — (L volvere, to twist round) Acute obstruction of alimentary canal. See twist.

To regurgitate stomach contents. Rare in horses and more likely via nostrils than mouth. Indicates rupture of stomach, grass sickness (qv) and/or impending death. | **vomit**

End part of external opening of genital tract of mare. Opens into vagina and consists of 2 prominent, rounded lips (labiae) which protect clitoris. **V.** merges on either side with the skin of perineum. **sloping v.** Poor conformation. See Caslick, Pouret. **winking of v.** Action of in-season or urinating mare in which clitoris is exposed. Adjective: vulval. | **vulva**

W

Waler See Australian.

walk See gait.

walking disease Result of cirrhosis (hardening) of liver due to plant toxins such as crotalaria and senecio, which contain alkaloids. Symptoms: walking in circles, pressing head against objects. Diagnosis: on jaundiced state and liver function tests (lowered blood albumin and increased serum enzymes). See poisons. American **W.** Pony Registry, PO Box 5782, Macon, GA 31208 (912 743 2321). **W. horse** See Tennessee.

wall Line/barrier. **w. eye** Lack of pigment in iris of eye, showing more white than usual around the pupil. Said to be a sign of bad temper. See behaviour, marking. **w. of foot** See foot.

wanderer See neonatal maladjustment syndrome.

warble fly (syn gad fly) Two species significant in UK because their larvae, or warbles, occasionally live in horses (cattle are natural hosts): *Hypoderma bovis* and *Hypoderma lineatum* found all over Britain, except in Orkney and Shetland Isles. Also live in Europe, Canada and USA. They are large flies resembling bees. *H. lineatum* is black with yellow or orange bands; *H. bovis*, black and yellow. They lay eggs on horse's coat and these stick to base of hairs – *H. lineatum* eggs in rows, as many as 20 to each hair; *H. bovis* eggs attached singly. 3–6 days later larvae about one-fiftieth of an inch long emerge and develop into maggots. These crawl down hairs, burrow into skin and migrate through host's body. In cattle, *H. lineatum* spend autumn in tissues of leg, chest and belly, then find their way to gullet. In February they migrate to skin under back causing swelling with small hole through which maggot breathes. Each maggot forms small abscess and 1–8 days later it moults to become third and last larval stage. The translucent larvae feed on inflammatory exudate and turn dark brown. After about 30 days they leave back through holes in skin, fall on ground and pupate. Adult flies emerge in May and life cycle is complete. As horse is an unnatural host, larvae may act unusually, eg migrate to flank or form abscesses and fail to break through skin. Larvae should never be squeezed; warm poultices will encourage them to emerge. Tracts leading to swellings are inflamed lymph channels and not, contrary to popular belief, tracts made by the maggot. Treatment: see derris.

45 Warble fly eggs
(*Hypoderma lineatum*)
attached to hair. Larva
(*Hypoderma bovis*)

(trade name: Warfarin) An anticoagulant which interferes with formation of clotting factors of blood. Can be given orally for therapeutic purposes. **warfarin**

Cross between cold- and hot-blooded. **warm-blooded**

(1) Breed, up to 18 h, very popular for riding. Also termed **Dutch W. American W. Soc**, 6801 W. Romley Ave, Phoenix, AZ 85403 (602 936 6621). **British W. Soc**, Moorlands Farm, New Yatt, Witney, Oxon, OX8 6TE (01993 868673) (2) Colloq (without capital W) for any **w.** type, eg Hanoverian, Trakehner. **Warmblood**

Fleshy or scaly growth on skin. See growth, milk wart, sarcoid. **wart**

Loss of weight. Symptom of red or whiteworm infestation, tuberculosis, liver disease, chronic infection, ragwort poisoning, diarrhoea, kidney disease or poor feeding. See metabolism. **wasting**

(chemical symbol: H_2O) Should always be available to horse, except in large quantities before hard work, eg race, or being anaesthetised. Washing **w.** through mouth without drinking usually symptom of colic. See dehydration, fluid balance. **water**

(L cera) (1) Colloq for dry colostrum at end of teat just before foaling. See birth. (2) Ear wax or cerumen. **wax**

White blood cell (qv) or white blood (cell) count. **WBC/w.b.c.**

Separation of mare and foal. Occurs gradually under natural conditions; feeding becomes less frequent and mare discourages foal by kicking, biting or hindering it. **W.** usually completed by 10–11 months, ie just before birth of next foal. Thoroughbred usually weaned at 5–6 months, by (1) taking group of foals from mares, confining foals to looseboxes for 2 or 3 days, until calling and anxiousness has died away (mares must be out of calling distance); (2) programme **w.**, kinder method in which group of mares and foals have one or two mares taken away at regular intervals of, say, 2 days, until finally one mare is left with all the foals. Then she is removed. Mares usually taken away as group are let free in paddock and weaned foals are returned to their own boxes at getting-in time. Method can be equally effective if mares and foals are out day and night. Group members should know one another and their paddock; mares with difficult temperaments should be taken first. **w., preparation for** Foal should be encouraged to eat away from its dam (with bars over small manger and creep feeding in paddock, ie rails foal can walk beneath, but mare cannot). After **w.**, protein in feed should be increased to compensate for loss of milk. (See food). **w. problems** Mare's udder **weaning**

weaning — may become hot, swollen and tender, but it rarely needs treatment. Milking udder to relieve pressure stimulates formation of more milk and should be done only in exceptional circumstances. Liniments, ointments etc on outside of udder are unnecessary. If extensive swelling develops and mare is reluctant to move or goes off feed, suspect mastitis (qv). Quantity of food can be reduced, but not drastically, as sudden cutback may be harmful to pregnant mare. Water intake should not be restricted as it may cause stoppage. Exercise is helpful. Foals may fret and go off feed, especially if method (1) was used. They may weave, crib-bite and box-walk, but pairing foals is unsatisfactory because fretting will develop when pairs are split. Grids between boxes may settle restless foals.

weave — To shift weight from one foreleg to the other and usually swing neck and head from side to side. Considered bad nervous habit which takes off condition and may weaken tendons of forelegs. See vice.

WEE — Abbr Western equine encephalomyelitis. See encephalomyelitis.

weight — Measure of heaviness. **birth w.** Measured to help determine maturity/immaturity. Thoroughbred: 50kg (approx 110lb); pony: 18–32kg (approx 40–70lb). **w. loss** See wasting, also metabolism.

WEIGHTS AND MEASURES
Mass
Metric

1 kilogram (kg)	= 15,432 grains or 35.274 ounces or 2.2046 pounds
1 gram (g)	= 15.432 grains
1 milligram (mg) (1,000mg = 1g)	= 0.015432 grains

Imperial

1 ton (2,240lb)	= 1,016 kilograms
1 hundredweight (112lb)	= 50.80 kilograms
1 stone (14lb)	= 6.35 kilograms
1 pound (avoirdupois)	= 453.59 grams
1 ounce (oz)	= 28.35 grams
1 grain (gr)	= 64.799 milligrams

Capacity
Metric

1 litre (l)	= 1.7598 pints
1 millilitre (ml)	= 16.894 minims
imperial	
1 gallon (gal) (160floz)	=4.546 litres

1 pint (pt)	= 568.25 millilitres or 0.56825 litres	*weight*
1 fluid ounce (floz)	= 28.412 millilitres	
1 fluid drachm (fldr)	= 3.5515 millilitres	
1 minim (min)	= 0.059192 millilitres	

Length
Metric

1 kilometre (km)	= 0.621 miles
1 metre (m)	= 39.370 inches
1 decimetre (dm)	= 3.9370 inches
1 centimetre (cm)	= 0.39370 inch
1 millimetre (mm)	= 0.039370 inch
1 micron (μ)	= 0.0039370 inch

Imperial

1 mile	= 1.609 kilometres
1 yard	= 0.914 metres
1 foot	= 30.48 centimetres
1 inch	=2.54 centimetres or 25.40 millimetres

Temperature

Centigrade	Fahrenheit	Centigrade	Fahrenheit
110°	230°	38°	100.4
100	212	37.5	99.5
95	203	37	98.6
90	194	36.5	97.7
85	185	36	96.8
80	176	35.5	95.9
75	167	35	95
70	158	34	93.2
65	149	33	91.4
60	140	32	89.6
55	131	31	87.8
50	122	30	86
45	113	25	77
44	111.2	20	68
43	109.4	15	59
42	107.6	10	50
41	105.8	+5	41
40.5	104.9	0	32
40	104	−5	23
39.5	103.1	−10	14
39	102.2	−15	+5
38.5	101.3	−20	−4

To convert Fahrenheit to Centigrade: subtract 32, multiply remainder by 5 and divide result by 9. To convert Centigrade to Fahrenheit: multiply by 9, divide by 5 and add 32.

weight

Tables can be used for direct transference of doses from one system to the other; but multiples should not be used as approximation might raise figure significantly. To convert grams per 100ml into grains per ounce, multiply by 4,375. To convert grams into ounces, multiply by 10 and divide by 283. To convert litres into pints, multiply by 88 and divide by 50. To convert kilos into pounds, multiply by 1,000 and divide by 454.

Approx equivalent doses in metric and imperial (apothecaries') systems *

grams (g)	grains (gr)	grams (g)	grains (gr)
10	150	2	30
8	120	1.6	25
6	90	1.2	20
5	75	1	15
4	60	0.8	12
3	45	0.6	10
2.5	40	0.5	8

milligrams (mg.)	grains (gr.)	milligrams (mg.)	grains (gr.)
400	6	6	$1/10$
300	5	5	$1/12$
250	4	4	$1/16$
200	$3^{1}/_{2}$	3	$1/20$
150	$2^{1}/_{2}$	2.5	$1/24$
120	2	2	$1/30$
100	$1^{1}/_{2}$	1.5	$1/40$
80	$1^{1}/_{3}$	1.2	$1/50$
75	$1^{1}/_{4}$	1	$1/60$
60	1	0.8	$1/80$
50	$3/_{4}$	0.6	$1/100$
40	$3/_{5}$	0.5	$1/120$
30	$1/_{2}$	0.4	$1/160$
25	$2/_{5}$	0.3	$1/200$
20	$1/_{3}$	0.25	$1/240$
15	$1/_{4}$	0.2	$1/300$
12.5	$1/_{5}$	0.15	$1/400$
10	$1/_{6}$	0.12	$1/500$
8	$1/_{8}$		

millilitres (ml)	minims (min)	millilitres (ml)	minims (min)
10	150	0.8	12
8	120	0.6	10
6	90	0.5	8
5	75	0.4	6
4	60	0.3	5
3	45	0.25	4
2.5	40	0.2	3
2	30	0.15	$2^{1}/_{2}$
1.6	25	0.12	2
1.3	20	0.1	$1^{1}/_{2}$
1	15		

1 fluid ounce=approx 30ml
1 fluid drachm=approx 4ml
15 minims=approx 1ml

Of Wales. **W. Cob** Good-natured breed developed from **W.** Mountain pony and with some of that breed's hardiness. Heavy type used in harness has high-stepping trot, but now dying out, leaving riding type. Usually 14–15 hands, compact and can carry 90kg (196lb) rider. Most colours including dun, but piebald and skewbald not favoured. **W. Mountain** Breed often thought most beautiful of British mountain/moorland types. Origins are lost but looks indicate Arab blood. Strong, willing, makes good child's pony. Some authorities believe breed more susceptible than most to cryptorchidism (see rig) and that condition inherited from free-running rigs. See pit pony. **W. Pony and Cob Soc**, 6 Chalybeate St, Aberystwyth SY23 1HS (01970 617501). **W. Pony Soc of America**, PO Box 2977, Winchester, VA 22601 (540 667 6195).   **Welsh**

See Fjord.   **Westland**

(*Triticum sativum*) Cereal plant, husk of which (bran) fed to horses. The grain should not be given as likely to cause laminitis or eczema and, in amounts over 3kg (7lb), death.   **wheat**

See physiotherapy.   **whirlpool treatment**

Noise made by horse unsound in wind, qv. See urine sample.   **whistling**

See albinism, coat colouring. **w. blood cells** (syns w.b.c., leucocytes) Cells in bloodstream, tissues and organs. 5 types: neutrophil (poly-morphonuclear leucocyte) which eats bacteria, dead cells and debris by amoeboid action; lymphocyte, which helps produce antibodies; eosinophil, which deals with allergic conditions and parasites; monocyte, which has similar function to neutrophil; basophil, which is part of inflammatory reaction (see also platelet, which helps clotting of blood). Normal **w.b.c.** count 5–10,000 per cu mm. Any increase (leucocytosis) indicates bacterial and (lymphocytosis) viral infection; decrease (leucopenia) suggests arteritis or other virus infection. See blood tests. **w. bryony poisoning** Caused by eating **w.b.** plant. Symptoms: sweating, severe purging, convulsions, stupor, sometimes death. No specific treatment available. **w. line** Junction of wall of foot with sole. Seen in upturned hoof as line inside circumference of wall. **w. muscle** See selenium, setfast.   **white**

Nematode (roundworm parasite) of order Ascaroidea. *Ascaris equi/equorum* largest roundworm in horses; male 15–30cm (6–12in), female 12–24cm (5–9½in). Life history is direct: adults live in small intestine, females lay eggs which pass out in droppings; infective larvae develop and are swallowed, then burrow through intestinal wall. Bloodstream carries them to liver, heart and lungs. From lungs they travel up windpipe to   **whiteworm**

whiteworm	throat and are swallowed. Larvae pass through stomach to intestines, where they grow into adults, completing the cycle in about 12 weeks. A female can contain 27 million eggs and lay 200,000 a day. The eggs live many months, are resistant to many chemicals and are most dangerous to young horses. Can cause unthriftiness, lung damage and occasionally rupture of gut. Diagnosis: on finding eggs in dung. Treatment: benzimidazole, carbon disulphide, piperazine salts.
whorl	(syn vortex) Spiral twist, eg in muscles around heart; hairs in coat (usually about 2.5cm (1in) on neck; see marking).
whorlbone lameness	(syn trochanteric bursitis) Lameness common in Standardbred (qv) after fall or strain in training. Caused by inflamed bursa beneath tendon of gluteus muscle where it passes over part of femur (great trochanter). Symptoms: pain on pressure over hip area, leg flexed at rest, weight put on outside of foot during action. Treatment: pain-killers and corticosteroid injections into bursa.
wild	Untamed; animal whose ancestors have never been domesticated. The 5 **w.** species of living Equidae: Przewalski, Asiatic wild ass, common zebra, mountain zebra, Grevy's zebra. Cf feral.
wind	(colloq for breathing) Important part of soundness examination, qv. **gone in the w.** Any fault in respiration. **heaves/broken w.** (syn emphysema) See broken **w. w. infirmities** Roaring, whistling, gurgling. All sounds made by horse with partially blocked nasal passages, **w.**pipe (trachea) or voice box (larynx). Obstruction may be wart or growth (rare), soft palate or vocal cords. If cartilage (arytenoid) and muscles of voice box are weak they will not pull aside cords when horse inhales; cords will stay in relaxed (exhaling) position, ie centre of voice box. (Cords are arranged like 2 half-cups facing upwards against sides of voice box. Air can easily escape, but cannot as easily enter, unless cups are pulled aside.) Diagnosis: on hearing noise as horse inhales at gallop, not to be confused with normal breathing-out sounds (cf soft palate, tongue swallowing). Viewing with laryngoscope (qv) can reveal lack of cord movement and deformed shape of voice box. See Figs 25–7 (p200). Treatment: Hobday or laryngeal operation. **w.**pipe (syn trachea) Cartilaginous tube from voice box to lungs; extends down front of neck, then branches into 2 main bronchi. Lined with epithelium (qv) which has tiny hairs (cilia). These wave in air flow to trap any particles, which can be coughed out.
windgall	(syn wind puff) Swelling of joint (articular **w.**, caused by arthritis) or of tendon sheath (tendinous **w.**) caused by sprain (tear-

ing of fibres in tendon or tendon sheath). Swellings also appear in general ill-health, eg allergy, infection. | *windgall*

Gulping of air. May be accompanied by crib-biting, qv. Nervous habit which impairs digestion and may increase foul-smelling flatus; considered a vice, qv. | **wind-sucking**

Colloq to open lips of vulva, exposing clitoris. Seen during oestrus and after urinating. See behaviour. | **wink**

Top of shoulders, between neck and back; formed by 3rd–9th thoracic vertebrae (see vertebral column). Highest point of **w.** usually higher than back (cf donkey) and used in measuring horse's height. See hand; fistulous **w.** | **withers**

(syns ataxia, incoordination) Condition of poor coordination, especially of hindlegs and sometimes forelegs. May appear from 3 months to 3 years, although older horses can be affected. Occurs mostly in the Thoroughbred, Quarterhorse and Morgan horse. Onset may be gradual or sudden; there is dragging of toes of hindlegs and unsteadiness in pulling up, backing or turning. Horse may be able to cope with condition but some cannot get up and have to be destroyed. Mildly affected mares could be used for breeding, but condition may be inheritable and in some cases it is unwise to allow stallion to mount. There is no proven treatment but arthrodesis (qv) may help. Dietary restriction and box rest for several months sometimes effective. Most insurance companies allow destruction on humane grounds and meet claims. Cause may be injury to spinal canal or cord, malformed or fractured cervical vertebrae, nutritional deficiency, abscesses. True **w.s.** may be inherited condition of malformed vertebrae. Cf neonatal maladjustment syndrome; cerebellar degeneration; segmental myelitis. | **wobbler syndrome**

See teeth. | **wolf tooth**

See uterus. | **womb**

See filter. | **Wood's filter**

Breach in continuity of skin made by kick, blow, sharp object, etc. **open w.** Cut. **lacerated w.** Tear, eg from barbed wire. **puncture w.** Small, penetrating hole produced by nail, pitchfork, etc. **W.** healing is by 1st intention (when edges of skin are stitched together and epithelium grows into direct union without scar tissue) or by 2nd intention (when proud flesh fills gap between edges of skin before epithelium grows). Treatment: wash with weak antiseptic and remove debris, stitch (suture) as soon as possible. Once granulation tissue starts to grow, ie | **wound**

wound after about 12 hours, 1st intention healing becomes more difficult. Lotion, eg of zinc sulphate, helps prevent proud flesh. Skin **w.** over bone heals better than over muscles, due to absence of swelling and oedema. All **w.**s heal faster in presence of oxygen, therefore dressing should be permeable, eg polypropylene sheeting (filmy plastic-like material used especially on site of operation). Antitetanus serum should be given unless horse has previously been immunised.

wry (Old English wrigian, to turn) **w. foot** (syn flare foot) See foot.**w. neck** (syn torticollis) Type of difficult birth (dystocia) where head of foetus is bent backwards. Difficult to straighten manually as neck vertebrae usually damaged. Dismemberment of foetus (embryotomy) or caesarean section usually necessary. **w.nose** Condition where nose is deformed by bend to one side. Results in narrow airway and may impair breathing if severe. Cf soft palate.

X   Female sex chromosome. See chromosome.

xerosis   (from Gr xeros, dry) Unusual dryness, as of mouth, eyes, coat. See dehydration, drycoat.

X-ray   (syn Roentgen ray) Energy wave of same type as light ray, but of much shorter wave-length (approx 5 x 10cm). Sometimes, with other imaging methods, brought under heading 'diagnostic imaging'. See radiation; veterinary.

xylazine   (trade names: Anased, Chanazine, Rompun, Virbaxyl) Sedative, analgesic and muscle-relaxant properties. Given by slow IV injection. Used for handling fractious animals, for medical examinations and premedication for general, local or regional anaesthesia.

Y | Male sex chromosome. See chromosome.

yellow | Lemon colour. **y. body** (syn corpus luteum) Structure in ovary formed after rupture of follicle and shedding of egg (ovulation); produces progesterone and lasts about 15–17 days. It is then destroyed – probably by hormone prostaglandin secreted in uterus. Follicle fills with blood clot; luteal cells grow into clot and organise themselves into **y.b.**, which controls dioestrus. **y.b. of pregnancy** One which lasts beyond usual span of 17 days (if a fertilised egg arrives in uterus during dioestrus). It is joined by accessory **y.b.**s which maintain pregnancy to about day 150. After this, foetus produces progesterone and ovaries become quiescent. **y. star thistle (Centaurea soostitialis) poisoning** Causes chewing disease, with firming of muscles of face and muzzle, in N California.

yellows | Colloq for jaundice, qv.

yew poisoning | Caused by eating **y.** (*Taxus baccata*), most poisonous tree native to Britain. Contains alkaloid taxine, which depresses heart action. Horse usually dies almost immediately. If death is delayed there may be intense inflammation of stomach. Diagnosis, on finding fragments of leaves in stomach and intestines. Treatment not usually possible. See poisons.

yolk sac placenta | Outgrowth of foetal gut, richly supplied with blood vessels. Nourishes foetus up to about 30 days' gestation and is then replaced by true placenta.

Yorkshire Coach horse | Virtually extinct draught type developed from Cleveland Bay, qv.

Z

zebra (Amharic, striped) 3 types: common or Burchell's **z.** (*Equus quagga burchelli*, has 44 chromosomes); mountain **z.** (*Equus zebra*); and, the largest and also most horse-like, Grevy's **z.** (*Equus grevyi*, 46 chromosomes). Each lives in parts of Africa, may eat leaves and shoots instead of grass and has dark stripes and ass-like conformation, ie large ears, thick neck, boxy hooves. Generally believed that the more primitive a species, the more striped or distinctly marked it is. Different types of **z.** unlikely to become one breed because cross-breds are usually sterile. Grevy's **z.** becoming extinct in natural habitat (Kenya and Ethiopia) but breed is protected in about 20 zoos world-wide. **Z.** sire and donkey dam produced what was claimed to be first 'zeedonk', a filly, in 1971 (Colchester Zoo, Essex). Filly had donkey body and **z.** (striped) legs. **z.**/donkey cross also called zonkey. See chromosome, coat colouring, quagga.

zeedonk See zebra.

Zeeland Heavy Dutch breed well known in Middle Ages but whose name is no longer officially recognised by Netherlands Ministry of Agriculture. More supple than its neighbour, Dutch Draught (qv) and has probably interbred with that massive type. Sometimes used as circus horse.

Zemaituka/s (from Zemaitifa, colloq for W Lithuania; pl Zemaitukai) Russian horse of great stamina, known in 13th century and probably developed from Przewalski (qv) and Arab. Up to about 15 h and most often dun or mousey with dorsal stripe.

Zhmud See Lithuanian.

zinc oxide White or yellowish-white soft odourless tasteless powder. Applied to skin in ointments, pastes and lotions as mild astringent and to protect. Heals saddle sores. **z. poisoning** Caused by taking in contaminated food or water (usually near brass foundry). More serious if lead is also ingested. Symptoms: constipation, gastroenteritis, arthritis, paralysed throat. See poisons. **z. sulphate** Colourless crystals or white crystalline odourless powder with astringent metallic taste. Solutions containing 10–25 per cent used to treat proud flesh. See wound.

Zmudzin Type of Konik, qv.

zonkey | See zebra.

zoonosis | **zoonosis** (zoo- combining form, relationship to animals from Gr zoon, animal + nosos, disease) Disease of animals which can be transmitted to man under natural (not experimental) conditions, eg tuberculosis, rabies.

zygote | (Gr zygotes, yoked together) Fertilised egg. See also embryology.

DRUG MANUFACTURERS

Agrimin Ltd, Brigg, Lincs DN20 OSP. Tel (01652) 688046

Alstoe Ltd, Melton Mowbray, Leics LE15 7ZU. Tel (01664) 411663

Animalcare Ltd, Common Road, Dunnington, York YO1 5RU. Tel (01904) 488661

Arnolds Veterinary Products Ltd, Harlescott, Shrewsbury SY1 3TB. Tel (01743) 441632

Bayer Plc, Bury St Edmunds, Suffolk IP32 7AH. Tel (01284) 763200

Bimeda UK, Liverpool L33 7XS. Tel (0151) 5473711

BioMar Ltd, Grangemouth, Stirlingshire TW1 3RH. Tel (01324) 665585

Boehringer Ingelheim Ltd, Bracknell, Berks RG12 4YS. Tel (01344) 424600

Boots the Chemist Ltd, Nottingham NG2 3AA. Tel (01602) 506111

C-Vet Veterinary Products, Leyland, Preston PR5 3QN. Tel (01772) 452421

Centaur Services Ltd, Castle Cary, Somerset BA7 7EU. Tel (01963) 350428

Cheminex Ltd, Corby, Northants NN17 2DS. Tel (01536) 265444

Ciba Animal Health, Whittlesford, Cambridge CB2 4QT. Tel (01223) 833621

Crown Veterinary Pharmaceuticals, Leyland, Lancs PR5 3QN. Tel (01772) 452421

Day Son & Hewitt Ltd, St George's Quay, Lancs LA1 5QJ. Tel (01524) 381821

Efamol Vet, Guildford, Surrey GU3 1NA. Tel (01483) 304441

Elanco Animal Health, Basingstoke, Hants RG21 6XA. Tel (01256) 353131

Fort Dodge Animal Health, Southampton, Hants SO30 4QH. Tel (01489) 781711

Forum Products Ltd, Redhill, Surrey RH1 6YS. Tel (01737) 773711

Glaxo Laboratories Ltd, Greenford, Middlesex UB6 0HE. Tel (0181) 422 3434

Hoechst Roussel Vet Ltd, Walton, Milton Keynes, Bucks MK7 7AJ. Tel (01908) 665050

Horse Health Products, Pulborough, West Sussex RH20 2HY. Tel (01798) 875337

Intervet UK Ltd, Science Park, Cambridge CB4 4FP. Tel (01223) 420221

Janssen-Cilag, High Wycombe, Bucks HP14 4HJ. Tel (01494) 567555

Britain and Ireland

Kruuse UK Ltd, Sherburn in Elmet, N. Yorkshire LS25 6ES. Tel (01977) 683171

Leo Animal Health, Princes Risborough, Bucks HP27 9RR. Tel (01844) 347333

J.M. Loveridge Plc, Southampton, Hants SO15 1BH. Tel (01703) 228411

3M Health Care Ltd, Loughborough, Leics LE11 1EP. Tel (01509) 611611

Mallinckrodt Vet Ltd, Uxbridge, Middlesex UB9 6LS. Tel (01895) 626000

Micro-Biologicals Ltd, Bury St Edmunds, Suffolk IP33 3SU. Tel (01284) 706778

Millpledge Pharmaceuticals, Retford, Notts DN22 9NA. Tel (01777) 708440

MSD Agvet, Hoddesdon, Herts EN11 9BU. Tel (01992) 467272

National Veterinary Supplies, Talke Pits, Stoke on Trent ST7 1XW. Tel (01782) 771100

Norbrook Laboratories Ltd, Great Corby, Carlisle BT35 6JP. Tel (01228) 562888

Norvartis Animal Health, Whittlesford, Cambridge CB2 4QT. Tel (01223) 833634

Paines & Byrne Ltd, West Byfleet, Surrey KT14 6RA. Tel (01932) 355405

Pfizer Ltd, Sandwich, Kent CT13 9NJ. Tel (01304) 616161

Pharmacia & Upjohn Ltd, Crawley, W. Sussex RH10 2LZ. Tel (01293) 582444

Rhone Merieux Ltd, Harlow, Essex CM19 5TS. Tel (01279) 439444

Robinson Healthcare, Chesterfield, Derbys S40 1YF. Tel (01246) 220022

Roche Products Ltd, Heanor, Derbys DE75 7SG. Tel (01773) 536500

Sanofi Animal Health Ltd, Watford, Herts WD1 8YJ. Tel (01923) 212212

Schering-Plough Animal Health, Welwyn Garden City, Herts AL7 1TW. Tel (01707) 363636

Smith and Nephew Healthcare, Hull HU3 4DJ. Tel (01482) 222200

Tulivin Laboratories Ltd, Belfast BT8 8DH. Tel (01232) 814188

Vet-2-Vet Marketing, Bury St Edmunds, Suffolk IP33 2QN. Tel (01284) 767721

Veterinary Drug Co Plc, Dunnington, York YO1 5RU. Tel (01904) 488444

Vetoquinol UK Ltd, Bicester, Oxon OX6 7UL. Tel (01869) 241287

Vetrepharm Ltd, Fordingbridge, Hampshire SP6 1PA. Tel (01425) 656081

Virbac Ltd, Science Park, Cambridge CB4 4WE. Tel (01223) 420404

Willows Francis Veterinary, Crawley, W. Sussex RH11 9BP. Tel (01293) 614141

Winthrop Laboratories, Guildford, Surrey GU1 4YS. Tel (01483) 505515

Wyeth Laboratories, Maidenhead, Berks SL6 0PH. Tel (01628) 604377

Young's Animal Health, Leyland, Preston PR5 3QN. Tel (01772) 457666

Britain and Ireland

Abbott Pharmaceuticals Inc, 14th and Sheridan, N Chicago, IL 60064. Tel (312) 937-7079

Adams Veterinary Research Laboratories Inc, PO Box 971039, Miami, FL 33197

Alcon Laboratories Inc, PO Box 1959, Fort Worth, TX. Tel. (817) 293-0450

Anthony Products Company, 5600 Peck Road, Arcadia, CA 91006

Astra Pharmaceutical Products Inc, 7 Neponset Street, Worcester, MA 01606. Tel (617) 852-6351

Ausonics Inc, 299 Adams Street, Bedford Hill, NY 10507

Bayer Corp, PO Box 390, Shawnee Mission, KS 66201-0390. Tel (800) 255-6517

Beecham Laboratories, 501 Fifth Street, Bristol, TN 37620. Tel (615) 764-5141

Bio-Ceutic Laboratories, 2621 North Belt Highway, St Joseph, MO 64502

Biocraft Laboratories Inc, 92 Route 46, Elmwood Park, NJ 07407. Tel (201) 796-3434

Boehringer Ingelheim Ltd, 2621 North Belt Highway, St. Joseph, MO 64502-2002

Bristol Veterinary Products, PO Box 4755, Syracuse, NY 13221-4755. Tel (315) 432-2000

Burroughs Wellcome Co, 3030 Cornwallis Road, Research Triangle Park, NC 27709. Tel (919) 541-9090

The Butler Co., 5000 Bradenton Ave. Dublin, OH 43017

Carter-Wallace Inc, Cranbury, NJ 08512

Ceva Laboratories, 10551 Barkley Street, Overland Park, KS 66212

Colorado Serum Company, 4950 York Street, Denver, CO 80216

Coopers Animal Health Inc, PO Box 419167, Kansas City, MO 64141-0167

Cutter Biological, 2200 Powell Street, Emeryville, CA 94608. Tel (415) 420-4167

Daniels Pharmaceuticals Inc, 2527 25th Avenue North, St Petersburg, FL 33713

Dupont Pharmaceuticals, 1 Rodney Square, Wilmington, DE 19898. Tel (800) 441-9861

NORTH AMERICA

North America

Elanco Products Company, Lilly Corporate Center, Indianapolis, IN 46285

EVSCO Pharmaceutical Corp, PO Box 209, Buena, NJ 08310

Farnam Companies, PO Box 12068, Omaha, NE 68112

CB Fleet Co Inc, 4615 Murray Place, Lynchburg, VA 24506. Tel (804) 528-4000

Fort Dodge Laboratories, 800 Fifth Street, Fort Dodge, IA 50501

Foster and Smith Inc, PO Box 100, Rhinelander, WI 54501

Geigy Pharmaceuticals, Ardsley, NY 10502. Tel (201) 277-5000

Granite Division (E.D.) Inc, PO Box 908, Burlington, NC 27215

Guardian Chemical, 230 Marcus Boulevard, Smithtown, NY 11787. Tel (516) 273-0900

Haver (Mobay Corp), Shawnee, KS 66201

Dow B. Hickman Inc, PO Box 35413, Houston, TX 77035. Tel (713) 723-0690

Hoechst-Roussel Agri-Vet Co, Route 202–206, PO Box 2500, Somerville, NJ 08876-1258. Tel (201) 231-2000

Janssen Pharmaceuticals, Titusville, NJ 08560

Johnson & Johnson Inc. 501 George Street, New Brunswick, NJ 08903. Tel (201) 52-0400

Lederle Laboratories, 1 Cyanamid Plaza, Wayne, NJ 07470. Tel (914) 735-5000

Leeming Div. Pfizer Inc, 100 Jefferson Road, Parsippany, NJ 07054. Tel (201) 887-2100

Eli Lilly & Co, 307 E McCarty Street, Indianapolis, IN 46285. Tel (317) 261-2000

Luitpold Pharmaceuticals Inc, One Luitpold Drive, Shirley, NY 11967

Merrell Dow Pharmaceuticals, Cincinnati, OH 45215. Tel (513) 948-9111

MSD Agvet, PO Box 2000, Rahway, NJ 07065

Norcliff Thayer Inc, 1 Scarsdale Road, Tuckahoe, NY 10707. Tel (914) 631-0033

Norden Laboratories Inc, PO Box 80809, Lincoln, NE 68521

Norwich Eaton Pharmaceuticals Inc, 13–27 Eaton Avenue, Norwich, NY 13815. Tel (607) 335-2565

Osborn Corp, PO Box 1590, Ford Dodge, IA 50501

Paddock Laboratories Inc, 3101 Louisiana, MN 55427. Tel (800) 328-5113

Parke-Davis, 201 Tabor Road, Morris Plains, NJ 07950. Tel (201) 540-2000

Pfizer Animal Health Inc, 812 Springdale Drive, Exton, PA 19341

Pioneer Brand Microbial Products, PO Box 258, Johnston, IA 50131

Pitman-Moore Inc, PO Box 344, Washington Crossing, NJ 08560

Proctor & Gamble, PO Box 171, Cincinnati, OH 45201. Tel (800) 543-0299

The Purdue Frederick Company, 100 Connecticut Avenue, Norwalk, CT 65856. Tel (203) 853-0123

North America

A.H. Robins Company, 1407 Cummings Drive, Richmond, VA 23220. Tel (804) 257-2000

Roche Animal Health & Nutrition, 340 Kingsland Street, Nutley, NJ 07110. Tel (201) 235-5000

Roxane Laboratories Inc, 330 Oak Street, Columbus, OH 43216. Tel (800) 848-0120

Henry Schein Inc, 5 Harbor Park Drive, Port Washington, NY 11050. Tel (516) 621-4300

Schering Corporation, PO Box 529, Galloping Hill Road, Kenilworth, NJ 07033. Tel (201) 558-4000

Schering-Plough Animal Health, 1095 Morms Union, NJ 07083

Sclavo Inc, 5 Mansard Court, Wayne, NJ 07470. Tel (800) 526-5260

Searle Pharmaceuticals Inc, Box 5110, Chicago, IL 60680. Tel (800) 323-4397

Seres Laboratories Inc, 3331 Industrial Drive, Santa Rosa, CA 95402. Tel (707) 526-4526

SmithKline Laboratories, 1500 Spring Garden Street, Philadelphia, PA 19101. Tel (215) 751-4000

Solvay Animal Health Inc. 1201 Northland Drive, Mendota Heights, MN 55120

Syntex Animal Health Inc, 4800 Westown Parkway, Suite 200, West Des Moines, IA 50266-6711

Techamerica Group Inc, 15th & Oak, Elwood, KS 66024

Travenol Laboratories Inc, One Baxter Parkway, Deerfield, IL 60015. Tel (312) 940-5387

Tyson & Associates Inc, 19725 Sherman Way, Suite 270, Canoga Park, CA 91306. Tel (213) 998-2161

The Upiohn Company, 7000 Portage Road, Kalamazoo, MI 49001. Tel (616) 323-4000

Vet-A-Mix Inc, 604 W Thomas Avenue, Shenandoah, IA 51601

Vetrepharm Inc, 383 Sovreign Road, London, Ontario, N6M 1A3, Canada

Vitaline Formulas, PO Box 6757, Incline Village, NV 89450. Tel (702) 831-5656

Winthrop Veterinary, 90 Park Avenue, New York, NY 10016. Tel (212) 907-2000

Wyeth Laboratories, PO Box 8299, Philadelphia, PA 19101. Tel (215) 688-4400

Zenith Laboratories Inc, 50 Williams Drive, Ramsey, NJ 07446. Tel (201) 327-3100

PROPRIETARY DRUG NAMES

Acetylpromazine	See acepromazine maleate		hoof care. See biotin.
Achromycin	See chlortetracycline hydro-chloride	**Biotrition**	See biotin
		Binixin	See flunixin meglumine
Achromycin	See tetracycline hydrochlo-ride	**Bisolvan**	See bromhexine
ACP	See acetylpromazine	**Buscopan**	Antispasmodic (qv) drug used to treat some colics and obstructed gullet
Adequan	See polysulphated gly-cosaminoglycan		
Amflpen	See ampicillin	**Calcium Disodium Versenate**	See sodium calcium edetate
Amikin	See amikacin	**Carbachol**	See carbachol
Anased	See xylazine	**Chanazine**	See xylazine
Androject	See testosterone	**Chloromycetin**	See chloramphenicol
Anectine	See suxamethonium chlo-ride	**Chorulon**	See chorionic gonado-trophin
Antepsin	See sucralfate	**Cidomycin**	See gentamicin sulphate
Arquel	See meclofenamic acid	**Cimetidine**	See cimetidine
Artervac	See equine viral arteritis	**Circulon**	See isoxsuprine hydrochloride
Aspirin	See acetylsalicylic acid		
Atrocare	See atropine sulphate	**Clamoxyl**	See amoxicillin
Aureomycin	See chlortetracycline hydro-chloride	**Collovet**	Iron tonic to treat anaemia
		Colvasone	See dexamethasone
Azium	See dexamethasone	**Cromovet**	See sodium cromoglycate
BCG	See BCG	**Crystapen**	See benzylpenicillin
BCK	See bismuth	**Cytacon**	Vitamin B_{12} liquid
Benylin	See diphenhydramine hydrochloride	**Dantrium**	See dantrolene sodium
		Daraprim	See pyrimethamine
Betnesol	See betamethasone sodium phosphate	**Decadron**	See dexamethasone
Betsolan/B. eye and ear drops	Drops containing betametha-sone sodium phosphate, qv	**Depocillin**	See procaine penicillin
		Depo-Medrone	See methylprednisolone acetate, cortisone
Biometh-Z	Compound preparation for		

Depopen	See procaine penicillin
Dermisol	Cleanser containing benzoic acid, malic acid, propylene glycol and salicylic acid
Dermobion	Contains neomycin sulphate, qv and nitrofurazone, qv
Dexadresson	See dexamethasone
Dexafort	See dexamethasone
Dextran	Synthetic plasma expander; used in blood transfusions
DMSO	Abbr dimethyl sulphoxide, qv
Dobutrex	See dobutamine
Domosedan	See detomidine
Dopram V	See doxapram hydrochloride
Dufulvin	See griseofulvin
Duphacillin	See ampicillin
Duphacort	See betamethasone sodium phosphate
Duphacycline	See oxytetracycline hydrochloride
Duphalyte	Parenteral fluid of sodium chloride, glucose, amino acids and vitamins
Duphapen	See procaine penicillin
Duphatrim	See trimethoprim
Duvaxyn	See Duvaxyn EHV 1,4; influenza
Econopen	See procaine penicillin
Ef-Cortesol	See hydrocortisone
Embacycline	See oxytetracycline hydrochloride
Emequell	See metoclopramide hydrochloride
Engemycin	See oxytetracycline hydrochloride
Epanutin	See phenytoin
Equidin	See oxybendazole
Equifulvin	See griseofulvin
Equip F and Equip FT	See Equip F
Equipalazone	See phenylbutazone
Equi-Sup	Compound multivitamin and mineral supplement
Equitac	See oxybendazole
Equiton	Compound multivitamin and mineral supplement
Equitrim	See trimethoprim
Equivite Resorb	Oral rehydration solution
Equivurm Plus	See mebendazole
Eqvalan	See ivermectin
Erythrocin	See erythromycin
Erythroped	See erythromycin
Estrumate	See cloprostenol
Excenel	See ceftiofur
Extra Tail	Fly repellent containing diethyltoluamide, dimethyl phthalate and citronella
Farrier's Formula	Compound preparation for hoof care
Finadyne	See flunixin meglumine
Fluothane	See halothane
Fluvac-Equine	Influenza vaccine with oil-water adjuvant, prepared in USA

Folligon	See serum gonadotrophin
Forgastrin	See attapulgite; bismuth
Fucidin	See fusidic acid
Fucithalmic Vet	See fusidic acid
Fulcin	See griseofulvin
Garamycin	See gentamicin sulphate
Gentamycin drops	See gentamicin sulphate
Grippequin	Influenza vaccine prepared in France
Grisovin	See griseofulvin
Grisol-V	See griseofulvin
Green Oils	Preparation for minor skin infections
Halothane	See halothane
Haemaccel	Reconstituted gelatin in Ringer's solution, qv
Haemo 15	Parenteral preparation of vitamins and minerals
Halathane	See halothane
Heparin	See heparin
Hexocil	See hexetidine
Hibitane	See chlorhexidine hydrochloride
Hyalovet	See sodium hyaluronate
Hylartil	See sodium hyaluronate
Hyonate	See sodium hyaluronate
Imaverol	See enilconazole
Imodium	See loperamide hydrochloride
Intra Epicaine	See mepivacaine hydrochloride
Intraval sodium	See thiopentone sodium
Ionalyte	Oral rehydration solution
Jexin	See tubocurarine chloride
Kenalog	See triamcinolone
Kerra Care	See biotin
Kerafac	Compound preparation for hoof care
Ketaset	See ketamine hydrochloride
Ketofen	See ketoprofen
Killitch	See benzyl benzoate
Kloxerate eye ointment	See cloxacillin sodium
Lanoxin	See digoxin
Large Animal Immobilon	See etorphine hydrochloride and phenothiazines
Large Animal Revivon	See diprenorphine
Lanoxin	See digoxin
Lasix	See furosemide
Lectade	Oral rehydration solution
LH 1500	See chorionic gonadotrophin
Lignavet Plus	Parenteral preparation of lignocaine hydrochloride and adrenaline
Lignol	Parenteral preparation of lignocaine hydrochloride and adrenaline
Locaine	Parenteral preparation of lignocaine hydrochloride and adrenaline
Locovetic	Parenteral preparation of lignocaine hydrochloride and adrenaline
Losec	See omeprazole

Maxitrol eye drops	Contains dexamethasone, hypromellose, neomycin and polymyxin B sulphate		**Pevidine**	See pevidine/iodine solution
Metronex	See metronidazole		**Phenobarbitone**	See phenobarbitone
Mycophyt	See natamycin		**PMS**	See serum gonadotrophin
Nandrolin	See nandrolone phenylpropionate		**PMSG**	Abbr pregnant mare serum gonadotrophin, qv
Navilox	See isoxuprine hydrochloride		**Pneumabort-K**	See Pneumabort-K
Negasunt	See sulphanilamide		**Pred Forte**	See prednisolone
Neostat	See neomycin sulphate		**Predsol**	See prednisolone
Neobiotic	See neomycin sulphate		**Prevac Plus and Prevac T. Plus**	See Prevac Plus
Norcuron	See vecuronium bromide		**Pro-Dynam**	See phenylbutazone
Norofulvin	See griseofulvin		**Protexin**	See probiotic
Nutrequin	Feed supplement containing vitamins, minerals, aminoacids		**Quinidine**	See quinidine sulphate
Nymfalon	See chorionic gonadotrophin		**Receptal**	See buserelin
Opticlox	See cloxacillin sodium		**Regumate**	See altrenogest
Orbenin	See cloxacillin sodium		**Rifadin**	See rifampicin
Oxytocin S	See oxytocin		**Rompun**	See xylazine
Oxytocin Leo	See oxytocin		**Saniphor**	See pevidine/iodine solution
Panacur and Panacur Guard	See fenbendazole		**Savlon**	See chlorhexidine gluconate
Panalog	Contains neomycin, nysnystatin, thiostrepton, triamcinolone acetonide		**Scoline**	See suxamethonium chloride
Panomec	See ivermectin		**Sedivet**	See romifidine
Parlodel	See bromocriptine		**Solupen**	See benzylpenicillin
Pavulon	See pancuronium bromide		**Soludex**	See dexamethasone
Pentothal	See thiopentone sodium		**Sputolosin**	See dembrexine hydrochloride
Pentoject	See pentobarbitone sodium		**Strongid-P**	See pyrantel tartrate
Pepto Bismol	See bismuth		**Sweet-Itch Lotion**	See pyrethrum
			Synacthen	See tetracosactrin acetate

Tagamet	See cimetidine	**Valium**	See diazepam
Telmin	See mebendazole	**Ventipulmin**	See clenbuterol hydrochloride
Terramycin	See oxytetracycline hydrochloride	**Vetalar**	See ketamine hydrochloride
Tetanus Antitoxin	See tetanus	**Virbaxyl**	See xylazine
Thiovet	See thiopentone sodium	**Vitamin B$_1$**	See aneurine hydrochloride
Timentin	See ticarcillin	**Vitenium**	Compound selenium and vitamin E preparation
Tocovite	See tocopheryl acetate		
Torbugesic	See butorphanol	**Warfarin**	See warfarin
Torgyl	See metronidazole	**Xylocaine**	See lignocaine hydrochloride
Tribrissen	See trimethoprim	**Zantac**	See ranitidine
Trivetrin	See trimethoprim	**Zovirax**	See aciclovir
Uniprim	See trimethoprim		